I0754618

S. Pancoast M.D.

PROCREATION — HEALTH — BEAUTY — LONGEVITY.

THE

# LADIES' MEDICAL GUIDE.

Επιγενεσις.—Καλοςγυννηνομος.

"*Now* is the time to store away in the garners of our minds the rich treasures of truth—*now* is the time to gather pearls of wisdom, and hang them around the neck of memory—*now* is the time to drink deep of the waters of life, fresh from the fountains of intelligence."

KNOW THYSELF.

Quæ Prosunt Omnibus.

BY S. PANCOAST, M.D.,

Professor Microscopic Anatomy, Physiology, and the Institute of Medicine in Penn Medical University, Philadelphia, Pa.; Author of "Curability of Consumption," "Boyhood's Perils and Manhood's Curse," etc.

Sixth Edition.

Philadelphia:
PUBLISHED BY JOHN E. POTTER,
No. 617 SANSOM STREET.
1865.

TO

THE MOTHERS AND DAUGHTERS

OF THE

UNITED STATES OF AMERICA,

THIS

INSTRUCTIVE TREATISE

ON THE

STRUCTURE AND FUNCTIONS OF THE REPRODUCTIVE ORGANS,
DISEASES OF FEMALES AND CHILDREN,

THE TOILET, ETC.,

SCIENTIFICALLY CONSIDERED IN REFERENCE TO

HEALTH, BEAUTY AND LONGEVITY:

UNDERTAKEN AT THE SUGGESTION OF MANY LADIES

AND

PROMOTED BY THEIR ENCOURAGEMENT:

IS MOST

RESPECTFULLY INSCRIBED,

BY THEIR SINCERE FRIEND AND WELL-WISHER,

THE AUTHOR.

# EXCERPTA.

"Truth must ultimately vanquish error, and vindicate its divine origin. There is no truth relating to this life only, so important as that which teaches the means of securing a 'sound mind in a sound body.'"

> "———— Immediately a place
> Before mine eyes appears, sad, noisome, dark;
> A lazar house it seems; wherein are laid
> Numbers of all diseased; all maladies
> Of ghastly spasm, or racking torture, qualms
> Of heart-sick agony, all feverous kinds,
> Convulsions, epilepsies, fierce catarrhs,
> Intestine stone and ulcer, colic pangs,
> Demoniac phrensy, moping melancholy,
> And moonstruck madness, pining atrophy,
> Marasmus and wide-wasting pestilence,
> Dropsies and asthmas, and joint-racking rheums.
> Dire is the tossing, deep the groans; Despair
> Tendeth the sick, busiest from couch to couch;
> And over them triumphant Death his dart
> Shakes, but delays to strike, though oft invoked
> With vows, as their chief good and final hope."

Bind up, then, the wound of these children of affliction—pour in oil and wine, but in so doing take heed

> "That the immaculate whiteness of your fame
> Shall ne'er be sullied with one taint or spot."

Woman has ever been the comforter and counselor in adversity and affliction—a follower of Christ: the last at the Cross, and first at the Sepulchre.

> "'Tis woman's smiles that lull our cares to rest,
> 'Tis woman's charms that give to life its zest;
> 'Tis woman's hand that smooths affliction's bed,
> Wipes cold sweat from aching brow—supports the sinking head."

Such is woman's sphere of action, and such is woman's mission. Go forth then into the world, and in all your future strivings, in all your labors, in all your pains and pleasures, may the strong arm of Jehovah Rophi—the Lord of the Healer—

> "Before, behind thee, and on every hand,
> Enwheel thee round."

# LIST OF ENGRAVINGS.

# GENERAL CONTENTS.



## PART I.

### ANATOMY OF THE FEMALE ORGANS OF GENERATION.

#### CHAPTER I.



#### CHAPTER II.

## CHAPTER III.



## CHAPTER IV.



## CHAPTER V.



## CHAPTER VI.



## CHAPTER VII.



## CHAPTER VIII.



## CHAPTER IX.



## CHAPTER X.

## CHAPTER XI.



## CHAPTER XII.



## CHAPTER XIII.



## CHAPTER XIV.



## CHAPTER XV.



## CHAPTER XVI.

## CHAPTER XVII.



## CHAPTER XVIII.



## CHAPTER XIX.



# PART II.

## DISEASES OF FEMALES AND CHILDREN.

## CHAPTER I.



## CHAPTER II.

## PART III.

### TOILET.

### CHAPTER I.



### CHAPTER II.

## CHAPTER III.



## CHAPTER IV.



## CHAPTER V.



## CHAPTER VI.

## NAMES OF AUTHORS

### QUOTED AND REFERRED TO IN THIS VOLUME.

Apelles.
Arnaud.
Aristotle.
Acton.
Apuleius.
Ainsworth.

Bedford
Billiard.
Busch.
Bulwer.
Barry.
Baer, Von.
Bischoff.
Baubine.
Beclard.
Banning.
Baum.
Barnum.
Boerhaave.
Bichat.
Blumenbach.
Balzac.
Bounett.
Bell, T.
Burdach.
Byron.
Blundell.
Buffon.
Bailey, Mrs.
Bond.
Bienvernu.
Bell, Sir Charles.

Coste.
Copeland.
Carpenter.
Coleridge.
Chobert.
Colombas.
Chroke, Jean.
Crawford.
Cribb.
Cuvier.
Cazenave.
Crosse.
Cowper.
Combe.
Chambers.
Croft, Sir Richard.
Campbell.
Colleredo.
Cruveilhier.
Collins.
Countess of Landsfelt.
Cooper, Sir Astley Paston.

De Graaf.
Denis.
Desgranges.
Dewees.
Darwin.
Donné.
Dunglison.
Daret.
Dzonde.
Dieffenbach.

Ætius.
Eginitus, Paulus.
Eisenmann.
Elliotson.
Evelyn.
Ellis.
Elbe.

Flourens.
Farne.
Farre.
Fournier.
Fowler.
Fuller.

Geoffrey, Isidore.
Gariel.
Greve.

Gockel.
Gardner
Galen.
Gardien.
Gross.
Godwin.
Good.
Giron.
Guersent.
Grellier.
Gough.
Gollman.

Hall, Marshall.
Hunter.
Huele.
Haller.
Home, Sir E.
Hufeland.
Hilaire.
Heuremaun.
Hogarth.
Hippocrates.
Harvey.
Hofacker.
Hood.
Heidricht.
Hassel.
Hanno.
Homer.
Holmes.
Hemple.

Jonnini.
Julien.
Jonės.
Joerg.

Kobelt.
Katsky.
Kirby.

Longshore, J. S.
Livy.
Lecot.
Lothidin.
Leriche.
Lempriere.
Lobstein.
Lavater.
Leibig.
Les Africanus.

Mûller.
Martial.
Mayer.
Meckel.
Melville.
Malphigi.
Maton.
Magendie.
Moseley.
Montgomery.
Morton.
Meigs.
Mead.
Milton.
Morgan, Lady.

Newport.
Nichols, T. L.
Naegele.

Otto.
Oldham.
Ovid.
Osgood, Mrs.

Parr.
Praxiteles.
Pouchet.
Potts.
Pliny.
Paré.
Petit.
Plato.
Pancoast.
Pamphigus.
Pagenstecker
Pope.
Pitt.
Petronius.

Ramsbotham.
Rudolphi.
Reil.
Rann.
Robertson.
Redi.
Raciboski.
Ryan.
Rouband.
Rousseau.
Reid.
Ririlow.
Roussel.
Rosen.
Robinson.

Socrates.
Saviard.
Schweikard.
Sibbard.
Soules.
Sampson.
Sharpey.
Spalanzani.
Starke.
Spence.
Sterling.
Shakespeare.
Sigourney.
Stackhouse.
Saddler.

Sougal.
Smith, Taylor.
Scudder.
Scott, Sir Walter.
Stowe.
Stubbs.

Tertullian.
Trallian.
Tulpius.
Thomson.
Turringen.
Tiedmann.
Tournefort.

Vauquelin.
Valentine.
Vaulevier.
Valentin.
Velpeau.
Veary.
Vogel.

Walker.
Walrecht.
Whitehead.
Wright.
Warren.
Weber.
Wardrop.
Withering.
Wilson.
Willis, N. P.
Wilson, Erasmus.
Wilkins, Sir Charles.
White.
Walferus.

Young.
Youatt.

Zacchias.

# NAMES OF BOOKS

## QUOTED AND REFERRED TO IN THIS VOLUME.

Arnaud's Works.

Abhandlung Kœnig. Akadder Wissenchaft zu Berlin.

Anatomical Exercitations concerning the Generation of Living Creatures.

Acton on the Reproductive Organs.

Acton on Prostitution.

Bedford's Lectures.

Busch's Works.

Bulwer's Anthropometamorphosis.

Barry's Works.

Banning's Works.

Baer's (Von) Works.

Balzac's Works.

Boyhood's Perils and Manhood's Curse. S. Pancoast, M. D.

Bulletins de la Faculté—of Paris.

Byron's Bride of Abydos.

Blumenbach uber den Biedungstinel.

Burdach's Physiologie.

Blundell's Refutations of the Doctrines of Imaginationists.

Buffon's Works.

Baubine's Latin Translations of Roussel.

Bell's (Sir Charles) Works.

Brooks' Letters from Turkey.

Curse Removed. T. L. Nichols, M. D.

Cyclopedia of Anatomy and Physiology.

Chambers' Cyclopedia.

Cooper's Works. Sir Astley.

Carpenter's Elements of Physiology.

Crawford's Mission to Ava.

Combe's Constitution of Man.

Cooper (Sir Astley) on the Breast.

Cours de Microscopié. Donne.

Combe's Management of Infants.

Copeland's Pathology of Irritation.

Cazenave's Works.

Copeland's Works.

Chambers' Encyclopedia.

Dissertation sur les Hermaphrodites.

Darwin's Works.

Donnes' Works.
Dewees' Works.

Ephem. Nat. Causes.
Economy of Human Life.
Evelyn's Discourse on Medals.
Edinburgh Medical and Surgical Journal.
Eadie's Dictionary of the Bible.

Fox's History.
Fowler's Lectures on Phrenology.

Gollman's Diseases of the Urinary and Sexual Organs. C. J. Hempel, M. D.
Gazette Méd. de Paris.
Gazette, Medical, London.
Graaf's Journal des Chirurgie und Augenheilkunde.
Greve's Fragments of Comparative Anatomy and Physiology.
Gardner's Sterility.
Godwin's Works.

Hall's Works, Marshall.
Hist. Gen. et Partic. du Devel. etc.
Hufeland's Journal der Prak.
Hist. de l'Acad. Roy. des Sc.
Histoire du Développement.
Hood's Diseases of Children.
Haller's Works.
Hood on Scarlet Fever.
Hassel's Works.
Hippocrates' Works.
Homer's Works.

Icones' Select. etc.

Journal de Med.
Jones' (Rymer) Works.

Kalogynomia, or the Laws of Female Beauty. T. Bell, M.D
Kobelt's Works.

Lempriere's Classical Dictionary.
Longshore's Lectures.
Lancet, London.
Lardner's Works.
Leibig's Works.
Ladies' Companion.

Morton's Anatomy. Dr. S. G.
Muller's Works.
Meckel in Reil's Arch.
Medical Repository, N. York.
Medical Journal, Buffalo.
Morgan's (Lady) Works.
Manuel Complet de Med. Ley. per Briand.
Medical and Physical Journal
Milton's Paradise Lost.
Medico-Chirurgical Transactions.
Martial's Works.
Meckel's Pathological Anatomy.
Medical and Surgical Reporter. Philadelphia.
Meigs' Works.
Montez (Lola) on Female Beauty.
Macasser (Rowland) on the Hair.

Neue Settene Beobachtungen zur Anatomie.

Observ. sur l'Hist. Nat. sur la Physique et sur la Peinture.
Oldham's Proceedings Royal Society.
Ovid's Works.

Pouchet l'Ovulation Spontanée.
Pouchet's Théorie Positive.
Phrenological Journal.
Philosophical Transactions.
Pancoast's Lectures.
Pardoe's (Miss) City of the Sultan.
Pope's Poetical Works.

Quarterly Review.

Recueil's d'Observations Chirurgicales.
Ryan's Medical Jurisprudence.
Ramsbotham's Midwifery.
Robinson's Essavs on Natural Economy

Sacred Scriptures.
Stael's (Madame de) Works.
Shakespeare's Works.
Sigourney's (Mrs.) Works.
Simon's Works.
Scudder's Works.
Sepulchral Monuments.
Scott's (Sir Walter) Marmion.
Sterling's Spanish Artists.

Trans. Coll. Phys.
Taylor's Medical Jurisprudence.
Thomson's Seasons.

Unique Collections.
Urban's Sermons.

Von Ammon's Die ersten Mutterfplichter und die erste Rurderpflegi.

Withering on Scarlet Fever.
Willis' (N. P.) Works.
Walker's Physiognomy.
Wardrop's Diseases of the Heart.
Wilson (Erasmus) on the Hair.
Water-Cure Journal.

Youatt's Works.
Young's Nights Thoughts.

Zacchias' Works.

# PREFACE.

The present work will be found one of delicate and peculiar interest to every female interested in the health, beauty, longevity, happiness, and general well-being of her sex. It has been written at the especial request of numerous matrons to supply a *desideratum* in medical literature, in respect to the functions and diseases of the Female Organs of Generation. It is true that there are many works extant which pretend to such expositions, but they may all be regarded as utterly worthless, gotten up by charlatans and impostors, destitute of principle and without any thing more than a mere smattering of Medical Science, upon which to base their miserable and mischievous productions. Hence they have all failed to accomplish the purpose claimed for them, and should accordingly be contemned as "catch-penny" volumes, calculated to delude and deceive instead of being of any practical benefit to the "better portion" of the human family.

As the subject of Generation and Procreation is one that must ever largely engross the public mind, particularly every married female anxious for the preservation of her own physical perfection from the exhausting drains upon the *vis vitæ* of the animal economy through gestation, excessive parturition, lactation, etc., the matter of the *Prevention of Conception* —the production of vigorous and healthy offspring—and the removal of the many complicated disorders incident to women and children—should be handled with extreme caution and delicacy by the medical practitioner, whether in the regular routine of his profession, or in giving to the world any treatise or published work on such important elements of human health and longevity. The author, accordingly, takes up the subject, in all its intricate bearings, with no little moral diffidence, and with a full consciousness of the responsibilities involved in the faithful execution of his obligations to the female sex and general society. He, however, deems it high time some really *scientific* work should be interposed, in order to render nugatory the prurient and imbecile efforts of medical pretenders and quacks of every hue and name, who have, of recent years, flooded the country with their trashy and ridiculous works. He is therefore emboldened to appear in the literary arena, and proclaim those solemn and important *truths* that so nearly affect the vital interests of the entire human race. Enjoying advantages possessed, perhaps, by few other physicians in the United States, in respect to information of this peculiar character, the author can safely say that all that is known of a *truthful and reliable* nature will be found embraced in this volume. The book is not intended alone for the female sex, but is a work which every intelligent physician will find an invaluable acquisition to his library, as a reference and guide in his general practice in all complaints and peculiarities incident to females especially. In these days of progressive intelligence, the author is happy to perceive that the pseudo-modesty which prevailed a few years ago, in regard to subjects pertaining to the sexual organism, is rapidly wearing away, while the glorious science of Physiology in connection with Hygienic information is being universally entertained, as a means by which man may "*know himself*," and realize something of the sublime mysteries and phenomena of his physical and spiritual existence. In truth, *Nature* is ever immaculate, and abhors every thing which is repugnant to her pure and simple laws. She has no secrets that may not be revealed to all—whether male or female—none that should ever cause the cheeks of the "pure in heart" to mantle with the crimson hue of shame—none to make man hang his head and fear to contemplate the attributes and perfection of Deity's most elaborate and exquisite piece of workmanship—*man* himself.

The portion of this work devoted to Pregnancy will be found full and pertinent, yet lucid and concise—giving advice to females, showing what course they should pursue during that period, as well as after the child is born, together with much valuable information in regard to the management of infants.

All the prominent diseases of females are noted, the symptoms given, and the means for their cure and amelioration suggested and presented, in order that females generally may be enabled to treat themselves, except in obstinate and complicated maladies.

The chapter devoted to the Female Toilet will be found most useful and attractive to the sex, presenting many curious facts not to be obtained from any other source, while giving remedies for beautifying the skin, etc., that have been tested and approved by many ladies of high rank and fashion in all parts of the world.

A reference to the title of the chapters and to the list of engravings, will more fully explain the object and character of this volume. The author believes that it is the most complete work of the kind that has ever appeared. Its matter is intensely absorbing, and can scarcely fail to be highly appreciated by every discreet and intelligent lady into whose hands this *morceau* may fall. If the author can succeed in his present effort to increase the *stamina* of the female organism, strengthen her vital powers, insure her general good health and longevity, elevate her character as mother, wife, sister, friend and companion, and add aught of embellishment to her natural dignity, grace and loveliness of physical and intellectual attributes, he will have achieved honors and triumphs sufficient to satisfy his highest ambition as a well-meaning philanthropist, and ardent admirer of pure and lovely *woman*, "Heaven's last best gift to man." He feels, in sooth, that he may safely leave this work on Kalogynomial Pathology in their hands, and await the verdict of a favorable appreciation of his humble labor in their behalf.

S. PANCOAST, M. D.

# PRIMORDIAL PHILOSOPHY.

## WOMANLY HEALTH AND BEAUTY.

### SEXUAL ATTRIBUTES.

My purpose is not to appear before the world as a vague speculator upon abstruse questions of philosophy, but as an humble teacher in relation to those organic elements which so nearly affect the health, beauty and longevity of the human female, and, through her, the well-being of the entire race of humanity. Like Socrates, I believe that SELF-KNOWLEDGE is the basis of human action, happiness and exaltation. "Tell me, Euthydemus," said he, "have you ever gone to Delphi?" "Yes, twice," said he. "And did you observe what is written somewhere on the temple wall—'Know thyself'?"

To *know* one's-self, is not merely to know one's own *name*, but to know one's abilities, and how to adapt them to the service of mankind. Those who know themselves, know not only what is suitable for themselves, but for their species. Socrates earnestly recommended those who conversed with him to take care of their *health*, both by learning whatever they could respecting it from men of experience, and by attending to it, each for himself, throughout his whole life, studying what food or drink, or what exercise, was most suitable for him, and how he might act in regard to them so as to enjoy the most vigorous and perfect health.

In exhorting Epigenes to exercise his body, he said: "The body must bear its part in whatever men do; and in all the services required from the body, it is of the utmost importance to have it in the best possible condition; for even in that in which you think there is least exercise for the body, *thinking*, who does not know that many fail greatly from *ill-health?* The loss of memory, despondency, irritability, and madness, often from ill health of the body, attack the mind with such force as to drive out all *previous knowledge;* but to those who have their bodies in good condition, there is the utmost freedom from anxiety, and no danger of suffering any such calamity from weakness of constitution. It is disgraceful, too, for a person to grow old in self-neglect before he knows what he would become by rendering himself well-formed and vigorous in body."

This plain, practical, common-sense teaching of Socrates, is as applicable to the generations of the nineteenth century, as it was to the Athenians four centuries before Christ. It is teaching, too, which the American people, especially, would do well to heed.

To keep the body free from pain and disease, is the universal desire of the *genus homo*—men and women. It is a most reasonable wish and worthy of universal accomplishment. It is an indisputable fact that nothing, in the economy of life, is more virtually neglected than attention to the preservation of health, and acquisition of that knowledge which conduces to ward off the circumstances and accidents likely to superinduce disease and lead to a premature termination of life. Few people seem to imagine that any care or concern is necessary in respect to *that* which is the groundwork of all comfort, and the jewel of existence, till they find themselves attacked by disease or infirmity, occasioned by gross ignorance of the corrective principles on which health and disease depend.

It is no small thing to be *perfectly* well. The case is one in our civilized and artificial forms of society extremely rare. If we look at the faces of a large majority of the men and women, or even the youth of the land, whether in town or country, they will be found any thing but the faces of perfect health; and yet nearly every cheek might be made to glow and sparkle with the lily fairness and roseate hue of bounding health, beauty and intelligence.

It is not to be denied that physical inferiority, in one form or another, is the rule rather than the exception. Seriously examined, what a condition does the health of the masses, particularly of the female portion of the community, everywhere, present. Probably one-fourth of the whole population of the country die of consumption or of disorders concomitant of a violation of Nature's immutable laws.

A too *feverish* life, mentally and physically, with too little physical calmness, and also a feeble paternity and maternity, are some of the main underlying causes of this frightful state of things. I am not disposed to grumble, or over-state the evil condition of the public physique. My purpose is to simply show how easily most of these deficiencies may be ameliorated and radically remedied. My theory is, that American men and women have mentality enough, but a most deplorable lack of normal physique.

It should be realized by every one that perpetual care is indispensable to health, beauty and longevity. It is just as reasonable to suppose that a man can squander his fortune at random, and still find it remaining at the end of many years, as that men and women can violate organic laws, and have their health, grace, power and loveliness remain. If we would have strength, beauty and activity—fine color in the complexion, grace in the movements, heartiness in the whole structure and appearance, we must all incontestibly return to primitive principles, to an obedience to the beneficent mandates of Nature and Nature's God. It is lamentable that for lack of a little knowledge, so much misery, deformity and disease should prevail in the great family of man. Let me at least inform the young that the years of their middle age ought to be those not only of their best performances, but of their best appearances, Then all has become ripe and mature: and surely the fully-ripened fruit or flower is far more beautiful and welcome than those which are ill-favored, or where the canker-worm is feasting on their heart-juices and delicious aromas.

Such are the reflections which must often arise in persons interested in the welfare of humanity, on seeing the manner in which American females, especially, scatter the rich treasure of their health, to grow old before their time, and to lose, perhaps, the best and mellowest portion of life—a happy middle, and a contented old age. Nearly every female may not only have exuberant health, but retain in perfection every physical grace and beauty to the last climacteric of human existence, if she will only resolve to do her duty to herself and, in resolving, act fully up to the simple requirements of Nature for the development and maturity of her peculiar organism.

While I am ready to admit that physicians and philosophers, in all ages, have labored to discover the "*vital elixir*," or sought to reveal the mysteries of the *vis medicatrix* of human existence, without avail, one thing is certainly evident, that in order to have vigorous health, and to prolong our stay on earth, it is necessary that we better understand what is *good* and what is *evil* in life. Every one should comprehend that there are *two* forces at work all the time, in animated as well as in vegetable forms—one *for* life, and one *against* it. These individual agencies are not only from *within*, but *without* the body corporate.

While, however, there are many causes at work to produce early decay, seemingly unavoidable, there are certainly very many which might be easily avoided. We cannot help the delicacy of enfeebled inherited constitutions; neither can we ward off the breezes which waft to us those *secret* and silent agencies which bring to us such epidemics as cut short the lives of thousands in a single day. We can, however, be temperate. We can have good air and pure cold water to refresh us internally and keep us clean externally; while our bodies may be suitably clothed for the variety of seasons, and fed with wholesome food, eaten at stated periods, with bodily and mental exercise sufficient to keep the *material* and *immaterial* well balanced. Our labor need not be protracted to our hurt; while our rest ought to be sufficient for our toils. The cares of life should not vex our spirit and enervate our nervous powers. The tone of mind is capable of elevation; society is susceptible of improvement; happiness is not unattainable; while we are surrounded by thousands of blessings calculated to sweeten our lives, and render pure our bodies and souls, if we would but discern them and appropriate them for the beatitude and perfection of humanity.

It has become a matter of recorded fact that the entire human race passes away and that the earth is repeopled every thirty years. It is not very agreeable thus to contemplate such brevity of human life, when observation teaches us that a principal cause of such mortality is man's own imprudence. This waste of life does not occur as a direct judgment of Providence, but from a natural effect of a violated law in our being.

The nearer a man follows Nature and is obedient to her laws, the *longer* he will live. The further he deviates from these, the *shorter* will be his existence. There is no general law paramount to this. It is a question often asked—To what age can a human being live? and What is the relative duration of his natural life? In answer to these questions, it can be clearly proven that the greater proportion of those who die under the age of one hundred years, *prematurely* end their days!

The period of *youth* in man is now complete in about twenty years. Other vertebrate animals of the largest and most advanced species, as the elephant, lion, camel, horse, ox, dog, etc., have lived, under favorable conditions, artificial as well as natural, *ten* times the length of their period of youth; but never much more than this period. Assuming the same rule for man as for other back-boned species, he should *now*, under *equally favorable* conditions with those species, live *ten* times *twenty* years, that is two hundred years! We see, at all events, in this supposition, that Scholasticus, who bought and kept a raven in order to learn whether the bird would live *two hundred years*, was not so great a simpleton after all; at least, if he had taken as good care of himself as he probably did of his raven. The idea of a human creature being capable of living for two hundred years, however, perfectly harmonizes with well-known facts in regard to human longevity. It is accordingly no matter of surprise that Methuselah should have lived to two hundred and fifty years, (not nine hundred and sixty-nine years, as literally recorded in the Sacred Writings). If we are to take the *Samaritan* version, Adam was even older than Methuselah—older by two hundred and ten *antediluvian* years, or about fifty-two and a half of our common years. We can readily believe that Terah should have lived two hundred and five years, and Abraham one hundred and seventy-five years, when we remember that at least ten instances are known, since the Christian era, of persons reaching one hundred and fifty years and upward. Petrach Czartew, a Hungarian, lived, as the record is, from 1587 to 1772, or one hundred and eighty-five years! Mark Albuna reached one hundred and fifty years, in Ethiopia; C. J. Drakenburg, one hundred and forty-six years, in Norway; M. Lawrence, one hundred and forty, in the Orkneys; and Louisa Truxo, a negress, it is said, lived to one hundred and sixty-five in Tucuman, South America. Every body has heard of Old Parr, who lived to one hundred and fifty years in England, and then died, not of *old age*, but from overfeeding while a guest of the British king. We thus find an agreement, a common character, about these long lives.

The probable fact of the simpler and more natural lives of the antediluvians agrees with the stated fact, that they lived so nearly a uniform period. It was at a comparatively late era that human lives began to differ so wonderfully in length, and that death began to make its most fearful mark on what should be the best years of life—those of childhood.

It would indeed seem plain enough, that by *excessive* physical and mental stimulation, with the present undue use of spices, tea, coffee, chocolate, etc., and the misuse of the living powers by subjecting them to the effects of a false cookery, of tobacco and alcoholic stimulants, many of which were unknown until a few hundred years past, we have at the same time hastened and shortened the life of the human animal in a corresponding ratio.

It would appear reasonable that anxieties, excitements, great mental activity, beget in man a craving for stimulants, and that these, in the form of condiments and exciting food and beverages, keep alive the passions and activities of all kinds; that they hurry on the operations of brain, stomach, and all the other vital organs, and thus intensify and shorten life.

It is also by the adulteration of food and beverages that men and women mutually poison and are poisoned. We cannot take poisons for food with impunity; and so, as a race, we necessarily die earlier than Nature originally designed that we should.

Truly, as Flourens expresses it, "*Man does not die*—HE KILLS HIMSELF."

This great activity of our mental and physical organizations, not only leads to *precocity*, but to premature decay and dissolution. It is accordingly high time to apply remedies to the social life, in order to the restoration of the physical *stamina* of the human creature. The whole moral force of mankind should constantly be directed to resist the *destructive* tendencies of the age. If for the next two hundred years we do something to check infant mortality and extend life more uniformly toward four or five score years, we shall prove ourselves worthy of the name of humanitarians and philanthropists. May we not hope, therefore, that when the truths of science and human experience shall have become better developed, the errors that now consign one half of all born to the grave within the first ten years of life, will yield before that perfect physiological law, upon which the greatest human endurance and longevity is based? Surely, though the *perfect* life is yet only an *ideal*, he errs fatally who does not daily strive to make it *reality*.

The physical stamina of the human creature is not to be fully developed by physical means and hygienic efforts alone. There are many moral considerations, which must ever act as powerful auxiliaries to promote his welfare and glory. Among these the desire for companionship and communion of the sexes is a prominent feature in the constitution of the *genus homo*. This is true, also, in a more or less degree, in all the lower forms of animated life. Man cannot live alone. The social organs are Amativeness, Philoprogenitiveness, Adhesiveness, Inhabitiveness, and Union for Life, or Connubiality. Adhesiveness seeks for fellowship, for affection, for paternity. It exists between men—between women—between men and women. The friendship which existed between David and Jonathan, Damon and Pythias, and between Ruth and Naomi, are instances of the most exalted kind. As a matter of course this faculty, added to that of Amativeness and Connubiality, greatly elevate and strengthen the love and affection existing between husband and wife. The primary office of Amativeness is the continuance of the race; but it may readily be asserted, that the normal action of the faculty does as much as any other to elevate, refine, and ennoble mankind. As respects Union for Life, or Connubiality, Man is by *nature* a MATING OR MARRYING being! Indeed, this propensity or predisposition is as much a law or institute of his being as is sexual love, or the procreant instinct, or the love of young. This mating instinct, or faculty of Union for Life, as a modern writer beautifully expresses it, " is the basis of marriage, and of the laws and customs which recognize the life-choice of one woman for one man." "That this faculty is a part of the mental nature of every well-constituted human being, scarcely admits of a doubt. If the consciousness or testimony of the inner life of ten thousand well organized and unperverted men and women could be obtained, it is probable that ninety-nine in a hundred would cordially respond to the presence of a strong desire to select one, and but one, sexual mate, and cleave to that one for life."

The fact is, Nature has her laws, and they must not be violated. This law implies and requires both mating and fidelity, and interdicts amatory promiscuosity in all its forms. Sexual conjunction is proper only when it is proper that it eventuate in its natural product—children—and when *both* parents can *together* bring up all their mutual children. Hence, the *family* state is Nature's institute. Of this the Philoprogenitive institute is an absolute proof and requisition.

While, however, we thus find marriage defined as a civil and religious contract between male and female, by which they engage to live together in mutual love and friendship for the purpose of procreation, yet there are many causes which disqualify the sexes for a connubial union. Certain diseases are aggravated by marriage, such as inveterate scrofula, epilepsy, confirmed phthisis. As these and other diseases may be communicated to the offspring, they should be justly considered as impediments to matrimonial union. Again, rickets is often transmitted to the infant; and this rickety predisposition in the female predisposes her to spinal and pelvic deformity; and it too often happens, in such cases, that the female, the day she hopes to be a mother, is consigned to the tomb. Mania and other forms of mental imbecility, are impediments to the marriage compact. It is necessary that there should be capacity to contract, and the consent of both parties. The various requisites for conjugal union, however, are seldom duly considered by society; in fact, few persons trouble themselves about them. The age, constitution, or health of the parties are scarcely ever considered, though highly important.

All physiologists agree that early or premature procreation is objectionable on many accounts, from the imperfect development of the parties, and the smallness of the pelvis, which exposes women to protracted suffering during parturition, and too often to loss of life. It is universally known to all practical obstetricians, that females, who become mothers at an early age, purchase the honor of maternity at a very dear rate. Such persons are liable to numerous disorders during gestation; the pelvis is unable to support the gravid uterus—it is too small for the passage of the infant; consequently, parturition will be laborious and protracted, and finally must be completed by artificial means; while the degree of pressure on the important organs of the pelvis, produced by parturition, causes great suffering and danger to the woman, and may be followed by deplorable diseases, or death itself.

It is a common belief, that gestation is a period of disease and suffering, and that parturition is inevitably a painful and dangerous process. Now, the great truth yet to be learned, is the very reverse of such impression. It is just as natural for a woman to bring forth children, as for a shrub to produce flowers and fruit. In a state of health, no *natural* process is painful. Pain, in all cases, is a sign of disease—it has no other significance. In its healthy condition, the uterus receives the germ of a new being, provides it with its proper nourishment, expands to make room for its development, and, at the time appointed by Nature, dilates its opening and contracts—a series of involuntary and painless muscular efforts—so as to throw the infant into the new existence which its growth demands. It performs its own proper functions, just as the lungs, the heart, or the stomach perform theirs; because it was formed by the same Infinite Wisdom and Goodness, who ordained that pain and sorrow should be the consequence of sin, and who ordains that health and happiness shall ever be the result of obedience to the laws of life.

When God looked upon his creation and pronounced it good, he could not have overlooked the most important function of his last and most important work. There can be no question that, in the original creation of woman, she was fitted to obey the command, "*Increase and multiply, and replenish the earth,*" without peril or pain. The very idea of the *curse* inflicted upon her, carries with it the belief that she was originally created perfect in this condition. Has there been any change? If so, what is its nature?

There is nothing to show that the bony pelvis has changed its form, or that the head or chest have been altered in their relative dimensions. In all healthy subjects, the pelvis is still found most admirably adapted to the size of the fœtus, at the period of its full development. The uterus, by nature, is not less adapted to its functions, than the eyes or ears are adapted to theirs. No; *Nature* has not *changed!* Woman, in her *healthy* condition, is still the same glorious being that she was when she first came from the hands of the Creator.

Then why is woman subjected to all her pains, sufferings, outrages, and perils in the performance of the great functions of her life? It is because the forbidden fruit of enervating luxuries and excesses is continually eaten. Indolence, self-indulgence, voluptuousness, and all sins against the laws which God has written in the structure of our bodies, bring with them the curse of deranged nervous systems, broken health, irregularity of function, disease, pain, and premature death. Every woman is an Eve, and forbidden fruits are all around her. If she listen to the voice of the beguiling serpent, hers is the woe. On the other hand, faith in God, obedience to his laws, and living in harmony with his works, assure to woman health, and beauty, and joy, and safety in fulfilling all her destiny. These truths are incontrovertible as the principles of Nature.

By the immutable laws of Nature, the sins of parents are visited upon their children, even to the third and fourth generations. Consequently, women are born scrofulous, weak, and often with bodies imperfectly developed, and tendencies to spinal and pelvic deformities, forbidding the possibility of healthy and natural labors. All such women must suffer; but even to them, obedience brings its rewards. In many cases their health can be greatly improved, and their unfortunate liabilities signally lessened.

In consequence of the wise adaptation of the human lungs and skin to the atmosphere, the free access of pure air, from the first moment of independent life, is of the highest necessity; yet our women, even more than our men, are smothered and poisoned all their lives; and while they should breathe pure air, day and night, at all times, they are almost continually deprived of it. In the curtained cradle, the close bedroom, the heated nursery, the crowded school-room, the unventilated church, ball-room, theatre, and through a whole life of falseness and luxury, the blood never gets its share of oxygen, and the whole system becomes loaded with impurities. Every organ becomes weakened, and every function deranged. What can we expect from such violations of Nature's laws? Thus, either as the doll-baby, or the slave of civilization, woman is wronged in her whole nature, and suffers for the wrong; and all society suffers with her.

Every violation of the laws of health, every injury to the organs of any other function, must entail mischief and disorder upon the reproductive system. It suffers, above all, from the irregular or excessive action of its own organism. Stimulated to premature development by the luxuries of artificial life, what should be the happiness, the delight, and glory of woman, becomes her dread, her misery, and her despair.

When the various causes of disease produce their legitimate effects upon the female constitution; when pallor and languor take the place of rosy health and energy; when there come loss of appetite, and nervous palpitations, and hysterical sobbings; when there is suppression of the menses, or painful menstruation, pain in the back, a sinking of the stomach, a dragging sensation between the hips; when to these symptoms of nervous and uterine disorder are added whites and falling of the womb, medical aid must be resorted to, and then begins, too often, a new catalogue of wrongs and abuses. Thousands of women, especially the young and delicate, suffer years of torture, before they can be forced to seek medical advice, and no one can blame them. It must be confessed that there is a deplorable ignorance of the causes, of the nature, and treatment of female diseases. Books, and professors, and practitioners, are alike in the dark. But there is something worse than mere ignorance. Where men do not know what to do, and are called on to do something, they are likely to do wrong. Thus women are drugged into an aggravation of their evils. They are outraged by frequent and useless examinations; they are made to wear useless or hurtful mechanical contrivances—the most miserable of all palliations; and, to crown the whole, they are leeched and cauterized, day after day, and week after week, until death itself would be a welcome refuge from their sufferings. I do not fear to denounce all such practices as ignorant, corrupt, and barbarous. There are very few cases of female diseases where an examination is necessary. Such exposure to a sensitive woman is worse than death. There is not one case in ten where doctors pretend to find, and where they honestly think they do find, ulceration, or schirrus, or cancer of the womb, that they really exist. There is not one case in ten, where they apply lunar caustic that it is needed, even by the rules of their own system. No man need burn when he knows how to heal. These caustic doctors are like the other quack who made every kind of sore a burn, and then sold his salve to cure burns.

These outrages are even more infamous and diabolical when the physician is called to the bedside of the parturient woman. Here, where august Nature should reign supreme, her laws are grossly violated and set at naught. Instead of preparing a woman to go through the process of labor with all the energy of her vitality, she is weakened by medication and blood-letting. Instead of being put upon a proper regimen, and a diet suited to her condition, she is more than ever pampered and indulged. Finally, when labor comes on, the chances are that the uterus will be stimulated into excessive and spasmodic action by the deadly ergot; and if a weakened and deranged system does not act as promptly as the doctor wishes, he proceeds to deliver with instruments, at the risk, often the certainty, of destroying the child, and very often the certainty of inflicting terrible and irreparable injury upon the mother. In numerous instances, the butcher of a physician will drag the infant into the world by the forceps, or plunge a perforator through its skull, or tear its limbs piecemeal from the abused and tortured victim of such barbarity. Who shall say how many of the still-born children in our land have not been "scientifically" murdered in this fashionable practice of midwifery!

I fearlessly appeal to the wise, the gentle, and the really skillful of the medical profession, if I have spoken too severely of the treatment of female diseases and the practice of midwifery, by professional mountebanks of high standing in the community? I am perfectly aware of the ground upon which I stand, and understand the abuses I propose to remedy. It is but justice to state that the practice I denounce has been pointedly condemned by some of the most distinguished men in the profession. Professor Bedford, of the New York University, Dr. Nichols, and others of that city, have very severely criticized these scandalous irregularities of the profession; while Marshall Hall, one of the most distinguished medical writers in Europe, in denouncing frequent examinations and the abuse of the speculum, in a late number of the *Lancet*, held the following very pertinent language:

"I have seen cases in which the speculum and caustic having been employed—and unduly employed, as I believe—the patient remained more miserably afflicted in mind and body than ever, as the effect of such treatment. I will not advert even to the epithets which have been applied to the frequent use of the speculum by our French neighbors, who are so skilled in these matters; but I will ask, what father among us, after the details which I have given, would allow his virgin daughter to be subject to this 'pollution'? Let us then maintain the spotless dignity of our profession, with its well-deserved character for purity of morals, and throw aside this injurious practice with indignant scorn, remembering that it is not the mere exposure of the person, but the dulling of the edge of virgin modesty, and the degradation of the pure minds of the daughters of England which are to be avoided."

Surely, if this abominable practice is thus so severely denounced in England, the fathers and husbands of the daughters of Columbia ought to be equally careful to preserve their spotless purity and honor. Truly, it is the disgrace of the medical profession that ignorant women — ignorant of these things, though instructed in a thousand matters of less importance — are imposed upon by unprincipled and mercenary doctors in this shameful and execrable manner.

As this volume is intended as a Gospel of Health to suffering woman, designed to present information which will tend to the improvement of her physical stamina, and the maintenance of her dignity, grace, beauty, and longevity, I have no apology to offer for the hints and sentiments which are yet to follow, as embodied in my interpretation of the Laws of Nature in regard to the functions of the female organism.

It may be deliberately and truthfully asserted, that more women owe the destruction of their health and the loss of their lives to the excessive use of the maternal functions, than to all other causes combined. Surely, none but woman herself has a right to control such functions. It is her privilege to say when and to what extent she will suffer; when she should have children, and what shall be the number of her progeny. By entering the marriage state, it does not follow that she shall be plundered of her health, in obedience to the sensual behests of her connubial companion. Indeed, no man of feeling, sense, decency, and justice, will be found willing to have his wife suddenly transformed from a beautiful and healthy being into a miserable, emaciated, and sallow spectre. *Excessive* venereal indulgence—excessive child-bearing — excessive nursing—are terribly destructive of the vital forces of woman's organization; hence, she is destined to suffer, to languish, to fade and die prematurely. Twenty years of a married woman's life, upon an average, are sacrificed to perpetual physical and mental misery—between nursing and breeding, there is scarcely a single hour left, in many instances, for the system to recuperate and regain its normal standard of health and vigor. Hence, they are slaves to an infamous law of civilization—to an outrage even sanctioned by religion! They are slaves to unrestrained sexual indulgence, slaves to their numerous progeny, yet dare not murmur against their deplorable fate. This slavish drudgery to maternal requirements is a cause of many distressing disorders, producing irritability of temper, and all those domestic *contretemps* which so often utterly destroy the happiness of the family relation, and bring disgrace and odium upon the marital institution, designed by the ordinances of Nature and Heaven for the highest felicity of man and woman in a state of terrestrial existence. Had woman the possession of herself, and the control of her own maternal functions and duties, instead of grievous sufferings and privations, she would have health and beauty, not only of her own organization, but would become the mother of children equally vigorous and lovely. To avoid these evils, who may estimate the amount of crime of infanticide and abortion, committed by wives in the paroxysm of despair? Is there no remedy for these deplorable consequences of the abuse of the matrimonial association of the sexes? "Is there no balm in Gilead" to remedy the distressing ailments and miseries concomitant of excessive venery and child-bearing? Is there no *unfailing preventive against pregnancy?* Most certainly there is, and one, too, entirely consonant with Nature, and one which may be employed without violation either of Divine or human laws. The farmer is careful to raise no more stock than he can afford to keep. How many families are there composed of swarms of children, whose parents are unable to provide for their proper support and education! Surely, nothing is more wicked than to bring into the world such numbers of helpless and innocent beings, to doom them to poverty, ignorance and crime, because of their parents' inability to make necessary provision for them. I by no means would sanction the destruction of embryotic life—such would be a crime deserving of the severest penalties. Nor need such wanton sacrilege upon Nature ever be necessary. Those who will reflect on this matter, will be guided in their line of duty to themselves and their Creator in the course of this volume.

Whatever may be said of woman's rights, needs, and dependencies, and man's prerogatives and tyrannies, I have never been able to discern why man and woman should be at variance in any respect. All discrepancies between them are imaginary, for they are contrary to the principles of universal nature. There are, no doubt, inharmonious relations arising out of the imperfect development of the race, but to say that there are natural opposing rights, duties and interests, is a palpable absurdity. The *genus homo* constitute man and woman, one and indivisible. They are equal in their attributes, and have no prerogatives and affections which are not mutual and necessary for the happiness and well-being of each—both together developing, and unfolding the *genus homo*. Hence the ultimatum of human development is the enjoyment of all the natural rights and prerogatives common to both as a *united* being. Neither man nor woman will ever enjoy permanent immunity from present suffering until a higher degree of development is secured. To attain such glorious results, every moral and social and physical means should be made available to the purpose.

Certainly, the highest and holiest duties of earth are consigned to woman: she is the one who moulds the physical form of her offspring, and rears it to the stature of a man, and shapes its moral and intellectual destiny. The embryotic being draws nutriment and subsistence from its maternal parent, and derives its vital impress from that of the parent stock. Loveliness begets loveliness; purity begets purity; wisdom begets wisdom; while vice begets vice; selfishness, selfishness; hatred, hatred; bad temper, bad temper; licentiousness, licentiousness; etc.

If such principles hold good, there is no reason to suppose that the human race is not susceptible of a culture and development of the highest physical and mental character. All highly-developed plants are capable of very great modifications by means of cultivation; and all highly-developed animals, in the same way, by means of education, climate, and mode of life. This doctrine is illustrated in the fact, that the *most perfect*—the naturalist would say, *monstrous*—double roses result by cultivation from the marsh-rose, with its single row of petals. Wheat and rice, in their original, wild state, bore grains having little farinaceous or life-sustaining material. The parent of all our numerous and delicious varieties of apples is the small and bitter Siberian crab. Even the luscious peach is, botanically, a *monstrosity*, a fleshy pericarp developed, by cultivation, from the tough rind covering a fruit originally resembling the almond. The transforming power of human care and a genial soil, over the strawberry, the cherry, the potato, in fact, the whole range of cultivated plants, is well known to all.

Variations equally striking are abundant in the animal world. The ill-shapen, vicious "Indian poney," or wild horse of this country, has become the intelligent and elegant specimen of the farm or carriage-horse. The wild hog has undergone a striking improvement in the domestic hog. Compare, in like manner, the difference between the head, forehead, and expression of the wild dog with a favorable specimen of the dog, in his higher state, as a companion of man.

In all these instances, and many more, we see the proofs of a large capacity for development. The improvement and higher elevation of the *genus homo*, can scarcely be an exception to the universal rule.

On the other hand, do we not know that man is liable to fall back into an inferior physical and mental condition, through the force of ignorance and adverse circumstances upon his organism? Do we not know that the rice and wheat which cultivation has produced from grass, like herbage, returns to the same low condition as before, when the hand of cultivation is withdrawn from them? Do we not know that this is the law of every "*improvement*" that man can make in animal or vegetable existences? None of these improvements are permanent. They are all forced states. They all lapse fast into wild nature again, so soon as the force that upraised them is withdrawn. Thus I deduce the conclusion that man is undoubtedly in a *transition* state—passing from an undeveloped or *rudimental* man, to man *perfect* and complete *as* man, in every element of physical, intellectual and moral attribute. Accordingly, I believe that the future mental and physical condition of man or woman is measurable fixed in the *moment of generation*, and also that most of the phenomena and possibilities of life are really pictured in the embryo from the moment of generation. These statements seem strictly rational and philosophical, when properly understood; but in order to make the idea more clearly palpable, I will endeavor to show what qualifications should be made in the expressions of the law, as here presented.

That children resemble their parents in body, in capacities, and in dispositions, is a general fact too well known to require a labored attempt at proof. It is the law of all offspring. Sensible men know that when they desire a colt to be distinguished for *speed* or strength, or *hardihood*, for *slenderness* or *weight*, they must choose a sire or a dam, or still better, both, that are distinguished for the same quality. Sensible men know that when all other conditions are favorable, they are not disappointed in the result at which they aim; but they know equally well, that such disappointment frequently befalls them, and that this is *not* because there is *no law* in the case, but because there are *other laws* which come into play subsequently to the fact of generation, modifying the action of the former, and resulting in apparent exceptions to the general rule.

What I desire to impress on the minds of my readers, is that, since every thing that shall, in the natural course of events, happen to modify the mind, character, and physical form of the child subsequently to the act of generation, is really determined, though not known beforehand; therefore it follows that the capabilities of the future man or woman *are* fixed by the conditions attending the fact.

It is not my present business to inquire, as does Walker in his instructive treatise on "Intermarriage," What particular portion of the face, form and disposition each parent contributes? I would merely remind the reader, that as an almost universal rule, sons and daughters do resemble both fathers and mothers, and then ask *Why* is this the fact? What can the merely material part or office of either father or mother do toward bringing out so wonderful and general a result? Is not this resemblance the work of the vital-force that parts from both parents to fix its lodgment within the new germ, and build up a new expression of its own origin and inherent nature? Does not this one fact of the *hereditary* transmission of corporeal and vital qualities sustain all that has been advanced relative to the indispensableness of an organizing force, a *vis vitæ* or *vis medicatrix naturæ*, which moulds and develops the materials of each living body at its will?

In summary conclusion of views in questions of so much importance, I may recapitulate certain general facts, principles, and consequences, as necessary for the development of physical and mental strength and beauty.

It is a *fact* that *matter* never moulds itself into *living* vegetable or animal forms, while as a *principle*, the course of Nature is *uniform*. That which has *once been*, is still under like conditions, possible; *consequently*, in and before every organized being there must be a typical organizing force, which acts upon matter and moulds it in harmony with its own inherent qualities.

It is a *fact*, that *offspring*, of whatever species, *resemble parents* in a vast majority of instances. It is safe to assume, hence, that such resemblance always exists, save where some *secondary law* has been brought to bear more powerfully, and so modified the product of parental action. *Consequently*, all offspring must have inherited their organizing force, or *vis vitæ*, from parents of the same species.

It is a *fact*, that offspring of one species never proves to belong to some other. Different species have never been known to successfully intermix, so as to produce a mongrel race capable of perpetuating itself. *Mules* always return by degrees to one parental species or the other; or else they perish. *Consequently*, species never intermix, or change from their essential characters. Necessarily, then, the *first* individuals of every species must have been *directly* created, and not gradually developed, the vegetable from the mineral, the animal from the vegetable, evolving man as the highest type of animal existence. In other words, man has not been developed from the tadpole, the sloth, the monkey to his present *status* as lord of the animal kingdom. He was created man—a rudimental man—and can only be developed into an *improved*, elevated, perfect man—remaining man and man only, whatever his retrocession or progress in physical and mental attributes. This doctrine simply declares the inability of *Nature*, by any process of evolution or germination whatever, to have furnished either the body or the *organizing* force of man or any other existing species; and the necessity of a primordial self-existing *Superior Creative* energy to accomplish all results of this kind.

*Finally*, I affirm that a human being is a complex unit—very complicate, mixed, various—but not really heterogeneous. Organized *matter* and *spirit*, or soul, meet in a common purpose, and by *vis vitæ* and other forces develop a living organized being.

This outline of my views will, I think, be amply sustained by the Physiological, Anatomical, Pathological and Morphological facts and revelations contained in the subsequent pages of this volume. I have carefully explored the latest and most reliable and improved authorities on all matters bearing on the development of the physical stamina of the Female Sex, and the Preservation of her Beauty, Health and Intellectual Faculties, and am warranted in believing that I have omitted nothing essentially important or worthy of being known. I claim for the work no especial originality of style or diction, having freely incorporated facts and ideas of numerous writers with such *data* as have come within the range of my own professional experience and philosophical deductions. I have, therefore, not thought it necessary to quote authorities literally in every instance, or to mar the general compilation with notes or references to a multitude of names and works not generally known—my object being solely to present the fullest amount of instructive and scientific information in the most portable or convenient form.

# PART I.

## CHAPTER I.

### ANATOMY, OR STRUCTURE OF THE FEMALE ORGANS OF GENERATION.

### THE FEMALE SEXUAL ORGANS.

THE generative or reproductive organs of the human female are usually divided into the internal and external. Those regarded as internal are concealed from view and protected within the body. Those that can be readily perceived are termed external. The entrance of the vagina may be stated as the line of demarcation of the two divisions.

### EXTERNAL ORGANS OF GENERATION.

The external organs of generation consist of the *Mons Veneris*, *External* and *Internal Labia*, *Clitoris*, *Meatus Urinarius* and *Hymen*.

1. MONS VENERIS.—This is the prominence situated over the symphysis pubis, consisting of the integuments or skin, (fatty or adipose tissue), and sebaceous follicles, and covered with hair at puberty.

2. EXTERNAL LABIA.—The labia majora (large lips),

are sometimes called the external lips of the vagina, and close the orifice of that passage, or canal. They are two thick membranous folds, constituting the sides of the external pudendum, and extending from the mons veneris above to the perinæum below. By their union below the perinæum, they form the forchette or frænum. At the posterior extremity, close to the extrance of the vagina, there is a small depression termed the *fossa navicularis.* Externally, the labia majora consists of a delicate skin covered with hair, continuous with that of the thigh and pubic region. The internal surface resembles a mucous membrane; is thin and smooth, of a reddish or pink color in young, and pale in old age; being supplied with sebaceous follicles or depressions which secrete an oleaginous substance. In the virgin both lips are closely united, forming a longitudinal slit. After frequent coition and parturition they remain, more or less, permanently separated by the labia minor (the smaller or inner lips), protruding between them. They are sometimes the seat of swelling and suppuration, which is frequently very painful and distressing to the patient. They occasionally entirely unite, which is caused by ulceration and the close approximation of each labia. They are sometimes found united in this way at birth. The diseases of these parts are frequently the consequences of uncleanliness.

3. CLITORIS.—This is a body which is seen immediately below the mons veneris, by separating the external labia. It is usually about one inch in length, and formed similarly to the male penis. It

consists of two corpora cavernosa; has a glans, prepuce and double frænulum, but no meatus urinarius. It is situated below the anterior commissure of the labia minor, and is covered by the prepuce. It is attached to the pubic bone or anterior part of the pelvis (*Fig.* 1, *f*); and by two crura from the as-

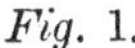

*Fig.* 1.

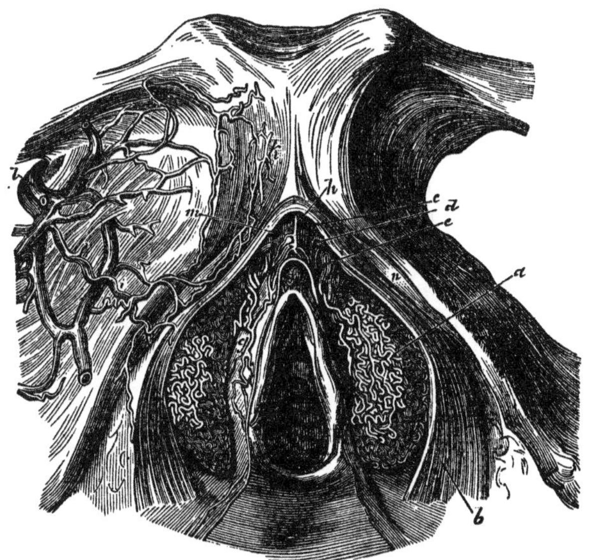


ANTERIOR VIEW OF THE EXTERNAL ORGANS. 1.—(*After Kobelt.*)

*a*, vestibular bulb; *b*, constrictor vaginæ muscle, according to Kobelt the compressor of the bulb. It is here represented as drawn back behind the bulb, which in the natural position is covered by it; *c*, anterior division of the muscle which passes over the body of the clitoris, serving to depress the organ, and to compress the dorsal vein; *d*, posterior tendinous division of the same muscle; *e*, pars intermedia; *f*, glans clitoridis; *g*, veins proceeding from the nymphæ; *h*, dorsal vein of the clitoris; *i*, branches communicating with the obturator veins; *k*, branches ascending to the epigastric veins; *l*, obturator veins; *m*, corpus clitoridis; *n*, crus clitoridis of the left side.

cending rami of the ischia, to each of which an erector muscle is attached. The corpora cavernosa unite under the symphysis pubis terminating in the glans of the clitoris which reaches beyond the prepuce in the shape of a roundish body of the size of a pea. It is united superiorly to the symphysis pubis by means of a frænulum, and inferiorly to the labia minora by means of another frænulum. This portion of the pudendum is richly endowed with nerves and vessels. It becomes erect during coition, and is the principal seat of the thrill or voluptuous sensation in the female. In nymphomania, the clitoris is sometimes cut by the knife and the parts cauterized, before this species of insanity can be permanently cured. The clitoris of the women living in a warm climate is usually larger than with those of colder zones. Such is its excessive length among the Abyssinian, Mendingan, and Ibbon women, that it is a popular usage to extirpate a portion of the obstruction. When the Abyssinians were converted to Christianity, this species of circumcision was abolished as a remnant of paganism. The men, however, soon rebelled against the innovation, when it became necessary for the Propaganda of Rome to send a surgeon to restore the ancient custom. The clitoris is sometimes four or five inches in length, and of the thickness of a boy's penis prior to pubescence. Such malformation has induced unnatural satisfaction of the sexual instinct between two women, or between a so-called hermaphrodite and a virgin. The so-termed "Lesbian love," or the lustful embraces of women of each other, arose from such abnormal condition of the clitoris. This revolting vice derived its name from the Island of Lesbos, where it was practiced by the celebrated poetess Sappho. In ancient Rome there was a society of these creatures who were called the "Tribades." Prior to the first French revolution, there was a similar society in Paris, who, as if to add mockery to their infamy, called themselves the "Vestals."

4. Internal Labia, or Nymphæ.—These are two distinct folds of membranes lying within the labia majora, (or external lips) and attached above to the clitoris and external labia below. Posteriorly they are closer together than anteriorly; externally they terminate in a cock's-comb-shaped, indented, free margin. They consist of a delicate crimson membrane, richly provided with nerves Between its external and internal layers is concealed a loose cellular tissue and a number of mucous glands. Each lip divides at the anterior and superior extremity into two crura. The lower ones unite with the clitoris, while the upper ones, above the clitoris, unite and form a sort of cap or prepuce.

In Hindostan, Persia, and Turkey, they are much elongated, and have to be removed with the knife on account of their interference in child-birth. In labor they protrude, and are not unfrequently lacerated, at the same time protecting the external labia. Among women, who have borne many children, such elongation is very considerable.

It is only in females in whom they do not protrude, that the labia minora have the rosy color of a mucous membrane. When they protrude they become dry, hard, and assume a brown color. If the sexual organs are abused they become much relaxed, and hang down like flaps of an inch in width. Among the women of the Hottentots and Bosjemans, they are sometimes from six to eight inches long, as described by travelers. Among the northern tribes of Africa, also, they are habitually so long that they have to be cut off.

5. URETHRA, OR MEATUS URINARIUS.—This is the opening into the bladder—about one inch below the clitoris, and one-third of an inch above the upper surface of the mouth of the vagina. The meatus urinarius forms a small, pad-shaped ring. It is situated in a little fossa, or lacunæ, or depression. Many females are under the impression that the urine passes along the vagina. The opening into the bladder terminates externally, and on a line with the external opening of the vagina. The internal labia give an external direction to the current of urine, and thus prevent it from passing into the vagina. It sometimes becomes necessary to draw off the contents of the bladder in females, for a considerable length of time. The patient herself, or some of her female friends, may soon become acquainted with the passage or use of the female catheter, and thus obviate the exposure which is very repugnant to a delicate female. The triangular space between the clitoris, meatus urinarius, and labia minora, is termed the *vestibule* of the vagina.

6. HYMEN, or VAGINAL VALVE.—This is a thin membrane of semi-lunar shape, and stretched across the orifice of the vagina, (*Fig.* 1.) It has generally one or more openings for the passage of the menses.

Imperforated hymen has been known to cause great distress in many females, at their first catamenial flow, the discharge of blood completely blocking up the vaginal canal and extending into the uterus or womb, thus causing hysterical paroxysms and other alarming symptoms. In such cases it must be ruptured and the discharge eliminated. It is usually ruptured at the first sexual congress. Sometimes, however, it is so tense and unyielding as to require the aid of a knife before the sexual act can be accomplished. In virgins the sexual delight is increased even by the pain which the tearing of the hymen causes.

The presence of the hymen was formerly considered a certain test of virginity, on account of its being ruptured during coition. This idea has long since been repudiated, for it is not unfrequently lost through accident, diseases, etc. In many instances, it does not give way in the first or subsequent connections and pregnancy. In such cases, the spermatozoa of the male work themselves through the opening in the hymen, and finally pass up through the vagina, uterus, and into the Fallopian tubes, where impregnation occurs. Therefore, medical writers no longer regard the presence of the hymen as proof of chastity, or its absence a proof of immorality.

When the labia and nymphæ are removed, a vascular erectile structure is brought to view, with the contractile muscle which surrounds the mouth of the vagina. These are called *Pars Intermedia, Bulbus Vestibule*, and *Constrictor Vaginal Muscle.*

*a. Pars Intermedia.*—This dorsal vein (*Fig.* 1, *h.*) of the clitoris gives off several branches which communicate with other branches given off anteriorly

These veins enter the body of the clitoris by two rows of apertures or canals along its under surface—then afterward pass out of the clitoris, (previously uniting with the veins from the glands of the clitoris, labia, and nymphæ), and form a series of convoluted veins, which pass down and terminate in the bulb of the vestibule. This is the structure termed by *Robelt*, the *Pars Intermedia*. (*Fig.* 1, *e.*)

*b. Bulbus Vestibuli, or Bulb of the Vagina.*—Lying on both sides of the entrance into the vagina, immediately behind the labia and nymphæ, are two bulbous masses, consisting of tortuous veins enclosed in a fibrous membrane. They are about the size of a chestnut when in a collapsed state. When well-filled with blood they may be compared to a leech, (*Fig.* 1, *a.*) They are continuous with the *Pars Intermedia* just described.

*c. Constrictor Vaginal Muscle.*—The clitoris, pars intermedia, and bulbus vestibuli, are enclosed in a thin muscle, which is called the Constrictor Vaginal Muscle, (*Fig.* 1, *b.* & *c.*) The fibres of this muscle interlace with the fibres of the sphincter ani enclosing the mouth of the rectum. The muscle becomes smaller as it ascends, and embracing the vestibular bulb, converges and meets at the root of the clitoris its fellow from the opposite side, where it (the muscle) terminates in a narrow tendon. The office of this muscle is to compress the dorsal vein, and at the same time the lower portion, by compressing the vascular apparatus of the vestibuli bulb, forces the blood upward into the body of the clitoris, and thus producing congestion and erection of that organ.—(*Cyclop. of Anat. et Phys.*)

## CHAPTER II.

### INTERNAL ORGANS OF GENERATION.

THE internal reproductive organs of the female consist of the *Vagina*, *Uterus*, *Fallopian Tubes* or *Oviducts*, and *Ovari*.

1. VAGINA.—This lies between the rectum and the bladder, and extends from the external labia to the neck of the uterus. It is about one inch in diameter in virgins, but much larger in those who have borne children. Its length is from five to six inches. The uterine end surrounds the neck of the womb and assists in supporting the same.

The Vagina consists of three coats or distinct membranes—the external being fibrous, the middle muscular, and the internal mucous. The latter secretes a mucus, which, when the female is in good health, is merely sufficient to keep the vagina in a moist condition. When it does more than this, the secretion is discharged externally, and called Leucorrhœa, or Whites. In coition this secretion is increased. The vagina in some females contracts powerfully when stimulated by the male intromittent organ, which increases sexual pleasures during the act of copulation. The office of this organ is to receive the seminal fluid and facilitate its passage into the uterus. During menstruation it also voids the catamenial flow, and it likewise transmits the fœtus and placenta during labor.

Abnormal conditions of the vagina occasionally exist. It some instances it has been found wanting there being no trace of any canal leading to the uterus observed. Sometimes this channel is so narrow as scarcely to admit a goose quill through its length, but such cases, however, are very rare.

A vertical septum occasionally divides the vagina through its whole course, thus exhibiting a double vagina and a double hymen. (*Fig.* 2.) Such mal-

FIG. 2.

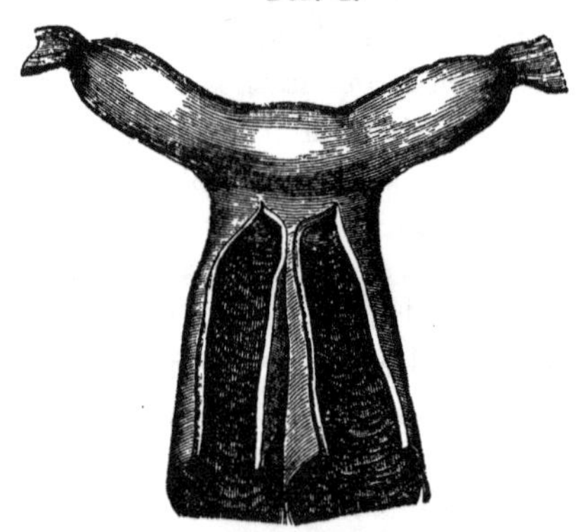

The body of the uterus divided into two halves, which are united at the cervix by a horizontal commissure representing the fundus. The os uteri and vagina are double. (*After Busch.*)

formation, however, does not prevent conception or parturition. In other instances, a transverse septum may obstruct the vagina more or less completely. Such obstruction is seldom perfect; hence, as there is usually some perforation, there may be no hindrance to impregnation. Such blockade may occur at any

Fig. 3.

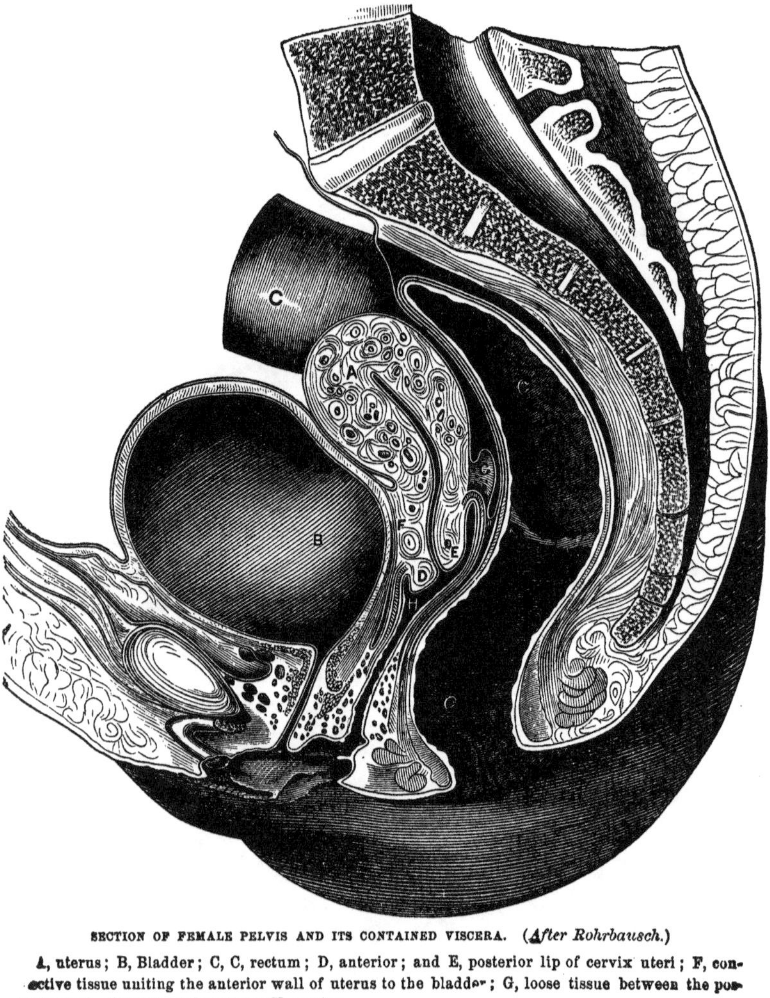

SECTION OF FEMALE PELVIS AND ITS CONTAINED VISCERA. (*After Rohrbausch.*)

A, uterus; B, Bladder; C, C, rectum; D, anterior; and E, posterior lip of cervix uteri; F, connective tissue uniting the anterior wall of uterus to the bladder; G, loose tissue between the posterior wal of uterus and rectum; H, vagina.

part of the vagina, and may result from the membranous folds being unnaturally developed, or it may occur from inflammation attendant upon disease or labor If these septums are complete, leaving no perforations, serious results may arise from the accumulation of the menstrual secretion. Laceration may occur during pregnancy, while fistulous openings into the rectum or bladder may be formed.

The vagina is liable to various forms of disease such as inflammation, ulceration, abscess, mortification, etc.; while cysts and tumors are not unfrequently found, all of which will be alluded to when describing the diseases of the organs of generation.

2. Uterus, or Womb.—The unimpregnated uterus lies entirely within the pelvis—the bladder being in front, the rectum behind, the Fallopian tubes on each side, or laterally, and the vagina below. (*Fig.* 3.) The form of the uterus has been compared to a flask with its mouth turned downward; also to a pear, or a truncated cone. Perhaps a flattened pear will convey the best idea of the natural appearance of the organ.

The uterus does not attain its full size or development until the period of pubescence. Previous to this time it is not much altered from its infantile condition. As the period of puberty approaches, there will be a gradual enlargement of the mammæ, which fact will indicate an increase in the bulk and weight of the uterus. After this period of development, it remains of the same size throughout life in the unimpregnated female. The average size of the womb at puberty, or after it has attained its full growth, is three inches in length, and two in breadth at the points of attachment to the Fallopian tubes. The diameter of the neck is much less, being usually about one inch.

The uterus is usually divided into three parts—called the fundus, body, and neck. The *fundus* is that portion above the insertion of the Fallopian tubes. It is very dense, ( *Fig.* 4, *a a*,) and firm in texture. It is a portion the least subject to disorganization from any cause. Other portions of the womb are liable to be destroyed by carcinomatous or cancerous ulceration, while the fundus remains uninjured. On the other hand, it is the part of the organ to which polypi that are not cervicle are found adhering. It is to the fundus, also, that the placenta is most usually attached.

The *body* of the uterus is included between the line above indicated and another (*Fig.* 4, *B B*) drawn through the narrowest part of the organ, or where the walls of the womb are in closest approximation. The body constitutes the principal portion of the uterus, and is that part which expands more than any other to invest the ovum. The walls here are usually half an inch thick and well supplied with blood vessels.

The *cervix*, or neck, (*Fig.* 4, *c c*) is cylindriform in shape, and composed of tissue similar to the body of the uterus. The walls are about the same thickness as the body, but do not approximate, thus leaving a spindle-shaped cavity, called the canal or cavity of the cervix. The part below the line (*D*, *D*) projects into the vagina and is called the *vaginal* portion. Around its base, the walls of the upper surface of the

FIG. 4.

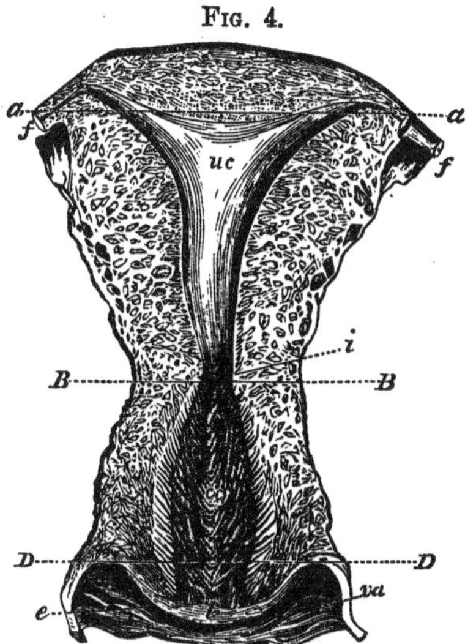


VERTICAL SECTION OF NULLIPAROUS UTERUS PARALLEL WITH ITS ANTERIOR AND POSTERIOR WALLS.

*u c*, uterine cavity; *c c*, cervical cavity or canal; *i*, internal os uteri; *e*, external os uteri; *f*, *f*, Fallopian tubes; *v a*, vagina. (*Ad Nat.*)

vagina is attached; hence, the neck does not lie immediately within the vaginal canal, but projects from its upper wall, and is there seemingly suspended. Sometimes the projection is so slight that there is difficulty in bringing the cervix or neck into view by means of the speculum. The position of the neck prevents the part from injury in coition. At the apex of the neck is observed a transverse fissure, which is the terminal end of the cervical canal. This opening is called the os-externum uteri, or the external orifice of the cervical canal. (*Fig.* 4, *e.*) This external orifice of the womb is bordered by two smooth lips, which are distinguished as the anterior and posterior lips of the os-uteri. The anterior lip is the smallest, and projects but slightly into the vagina. This unequal form of the two lips has given rise to the term os-tincæ—the orifice of the uterus. In the virgin this part of the uterus is smooth and firm, like soft cartilage. After the birth of many children, it becomes much enlarged, soft, flaccid and of irregular form. The uterus being a hollow organ, possesses both an internal and external surface. The external surface is partially covered by a reflection of the peritoneum, which is a dense, smooth fibrous tissue that lines the whole abdominal cavity. It is by the reflection of this membrane that the broad ligaments are formed which we shall presently describe. The internal cavity of the uterus in the unimpregnated state is nothing more than a narrow triangular interspace between flattened walls, which are either in immediate contact or are separated slightly from each other, and the space filled with mucus. The Fallopian tubes after passing into the uterus expand, trumpet-like, and meet the cervical canal opening upward, and the three openings expanding in this way, thus form the triangular cavity of the uterus.

By studying the form of the cavity of this organ, all the phenomena of the entrance of the ovum into the uterus and its detention there before it becomes detached to the uterine walls, may be perfectly understood. This cavity is lined by a mucous membrane of a pale pink color, except in cases where death has occurred during menstruation, when it is of a deep red hue. This membrane is not smooth, as it appears to be when viewed with the naked eye, but is perforated everywhere by the orifice of minute canals or follicles. (*Fig.* 4, *i.*)

The membrane lining the cavity of the cervix or neck of the womb is arranged in numerous folds or plicæ, (*Fig.* 4, *c*, *c*) which gives a large amount of secretory surface to a comparatively limited space. This mucous membrane is largely supplied with crypts or follicles, which secrete copiously when diseased.

After repeated pregnancies these folds become prominent and thickened, presenting a bulbous appearance, resembling the branches of a tree; hence the origin of the old term *arbor vitæ,* by which this structure was commonly designated.

As before remarked, the internal surface of the uterus presents, when examined under a microscope, a large number of small follicles or canals, which pursue a tortuous or meandering course and ramify in the substance of the mucous membrane. Besides these mucous canals there is a number of small closed follicles, which have an important bearing upon the functions of the uterus, as will be explained in another place.

All mucous membranes are formed of cells called epithelium, and arranged in several layers of cells or in a single layer. The single layer is called the cylindrical epithelium, while the several layers are called pavement or scaly epithelium. To some parts of the cylindrical epithelium, there is a small fibre-like appendage or projection, which modification is called cilia. The cilia are in motion in the living body, which motion resembles the appearance of a field of grain when influenced by the wind, causing an undulating or wave-like oscillation.

The vagina and outer portion of the cervix is covered by the scaly epithelium, which form of epithelium is never ciliated. Within the cervical canal the epithelium changes its form, becoming cylindrical and ciliated. Above the cervix it again becomes changed to the pavement or scaly epithelium. It will be necessary to allude to the different forms of the epithelium of the uterus when treating of leucorrhœa and conception.

It is supposed that the movement of the cilia is to assist the spermatozoa of the male semen in passing into the uterus through its cervical or narrow portion. Immediately below the epithelium membrane and upon which it rests is a thin layer of albuminous liquid, called basement membrane, containing numerous granules, which form the nuclei of the cells of which this membrane is composed. This liquid is the matrix of these cells, and is derived from the blood-vessels, which form a capillary network, underlying the whole epithelium surface.

The lining membrane of the uterus, with its crypts and ramifying follicles or canals, secrete a mucus, which is eliminated or poured out upon its surface, keeping it in a moist condition, when the female is in good health. When the same membrane is inflamed, or irritated, the secretion is increased and changed, constituting disease.

The body of the uterine walls consists of muscular tissue, lined, as before stated, on the outside, by reflections of the peritoneum, which line the whole abdominal cavity, and internally by the epithelium or mucous membrane. This portion of the uterine walls is remarkably firm and solid, and constitutes the greatest bulk of the organ.

All muscular fibre in the living body possess inherent contractile power, which is made manifest when a stimulus is applied. In the uterus, after the fœtus has arrived at maturity, which is nine lunar months, there is a peristaltic contraction taking place, but which does not extend to all parts of the muscular tissue of the uterus alike. The object is to press out the contents of the cavity; hence the contraction or force must be applied to the fundus and body of the uterus, while that of the cervix becomes relaxed. In this way contraction of the upper and relaxation of the lower part of the uterus continues until the fœtus is expelled into the vagina. The contractile power of the uterine walls is dependent upon an exciting cause—which cause is, no doubt, that of the fœtus increasing in innervation or nerve-force, which acting upon the muscles causes the peculiar contraction in child-birth. The uterus is largely supplied with blood-vessels, lymphatics and nerves. The nerves are derived from the spinal and sympathetic nervous system.

4. Ligaments of the Uterus.—These terms are applied to several duplications of the peritoneum, as well as to strands or bands of muscular or fibrous tissue. The ligaments connect together the appendages of the uterus, support it, and limit its motion within the pelvis. There are four of these ligaments—the round, broad, utero-sacral and the utero-vesicle.

*a. Round Ligaments.*—These are sometimes called the sub-pubic ligaments. They consist of flattened cords or bands of muscular and fibrous tissue. These bands arise in the tendons of the internal oblique and transversalis muscles of the abdomen, near the symphysis pubis, or front bone of the pelvis, and are inserted into the uterus near the commencement of the Fallopian tubes. (*Fig.* 5.) The ligament of the right side is generally shorter than the left. Hence in pregnancy the uterus usually inclines to that side. The round ligaments are composed of smooth muscular fibres arranged in bundles and derived from the uterus.

*b. Broad Ligaments.*—The peritoneum, after covering the front, back and fundus of the uterus, extends off in two folds or layers to the side and base of the pelvis, to which they are attached. By the arrangement of these ligaments the cavity of the pelvis is divided into two chambers—the anterior one containing the bladder, and the posterior, or deeper, holding the rectum and portion of the small intestines—while the uterus occupies the septum between them. (*Fig.* 3.)

To the upper border of the broad ligaments are three folds, called the lesser wings. The central or superior of these contains the Fallopian tubes, and is called the mesentery of the tubes. The smaller posterior fold invests the ovary, together with its proper ligament; while the third or anterior fold inclines obliquely toward the uterus, and constitutes the covering of the round ligaments. (*Plate* 5.) Between the laminæ or folds of these ligaments are found the

Fig. 5.

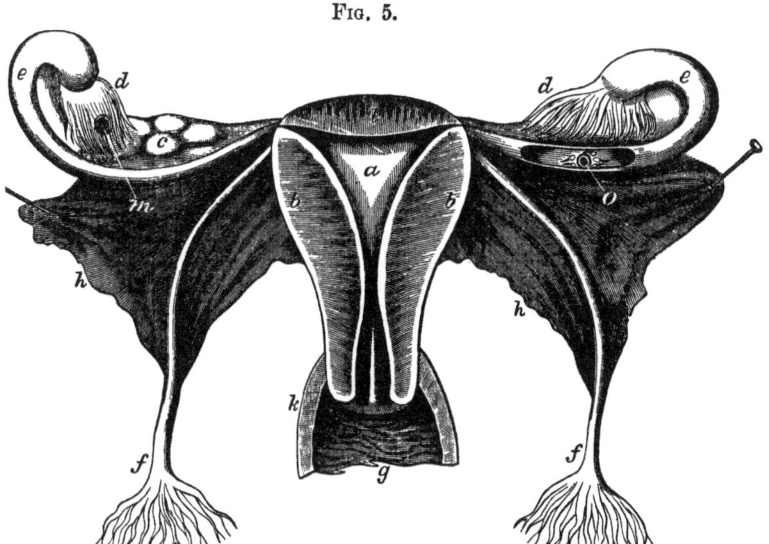


FRONT VIEW OF THE UNIMPREGNATED UTERUS AND ITS APPENDAGES AND SECTION OF THE VAGINA.

*a*, cavity of uterus; *b*, body of uterus; *d d*, fimbriated extremity of Fallopian tubes; *e*, Fallopian tube; *f*, round ligaments; *h*, broad ligaments; *k*, walls of vagina; *l*, fundus of uterus; *g*, vagina; *m*, fimbriated portion of tube grasping an ovum; *o*, ovum surrounded by spermatozoa in lower third of Fallopian tube during its passage toward the uterus. It is in this part of the tube where impregnation usually takes place.

blood-vessels, lymphatics and nerves, which supply the uterus and its appendages. The broad ligaments are considered by some writers more as a mesentery than a ligament, on account of their investing the uterus. Its appendages are attached to the pelvis in the same manner as the mesentery attaches the intestines to the spine—the space between the folds sufficing for the conveyance of the blood-vessels and nerves.

*c. The Utero-Sacral Ligaments.*—From the back side of the neck of the uterus, two folds of peritoneum proceed toward the rectum. Between these folds are two corresponding bands of fibrous tissue which extend from the substance of the neck or cervix of the uterus and are inserted into the sacrum. The office of these ligaments is to prevent the womb from being forced upward in the act of conjunction, and to limit the descent of the organ in erect posture of the body.

*d. The Utero-Vesicle Ligaments.*—Opposite to the point of junction of the body and neck of the uterus, where the peritoneum is reflected forward on the bladder, are observed two lateral folds containing bundles of fibrinous tissue. These constitute the anterior or utero-vesicle ligaments.

4. FALLOPIAN TUBES OR OVADUCTS.—The Fallopian tubes are the excretory ducts of the ovaries, as the vas deferens are the excretory ducts of the testicles. The Fallopian tubes differ from the vas deferens, as well as every other excretory duct in the animal economy, on account of being entirely detached from the glands or ovaries. The Fallopian tubes or ovaducts are equally developed on both

sides of the body in all vertebrate or back-bone animals, except in the class of Aves or birds. (*Fig.* 26, *g.*) With this class the right tube becomes atrophied at an earlier period, while the left continues to develop.

Each ovaduct has the form of a conical tube, the base of which being free and directed toward the ovary, while the apex is attached to the uterus. The shape of the tubes resembles a horn or trumpet, particularly when straitened out. The length of these tubes varies in different subjects, but the average length is four and a half inches. The diameter of the tubes will only admit of a bristle, but the canal at its external or free surface will admit of a quill of ordinary size. The outer edge of the tubes are broken into a number of fringe-like processes of unequal length, constituting the fimbriated portion, or *corpus fimbriatum,* in the centre of which is seen the orifice called *corpus abdominali.* The tubes themselves are composed of strong fibrous tissue, similar to the uterus, and are invested like the latter organ, with the peritoneum, by being placed between the folds of the broad ligaments as before described. The internal coat is a mucous or epithelium membrane, but different from that which lines the uterus. Here are found no crypts or follicles as exist in the lining membrane of the uterus, but a very delicate pink layer of undeveloped tissue, mixed with numerous formative cells.

Under ordinary circumstances, and when these organs are in health, the canals of the Fallopian tubes contain only a small quantity of viscid mucus. When death takes place during the menstrual period, this

Fig. 6.

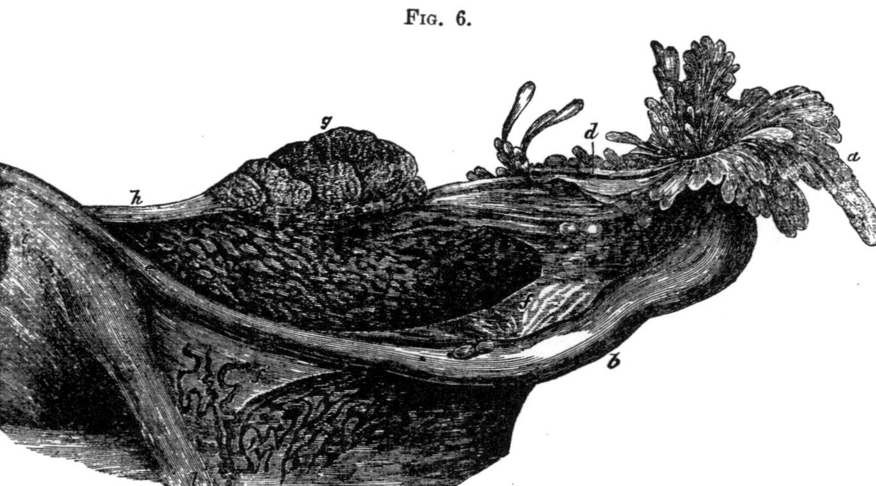


LEFT FALLOPIAN TUBE FROM AN ADULT. (*After Richard.*)

**a, fimbriæ; b, body of the tube; c, abdominal orifice; d, tubo-ovarian ligament and fringes; e, commencement of the tube; ff, tubal mesentary or broad ligament; g, ovary; h, ligament of the ovary; i, uterus; l, round ligaments.**

fluid is found to be replaced by uncoagulated blood of a dark color. The fimbriated portion or *infundibulum*, performs an office of more importance than it usually has the credit of doing. It is this portion of the tube that grasps the surface of the ovaries, receiving and conveying the ova to the uterus.

From illustrations given in works a very poor idea of the beauty of this structure can be obtained. To comprehend the wonderful peculiarity of the delicate plicæ or fringes with which the expanded mouthpiece of the tubes are beset, they should be examined under water. When thus inspected in the young and healthy subject, the funnel-shaped projections are arranged in numerous folds and leaflets, which are merely continuations of the similar plicæ which line the cavity of the tubes. The office of these delicate and down-like folds is doubtless to receive and entangle the delicate ovum in one of the numerous channels which are formed between the leaflets and to conduct it into the cavity of the tube toward which they are diverged. (*Plate* 6.)

There are a great variety of forms of these funnel-shaped projections—no two subjects presenting the same appearance. They seem to bear a certain relation to the age of the persons in which they are found. In the young subject at the age of puberty, and in those who have borne a few children, they exhibit that richness and profusion of folds already described.

*Tubo-ovarian Ligament.*—This so-called ligament consists of one of the fimbriæ prolonged upon the outer margin or base of the broad ligament or mesentery of the tube. (*Fig.* 6, *d.*) It was supposed by the older anatomists that the office of this ligament was to draw the end of the tube upon the ovary. This view is not entertained at the present day. Its office is to keep the fimbriated extremity of the tube within a certain distance of the ovary, and permit the orifice to be easily applied over the gland or ovary when it is required. By this arrangement the tube is enabled to enclose any portion of the ovary that may be needed. The length of this ligament is one and a half to two inches in length.

5. Office of the Fallopian Tubes.—The Fallopian tubes perform a double office, receiving the ova from the ovaries, and conveying them into the uterus. and also receiving the spermatic fluid of the male and conveying it from the uterus in the direction of the ovaries, the tubes being the seat of impregnation.

These conclusions are derived from observation upon mammalian animals as well as the human female, the functions in either case being essentially the same. It is accordingly quite clearly demonstrated that the office of the fimbriated extremities of the Fallopian tubes is to become expanded over a certain portion of the ovaries—the extent of the surface depending upon the relative size of the ovaries.

In some mammalia, as the cat, for instance, the extremity of the tube is sufficiently large to encompass the entire ovary, so that an ovum escaping from any part of its surface, will be conveyed or fall into the orifice, and be drawn into the canal. In many other animals, however, as well as in the human female, the size of the tube is only large enough to cover one-third or one-half of the ovary at one time, so that, in all cases, a selection must be made of the exact spot where the ovum is discharged, or else the ovum will be lost by falling into the cavity of the abdomen.

Sterility in the female is sometimes caused by a morbid adhesion of the tube to a portion of the ovary. By what power the mouth of the tube is directed toward a particular portion of an ovary, from which the ovum is about to be discharged, remains entirely unknown, as does also the precise nature of the cause which affects this movement.

The tubo-ovarian ligament (*Fig.* 6, *d.*) serves at all times to keep the extremity of the tube in contiguity with the ovary, but by what agency the orifice of the tube is drawn toward and the fimbriæ become expanded upon the ovary cannot be satisfactorily explained. The only way to account for the movement is the contraction of the low contractile form of fibre of which this ligament is composed, which is found in some of the lower-order animals. It was formerly supposed that the approximation of the mouth of the tube and the ovary occurred under the influence of sexual orgasm — an inference natural enough so long as it was believed that the ova were discharged from the ovary during and as a consequence of sexual congress. This cannot, with our present knowledge of physiology, be admitted; for it is now a well-settled fact that in all mammalia, including the human female, the discharge of the ova or eggs takes place during the menstrual discharge and not during sexual congress. The approximation of the Fallopian tube to the ovary at such times is to be regarded as a movement providing for a safe passage of the ova to the uterus, and not that the venereal orgasm is the cause of the movement.

The period of time occupied for the passage of the ovum through the tube is usually a few days. In the bitch, the ovum remains in the tube susceptible to impregnation during six or eight days. In the guinea-pig and rabbit, the ovum makes its transit in about three days. Less is known respecting the time of such passage in the human female. With the exception of abnormal cases, there are but two instances recorded in which the human ovum has been actually seen on its passage to the uterus.

An attempt has been made to ascertain the time an ovum is passing in the human female, by comparing the condition of early ova found in the uterus, or prematurely expelled from this organ, with the last known date of intercourse or of menstruation; but neither of these modes of calculation can afford any certain information. The analogies furnished by observation with the higher order of animals lead to the supposition that the time occupied for the passage of the ovum through the tube in the human female is not materially different from that of animals, which is from six to twelve days.

The office of the tubes, as before intimated, is two-fold, namely, the passage of the ovum from the ovaries to the uterus, and for the conveyance of the spermatozoa toward the ovaries. The rapidity with which the spermatic fluid is capable of reaching and entering the Fallopian tubes in some animals is very remarkable. *Bischoff* observed spermatozoa in the ovaduct of a guinea-pig in three quarters of an hour after coitus. The power by which the semen reaches the tubes is partly by its ejaculation from the male organ toward the mouth of the uterus, and by the ciliary covering of the membrane lining the neck of the womb, which assist the movements of the spermatozoa to ascend into that organ, by their own inherent power. In this way they are enabled to pass up into the tube, where their progress is then arrested by the cilia lining, the tubes having a downward movement for the purpose of conveying the ova toward the uterus, and retarding the movement of the spermatozoa. By this arrangement of the ciliated lining membrane, the egg or ovum and spermatozoa are brought together in the middle and lower third of the Fallopian tube, where impregnation usually occurs.

This explanation properly belongs to the article on Conception, to which the reader is referred.

In order to show the precise limits of the functions of the ovaducts, it will be necessary to examine particularly the evidence which serves to show that the ovary is the part in which the ovum is formed, and that the uterus is the place in which it is inverted or developed; and also that the Fallopian tubes are the conducting media by which the ovum is transmitted from the formative to the recipient organ: likewise, that these tubes are the seat where the ovum becomes impregnated by contact with the spermatozoa while on its passage to the uterus. (*Fig.* 5.) One of the most remarkable circumstances connected with the generative process is the periods of separation of the ova from the ovary and their passage along the Fallopian tubes to the uterus, which will be more particularly explained in the article on Conception.

### DEFECTS IN THE STRUCTURE OF THE FALLOPIAN TUBES.

*Chaussier* mentions the case of a woman who, notwithstanding she had but one ovary, one Fallopian tube, and one side of the uterus absent, had borne ten living children. Her death having occurred a short time after the birth of her last child, a good opportunity was afforded for examining the parts, when this curious fact was abundantly established. Hence the absence of one tube and ovary will not cause sterility, although such a misfortune must necessarily follow when they are entirely wanting. Sometimes the tubes are short and there may be an absence of the fimbriæ. The former might not cause sterility, but the latter would.

Adhesions not unfrequently take place from inflammation between the tubes and peritoneum and intestines, which is apt to displace the arrangement of the parts. This is one of the most frequent causes of sterility, and is of that nature that cannot be obviated. The tubes may become distended with blood accumulated from the menstrual flow. A case of this kind is stated in the American Journal of Medical Science, No. xxxv. It is that of a woman who, after her second confinement, had an attack of inflammation of the uterus, which terminated in a union of the uterine walls. Behind this obstruction the menstrual flow accumulated, until the Fallopian tubes

Fig. 7.

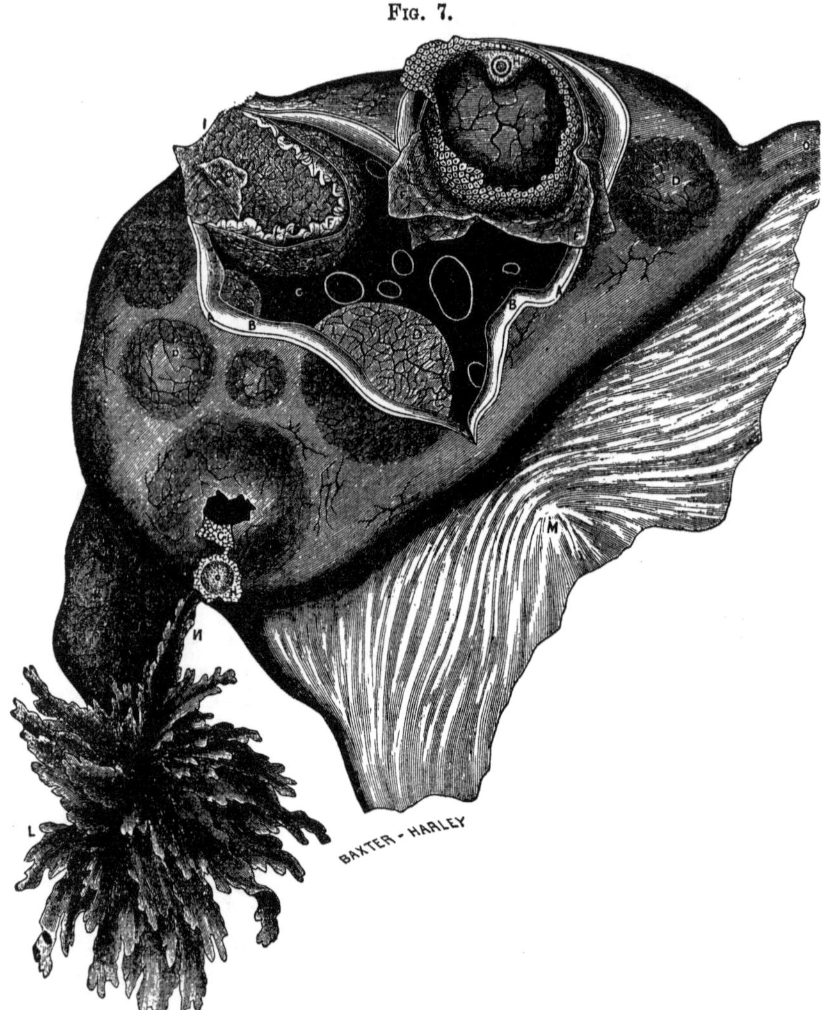


OVARY ENLARGED FOUR TIMES THE NATURAL SIZE, AND DISSECTED TO SHOW. (*After Coste.*)

A, peritoneum ; B, tunica albuginea ; C, stroma ; D D D D, Graafian follicles in various stages of growth ; E E, outer coat of the follicle ; F F, inner coat of the follicle ; G G G, epitheleal lining or membrana granulosa ; H H, ovum and camulus ; I, orifice by which the follicle has discharged an ovum ; K, Fallopian tube , L, fimbriæ ; M, broad ligament ; N, tubo-ov rian ligament ; O, ligamentum ovarii.

became enormously distended, when, at length, one of them burst, thereby causing death from the escape of blood into the abdominal cavity.

6. OVARY.—The ovaries constitute the glands appropriated to the formation of the female ova or eggs. The ovary is not fully developed until about the period of puberty. It is usually about the size of a large chestnut when fully developed, their weight being about one-quarter of an ounce. They lie imbedded in the broad ligaments between the uterus and fimbriated extremity of the Fallopian tubes. Besides the connection which it has to the uterus through the intervention of the broad ligaments, it has another uniting it to the womb, known as the *ligamentum ovarii*, or ovarian ligament, (*Fig.* 6, *h*) while it is also connected to the Fallopian tube by another ligament called *tubo-ovarian ligament*, already described. (*Fig.* 6, *d.*)

During pregnancy the ovaries change position. As the uterus expands it carries them along with it into the abdominal cavity.

*Structure of the Ovary.*—The ovaries, like the uterus and Fallopian tubes, are covered with the peritoneum, derived from broad ligaments, which form their outer covering. (*Fig.* 7, *a*, *a.*) Below this outer coat, we find another composed of dense fibrous tissue, and called the *tunica albiginea* or *tunica propria*, (*Fig.* 7 *B B.*) This forms a complete investment for the ovary.

After removing this investment or tunic another is brought into view, which is called the stroma or parenchyma. It lies immediately below the tunica proper, (*Fig.* 7, *c*) thus forming a bed for the germs, and protecting the ova from injury. This structure is largely supplied with blood-vessels, which give it a bright red color. When the microscope is applied to this structure, it will be found to consist of blood-vessels principally—the space between the vessels being filled up with fibrous tissue, which bind the vessels together.

## OVASACS OR GRAAFIAN VESICLES.

On cutting into a healthy ovary of a subject not too far advanced in life, a number of small vesicles or bladders (so small as to require the aid of the microscope to see them) may be readily separated. These vesicles are named after De Graaf, their discoverer. In infants and young subjects these vesicles or ovasacs are found only upon the periphery, (*Fig.* 9,) where

FIG. 8.

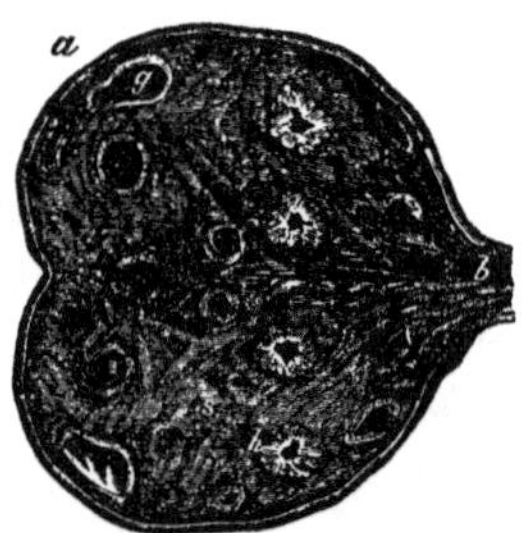


LONGITUDINAL SECTION OF ADULT OVARY.

*a*, distal ; *b*, proximal end ; *s*, stroma ; *g*, Graafian follicles of the ordinary size before enlargement ; *h*, stellate remains of follicles which have burst and shrunk after discharging their ova.

they form a thick rind. The spaces between them are filled with blood-vessels and fibrous tissue, the latter affording support for the vessels, and is called as before stated, the *stroma.*

After puberty these ovasacs become buried deeper in the structure, even to the very base of the organ. They are always, however, the most numerous upon the outer surface. The number of developed vesicles in each ovary visible to the naked eye was formerly computed at from twelve to twenty, while it was supposed that when these were exhausted by child-bearing and miscarriage, the power of procreation ceased. Recent and careful observation, however, has shown that the number of vesicles in each ovary amounts to thirty, fifty, one hundred, and even two hundred, while in very young subjects the number exceeds all computation.

The vesicles are most easily seen in the adult ovary by making a perpendicular section. In this way from ten to twenty may be brought in view. (*Fig.* 8.) A similar section in the ovary of an infant, and examined with a microscope, will reveal several hundred. (*Fig.* 9.) Each Graafian follicle or ovasac is of an

FIG. 9.

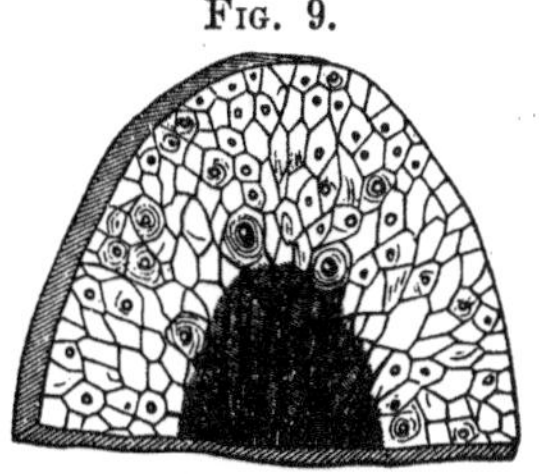

**Section of part of the ovary of an infant aged twenty months. The central portion consists of stroma and blood-vessels only. The lighter peripheral part is composed entirely of close-set ovasacs, containing ova of various sizes**

oval form, the contents of which will be now carefully analyzed in order to have a clear comprehension of the changes which occur in them during pregnancy, and which result in the formation of the body termed the *corpus luteum.*

## STRUCTURE OF GRAAFIAN FOLLICLE.

Each Graafian follicle is lined bv three distinct membranes:—

*a. External, Fibrous or Vascular.*—(*Fig.* 7, *E.*, and *Fig.* 10, *o*, *v.*) This membrane closely embraces the ovasac and is derived from the parenchyma or stroma of the ovary. If examined with the microscope, it will be found very vascular. Its office is to give increased support and protection to the ovasac which it surrounds.

*b. Second or Middle Coat.*—This is an independent membrane, and in uniting with the external, forms the Graafian follicle. (*Fig.* 7, *F*, *F* and *Fig.* 10, *o*, *v.*)

*c. Internal Lining, called Epithelial Membrane, or Membrana Granulosa.*—(*Fig.* 7, *G*, *G*, and *Fig.* 10, *m*, *g.*) This membrane consists of nucleated cells forming an epithelial lining, the cells of which are so lightly held together that it is doubted whether it is entitled to the name of membrane. This structure plays an important part to the ovum, which is always found lodged within it. As the ovasac develops, this membrane arranges itself into three distinct layers of granules. The *membrana granulosa* forms the outer layer. (*Fig.* 11, *c.*) The second portion aggregates around the ovum, constituting its special investment.

Fig. 10.

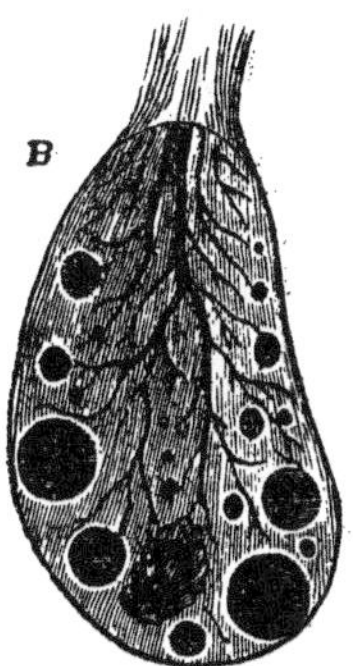


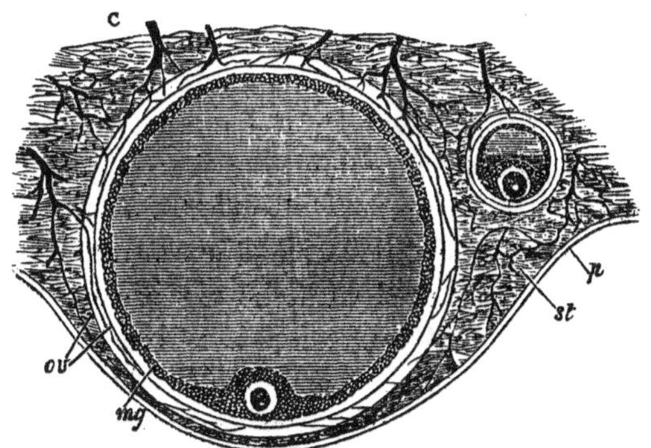


LONGITUDINAL SECTION OF HUMAN OVARY.

B. Transverse section of human ovary, to show the general arrangement of the developed Graafian follicles toward the surface; twice the natural size.

SECTION OF TWO GRAAFIAN FOLLICLES IN THE HUMAN OVARY.

C. Diagrammatic representation, in section, of two Graafian follicles, in different stages of advancement in the ovary of a human female, enlarged about ten diameters. *p*, peritoneal covering of the ovary; *s t*, ovarian stroma; *o v*, the two layers of the ovasac; *m g*, membrana granulosa, near which is the discus granulosus, with the ovum imbedded.

Fig. 11.

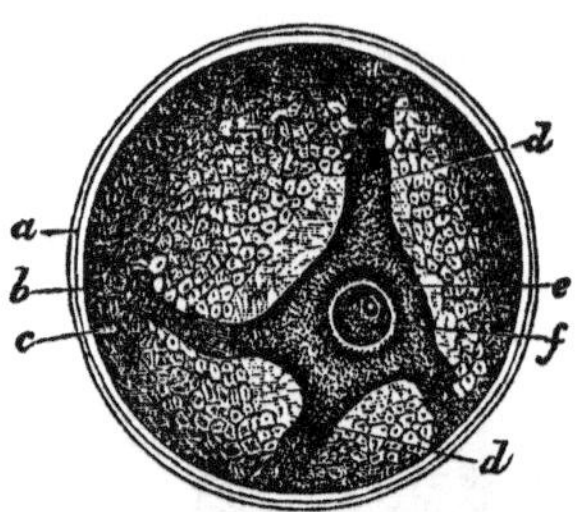


GRAAFIAN VESICLE OF THE RABBIT × 100 DIAMETERS.—(*After Barry.*)

*a*, outer coat or tunic of the ovasac; *b*, ovasac; *c*, epithelial lining or membrana granulosa, a portion of which has been removed in order to display, *d d*, retinacula (here too distinctly marked); *e*, tunica granulosa of Barry immediately surrounding the ovum, consisting of, *f*, zona pellucida, within which is the yelk and germinal vesicle and macula.

This is called *tunica granulosa* of Barry. (*Fig.* 11, *e.*) The third collects to form a structure composed of the central mass, in which the ovum is imbedded, corresponding with the cumulus of Baer (*Fig.* 7, *H*, *H*), of certain cords or flattened bands, from two to four in number, which pass off from the central mass outward, to become united with the *membrana granulosa* lining the Graafian follicle. These bands or cords are termed by Barry the *retinacula* (*Fig.* 11, *d*, *d*), from their supposed office in suspending the ovum and retaining it in its proper situation in the Graafian vesicle. These bands are not a necessary structure, for they are deficient in some animals. As this part of the descriptive anatomy seems intricate and difficult for those unacquainted with the structure of these parts, a more general and familiar explanation will be presented to the comprehension of the ordinary reader.

The ovary may be compared to a honey-comb, the walls of the comb formed by stroma or parenchyma, as already described, lining these cells; or, the Graafian vesicle are two membranes, which we will call the inner and outer coat of the Graafian vesicle. (*Fig.* 10, *o v.*) Besides this, there are a number of cells which De Graaf divided into three distinct layers or distinct membrane. In the midst of these cells is found the little ovum imbued with all the peculiarities of its parent, the human female, and destined to become a living being endowed with physical and spiritual life. Besides this structure, the Graafian follicles contain albuminous fluid of a slight yellowish color, which is coagulable by heat. In this fluid float granules and oil globules.

7. Office of the Ovary.—The ovary is to the female what the testis is to the male. It is the germ-preparing organ, and therefore the most essential part of the generative apparatus, all the other structures being only its accessories. The ovary is not merely an organ for the formation of the ova, but is designed also for their separation and expulsion when they have reached maturity. This process is usually termed ovulation, and takes place without the assistance of the male. The ova which are formed at an early period are not called into activity until the system is sufficiently developed for the parturient act to take place without serious detriment to the system.

In some of the lower order of animals the whole of the vital energies of the parent is exhausted by one effort of reproduction. It is probable that long before the time arrives for the development of the ova, many of them have perished, their places being continually supplied with new formations. On the other hand, at the decline of life the power of reproducing and emitting ova altogether fails. Hence the limitation of the office of reproduction is allotted to that period in which the vital energies are at their fullest vigor, when the parent may transmit to the offspring a strong and vigorous constitution.

Most parents overlook the fact that all the weaknesses, peculiarities and idiosyncracies of the parent are conveyed to the germ at the time of conception, and will unfold with it and become part and parcel of the constitution of the new being. Until this is fully realized by parents and the difficulty remedied, it is but reasonable to suppose that the vital *stamina* of each subsequent generation will greatly degenerate or deviate from perfect original or normal health. There is not an observant physician living who is not able to trace distinctly the weaknesses and constitutional imperfections of the parents, and show that they are more fully developed in the offspring, when they partake of them, than in the parents themselves.

The husbandman expects when he plants imperfect seed to reap the fruits of such labor. The same is the case in raising unhealthy stock. "A corrupt tree cannot bring forth good fruit," neither can an unhealthy human being generate vigorous offspring. The principles of Nature are self-apparent in this regard. There can be no violation of her simple laws without entailing some evil or abnormal consequence.

From what has been already stated, it will be perceived that the ovary in the human female has three noticeable periods. The first is that of preparation, extending from birth or infancy to puberty. The second is that state of activity which extends from puberty to the decline of life; and the third period is that of decay during the decline of life.

*a. The First Period.—Origin of the Graafian Vesicle.*— There has been found no trace of the Graafian vesicles before birth. The first evidence we have of their formation is soon after birth, when they consist of a little transparent vesicle surrounded by granular cells, which are filled with a clear fluid containing cell nuclei and granules. Surrounding this is observed traces of the ovasac becoming developed, which continue until a Graafian vesicle is formed. If the ovary of an infant be examined, when it is a few months old, by dividing it longitudinally, as in *Fig.* 9, it will be seen that the outer surface contains a large number of Graafian vesicles and ova in various stages of development, while the central part is made up of blood vessels and connecting tissue, which ultimately becomes similarly formed to the outer or peripheral portion.

*b. The Middle Period, or Second Stage of Growth and Maturation,* is the one to which the most interest is attached. During certain portions of this period or epoch the ovary is employed in ripening and emitting ova, and is a *periodic* occurrence in the human female as well as in the various orders of animals. The emission of ova will occur at different periods in different animals, these differing again from those occurring in the human female.

In the roe, for instance, Bischoff has discovered that she emits ova only once a year, which is the latter part of July and during August; and, also, that it is only at this period of the year that the ovary of the female contain ripe ova and the testes of the male ripe semen: hence, this is the only time when the animal can become impregnated.

In many animals the ripening of the ova and discharge occur more frequently. Especially is this the case in the human female, such periodicity occurring, no doubt, once a month, or during the menstrual discharge. This will be found more fully demonstrated in the article on Menstruation.

The office of the ovary from puberty to decline of life, is to mature ova and discharge them monthly, during which operation the whole energy of the ovary is called into action. After an ovum has been expelled, the wound made in the walls of the ovary becomes healed, and the action is transferrred to another set of follicles, which ripen and pass through the same order of changes as before.

The ovary cannot be said ever to be, during this period of life, in a perfect state of rest. New ova are all the while undergoing development; hence, ova may be found in the ovary in all stages of ripening.

There are two circumstances which arrest the process of ovarian development, namely, utero-gestation or pregnancy and lactation or nursing. Occasionally exceptions may be made to this rule; nevertheless, the evidence collected favors the belief that pregnant women, and those who suckle, emit no ova during the continuance of either.

When the period approaches, or has already arrived at which the female is in a condition to propagate, and ready to receive the male, a number of Graafian follicles increase in size and approach nearer the surface of the ovary, presenting the appearance of round grains, so close set as to give the semblance of a bunch of grapes. (*Fig.* 12.) When these enlarge in

FIG. 12.

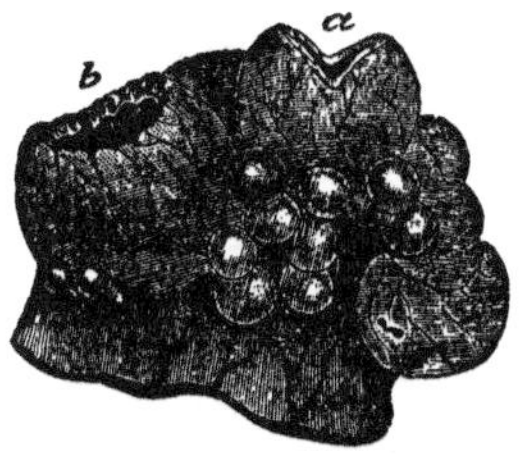


Portion of ovary of the Sow. The Graafian follicles project above the surface of the ovary. Two of them (*a*, *b*) have already burst and eliminated their contents.

size it is occasioned by an increase of the fluid in the follicle, the same being supplied by the minute capillaries or blood-vessels, giving it a bright red color. While these changes are going on within the follicle, preparations are being also made externally for the rupture of the walls of the ovary. (*Fig.* 7, *D D*, and *Fig.* 12, *a*, *b*.) The part to be thus broken becomes exceedingly red from the accumulation of blood, while the membrane which encloses the Graafian follicle becomes thinner and thinner, by pressure and absorption, until they are finally ruptured, (*Fig.* 7, *H*, and *Fig.* 13) and the ovum expelled, leaving a clot of blood and a bloody fluid.

Fig. 13.

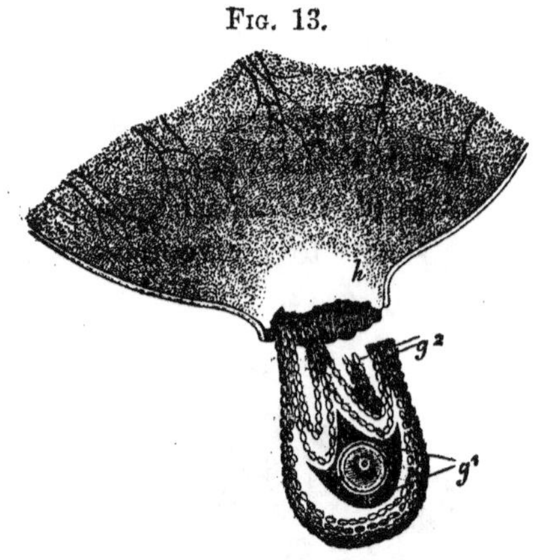


OVUM OF THE RABBIT IN THE ACT OF ESCAPING FROM A RUPTURED GRAAFIAN FOLLICLE. (*After Barry.*)

The ovum is surrounded by the tunica granulosa, $g^1$, and draws after it the portion of membrana granulosa termed the retinacula, $g^2$; at $h$, where the rupture has taken place, the coats of the follicle are attenuated, and toward this spot numerous vessels converge.

If an examination be made of a healthy woman who has previously menstruated regularly up to the time of death, there will be found in each ovary one or more Graafian follicles in the condition just described. As the Graafian follicles repair, they come toward the outer margin or periphery as represented in (*Fig. D D*, 7.) Only one of these ripen, as a general rule, at one time. Sometimes two or three are developing and preparing for being ruptured at the same period. If the bloody fluid be washed out of the Graafian vesicle after the ovum has been expelled, its inner surface will be found intensely red, looking like an inflamed surface.

8. Period of Rupture of Graafian Follicle and Escape of the Ovum.—This period is called by Pouchet the period of parturition of the follicle. This is after the ovum has passed through its various changes of development, and is expelled from the Graafian follicle in order that it may enter the Fallopian tube. Therefore the ovary is to the ovum what the womb is to the fœtus. It nourishes it, and when it is matured, expels it into the Fallopian tube, where it passes through other changes, provided it becomes impregnated by the spermatozoa while traversing this channel.

In animals where the egg is large, it (the egg) will assist in rupturing the ovasac. In the human female the ovum is too small to effect any such purpose in order to liberate itself. It lies in the Graafian vesicle perfectly passive and uses no mechanical effort whatever for its own liberation. The process by which this takes place is compared to the bursting of an abscess, with which mode of rupture nearly every person is familiar. The accumulation of the liquid before described within the follicle causes a pressure against its walls, and this kept up for a short time, will render them so thin by absorption, that a very slight force is sufficient to rupture the sac and expel the core and contents of the same.

As has been already stated, there are four membranes that must be ruptured before the ovum can be expelled from the Graafian follicle; namely, the two membranes forming or enclosing the contents of the Graafian follicle, and the two membranes of the ovary known as the peritoneal coat and tunica albuginea.

When these four membranes are sufficiently absorbed to admit of a rupture, it takes place, and the ovum, with its *membrana granulosa* or those layers of cells before alluded to, in which the ovum is imbedded, is expelled—which expulsion is beautifully shown in *Fig.* 13.

Here is represented a ripe Graafian vesicle which has just discharged its ovum with the tunica granulosa ($g^1$), and dragging after it a portion of the retinacula, ($g^2$). In the human female two or more follicles may become matured or ripened at the same time, and burst simultaneously. Should this occur, and each become impregnated in the Fallopian tube, they will severally develop a new being. In this way, twins and triplets are produced at the same time.

There are some remarkable features about the healing of the rupture of the membranes of the Graafian follicle, after the ovum has been expelled, as well as in the changes that take place in the follicle itself. The changes are very different if pregnancy does not occur after the ovum is expelled, from those changes which take place when impregnation is effected. In order to the comprehension of this subject in a proper manner, it will be necessary to speak first of the changes that take place in the follicle and its obliteration without pregnancy, and those which occur when fecundation follows the rupture.

*a. Without Pregnancy.*—Immediately after the expulsion of the ovum, the ruptured membranes gradually approximate, the redness disappears, and an exudation is thrown out, which causes the part to become agglutinated, precisely as is observed in a boil after it has discharged its contents. When the parts become united there remain the common cicatrix observed in the healing of other tissue. While the healing is going on, the follicle itself shrinks to a very small dimension, and by the time one or more follicles have passed through the same series, which will require a month or two, the cavity of the follicle will be shrunk so as scarcely to admit of a body of the size of a small pin-head, (*Fig.* 8, *h*) the membrane lining the same appearing puckered. The follicles continue to decrease in size until they become entirely obliterated, giving room to other vesicles or follicles, which pass through the same stages of growth and decay. By this frequent obliteration of the follicles, which is continually taking place during the menstrual period of the female, the ovaries, in advance life, exhibit a large number of pits and furrows, (*Figs.* 14 and 15)

FIG. 14.

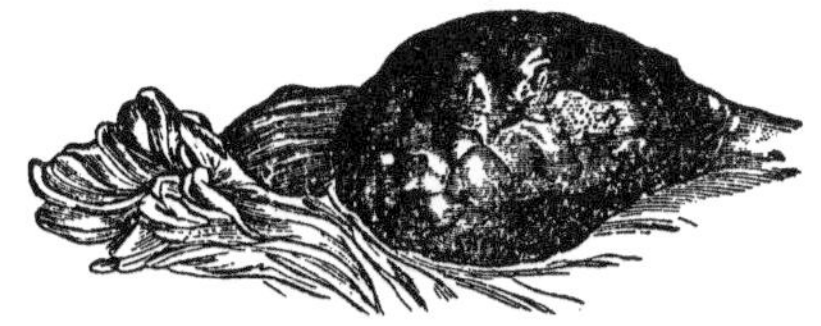

Ovary about the time of cessation of menstruation. (*Ad. Nat.*)

FIG. 15.

Ovary in old age. (*Ad. Nat.*)

at once affording a striking proof that the discharge

of ova or eggs from the ovary occurs independent of sexual congress.

*b. After Pregnancy.*—Very different are the changes which take place in the Graafian follicles when impregnation occurs from those which appear in the absence of impregnation. In both cases, it is true, there is the same obliteration of the follicle, but in the latter it is much slower than in the former case. The cicatrix will form in about the same time in each, while the obliteration of the vesicle after pregnancy may not be effected under thirteen or fourteen months. This process is also upon a very extensive scale. When impregnation has occurred, all parts of the generative apparatus are brought under the influence of a common stimulus. This is particularly the case with the uterus, which very soon receives a large supply of blood. The blood-vessels of the ovaries and uterus, together with their nerves, being so intimately associated, any stimulation of either will act similarly upon all the others. The vessels becoming loaded with blood, a greater amount of vital action takes place both in the ovary and the uterus. This is not the case when impregnation does not occur. When the ovum is thrown off from the ovary, it gradually subsides into a quiescent state, while the lacerated membranes of the vesicle and ovary unite and thus obliterate the follicle.

The stimulus consequent upon the union of the male and female germ seems to retard these changes—setting up new ones, that accomplish the same ends, although requiring a longer time for their accomplishment. In impregnation, the inner membrane of the follicle becomes thickened by a deposit of yellow oil granules. The Graafian follicle, at the time of rupture, may occupy from one-fourth to one-half of the ovary, and will continue to occupy this space until the third or fourth month of pregnancy; while if this does not occur the follicle will disappear in a month or two months. After four months of pregnancy, the follicle gradually diminishes—the inner coat rapidly increasing by a deposit of the oil globules, and this thickening encroaching upon the cavity, causing its diminution. The parts surrounding the follicle at this time become hard and swollen; likewise the ovary, which is larger than its fellow. (*Fig.* 16, and 44, *c.*)

FIG. 16.

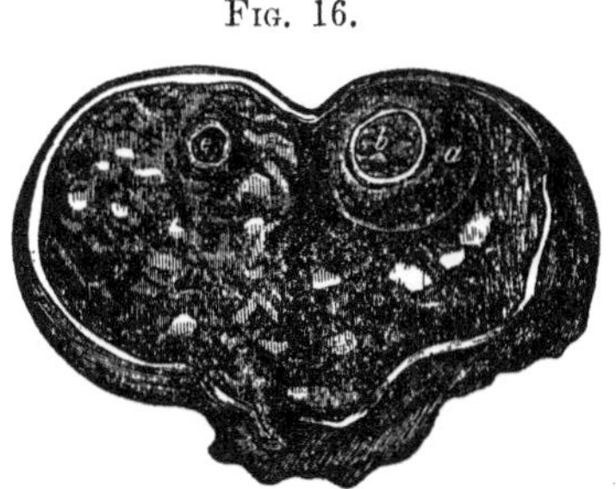

Section of the ovary of a woman who died at the end of the fourth month of utero-gestation. The Graafian follicle of the ovum which had been impregnated projects above the stroma. (*Ad. Nat.*)

The deposit of thin yellow oil globules within the follicle has given rise to the supposition of the formation of a new membrane, thus leading to erroneous conclusions in regard to a *corpus luteum*, to be presently described. After the fourth or fifth month of pregnancy the follicles begin to diminish more rapidly, and so continues until the time of birth, or nine months, when the ovasac will have lost much of its brightness, the cavity being nearly filled. Some four or five months after delivery, the cavity is entirely obliterated, the yellow appearance subsiding into a pale or white line, the cicatrix also disappearing meanwhile. (*Fig.* 44, *c.*)

## CORPUS LUTEUM.

*What is it?*

The Corpus Luteum is the yellow body which is left in the ovary in consequence of the bursting of a Graafian vesicle. (*Fig.* 17.)

Fig. 17.

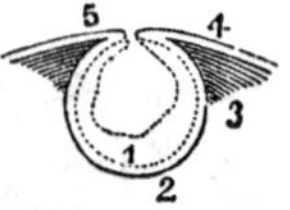


GRAAFIAN FOLLICLE AND CORPUS LUTEUM. (*After Von Baer.*)

Fig. 17 represents a corpus luteum taken from a female who destroyed herself by drowning, eight days after impregnation. 1, mucous tunic of the Graafian vesiclo sprouting from the circumference toward the centre; 2, external tunic of the vesicle; 4, ovarian stroma; 5, ovarian membrane; point at which the ovulum escaped from the Graafian follicle.*

Modern physiologists and anatomists look upon it as an obsolete term. The expression belongs to a time when anatomists were in the habit of designating by the word *body* or *corpus*, any part of the animal economy whose nature or relation with other parts was not understood. *Farre* thinks it is an unfortunate circumstance that such a term should ever have

* Morton's Anatomy, p. 361.

been applied to the Graafian follicle—the more so, since it was employed without any definite meaning.

The difference in the yellowness of the Graafian follicles in the impregnated and unimpregnated state, has caused the name of *corpus luteum* to be used without expressing any thing more than a yellow body. The one was called a *true* and the other a *false* CORPUS LUTEUM. With the same propriety a child might be called a *false* man. The term is arbitrary and unscientific. It is calculated to mislead to the supposition that the *false* and *true* corpus luteum are really different bodies, whereas they are the same, only in different stages of growth and decay, as has been already intimated.

## DOES THE DISCHARGE OF OVA TAKE PLACE WITHOUT SEXUAL CONGRESS?

Much controversy has occurred, at various times, in regard to the discharge of the ovum. All observers down to *Barry* contend that coitus was the sole cause of such phenomena, and that it could only take place during sexual congress. Late observers have exploded this idea. *Coste*, *Bischoff* and other modern physiologists, now regard coitus as having nothing to do with the discharge of ova, and clearly demonstrate that they ripen and are discharging periodically without reference to conjunction, and thrown off from the uterus. This is the case in all mammalia, including the human female. This subject will be found more fully treated in the article on *Menstruation*.

## THE PERIOD OF DECLINE OF LIFE.

This period commences at the termination of the catamenia, or menstrual flow, when if the ovaries be examined they will present a wrinkled, corrugated appearance, full of pits and tortuous lines. If a section be made in the ovary, there is found no trace of Graafian follicles, or one or two may be observed disintegrated into small masses or sacs of cartilaginous hardness. Generally, however, nothing remains except the dense parenchyma or stroma which forms the interior of the ovary.

On the other hand, if the ovary be examined from puberty to the critical period or change of life, it will be found largely supplied with blood-vessels, which may be seen ramifying all its parts. After the process of ovulation has entirely ceased, the ovary begins to suffer the wasting of age, presents a general pallor, and receives only that sufficiency of blood to answer for the nutrition of the shrivelled organ.

## EFFECTS OF EXTIRPATING THE OVARIES.

The removal of one ovary does not affect materially the reproductive power. *Hunter,* in order to test the effects of extirpating one of them, procured two young sows of the same farrow, and removing one of the ovaries from one of them, kept both animals under the same circumstances, in order to observe the effects of breeding upon them. They commenced engendering when two years old, the spayed animal took the boar earlier than the perfect female, and both continued to breed at nearly the same time. The mutilated sow produced her litters until she was six years old, at which time she had had eight farrows and brought forth seventy pigs altogether, and would not take the male afterward. The other continued breeding until she was eight years old and had thirteen farrows, yielding one hundred and sixty-two pigs, when she ceased to breed. The result was that the perfect animal continued to breed two years longer, and produced more than double the number of the spayed one.

Mr. *Potts* removed both of these organs in the human female, in the St. Bartholomew's Hospital, on account of swellings of both groins attended with much pain. The woman was in full health, large breasted, and had menstruated regularly. These tumors proved to be the two ovaries which had descended in the form of double hernia. The woman subsequently enjoyed good health; became thinner but more muscular, while her breasts disappeared and her menstruation ceased altogether after the operation.

An interesting example of the arrest of development of the ovaries is preserved in the Museum of King's College, London. The preparation consists of the entire internal organs of a young woman who died at the age of nineteen, without having menstruated. The ovaries, as well as the rest of the organs, are no larger than a child's of three years. The mammæ are small, the external organs only partially developed, while the whole frame is formed upon a very feeble scale.

## CHAPTER III.

### ANATOMY OR STRUCTURE OF UNIMPREGNATED OVUM.

### ITS ORIGIN AND FORMATION IN HUMAN FEMALES.

THE ovum may be described as a spheroid mass of organized substance, enclosed in a vascular membrane, and when fecundated by the sperm of the male undergoes various changes or development, until it is unfolded into an embryo. All animals with the exception of some of the lower, as the Infusoria, propagate their species and maintain them by means of the ova and sexual generation. It seems to be a law of Nature that species can only be propagated in this way. The result of fecundation is the formation of an embryo from the ovum, which by progressive growth arrives at maturity and assumes the form, structure and habits, as well as weaknesses and imperfections of its parents

The ovum has two phases or stages of existence. The one is in connection with the female organ, which provides material for its development until it arrives at the stage of maturity, when it is expelled from its bed or Graafian vesicle. The other is the influence exerted over it when it comes in contact with the fructifying principle of the male, in which a new power is awakened and developed. The ovum, therefore, cannot be considered as having arrived at maturity (though such is the case, so far as its own structure is concerned) until it is united to the spermatozoa of the male; for without it, its progress is arrested so far as regards its ultimate development.

On examining a fully developed ovum, after it has been expelled from the Graafian follicle, its structure will be found arranged as follows (*Fig.* 18):

FIG. 18.

OVUM. (*After Barry.*)

*a*, germinal spot; *b*, germinal vesicle; *c*, yelk; *d*, zona pellucida; *e*, tunica granulosa of Barry; *f*, adherent granules of cells.

1st. Portion of membrana granulosa uniting to its walls.

2d. Zona pellucida, enclosing the yelk or vitellus.

3d. Yelk or vitellus.

4th. Germinal vesicle.

5th. Germinal spot.

The zona that embraces the yelk, consists of a dense, thick, colorless albuminous membrane.

The yelk consists of granules and globules imbedded in a fluid substance contained within the yelk.

The germinal spot lies within the germinal vesicle.

9*

It consists of fine granular matter, and strongly reflects light.

The eggs of different animals vary in size. The eggs of birds increase in size in relative proportion to the size of the creature. The egg of the *Æpyorus*, an extinct bird, is very enormous. The remains of one of these, with its egg, was recently discovered in Madagascar. The circumference of this egg, in its long diameter, is said to be three feet, and its short diameter two feet four inches. It must have contained within its shell, according to *M. Isidore Geoffroy*, ten quarts, or nearly six times as much as an ostrich's egg, or one hundred and forty-eight times as much as an ordinary hen's egg, or fifty thousand times as much as a humming bird's egg.* The human ovum is not more than $\frac{1}{200}$th of an inch in diameter, and its weight about $\frac{1}{2000}$th part of a grain. In the fowl, the entire egg, when newly laid, weighs two ounces, or nine hundred grains, and is nearly $\frac{1}{22}$d part of the adult body, supposing it to be under three pounds; while the weight of the human ovum is about $\frac{1}{1000000000}$th part of that of the human female.

Number of Ova.—The number of ova developed in the female sex during the whole of her life, vary very much, and probably cannot be definitely ascertained.

The ovary of a herring has been found to contain twenty-five million eggs. In the ovaries of a halibut, weighing one hundred and fifty pounds, three million have been counted. The African ant is said to lay

* Cyclop. Anat. and Phys.

eighty thousand eggs in twenty-four hours, and the common hair worm eight million in less than a day. In birds and those animals that have large eggs only a few of them arrive at maturity. In the common fowl that lays daily two-thirds of a year, a product amounting to thirty pounds, or ten times the weight of the animal, is the result, while the number of eggs produced in the course of the bird's natural existence will not be less than twelve hundred. The number of ovula in the common hen will amount to thirty or forty thousand; hence, as twelve hundred eggs are only produced on an average from each, it will be seen that a large number of ovula never arrive at maturity.

In the human female but few ova ripen or come to maturity at a time. Thus several ova may be discharged at every menstrual period for about thirty years of life. The number thus discharged can scarcely be less than four hundred (probably many more), each one of which if fully developed, by being brought in contact with the fructifying seed of the male, would be capable of bringing forth a living being. It has been stated that the human ovum is about $\frac{1}{200}$th of an inch in diameter, or of the size of a pin's point; but small as it is, each one is capable of unfolding a human being.

It is interesting to trace the ovum and observe the changes which take place as it passes through the Fallopian tubes. Its development in the ovary and expulsion therefrom has already been noticed; while a description of its structure has been given, together with the manner in which the fimbriated portion of the tube has grasped the ovum. As these changes take place before the egg reaches the uterus, it will be necessary to dwell somewhat particularly upon such processes or phenomena. This part of the subject, perhaps, belongs more properly to the article on Conception or Fecundation, but the whole will be better understood by presenting every thing that necessarily has a bearing upon all such changes. The changes that take place in the ova of animals, during their passage along the tubes, will also be explained, as there is a close analogy between the functions of the reproductive organs of animals and the human female.

# CHAPTER IV.

## OVUM OF THE HUMAN FEMALE AND ANIMALS.

### THE CHANGES THAT TAKE PLACE DURING THE PASSAGE OF THE OVUM ALONG THE FALLOPIAN TUBES.

THE way in which the ovum is conveyed along the passage of the Fallopian tubes after its reception in the fimbriæ of the ovaduct, is explained by the peculiar structure of the parts. The tube is lined, as before stated, by delicate ciliated membrane, the movements of which cilia, according to *Henle*, is toward the uterus, which is sufficient, with the peristaltic action or contraction of its walls, to convey the ovum into the womb.

The time occupied for the passage of the ovum through the Fallopian tubes, is not definitely known; but judging from observations made on animals, the period is supposed to be from six to twelve days. In the bitch and rabbit it is from six to ten days.

An ovum, after being expelled from the ovary, is invested by a portion of the *membrana granulosa*, which formerly lined the Graafian follicle, (*Fig.* 13, *g*, *Fig.* 18, *e*,) and in this condition is received into the Fallopian tube. These cells are closely attached to the *zona pellucida*, or outer membrane of the ovum. They give the egg the appearance of being surrounded by rays. (*Fig.* 19.) This is characteristic of a fully devel-

FIG. 19.

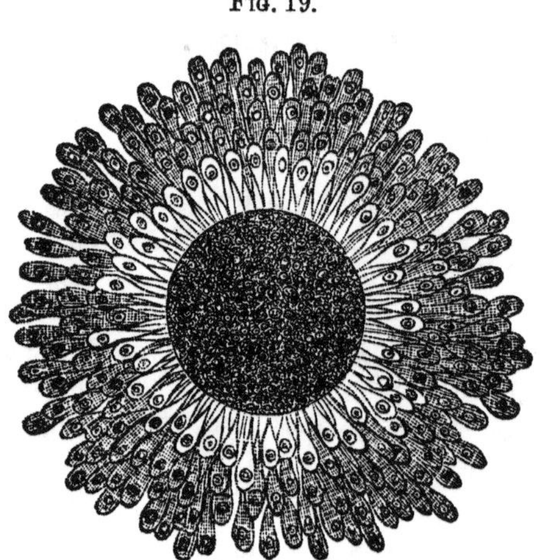

Ripe ovum from the ovary surrounded by cells which are attached to the zona pellucida. The cells are so arranged as to present the appearance of rays,

oped and ripened ovum. After its passage into the tube, the great change it undergoes is the stripping off of the ray-like appendage of cells. This is effected during its transit along the upper third of the tubes. (*Fig.* 20.)

If impregnation does not now occur, the ovum or egg perishes. It cannot proceed any further in its development toward the production of an embryo. If the ovum should become impregnated several important changes take place, which are as follows: The zona pellucida, or outer membrane of the egg, having thrown off its outer cell-covering, presents the appearance as represented in (*Fig.* 21), which being

Fig. 20.

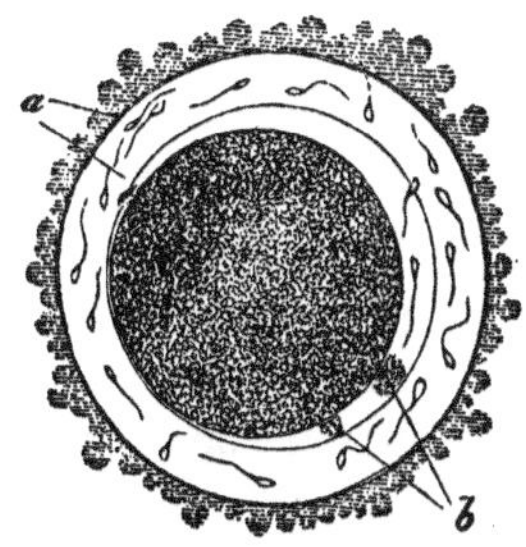


THE OVUM ON FIRST ARRIVING IN THE FALLOPIAN TUBE. THE RAY-LIKE APPENDAGES ARE NEARLY STRIPPED OFF. (*After Bischoff.*)

*a* zona pellucida ; *b*, granular bodies between the zona pellucida and yelk.

divested of the obstruction that invests it, the spermatozoa have no difficulty in penetrating the soft albu-

Fig. 21.

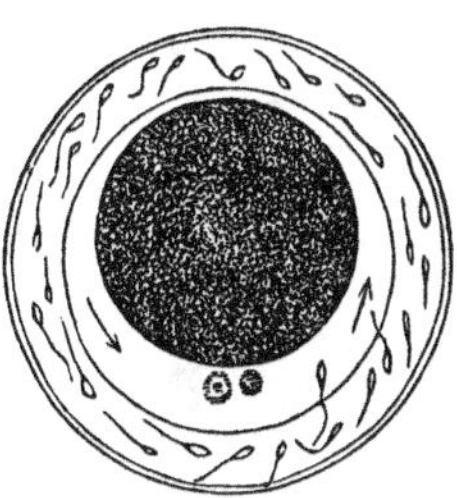

THE OVUM A LITTLE MORE ADVANCED IN THE TUBE. (*After Bischoff.*)

The surface is perfectly smooth. Spermatozoa have penetrated the zona pellucida. The respiratory chamber is formed between the latter and the yelk. The rotation of the yelk has commenced, as indicated by the arrows. The granular bodies appear preparatory to the segmentation of the yelk. Several of the stages are seen commencing in the preceding figure.

minous membrane that encloses the yelk. When the

spermatozoa penetrate the zona, the yelk contracts. This fact was first observed by *Newport*, who called the space the "*respiratory chamber*." This interspace is filled with a transparent fluid. After the contraction takes place another remarkable change occurs, which is the revolving of the yelk. This rotation is indicated by the arrows of the cut, (*Fig.* 21,) and is effected by the aid of *cilia* which line the inner surface of the yelk. About this time a small body, or there may be several bodies, seen in the "respiratory" space between the yelk and zona which is supposed to have some connection to the cleverage of the yelk, which is about commencing.

The experiments of Newport settle beyond dispute, that segmentation or divison of the yelk is the result of pregnancy alone, and never takes place without it. The segmentation commences first by a cleverage of the yelk into two equi-divisions, (*Fig.* 22,)

FIG. 22.

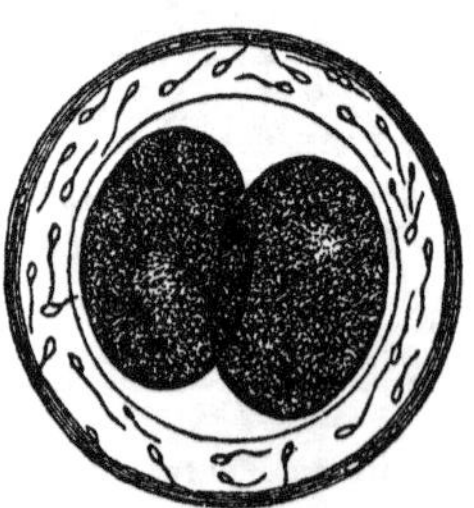

THE OVUM STILL MORE ADVANCED IN THE TUBE. (*After Bischoff.*)
The first stage in the segmentation of the yelk has taken place.

then into four equal parts, (*Fig.* 23,) and so continue dividing in geometrical progression until the yelk is broken up in fine granular masses, with which the generative force of the male sperm is equally divided.

FIG. 23.

THE OVUM FROM THE LOWER OR UTERINE END OF THE FALLOPIAN TUBE. (*After Bischoff.*)

The yelk exhibits four divisions.

How the yelk divisions take place before the ovum reaches the uterus is not certainly known. The fifth division, however, has been observed by *Bischoff* at the lower extremity of the Fallopian tubes similar to what is exhibited in (*Figs.* 24 and 25.)

FIG. 24.

THE ADDITION OF A LAYER OF ALBUMEN IN THE LOWER PORTION OF THE TUBE—(OBSERVED ONLY IN THE RABBIT.) (*After Bischoff.*)

The yelk exhibits eight divisions.

Fig. 25.

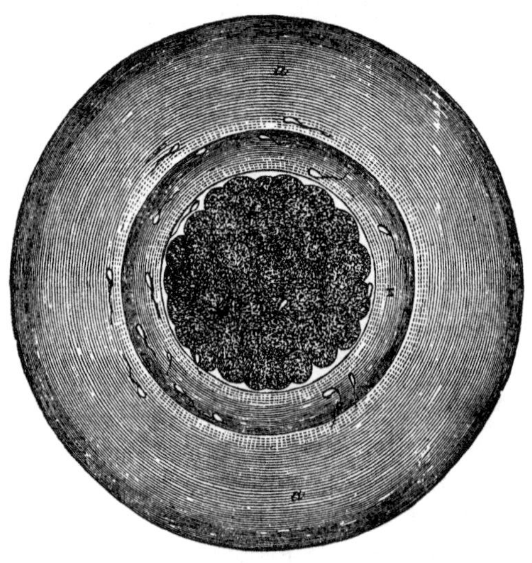

OVUM OF THE RABBIT FROM THE FALLOPIAN TUBE WITH SPERMATOZOA.

The accompanying figure is introduced to show the usual position of the spermatozoa in relation to the zona and albuminous layer in the ovum of Mammalia during and after impregnation. This ovum is magnified two hundred and fifty diameters. It was taken along with five others from the lower part of the Fallopian tube, sixty-eight or seventy hours after impregnation. The segmentation appears to have proceeded to the fifth stage. There is a thick covering of albumen over the zona, and a number of spermatozoa are represented involved in the albuminous substance; some were also seen on the surface of the zona, and some, varying in number in the different ova observed from five to seven or nine, were clearly ascertained to be situated within the zona on the surface of and in the grooves between the yelk segments. The position of these last is not sufficiently clearly represented in the figure.

The only additional change observed taking place in the tubes is a deposit of albumen around the zona pellucida, (*Fig.* 24) which takes place when the ovum is passing the middle and lower third of the tube. These occurrences are so uniform that the different offices for different portions of the Fallopian tubes may be readily determined.

The first or upper third is appropriated to the reception of the ovum, and for removing the adventitious covering of cells, while it also prepares the ovum for the operation of the spermatozoa. In the middle third, the respiratory chamber is formed, and here the rotation of the yelk commences. In the lower third the cleverage takes place, as also the deposit of albumen.

If these views of *Bischoff* be correct, it must be in the middle or lower third of the tube that impregnation occurs, or the ovum will perish. By the time the ovum reaches the lower third, in most animals, particularly the dog and guinea-pig, the *heat* is passed, and the animal will not permit coitus.

To sum up the offices of the Fallopian tubes, they may be stated as follows:—

1st. To receive the spermatic fluid from the uterus, and convey it upward through the entire canal.

2d. To receive the unimpregnated ovum from the ovary, and convey it in a directly opposite course for the purpose of meeting the male sperm.

3d. To afford protection to the ovum during its brief pilgrimage through the tube, and to deposit on its outer surface additional material, increase its bulk, and finally convey it into the cavity of the uterus.

The next question which arises in connection with this subject is—How far are these conclusions applicable to the human female in regard to gestation?

In the human female, that marked indication of sexual excitement known as *heat* in animals is rarely ever manifested, although it exists to some degree at each menstrual period. It is well known that the liability to impregnation is much greater immediately after the cessation of the menstrual flow than a little later during the intervals of the monthly turn. Observation would seem to strengthen the view which has been advanced, that impregnation occurs, as a rule, within twelve or fourteen days after the cessation of the menstrual discharge. It has also been known to occur after this period, but very seldom. This may be explained by the casting of an ovum during an intermenstrual period which was nearly ripe at the cessation of the previous discharge; while it is quite possible, also, that an ovum may be retained in the tube longer than the period named, owing to some retarded action of the regular functions of the co-relative parts. It may, however, be safely stated, as a general rule, that impregnation takes place within fourteen days after the cessation of the catamenial period. There are exceptional cases, as a matter of course to every law.

## CHAPTER V.

### DEVELOPMENT OF OVA IN BIRDS AND OTHER OVIPAROUS ANIMALS.

THE difference in the amount of formative material in the ovum of the bird is owing to the manner in which the embryo is supplied with its sustenance. Here the whole amount of nourishment required, is provided in the egg before it is detached from the parent. In the human female and viviparous,animals, the material for growth is derived from the maternal parent, whether afforded by the placenta or some analogous structure.*

The egg of the ordinary domestic fowl may be regarded as the type of oviparous animals. A knowledge of its development will enable any one to comprehend the difference which exists between the eggs of the human female and viviparous animals, or those that develop with the egg the necessary material for growth independent of the parent. In such cases, normal temperament and a supply of oxygen are all that is necessary for development of the young, provided the egg has been fecundated before being

* Viviparous—(*vivus*, alive; *pario*, to bring forth)—a term applied to animals which bring forth their young alive and perfect, as distinguished from *oviparous* animals, which produce their young from the egg.

thrown off by the female. A varnished egg will not hatch, nor can this take place if one half of the shell be thus treated.

The average size of a fowl's egg is two and a quarter inches in long diameter and one and three quarters in the short diameter, the average weight being two ounces. Double-yelked eggs usually weigh about three ounces. The weight of the yelk is about one-third of the whole, while that of the albumen and shell are equal to the other two-thirds. If eggs are kept exposed they become lighter, losing about one grain per day, which is owing to evaporation through the shell, it being of a porous nature. During incubation or hatching of the eggs they lose rapidly, amounting in twenty-one days from sixteen to twenty per cent., or about one-sixth of the entire substance. Out of this amount of loss only five or six per cent. consist of water, the balance is the result of chemical decomposition, or most probably of combustion, by the union of oxygen with carbon, producing carbonic acid, which passes off through the shell. The shell of the egg consists principally of carbonate of lime, held together by animal matter, while the white is chiefly pure albumen. The yelk is of oily matter, albumen, and about two per cent. of salts, with fifty-four per cent. of water. The albumen with the sulphur and salts are immediately employed in the growth of the embryo, while the oily matter serves for combustion in keeping up the temperature during incubation. If an egg be examined immediately after being laid, there will be found directly under the shell at the larger end, a small space, called the airspace, which increases the longer the egg is kept. This space also increases very rapidly during incubation, being caused by the evaporation of water and chemical decomposition, as before stated.

## STRUCTURE OF THE EGG—PROCESS OF FORMATION.

Many fowls lay an egg every twenty-four hours during a portion of the season, while others lay every second day, or for two or three days in succession, at a later hour each day, and then intermit for one day. Other fowls lay regularly every thirty-six hours. As already intimated, the time occupied in the passage of the egg through the ovaduct in the dog, guinea-pig, rabbit, and human female is from six to twelve days. In a fowl this transit is about twenty-four hours. If a fowl that has laid daily, be killed six hours after the last egg is passed, the ovaduct will be found blocked up with a yelk that has been taken up by the fimbriated extremity of the tube, or it may be just grasping it, as is seen in (*Fig.* 26, *b*). Sometimes the fimbriated extremity of the tube unfortunately fails to enclose the yelk when expelled from the ovary. In such cases it falls into the abdomen and may be removed by absorption, or it may produce peritoneal inflammation and death to the fowl.

During the passage through the upper or first two-thirds of the ovaduct, the albumen of the egg is deposited in a period of from three to four hours, according to *Coste*.* It is proper here to remark, that

* Hist. Gén. et Partic. du Dével, etc.

FIG. 26.

**OVARY AND OVADUCT OF A LAYING FOWL, KILLED TWELVE HOURS AFTER LAYING THE LAST EGG.**

*a*. Left ovary; *b*, opening of the infundibulum of the ovaduct and grasping an ovum about being expelled from the ovasac; *c d*, glandular portion of the ovaduct; at *d*, the isthmus; *e*, an egg in the uterine portion of the ovaduct, in which the shell is begun to be deposited; *f*, the rectum, ending in the cloaca; *g*, the undeveloped right ovaduct occasionally met with in birds.

the yelk of the egg when it is expelled from the ovary, is the same in structure as that of the rabbit and human female, before described; and that it is during the passage of the egg through the tube, that the white and shell of the egg is formed, but it is not entirely perfected until after its lodgment in the uterus. (*Fig.* 26, *e.*)

*White of the Egg.*—This constitutes several layers, and commences forming as soon as it enters the Fallopian tube. At first it is a thin layer immediately investing the yelk, which subsequently becomes condensed into the chalaziferous membrane and the two narrow cord-like appendages, which were first albumen but afterward become twisted and form the chalazæ. (*Fig.* 27, *A.*) As the yelk descends, the faster is the accumulation of the albumen round the yelk and chalazæ, giving to the egg its oval shape. (*Fig.* 27, *C.*) During the passage of the egg and formation of the albumen and shell, there is a great determination of blood to the several parts of the duct. The egg does not descend in a straight line, but in a spiral manner, (*Fig.* 27, *D*) which gives the spiral shape to the white of the egg and the twist to the chalazæ. The egg remains in the uterus from twelve to eighteen hours, in order to complete the formation of the shell. The lining membrane of the uterus is different from the membrane lining the oviduct—the former containing follicular glands which secrete the substance for the shell. As soon as the egg enters this part of the tube, a thick white fluid is poured out which is soon deposited and coagulated on a thin membrane covering the white. At first the shell is

Fig. 27.

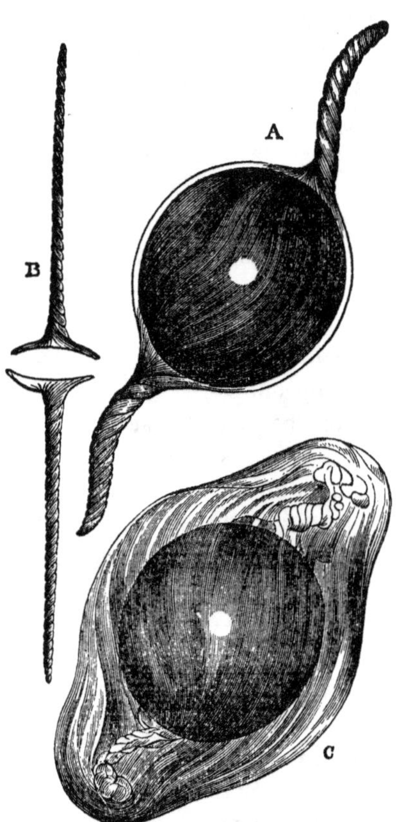


MANNER IN WHICH THE CHALAZÆ, ALBUMEN, ETC., ARE DEPOSITED ROUND THE OVARIAN OVUM OF THE FOWL.

A. Yelk from the upper part of the oviduct soon after it has entered it, showing a thin covering of albumen on the yelk, forming the chalaziferous membrane, and he twisted chalazæ extending from the opposite poles of the yelk. The twisting in these is represented more strongly than it can be seen at this period.

B. Sketch of the fully formed chalazæ from opposite sides of the yelk, stretched to their full leng*h, and showing the opposite direction of the spiral in each.

C. Egg from above the middle of the oviduct; the first layers of albumen deposited round the yelk and chalazæ.

FIG. 27.

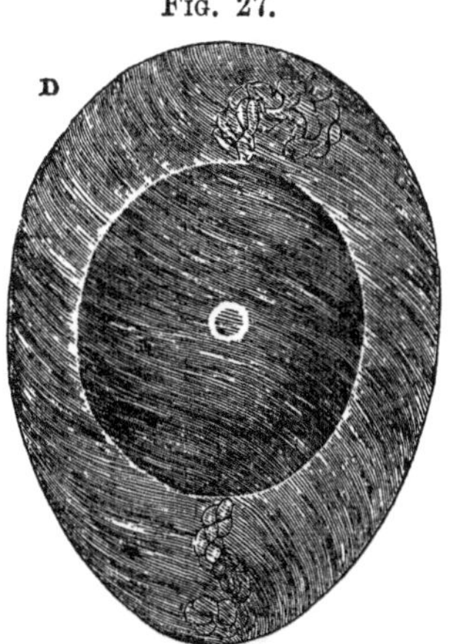


D. Egg from the lower part of the glandular oviduct near the isthmus, when the deposit of albumen is complete; the spiral arrangement of the albumen made manifest by slight coagulation.

soft, but it soon acquires the hardness which is characteristic of the egg when laid.

In reptiles a similar arrangement is observed during the passage of the ova along the Fallopian tube. Instead of one, there are several in the tube at the same time, as is seen in (*Fig.* 28); the same with rabbits, as seen in (*Fig.* 29, *A.*)

FIG. 28.

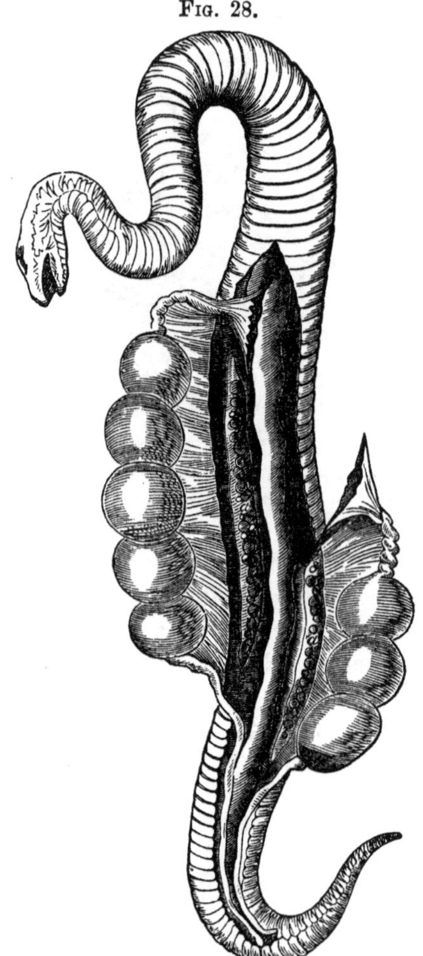

Common adder, in which the ova have descended to occupy both ovaducts, five in the right, and three in the left; the infundibulum is shown in each oviduct *a a*, the right and left ovaries, each forming a sac, opening anteriorly near th infundibulum for the discharge of the ova, which, when ripe, fall into the interior the sac, and thence pass into the ovaduct.

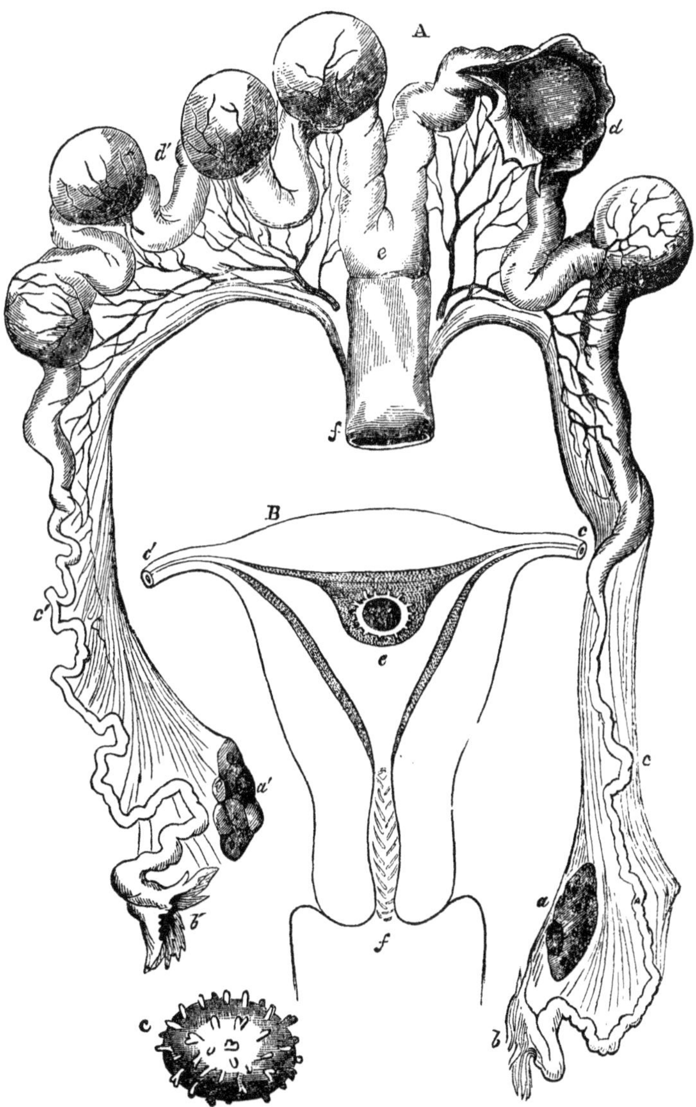


RELATION OF OVARIES, OVUM, OVADUCT, AND UTERUS IN MAMMALIA. (*From Cyclo. Anat. et Phys.*)

**A.** Reproductive organs of the rabbit, ten days advanced in pregnancy; *a a*, right and left ovaries, four corpora lutea in the right and two in the left; *b b*, fimbriated openings of the Fallopian tubes; *c c*, the Fallopian tubes; *d d*, right and left cornua of the uterus; with four dilatations on the right and two on the left containing ova, one of the right ova is exhibited by a division in the left horn of the uterus; *e*, the body of the uterus; *f*, the vagina.

**B.** Transverse section of the human uterus twelve or fourteen days after conception; *e*, the uterine cavity, in which the ovum with its villous chorion is imbedded in the decidua: *c c*, the Fallopian tubes cut short, by one of which the ovum has just descended while still of same size.

**C.** Enlarged view of the exterior of the human ovum twelve or fourteen days after conception, sh wing the villi of the chorion projecting from its surface.

# CHAPTER VI.

## MALE ORGANS OF GENERATION.

As we have given a full description of the male organs of generation in a work, entitled "BOYHOOD'S PERILS AND MANHOOD'S CURSE," those who may desire a knowledge of their structure are referred to that Treatise. It will accordingly only be necessary to give some idea of the Testes, the organs that secrete the male sperm, in conjunction with the subject-matter of the present volume.

### THE HUMAN TESTES.

The testicles are two glandular bodies that are suspended by the spermatic cord and scrotum. The size of the glands depends upon the age and sexual indulgence of the individual.

The scrotum consists of a simple integument, covered with hair. Within this there are four tunics or membranes, which, by comparison, may be compared to the peelings of an onion. The internal structure consists of tubes that are so convoluted or twisted upon themselves as to constitute lobes. As a description of these membranes would not be interesting to the general reader, it will only be requisite to present some idea of the glandular structure, or of that part which secretes the spermatic fluid.

As before remarked, the secreting structure of the testicles consists of tubes which form lobes. (*Fig.* 30, 1, 1 and *Fig.* 31, 1, 2, 2.) If these lobes be examined

Fig. 30

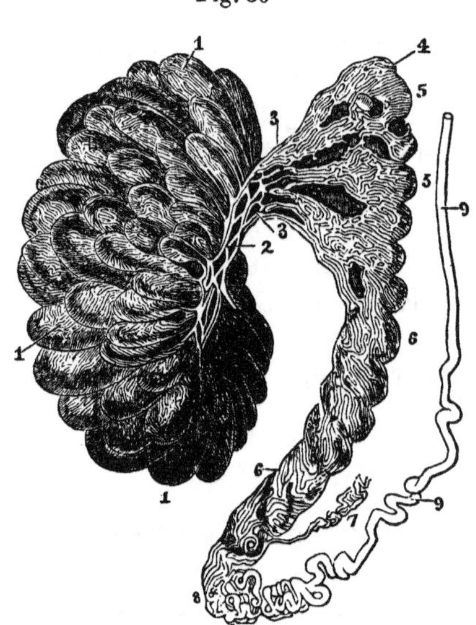


TESTIS INJECTED WITH MERCURY, AND DEPRIVED OF THE TUNICA ALBUGINEA. (*From S. G. Morton.*)

**Testis injected and divested of the tunica albuginea; 1, 1, lobules formed by the tubuli seminiferi; 2, rete testis; 3, 4, coni vasculosi, formed by the seminiferous tubes; 5, 6, the epididymis; 7, appendix of the epididymis; 8, termination of the epididymis in the vas deferens; 9, 9, vas deferens.**

carefully they will be found to consist of minute tubes, called *Tubuli Seminiferi.* Each tube is about seventeen feet long and $\frac{1}{170}$th of an inch in diameter. The tubuli of each lobe coalesce into twenty or thirty straight tubes, called *vasa recta,* (*Fig.* 31, 3.) The vasa recta are twice the diameter of the seminiferous tubes, and penetrate a fold of the tunica albuginea, (the immediate investment of the testicle) which forms what is called the *corpus highmorianum.* In this cor-

Fig. 31.

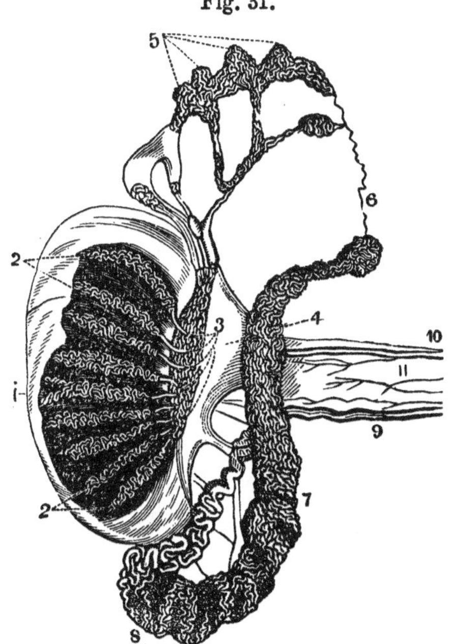


THE STRUCTURE OF THE TESTICLE INJECTED WITH MERCURY, AND ITS SEVERAL PARTS UNRAVELED. (*After Sir A. Cooper.*)

1, 2, 2, Tubuli seminiferi; 3, vasa recta, forming the rete testis; 4, corpus highmorianum; 5, vasa efferentia, forming the coni vasculosi; 6, a single tube formed by the junction of the vasa efferentia. This tube then becomes convoluted upon itself to form the epididymis; 7, 8, beginning of the vas deferens; 9, the vas deferens becoming a straight, isolated tube in its ascent to the abdominal ring; 10, spermatic artery; 11, spermatic cord spread out.

pus or body, an anastomosis of the tubes takes place, which is called the *rete testis*, (*Fig.* 30, 2.) The rete testis gives off from twelve to twenty ducts or tubes, which again penetrate the corpus highmorianum in passing out, and form the *vasa efferentia*, (*Fig.* 31, 5.) Here the tubing again form into cones or lobes, called *conus vasculosus*, which correspond in number to the vasa efferentia that form them, and afterward terminate in a common tube, (*Fig.* 31, 6.) This tube becomes again convoluted or twisted and forms the *epididymis*, (*Fig.* 30, 5, 6, and *Fig.* 31, 7.) The epididymis terminates at its lower margin in a common tube, called the *vas deferens*, (*Fig.* 30, 9, 9, and *Fig.* 31, 9.) The vas deferens is tortuous when it leaves the epididymis, but becomes straight as it passes up and forms a part of the spermatic cord. It finally leaves the cord and passes up laterally on the posterior part of the bladder. It then passes forward to meet its fellow from the opposite side, when the two unite, and by their junction form a duct about one inch in length, which terminate in the *urethra* of the male penis. This duct is called the *ductus ejaculatorius*. The vas deferens is much larger than the other parts of the tube, and is about the eighth of an inch in diameter.

The structure of the testicles will compare with that of the ovary and Fallopian tubes, as respects their peculiar beauty and arrangements. It has been estimated that there are eight hundred and forty tubuli in the two testicles, twisted in such a manner to make each tube seventeen feet in length as before stated. This will give 14,280 feet of tubing. This is lined by a delicate membrane, which secretes or forms granular cells—each granular cell, when developed, will form hundreds of spermatozoa, capable of unfolding a human being, when united to the ovum of a female. Truly, great and marvelous are the works of Nature thus to develop the human being out of such tiny microscopic atoms! A careful study of this wonderful structure will show the importance of very small particles of matter, in the hands of the All-wise Creator, able to endow them with vitality and unfold from them strong and powerful physical and mental organic structure.

## CHAPTER VII.

### FUNCTIONS OF THE HUMAN TESTICLES.

THE office or function of the testicles is to secrete the male sperm, a substance that appears to the naked eye like ordinary mucus devoid of life. If the microscope, however, be applied to a small quantity of this secretion, taken from a healthy male who has arrived at puberty, it will be found alive with minute, thread-like, bodies. So numerous are these that, at first sight, the semi-liquid mass seems to be almost entirely made up of them. They are called the *seminal animalcules*, or *spermatozoa*. There are also found in this *liquor seminis*, minute round corpuscles called *seminal* cells.

### ORIGIN OF SPERMATOZOA.

SPERMATOZOA in man, as well as in animals, and some of the higher order of plants, have their origin in cells, which are denominated seminal cells or *spermatophori*. These cells are filled with granular matter, (*Fig.* 32) each granule capable of being developed into a *spermatozoon*. These germ cells are developed in the tube composing the testicles. It is within the tubes these cells burst, when the thread-like bodies escape, and take on those peculiar motions which have

FIG. 32.

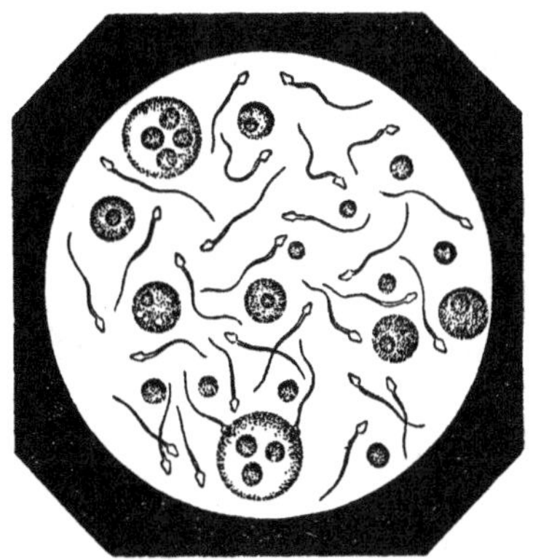

MICROSCOPIC APPEARANCE OF HEALTHY HUMAN SEMEN MAGNIFIED FIVE HUNDRED DIAMETERS.

given rise to the opinion that they are *distinct animalcules.* Some physiologists do not regard them as possessing distinct animal characteristics any more than is attached to the *cilia* that line the cells of the neck of the uterus and Fallopian tubes. Hence they have been called cell-germs, furnished with peculiar moving power.* On the other hand, *Pouchet* asserts that these *zoospermata* have a *digestive* apparatus, which is called by him *cephalo-thorax,* as represented (*Fig.* 33 ;† also, *Fig.* 34, *g.*) The (*Fig.* 34) gives the spermatozoa of different animals. The form of development is somewhat different, and the motion will correspond with the development. Those with tail-like appendages resemble the

* Carpenter's Elements of Physiology, § 240.

† Pouchet L'Ovulation Spontanée. (Plate 11, Fig. 4.)

FIG. 33.

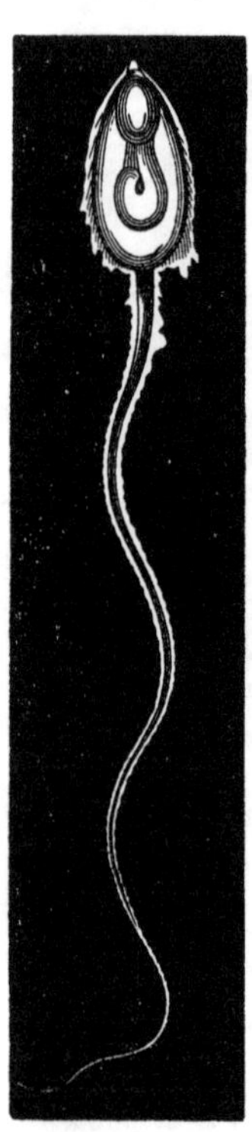

SPERMATOZOON FROM THE HUMAN TESTICLE. (*From S. G. Morton.*)

motion of an eel in water. Those with the spiral development have the spiral motion. From observation it has been ascertained that spermatozoa will retain their moving powers twenty-four or thirty hours after they enter the uterus and Fallopian tubes.

In the young and vigorous, the spermatozoa are abundant and active, In debilitated persons, those that have weak constitutions and where the vital forces are depressed, the spermatozoa will not only be found very scanty but exceedingly feeble. Such scantiness and feebleness will correspond with the vital energy or debility of the individual in whom they are developed.

In consumptives, and those who have broken down their constitution by over sexual indulgence and onanism, the action of the spermatozoa is slow and their development imperfect. In aged persons they disappear, while the testicles, like the ovaries of aged females, cease to perform the functions allotted to them in the prime and vigor of life.

The *natural* secretion of the vagina and uterus of the female is favorable for the maintenance of spermatozoa. When these become changed to acid secretions, they act as *poisons* and quickly destroy the

Fig. 34.

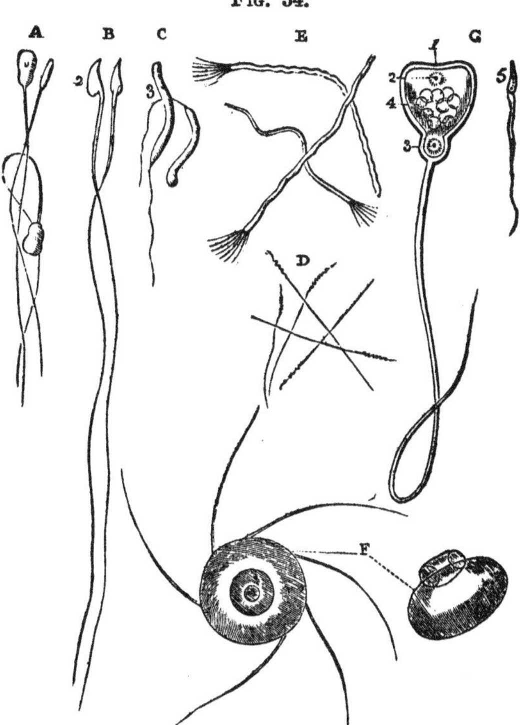


VARIOUS FORMS OF SPERMATOZOA. (*From Muller.*)

A. Spermatozoa from the dog; B, from the common mouse; and C, green woodpecker—after *Wagner*. D. Spermatozoa from the common water snake; E, second form of spermatic animalcules from the same animal; F, bodies contained in the semen of the crab—after *Siebold*. G. Spermatozoon of the bear—after *Valentine*. 1, anterior margin excavated; 2 and 3, two very dark circular spots regarded by Valentine as the mouth and arms; 4, a number of circles, supposed by Valentine to be outlines of gastric vesicles of an hepatic organ on the convolutions of an intestinal canal; 5, the same animalcule, less highly magnified and viewed laterally.

spermatozoa. Hence, one of the causes of sterility in the female is owing to the change in the secretions of the os cervix uteri and vagina.

The spermatozoa in man are exceedingly small—being about $\frac{1}{50}$ of an inch in length, and $\frac{1}{500}$ of an inch in diameter. The seminal animalculæ are said to be no larger in the whale than in the mouse. They are much larger in insects, mollusca, and others of the lower animals than in man. They are considerably larger in the mouse than in the horse, and in the snail fifty-four times larger than in the dog.

The office of the spermatozoa, as before stated, is to impart new life to the female ovum. This takes place in the Fallopian tubes during the passage of the ovum toward the uterus. The quantity of semen eliminated at one *coitus* is from one to three drachms, of which, perhaps, only about one-hundredth part consists of spermatozoa.

It is generally conceded that but two or three drops of semen proper, or spermatozoa, are ejected from the testicles at one conjunction of the sexes. The balance is an albuminous fluid secreted by the vesicula seminalis and prostate gland, which secretions are thrown off at the same time as that from the testicles. The use of this superabundant fluid is for the purpose of protecting these thread-like animalculæ and assist their movements. It possesses the right density or specific gravity for this purpose. If the density be increased the movements of the spermatozoa will be impeded; if reduced, they are destroyed upon the principle of endosmose.

I have in several instances placed a drop of semen from the vas deferens under the microscope, which semen is usually very thick, and always found that the motion of the spermatozoa was exceedingly slow.

They presented the appearance of a tangled mass of thread-like objects unable to extricate themselves. The moment, however, a drop of blood was applied, they found no difficulty in disentangling themselves. They would turn around once or twice and lash their tails, which seemed to unite the two liquids, and put the whole mass of animalculæ in motion.

The cause of motion of spermatozoa is not certainly known, but it is supposed to be similar to the wave-like motion in the ciliated cells of the uterus and Fallopian tubes.

In cold-blooded animals, the fishes for instance, they retain their power of motion longer than in warm-blooded animals. In the former they continue to move for days after being expelled from the male. Their movements continue for a longer period in the interior of the female organs of generation. In some species of insects (as the *Gasteropoda*), the spermatozoa will continue their movements for months when brought in contact with the female organs of generation.

In the human female it is supposed that the spermatozoa will retain their moving power for thirty-six hours after coitus. Common water at low temperature rapidly arrests their movements, while dilute saline solutions, or sugar and water, on the other hand, appear to have very little influence upon their actions. Such is also the fact with common saliva, or bile, or pus. Urine has rather an injurious influence upon their movements, especially when it has an acid reaction. The chemical agents are the only ones that have positive injurious effects upon the movements of spermatozoa. They not only stop their operations, but dissolve their structure and change their composition. For instance, alcohol, acids, metallic salts, narcotics, strychnine have similar effects to common cold water.

Heat and cold seem to affect their movements, although the action of the spermatozoa of frogs and fishes continue after the media in which they are surrounded sink below zero. The electric spark destroys the motion of spermatozoa instantly, by changing their structure, while Galvanism has no perceptible influence upon them, which fact is somewhat remarkable. I have made a number of experiments with chemical re-agents, under the microscope, and always found that mineral and vegetable acids dissolve spermatozoa instantaneously as electricity. The same is the fact with mineral and vegetable astringents. The *Figs.* 36, 37, 38, give the appearance of spermatozoa under the microscope when these re-agents are

Fig. 36. Fig. 37 Fig. 38.

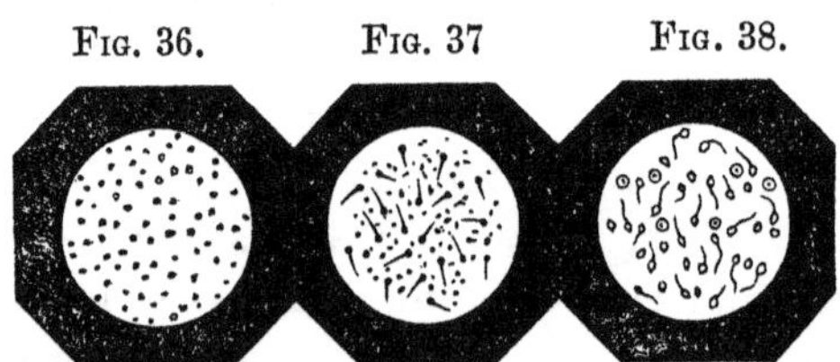

Fig. 36. Appearance under the microscope of semen after the application of vegetable acids. The spermatozoa are broken up into granules.

Fig. 37. Appearance presented under the microscope after the application of mineral and vegetable astringents.

Fig. 38. Appearance of spermatozoa under the microscope in those who have over-indulged and masturbated to great excess—such undeveloped spermatozoa cannot propagate. If conception should take place under such circumstances, the offspring will have a weak and delicate constitution and be short lived.

applied, and show the contrast between healthy and diseased spermatozoa.*

On the first discovery of the seminal animalculæ, there were many hypotheses advanced concerning them. By some they were considered the cause of sexual enjoyments or venereal propensities. Others supposed that the spermatozoa were of different sexes, and believed that if a female spermatozoon happened first to penetrate the ovum a female offspring was the result, and the reverse when a male spermatozoon succeeded in fecundating the egg. Another class imagined that a spermatazoon possessed all the organs of a human being in a compressed state, which became developed or unfolded by the female generative organs—in other words, that a spermatozoon was a miniature human being.

Such absurd theories require no refutation. They were advanced in a hypothetical age of the world.

* As it is woman's destiny and fate to bear the pangs, privations, anxieties, and personal sacrifices pertaining to maternity; no sane person will dispute her *inalienable right* to determine when and how often she shall endure the tortures and trials of child-bearing. And while morality, religion, law, and maternal duty alike reprobate the murderous and destructive habit, indulged in by too many women, both married and single, of producing abortion, after conception has once ensued, and which every true physican ever discountenances and condemns—there can be no scruples against preventing conception taking place. This process violates no moral and physical law, but effectually stays the consequences of sexual intercourse without interfering with the health or religious feelings of parties who desire a freedom from the responsibilities of large families—and the physical evils resulting from repeated and excessive child-bearing.

In order to relieve myself from the charge of favoring licentiousness, by guarding parties against the consequences of illicit intercourse, and to dispense my means of avoiding conception only among such as are worthy; the author has seen proper to withhold from the public the only effectual and safe means of attaining this object, which will only be communicated by letter.

# CHAPTER VIII.

## HERMAPHRODISM.

THERE are two distinct varieties of Hermaphroditic malformation—the *spurious* and the *true.*

The spurious comprehends such as have the generative organs approximating the natural organs in appearance and form. The true hermaphrodism includes an actual mixture or blending of the male and female organs upon the same individual.

### 1. SPURIOUS HERMAPHRODISM.

*A. In the Female.*—Errors have occurred in regard to the true sex of an individual, from enlargement of the clitoris and prolapsus of the uterus—the former being taken for the penis and the latter for the testicles.

In some females at birth the clitoris is not much behind that of the male penis in size at the same period of life. After this period it ceases to grow as rapidly as the other external genital organs, and at puberty it is from half to an inch in length, as a general rule. In other cases, the clitoris continues developing up to adult life, and resembles the penis of the male.

Large-sized clitores are less common among the inhabitants of temperate and cold climates than in the tropics. The frequency of them in Arabia and Egypt led the ancient surgeons of those countries to amputate the organ. *Ælius* and *Paulus Eginetus* speak of this amputation having been practiced among the Egyptians. According to *Jonnini*, circumcision is still performed upon females of that country.

This variety of conformation of the female parts was well-known to the ancient Greeks, as a number of their writers mention such women under the name of Τριβαδες, *Tribades*, and Εταιριοτριαι, *Etairiotriai*, among which class the celebrated *Sappho* is known to have been included. *Martial*, *Tertullian*, and other Roman writers have noticed the same malformation, and spoken of the depravity to which it led.

The clitoris is not unfrequently found two and three inches in length. In some instances it has been found from ten to twelve inches. *Chobert* mentions one case where the clitoris was twelve inches in length, and *Haller* two cases where it was seven inches long.

The clitoris of some of the lower orders of animals resembles very much the penis of the male of the same class of creatures. A very striking analogy is observed in this regard, in the lioness, raccoon, bear, cat, etc.

In the human female when the organ is large, it not only resembles the penis of the male in size, but there is an indentation corresponding to the orifice of the urethra. In other cases, the vagina is much contracted or nearly closed by a strong muscular membrane or hymen, giving the appearance of the perinæum of the male. The labia also unite and present the semblance of testicles. In such females the mammæ are but slightly developed; the voice is deep-toned; the chin and upper lip are sometimes covered with hair, while the features and muscles are hard, resembling those of the male. In short, the whole external peculiarities partake more of the characteristics of the male than of the female.

*Dr. Ramsbothem* has given a description of an infant that was christened as a boy, which proved after death to be a female, (*Fig.* 39). The uterus and Fallo-

FIG. 39.

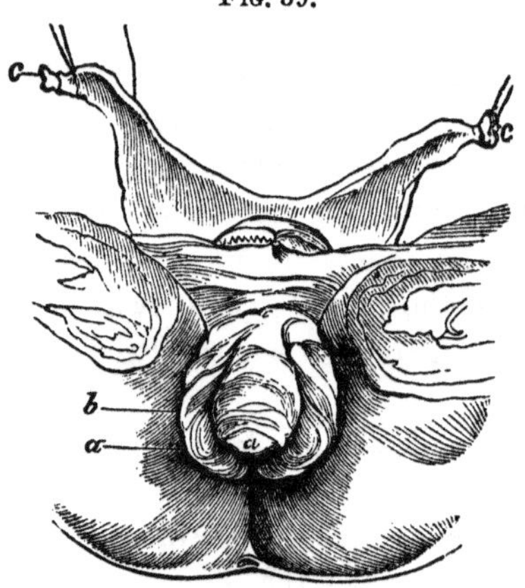


APPEARANCE OF A FEMALE'S EXTERNAL ORGANS OF GENERATION, WHICH WERE SUPPOSED TO BE THOSE OF A MALE UNTIL AFTER DEATH. (*From Cyclo. Anat. et Phys.*) *c*, *c*, *c*, Fallopian tubes and uterus; *b*, clitoris; *a*, gland of clitoris.

pian tubes were apparently naturally developed, while the clitoris was large and resembled the male penis.

*Colombos* and *De Graaf* give two similar examples in children, where the true sex was not discovered until after death.

*Arnaud* gives a description of Galloy, the celebrated hermaphrodite, whose clitoris after death was found to be three and a half inches long and four lines (one-third of an inch) in circumference. The glans and prepuce were well developed, while the urethra ran through the whole length of the penis. The external and internal female organs were naturally developed. She was married, but never became pregnant; her menstruation was natural, but she had hair on her face, while her voice was harsh like that of a male.

While a student, I had an opportunity of witnessing a female who had a clitoris three inches in length, which resembled the male penis in structure, except that the urethra was absent. At the orifice of the glans there was a depression which would be readily taken for the opening of the urethra unless closely examined. Her general appearance was masculine. Her history was not well known, and therefore I am unable to give her habits of life. There was no appearance that she had ever borne children.

*M. Beclard* has given an interesting description of a case in the *Bulletins de la Faculté* of Paris, for 1815. This case was exhibited in 1814 in Paris, and was at that time aged sixteen years. Her name was Marie Madeline Laforte. The form of her shoulders, pelvis and chest was masculine; the tone of the voice was like that of the male. Her beard commenced growing on her chin, upper lip, and along the side of the face. The symphysis pubis was elongated, as in a man, and the mons veneris rounded, while the labia externa were covered with hair. The clitoris was ten and a half inches long when at rest, but somewhat larger when distended. There was no urethra, but the head of the glans was covered with an imperfect prepuce. The labia were narrow and short, and the vulva between them was narrow, and blocked up by a dense membrane. Below the clitoris there was an opening which was capable of admitting an ordinary sound. Through this aperture both the urinal and menstrual fluids escaped. She had menstruated since she was eight years of age. She regarded herself as a female, and preferred the society of men. There was no appearance of testicle, while regular menstruation left no doubt of her sex.

*Arnaud** has also described an interesting case at great length. The subject was aged thirty-five, and passed in society as a female. She came to Arnaud complaining of a small tumor in the right groin (*Fig.* 40, *e*,) which had incumbered her much during life. On examination, he found a similar tumor on the left side. These bags represented the external labia. The clitoris was nearly three inches in length. The glans was well-formed and presented a small depression which ran backward along the whole under border of the clitoris, indicating the situation of a collapsed urethral canal. The orifice from which the urine escaped was in the same position as in a female when the organs are natural. There was no vagina, and the menstrual discharge took place from the anus. At each menstrual period, the tumor (*d*) gradually increased, becoming in the course of two or three days of a size of a hen's egg. When the tumor reached

* Dissertation sur les Hermaphrodites, p. 265.

FIG. 40.

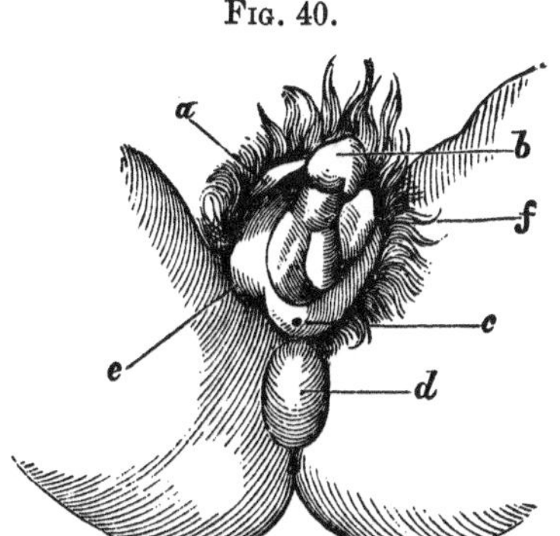


EXTERNAL APPEARANCE OF THE ORGANS OF GENERATION OF A FEMALE. (*After Arnaud. From Cyclo. Anat. et Physiol.*)

*a*, clitoris; *b*, glands of clitoris; *c*, orifice for passage of urine; *d*, tumor in perinæum; *e*, small tumor in right groin; *f*, small tumor in left groin.

this size, the discharge of blood commenced from the anus. As alarming symptoms had always occurred at these periods, Arnaud was induced to puncture the tumor, in which he found a cavity two inches in circumference and about two and a half in breadth, having a projection at one point which he supposed to be the *os uteri*. At the next menstrual period, the discharge came from the opening in this tumor, and was not attended with any of the alarming symptoms that had previously occurred. This opening, after a time, through neglect, was allowed to close, when the discharge flowed from the anus, as usual, with all the former alarming symptoms. This female's skin was thick and rough; she had a soft black beard; her chest was narrow; her breast small, like the male; her hands large and her fingers long. Her voice was coarse; the upper part of her body was masculine, while the lower part partook of the female characteristics—large pelvis, buttocks, legs, etc., with small feet. The regular menstruation of this person left no doubt in regard to her sex. The tumors surrounding the clitoris in the groin must have been the ovaries, which had descended.

The same malformations have been found to exist in the lower animals. *Rudolphi* noticed a mare that had a clitoris so large as almost to close up the entrance to the vagina. *Lecoq* has also mentioned a case of a calf of a similar character, while *Mery* speaks of a monkey which had a clitoris so large that his keeper thought the animal was a male.

*M. Veary*, physician at Toulouse, has given in the "Philosophical Transactions" of London, Vol. xvi., p. 282, an account of the case of Margarete Malause or Malaure, who entered as a patient in the Toulouse hospital in 1686. Her trunk and face presented the appearance of a female, but in the situation of the vulva, there was a body eight inches in length that resembled a well-formed male penis, except that it had no prepuce, though a canal perforated the organ through which the urine and menstrual fluid was voided. After being examined by several physicians, all of whom pronounced her sexual characteristics more those of a male than a female, the authorities ordered her name to be changed from that of Arnaud and to wear male attire.

In 1693, she visited Paris in male dress and boasted that she was endowed with the powers of both sexes. The Parisian physicians agreed with those of Toulouse in respect to her sex, until *M. Saviard* detected the supposed penis to be a prolapsus of the uterus. He reduced the protruded organ and cured the patient.* The king, afterward, at her own request, allowed her to assume her female name and dress.

*Sir E. Horne* and *Valentini*, both mention analogous cases of *False Hermaphrodism*. Numerous other instances of a similar character are on record, which will not require to be noticed at the present time. It may be observed, however, that there are on record also equally remarkable cases of spurious Hermaphrodism in the male as in the female sex, which have given rise to many curious mistakes and incidents, from the time that *Iphis*, daughter of *Ligdus*, king of Crete, was supposed to be changed into a man by the miraculous power of Isis, down to the present day. *Pliny*, *Trallian and Livy*, all have detailed interesting cases of this description of Hermaphrodism.

The case of Magdelain Mugnoz, a nun of the order of St. Dominique, in the town of Ubeda, mentioned by *Jean Croke*,† is somewhat extraordinary. It was supposed that she was changed into a male seven years after having taken the vow, when, in consequence of exhibiting strong sexual desire, and being accused of the perpetration of a rape upon a nun, she came under ecclesiastical displeasure and was expelled from the convent, after which he assumed male attire and changed his name to Francois.

A number of similar instances are mentioned by

* Recueil d'Observations Chirurgicales, p. 150.

† Fox, History, Cent. I.; and Arnaud, Dissertation sur les Hermaphrodites, p. 200; and Cycl. Anat. et Phys. Vol. II.

*Parè* and *Tulpius,* where malformed males were unexpectedly discovered at puberty, owing to excitement of the sexual passions.

*Schweikard* * mentions the case of a person baptized and brought up as a female whose true sex was not discovered until she was forty-nine years of age, when he requested permission to marry a young woman who had become pregnant by him. On examination, the penis was slender, and not over two inches long, while the testicles had not descended out of the abdomen and the urethra opened at the root of the penis.

*Otto*† has reported a remarkable case of a person who had lived for ten years in a state of wedlock with three different men. At the age of thirty-five her third husband brought an action of divorce against her, alleging that she was afflicted with some sexual infirmity, which rendered the connubial act on his part extremely difficult and painful. On examination being made by two physicians, they decided that she was not a female but a male. The members of the Royal Medical College of Silesia subsequently confirmed this decision. The penis was imperforated and about two inches in length. There was a perineal fissure forming a false vagina, that was sufficient to receive the penis of the husband for an inch and a half in depth. The general conformation of this individual was strong and muscular, although the

* Hufeland's Journal der Prak. Heilkunde, Bd. xvii. No. 18.

† Neue Seltene Beobachtungen zur Anatomie, etc., p. 123; and Cyclop. Anat. et Phys., Vol. II.

beard was thin and soft. The face, mammæ, chest, pelvis and extremities were masculine.

The case of Maria Nuzia given by *Julien* and *Soules** is one that may be classified with the preceding. This individual was born in Corsica in 1695, was married twice as a female, and divorced by her second husband in 1739, after sixteen years of wedlock. Her person was masculine; she had beard, but her breasts were tolerably developed, although the nipple of each was surrounded with hair, while she menstruated regularly.

The celebrated case of Hannah Wild, detailed by Dr. *Sampson*,† is another example equally curious with the foregoing. She had the male genital organs malformed, while her menstrual discharges were very regular.

B. TRUE HERMAPHRODISM.—True Hermaphrodism is found to exist naturally in several classes of the animal and vegetable kingdoms.

Those plants that are included under the term *phanerogamic*, except the class *Diœcia*, are furnished with male and female reproductive organs, which are either placed upon the same flower or on different flowers on the same plant.

In the animal kingdom, among the Entozoa, Mollusca and Gasperopoda, and some other species, the fecundation of the female is accomplished by its own male organ. As we ascend in the scale of animal

* Observ. sur l'Hist. Nat. sur la Physique et sur la Peinture, tom. 1, p. 18; and Cyclop. Anat. et Phys., Vol. II.

† Ephem. Nat. Curios., Dec. 1, 1666, p. 323; and Cyclop. Anat. et Phys., Vol II.

organization, this bisexual development ceases, except in certain peculiar cases, which will be enumerated. It is not proposed to give any minute history of true Hermaphrodism, but merely some interesting and curious cases that have come under the notice of physicians at different periods of the world, with a view to remove the skepticism which is now generally prevalent about the existence of any species of Hermaphrodism. The authorities here presented will leave no room for doubt on this subject.

In 1754* a young person died in the Hôtel Dieu of Paris, in whom, on dissection, the reproductive organs were found to be malformed in the following manner: On the right side there was a testicle and vas deferens, terminating in a corresponding vesicula seminalis. On the left side there was found, in the place of a testicle, an ovary, a Fallopian tube with its fimbriated extremity, a small oval uterus, and broad and round ligaments. The external organs resembled those of the male, although the penis was only about two inches in length. The mammæ were large, and the individual had always been regarded as a male. Here was a case of lateral Hermaphrodism, similar to what may be found, though not so perfectly developed, in the vegetable and lower forms of the animal kingdoms.

Another celebrated case of lateral Hermaphrodism has been reported by *Mayer*.† This person was named

* Abhandlung. Kœnig. Akad. der Wissenchaft zu Berlin für 1825, § 60; Cyclop. Anat. Phys. Vol. II.

† Gazette Méd. de Paris, 1836, No. 39; Lancet, V. I. for 1836-7, p. 140; or London Medical Gaz. for Oct. 29, 1836; and Cyclop. Anat. et Phys., Vol. II. p. 699

Marie Derrier or Charles Doerge, and had been baptized and brought up as a female, but at forty years of age, changed his name and dress to that of a man's. This person, after death, was examined by Professor Mayer, who discovered the existence of a uterus, a vagina, two Fallopian tubes, a testicle, prostate gland and penis. The penis was two inches and three quarters in length, but concealed below the mons veneris. During life it was capable of erection and of elongation to more than three inches. The prepuce covered only half the glans. The vagina was a little over two inches in length, and rather less than an inch in breadth, and terminated above in a fluid isthmus, which represented the fluid orifice of the uterus. The general characteristics of this individual were a mixture of the male and female; the breasts were small, and there was no distinct mammary glandular structure; the stature was five feet; the head and face presenting the appearance of those of a woman. As age advanced the beard grew, while he menstruated three times during his twentieth year. Professor Mayer likewise states that he had manifested a certain predilection for females, without feeling any special sexual desire.

In a note appended to a case published by M. Petit,* he states that a man consulted him who menstruated regularly every month from his penis, without any pain or troublesome symptom. This man no doubt had a concealed uterus. In the *Cyclop. Anat. et Phys.*

* Hist. de l'Acad. Roy. des Sc. for 1720, p. 38; and Cyclop. Anat. et Phys., Vol. II.

Vol. II., p. 709, two similar cases are mentioned. One was that of a young man seventeen years of age; the other a man who had been married several years, his wife having no children. In both these instances there was a copious menstrual discharge regularly every month from the penis. There was no opportunity of examining these cases after death; but there is no reason to doubt that there were internal female organs that communicated with the bladder and urethra.

*Mayer*, in his work, to which reference has already been made,* has delineated five cases, all of which he dissected. The first case, (*Fig.* 41,) was in a fœtus of four months, in which he found the bladder, the testicles (*a a*), with the epididymis and a two-horned uterus (*c*) terminating in the vagina (*d*) and opening into the posterior part of the bladder (*e*). From the left testicles a contorted vas deferens (*f*) arose, and ran down to the vagina (*d*); the right vas deferens (*g*) was shorter and disappeared near the corresponding corner of the uterus. The external organs were male, the glans penis being imperforate.

It has been already stated in the present work, that menstruation depends upon a change that takes place in the ovaries, and that such change exerts a marked influence over the general system. *Vaulevier*† mentions an instance where menstruation ceased in a

* Icones. Select., etc., p. 8–16. Also Walker and Graaf's Journal des Chirurgie and Augenheilkunde, Bd. vii. Hft. 3, and Bd. vii. Hft. 2.

† Journ. de Méd., tom. lxix., and Meckel in Reil's Arch. Bd. xi. s. 275. Also, Cyclop. Anat. et Phys. Vol. II. 716.

young girl enjoying good health, without any apparent injury to the system, when, soon afterward, a heavy beard began to grow upon her face.

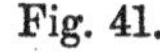

Fig. 41.

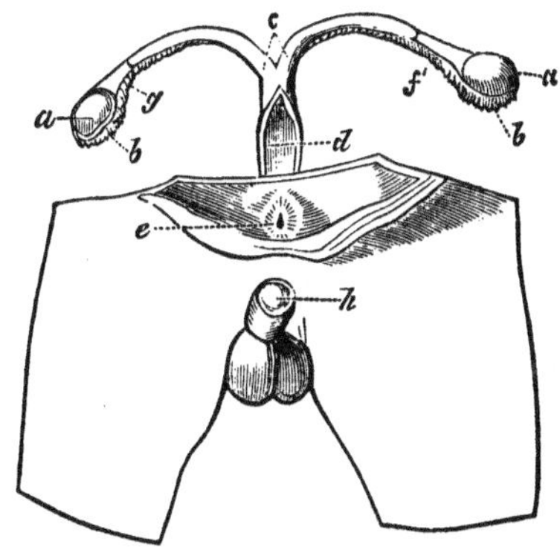


A COMPLETE CASE OF HERMAPHRODITIC MALFORMATION IN THE HUMAN SUBJECT.
*(After Mayer, from Cyclop. Anat. et Phys.)*

*a, a,* Testicles with their epididymis *b, b,* and a two-horned uterus *c,* which terminates in the vagina *d,* and which opens into the posterior part of urinary bladder *e.* From the left testicle a contorted vas deferens *f,* arises and extends down to the vagina; the right vas deferens, *g,* is shorter and terminates in the right of the uterus. The glans penis *h,* is imperforate.

Similar remarkable changes have been observed to take place in birds. *Greve,* in his "Fragments of Comparative Anatomy and Physiology," states that hens whose ovaries become diseased, will crow like cocks, while they acquire tail-feathers and spurs resembling the male fowls.

The male and female organs seem to be analogous in structure; and from a defect in the formative or typical force of their unfoldment or development, one side may be masculine and the other feminine. M. *St.*

*Hilaire* has offered the following table to show this analogy:—

| *In the Male.* | | *In the Female.* |
|---|---|---|
| Testicles, | = | Ovary. |
| Epididymis, | = | Fallopian Tubes. |
| Vas deferens, | = | Corum of Uterus. |
| Vesicula Seminalis, | = | Body of Uterus. |
| Sheath of the Penis, | = | Vagina. |
| Penis, | = | Clitoris. |

An interesting case of Hermaphrodism has been given by Dr. *Hendry*, of New York, in a letter dated from Lisbon in 1807.* The subject was a Portuguese, aged twenty-eight years, of a tall and slender muscular figure. The penis and testicles were in their usual situation, and in form and size resembled those of a male about the same age. The urethra extended to about one-third the length of the penis. The beard had a tendency to grow, but was kept cut short. The female parts resembled those of a well-formed person, except the labia, which were not prominent. The external organs appeared to be situated near the rectum. The breasts were small, voice and manners like those of a female. She menstruated regularly; was twice pregnant, and miscarried in the third and fourth month of gestation. During copulation, the penis became erect, but there never was a desire for copulation with the female sex.

## CAUSES OF HERMAPHRODISM.

The more prominent cause of Hermaphrodism will

* New York Medical Repository, Vol. XII., p. 86.

be found treated of in the Chapter on Termatology or Monstrosities. One of these causes appears to be an arrest of development of the sexual organs in their evolution, or to some morbid influence exerted on the embryo, changing its type of unfoldment.

It is known that a division may be made in the perineum, and the fissure remain, from the accumulation of urine in the urinary canal, on account of the imperforate urethra. The cause may also be hereditary in some families. *Heuremann* speaks of a family of females, who gave birth for several generations to males who were all affected with *Hypospadias*, or an opening of the urethra on the under surface of the penis, not far from the pubes.

*Lecat* says that this malformation is not uncommon in Normandy. *Baum, Walrecht, Gockel, Rann, Boerhaave, Naegele, Katsky, Saviard* and *Sir Everard Home*, have mentioned similar cases. Hereditary malformation of the genital organs of cows have been observed by *Hunter, Thompson*, and *Lothidin.*

*Sir Everard Home** mentions that in warm countries nurses and midwives have a prejudice that women born twins with males, seldom breed. The same notion exists among the lower classes of Scotland. This impression, however, has been refuted by *Cribb*, who gives the history of forty-two married females who were born twins with males—thirty-six of whom were mothers of females, and six had no children, though married for a number of years. Two of these females who had families were born triplets with males. The *Medical Repository* of 1827, (p. 350,) mentions an in-

* Comp. Ant., Vol. III., p. 333–4.

stance of quadruplets consisting of three boys and one girl, all of whom lived. This female afterward became the mother of triplets.

To those individuals in whom the male characteristics predominate, the term *Androgyni*, is applied, while *Androgynæ* embrace those Hermaphrodites in whom the female peculiarities are the most apparent. Thus in an *Androgynus* the general figure of the body may be that of a female; the male voice is wanting, and there is no beard. On the other hand, in the *Androgyna* the masculine developments are the most apparent.

These subjects are regarded as incurably impotent, and the malformation always such as to justify a divorce, but it is no ground for depriving a being of inheritance; nor is the calling of an Hermaphrodite actionable unless it has been attended with some especial damage. A dancing-master once brought suit in England against a party who called him an Hermaphrodite; but the judge and jury decided that the dancing-master had sustained no injury, from the fact, that in the line of his profession he was a much safer person, and none the less qualified than an individual who was more perfectly developed.

## CHAPTER IX.

### MENSTRUATION.

THE uterus is the efficient instrument in Menstruation, but the organs that cause and regulate it, are the ovaries. These exert a powerful influence not only upon the uterus, but over the entire organism. If the ovaries be removed in a female menstruating regularly, such catamenial flow will immediately cease, whereas it has never been known to occur in females who had no ovaries.

Menstruation consists of a sanguineous discharge, which escapes from the external orifice of the vagina in a female who enjoys health, periodically, except during lactation and pregnancy.

The discharge commences at puberty, and is an evidence that the female has arrived at that period of life. In the tropics puberty occurs from the tenth to fifteenth year; in temperate climates from twelve to sixteen years. Menstruation occurs in a healthy female every twenty-eight days, or every lunar month, and continues on an average for thirty years.

Mr. Robertson has given this subject his attention for many years, and prepared a table of four hundred and fifty women, which shows the period of their first menstruation respectively, as follows:—

| | | |
|---|---|---|
| In the 11th year | 10 | women |
| " 12th " | 19 | " |
| " 13th " | 53 | " |
| " 14th " | 85 | " |
| " 15th " | 97 | " |
| " 16th " | 78 | " |
| " 17th " | 57 | " |
| " 18th " | 26 | " |
| " 19th " | 23 | " |
| " 20th " | 4 | " |

It must be borne in mind that this table was formed from observation of females in England.

A remarkable case of early puberty is mentioned by Dr. *Gardner*, in his work on "Sterility." Her name was Phœbe Anna Baker, and was exhibited at Barnum's first "Baby Show" in New York. The Doctor states that he saw her at his office, July 27, 1855, and took the following notes:—

"Phœbe Anna Baker was born at Sing Sing, New York, January 19th, 1851. Her mother has one other child, a boy of seven years. Parents both American. At birth she weighed fourteen pounds, and has always since been large. When ten months old, a bloody flow was noticed from the pudendum, and this has continued periodically ever since, until the present date, without at any time going longer than six weeks (and when thus protracted showing signs of physical disturbance) without its appearance. About the time this flow commenced, a marked enlargement of her breast was noticed, and these very soon attained to their present size, being now equal to those of most girls of sixteen years, of perfect shape, having a well-formed, but not very protuberant nipple, and an areola of a light brown color. She weighs sixty-four pounds, and is of remarkable size for her age, fully developed in form and of a maturity of appearance most noticeable. The hips are full, the limbs rounded, and her form would indicate that she had attained maturity and puberty."

The Doctor further states that when he saw her, as above described, the flow had been retarded for some two weeks longer than usual, and the mother seriously supposed her pregnant, as she had discovered a man (for which sex she evinced great fondness) in an improper situation with her. This man the mother had arrested and detained in prison several days, until the menstrual flow in the girl returned.

This function is so regular in some women that the day and very hour of its occurrence may be predicted with a certainty. The flow usually continues from three to five days—sometimes for seven days—the interval between being from twenty-one to twenty-five days. In the majority of women this regularity is not observed. In some it occurs two or three days before, or it may be retarded the same length of time without any injury to the system. It has already been stated that menstruation does not occur during pregnancy and lactation. There are exceptions to both these rules. When menstruation takes place during pregnancy, it may occur from the placenta being placed over the os-uteri or neck of the womb, or arise from the vaginal portion of the cervix of the uterus.

Mr. *Whitehead* invariably found when menstruation occurred during pregnancy, that the discharge came from the diseased surface of the neck of the womb. A *true* catamenial flow is impossible during gestation or pregnancy, and when it occurs it indicates something wrong, either at the neck or head of the womb.

The quantity of menstrual fluid discharged at each monthly period has been variously estimated, but the usual quantity in females enjoying good health, may be stated at from two to five ounces. The estimates made by different observers, however, are much higher than this. *Hippocrates* and *Galen* state the quantity equal to an attic hemina, which is about eighteen ounces. *Haller* gives the average at six to ten ounces. Drs. *Whitehead* and *Farne* make it from three to four ounces.

NATURE OF THE DISCHARGE.—It was formerly supposed, and so stated by *Pliny* and others, that the menstrual fluid contained principles of a noxious and poisonous character. Pliny informs us that the presence of a menstrual woman turns wine sour, causes trees to shed their fruit, parches up their young shoots, and makes them forever barren, dims the splendor of mirrors and the polish of ivory, turns the edge of sharpened iron, converts brass into rust, and is the cause of canine rabies.*

The menstrual fluid in health has a peculiarly heavy odor, which is characteristic of it, as well as the gravis odor puerperii of the lochial and other discharges of child-bed, which may have led Pliny

* Plinii Nat. Hist., liber vii., § xiii., ed. Cuvier, 8vo., Vol. 1. Paris, 1827.

to arrive at such erroneous conclusions. This, as well as the peculiar odor of the breath of some females, no doubt results from the decomposition of the fluid, as it slowly collects in the vagina of the female, and from its absorption into the system.

The fact that the menstrual fluid will not coagulate, may have led to the different opinions advanced in regard to its real character.

When it is first formed, it appears to be real blood, but on its passage through the vagina it comes in contact with an acid secreted by that organ, which dissolves the fibrin and destroys its coagulating properties. The composition of the menstrual fluid, according to M. *Denis*, is as follows:—

| | |
|---|---|
| Water, | 82.58 |
| Fibrin, | 0.05 |
| Hematosine, | 6.36 |
| Mucus, | 3.63 |
| Albumen, | 4.83 |
| Oxide of Iron, | 0.85 |
| Osmazome and Cruovine, of each, | 0.11 |
| Salts and fatty matter, | 1.59 |
| | 100.00 |

The discharge is different when taken directly from the uterus for examination. It is then found to coagulate as readily as blood and possesses all its characteristics. There are many modern physiologists who advocate that menstrual fluid is not blood, but a secretion, from the fact that it contains a small quantity of fibrin. I have explained this by stating that the secretions of the vagina dissolve the fibrin.

*Haller* and *Hunter* also regarded the menstrual fluid a natural evacuation of blood.

It is generally supposed that the menstrual flux is eliminated by the vagina, os and cervix and body of the uterus. These views are mainly correct, although the principal portion of it is derived from the lining membrane of the uterus.

If the uterus of a female who died during menstruation be examined after death, the lining membrane will be found highly congested, the blood-vessels particularly, the capillaries quite enlarged; while, if a slight pressure be made with the hand, small streamlets of blood will ooze out from the little pores or orifices in the lining membrane. This congestion, however, does not extend lower than the neck of the womb.

The mode in which the discharge takes place has led many to maintain that it is eliminated in the form of secretion, the same as takes place from ordinary glands. From the fact that blood corpuscles are found in the fluid, they must come from the capillaries, which are ruptured by their distension, and that it presents all the appearance of blood, it is unnecessary to reason further against the secretion theory, or in favor of the non-secretion hypothesis. It is most probable that the discharge takes place from capillaries with open mouths — such arrangement being known to exist in the capillaries of the uterus.

THE OBJECT OF MENSTRUATION.—The mere escape of blood from the uterine walls is of slight importance compared to other purposes which it serves, and which comprehends much significance.

The French term "*fleurs*" and the English "*flowers*," formerly used, had their signification of the office of menstruation. The term suggested, that as a tree before it bore fruit blossomed, so a woman before she bore a child, or became pregnant, also had her flowers.

I have already intimated that a woman does not menstruate until she arrives at puberty, and until her ovaries reach a certain stage of development; and, also, that such catamenia continues as long as ovulation is prolonged. I have likewise stated that when the ovaries were removed that menstruation ceased; also, that when the ovaries are congenitally deficient, no menstruation occurs. Hence the presence of ovaries is essential for menstruation. When they cease to develop and emit ova, as during pregnancy and lactation, menstruation is likewise arrested. These facts seem to be fully established by modern physiologists.

In addition to this relationship between menstruation and ovulation, there is a direct correspondence existing between each menstrual discharge and the ripening of the ovum. It is the ovaries that produce the pain during the menstrual evacuation. This has been fully proven by the following case, recorded by Dr. *Oldham*, in the Proceedings of the Royal Society, Vol. VIII., p. 377.

Both ovaries descended through the inguinal canals and there permanently lodged. After an interval of three weeks both ovaries were observed to become painful and tumid. The swelling increased for three days, remained stationary for three more, and then declined—the time being from ten to twelve days.

These facts, and others that have been mentioned in speaking of the functions of the ovaries and Fallopian tubes, fully confirm the theory that menstruation is caused and maintained by the ovaries, during the process of preparing and ripening the ova, and that when the ovum is expelled the excitement of the ovary ceases, and with it the exciting cause producing the discharge from the uterus—the vessels of which contract and arrest the flow of fluid until another period of menstruation arrives.

Having considered the *cause* of Menstruation, the *purpose* of such provision may now be stated. It has been affirmed that the quantity of discharge is from three to five ounces, and that the process is repeated in the unimpregnated and healthy female once in every lunar month, or thirteen times a year, for about thirty years. If three ounces be eliminated, it will amount in this period to nine gallons, or seventy-two pounds. If five ounces, to fifteen gallons, or one hundred and twenty-two pounds. The only satisfactory conclusion that can be arrived at in regard to the purposes of Nature in throwing off so large a quantity of blood, is the supposition that it is intended to relieve the congestion of the ovaries that is known to exist during the ripening of the ova. There is no doubt that the Fallopian tubes as well as the uterus, assist in relieving this congestion. If impregnation follows ovulation, the excitement is diverted to a new channel, the uterus, in order to prepare it for the impregnated ovum, which excitement continues until the termination of pregnancy.

Menstruation does not in all cases seem essential to fertility; women sometimes breed without menstruating, while the suspension of the catamenial flux during lactation is not a positive prevention of conception. Girls have also been known to become pregnant before the menstrual age had arrived.

Having shown the causes of Menstruation and the purposes it serves, it would seem next in order to speak of the difficulties which attend it, and the medical aid required for its rectification. Such remarks, however, will be found more appropriate to the chapter which treats of the "Diseases of Females," and accordingly, the reader's attention is directed to that portion of the present work for the information that may be desired.

# CHAPTER X.

## GENERATION.

THIS is considered the most interesting and important part of a work of this character, particularly of late years, when so many different theories have been advanced and strongly maintained by some of the brightest lights that adorn the medical profession. The reader may, perhaps, readily anticipate the views of the author of this volume from what has been already advanced in the preceding pages. The work, however, would be imperfect without a fair presentation and comparison of the facts and opinions of former writers with the latest observations made upon this subject. Hence they will be succinctly stated and analyzed according to their relative importance.

The process of generation is that by which the young of living organized bodies are produced and the species continued. Some animals propagate by a division of their bodies into pieces, each one becoming endowed with an independent existence similar to the parent. Others propagate by buds upon the parent stem, which buds, when they arrive at maturity, separate and retain an individual existence. Another class of animals throw off from their bodies a portion of organized matter, which, after undergoing various processes of development, acquire all the peculiarities of the parent. In the fourth and last class, the process is more complex than in either of the others. In this last division, the union of the male and female sexes is necessary for procreation. The reproductive functions require more complicated processes in the higher than in the lower order of animals, in order to the perpetuation of the different species through an undeviating succession of generations.

While speaking of the process of generation in man, it will be appropriate to present some interesting facts respecting reproduction in some of the series of the animal kingdom inferior to the *genus homo*, or man. From what has been advanced in the forepart of this work, the reader will understand that the egg furnished by the female is perfectly *barren* so far as regards progressive development, unless it receives some influence from the product of the male generative organs. This is equally the fact in regard to the product of the male. To render either *fruitful*, there must be a *union* of the two several products of the male and female.

The scientific man, as well as the more ignorant, in all ages, have contemplated with wonder and admiration the phenomena by which the young of animals are brought into existence. The gradual construction of the frame-work of the animal body—the changes necessary for the formation of the brains and nerves, by which man thinks and feels—the muscles that induce locomotion—the process of nutrition, by which the various organs are formed and nourished—all proceeding from the comparative simple structure of the egg—are well calculated to inspire wonder and admiration of the works of Nature, and lead man to indulge in many absurd and unwarranted hypotheses and speculations, as to the origin and perpetuation of the various animal species.

The ascertained fact that the egg possesses an inherent *vital* power in itself, derived from the parent, and the mode of its being called into action by external physical agents—such as heat, moisture, oxygen and light—the influence exerted on it by being brought into contact with the male sperm—the preservation of the distinct species from generation to generation in undeviating succession—the transmission of hereditary weakness and constitutional peculiarities of form, resemblance and mental traits—all have a tendency to throw an air of mystery over the functions of reproduction.

There is one fact that must be borne in mind, which is, that all the scientific and learned can do, is to investigate matter and observe the laws which control and change its elements. The same elements that now exist, and the same forces, have existed from all eternity. It is the operations of these forces upon these elements, in the formation of new compounds, that we are to study, and this is all that man can do in this life. This investigation constitutes science, and beyond the light of such knowledge no man can safely venture. Hence it is apparent, all that is necessary for the generation of a new being is *matter* endowed with a *vital* force. This force calls to its assistance other physical agents in unfolding organic forms. Such agents are heat, light, moisture, and oxygen. It was from the action of the vital force upon matter, with the assistance of the agents named, that the first plant or first animal was formed.

An egg healthily developed, when brought in contact with the male principle, has this vital power awakened in it, and if it can then draw to itself the aid of the several agents already named, will gradually develop a human being, endowed with all the peculiarities of its parent, simply because the *unfolding* or vital principle in the egg and male sperm, is a part and parcel of the parental stamina. It is an established law of Nature, that "*Like* begets *like.*" Should there be any interference with such unfolding or vital force there will be an imperfect development, denominated malformation. This vital principle is the *constitution* of the new being, and has imbedded in it, or united with it, all the peculiarities or idiosyncracies, and all the hereditary weaknesses and ailments of its parents. *Females should remember this immutable law, before selecting a partner for life, if they would not entail upon posterity constitutional defects that can never be remedied.*

It is somewhat amusing to contemplate the various theories that have been advanced in regard to generation, in various ages of the world.

*Drelincourt*, a distinguished author of the last century, names no less than *two hundred and sixty-two* groundless hypotheses of generation, from the writings of his predecessors. *Blumenbach* justly remarks that nothing is more certain than that Delincourt's theory formed the two hundred and sixty-third.*

* See Blumenbach über den Bildungstinel, 12mo., Gotting. 1791; or Cyclop. Phys. et Anat., Vol. II., p. 427.

As it would be an endless and fruitless task to wade through all such theories, a few of the more plausible and remarkable ones may be briefly presented in the present place.

One of the oldest theories was that of the *Ovists.* These philosophers maintained that the female afforded all the material necessary for the development of the offspring—the male doing nothing more than awakening this dormant principle in the female. This was the celebrated *Pythagorian* theory. It was also *Aristotle's*, somewhat modified. Some of the old authors who entertained this theory, supposed that the embryo was formed from the menstrual fluid which descended from the brain during sexual union.

Another theory which had many advocates was that of the *Spermatists.* They supposed that it was the male semen alone which furnished all the vitality that was essential for the new being—the female organs simply furnishing a fit place or matrix, together with the materials necessary for its nourishment and unfoldment. This was *Galen's* favorite theory.

After the discovery of *Spermatozoa*, those that had supported Galen's hypothesis, now maintained that the spermatozoa were miniature representations of men, and called them *homunculi*—some even going so far as to assert that they discovered in them the body, limbs, form of face and expression of countenance of a full-grown human being. They also entertained the idea that these were male and female homunculi—that if a female homunculum was deposited a human female was developed, and the same of the male.

Another theory was that of *Syngenesis* or *Combination*, which supposed that the male and female both furnished semen, which united in the uterus with a third product and developed the egg.

All the theories advanced prior to the seventeenth century are erroneous, on account of the want of knowledge of the character of the egg in reproduction. It was not until Harvey established his dictum of "*Omne vivum ex ova*" that more rational ideas of reproduction began to be entertained. Upon Harvey's notions have been based all modern investigations. It led to a discussion of the two theories of *Epigenesis* and *Evolution*. The first is that of non-sexual generation, in which each new germ is an entirely new product of the parent. The other is a theory of non-sexual generation, in which the first embryo contains within itself, in miniature, all the individuals of that species which shall ever exist, and contains them so arranged that each generation shall not only include the next but all succeeding generations.

*Harvey* and *Malpighi* were the first who endeavored to sustain the theory of *Epigenesis*, as opposed to the old views entertained by the *Ovists* and *Spermatists*. During the middle of the last century, *Haller* and *Bonnett* advocated the opposite theory of *Evolution*.

Those who advocate the Epigenesis system maintain that there is no appearance of the *new animal* to be found in a perfectly impregnated egg before the commencement of incubation, or the beginning development of the new being, until heat, oxygen, and other agents are applied, when a formative or generative process is established, by which means the parts of the new being are put together or built up by the union of the molecules of matter of which the egg is composed. In other words, to be more explicit, this is what may be termed the *material* or *chemical* theory of generation, which signifies that the elements of matter are developed or unfolded into organic forms, by *chemical* changes taking place in said matter without the aid of any *vital* or inherent force.

*Haller* supported the opposite theory of *Evolution*—that the animal or fœtus pre-existed in the egg in an invisible condition, and that by the aid of heat, oxygen, and other conditions necessary for growth, the new being is developed.

*Bonnet* carried this theory much further than Haller. He maintained that not only all the parts of the animal pre-exist in the egg, but that the germs of all animals which are to be born pre-exist in the ovaries of the female—that in the genital organs of the first parents of all species is contained the *germs* of all posterity. In other words, in the ovaries of our great grandmother Eve, were contained the germs of every human being that has since existed—that every organic form that now exists, existed in the first parents of the same species and family.

Such are the two extremes that were advocated with much energy and bitterness during the last century.

The theory of Bonnet was called the theory of *Emboitement*, to distinguish it from Haller's hypothesis of Evolution. Recent writings are not altogether free from the vague notions of the older authors. The electric, mechanical, and spontaneous motive theories have all had their advocates, and are still adhered to by many.

Prof. *Burdach* very properly and justly remarks that the generative function in the fruitful egg and the generation of a young animal from it, are *natural* phenomena and no more a secret than other phenomena occurring in organized bodies.

The illustrious *Harvey*, who was a supporter of the theory of *Epigenesis*, so far as the building up out of the elements of matter composing the egg is concerned, believed there is something behind all this phenomena, which controls and directs the physical forces concerned in the unfoldment of animal forms. He states: "A more sublime and diviner Artificer (than man) seems to make and preserve man; and a nobler agent than a cock doth produce a chicken out of the egg. For we acknowledge our omnipotent God and most high Creator to be everywhere present in the structure of all creatures living, and to point himself out by his works; whose instruments the cock and hen are in the generation of the chicken. For it is most apparent that in the generation of the chicken out of the egg, all things are set up and formed, with a most singular providence, divine wisdom, and an admiral and incomprehensible artifice." "Nor can these attributes appertain to any but to the Omnipotent Maker of all things, under what name soever we cloud him; whether it be the *mens divina*, the divine mind with Aristotle; or *anima mundi*, the soul of the universe with Plato; or with others *natura naturaus*, nature of Nature himself; or also Saturnus or Jupiter with the heathen, or rather as befits us, the Creator and Father of all things in heaven and earth; upon whom all animals and their births depend; and at whose beck and mandate, all things are created and begotten."*

A subject closely connected with the present, yet somewhat speculative in character, is worthy of examination in this place. It is the theory of

### SPONTANEOUS GENERATION.

All organized beings are subject to death, yet no species of animals or plants become extinct, but continue through an undeviating succession of generations. The mineral owes its origin to the simple union of the particles of which it is composed; but the generation of species of organic forms constitute an *uninterrupted* chain, extending from the first creation of organic matter, while every new link that is added to this vast chain of organic structure is but an attachment to that by which it was preceded. Indeed, so complete is the law of continued reproduction of organic bodies, that many naturalists have adopted the circumstances of reproduction as the only means of determining which individual ought to be regarded as belonging to one species.

There was a time when it was supposed that some animals might be produced artificially, such as various kinds of worms and molluscous (soft-shelled) animals. The observations of *Redi* and others have proven these views to be erroneous. Spontaneous genera

* Anatomical Exercitations concerning the Generation of Living Creatures. London, 1653, p. 310, *et seq.*

tion, however, seems to take place in some of the very lowest forms of organized beings; yet, as science progresses, it may be proven that such organic productions are governed by the same general laws of reproduction, by the separation of a living portion from a parent body.

The supporters of spontaneous generation maintain that certain changes of organic molecules are the sole cause of the formation of different kinds of animalculi, as are observed in drops of water, starch, gum, etc., when they enter into putrefaction. The formation of these animalculi will depend upon conditions existing at the time of generation, such as the degree of heat, character of the air, amount of decomposition, and the proportion of water.

*Spallanzani*, a strong supporter of this theory of generation, discovered that an exclusion of air completely prevented the generation of animalculi, and hence came to the conclusion that they existed in the atmosphere.

The experiments of Mr. *Crosse*, a few years ago, in the production of animalculi from solutions of granite, silex, etc., wonderfully elated the advocates of this hypothesis. Not much confidence, however, has been placed in his experiments, from the fact that they have failed in the hands of others who followed implicitly his directions in their manipulations.

Reproduction of the present day may be divided into sexual and non-sexual.

A. NON-SEXUAL REPRODUCTION.—The Non-sexual Reproduction may be divided into three kinds or classes: *First*, by simple division; *Second*, by attached buds; and *Third*, by separate *gemmœ*.

The *first* is observed in the *Infusoria*. By dividing the animal into a number of pieces, each one, endowed with an independent life, will develop an individual similar to the parent with all its peculiarities. If a *hydra viredis* be divided longitudinally or transversely, each part will grow and develop that portion of its body of which it has been divested by the division. The tape-worm is another example of this kind. It will live and grow after its segments have been divided into fragments.

The *second* variety—that of *budding*—is best seen in coral and polypi. The young is first seen attached to the body of the parent, and consists of a small conical eminence on the body of the parent. This gradually enlarges cylindrically, while a small cavity forms in the interior, which afterward communicates with the stomach of the parent, so that food taken into the stomach of the parent penetrates that of the offspring. As the young polypus grows a small opening is next observed in this cavity. This is the mouth, while it is also furnished with tentaculi (feelers). After this, the animal obtains food for itself. The cavity between it and the parent is now closed, and it in turn progagates new offspring.

The *third* form of reproduction is that arising from small detached masses or sporules. These bodies are generally round, and may be represented as buds thrown off from the parent stem. They bear the same relation to the parent as the egg in higher animals. To this class belong the sponge. After being thrown off, it undergoes a process of development into an animal similar to the parent.

B. Sexual Reproduction.—In this form of Reproduction, there must exist two animals, male and female. The product of the female is called an ovum or egg; that of the male is a whitish fluid called male sperm or semen. The structure of the ovum has already been given, as well as the characteristics of the male sperm or semen. This form of generation is divided into the two divisions of *viviparous* and *oviparous*.

To the viviparous belong those animals which bring forth their young alive. The human species belongs to this class. To the oviparous belong those that hatch from eggs laid by the female parent. To this class belong birds, reptiles and fishes. In both of these classes the ova are formed in the ovary, and are fecundated by the male within the female.

These general views will now prepare the reader's mind for a clearer comprehension of the most important and interesting portion of this subject, as embraced in the

## REPRODUCTIVE FUNCTION IN MAN.

The period of life at which the human being is capable of reproduction is termed *puberty*. At this period important changes are observed in the structure and functions of the system. These changes are more marked in the female than in the male, which may be attributed to the female affording nourishment for the children during the whole of intra-uterine life, while the male furnishes only the material for fecundation.

In infancy and youth the two sexes do not differ materially in their general physical conformations, nor in their mental characteristics. At the period of puberty, however, there is observed a marked antagonism both of the intellectual and anatomical developments. The broad chest and wide shoulders of the male, and the large pelvis and abdomen of the female, constitute the chief peculiarities of difference between the male and female sexes. The body of the female is smaller, in weight about one-fourth less than that of the male. Her frame is more tapering, the muscles less prominent, the limbs are round and symmetrically proportioned, the bones small, the skin delicate and fine, the voice soft and feminine, while there is that chaste and reserved modesty of demeanor, which is so irresistibly captivating to the other sex. In the male there is the low, rough voice, owing to the large size of the larynx and vocal cords; hair appears on the skin and all over the body and limbs, indicating great physical powers and activity, enabling him to endure much fatigue and excel in deeds of strength and daring. In the male, at puberty, there is also an enlargement of all the generative organs, which is accompanied with sexual feelings and the secretion of semen by the testicles, prostate glands and vesicula seminalis, with occasionally a spontaneous emission occurring at night, generally during dreaming.

In the female there is likewise an enlargement of the breast and genital organs, while there is a peculiar discharge from the latter, termed the "menstrual" flow. It is not out of place here to mention that there is no discharge from females during sexual congress, as many suppose, equivalent to that emitted from the male during such conjunction of the sexes. There is, however, a secretion from the glands of the vagina which serves to lubricate the parts during coition and increases sexual pleasure. The excitement attendant upon coition is paroxysmal in both male and female, the seminal discharge taking place only from the former at the height of such paroxysm.

The period during which the genital functions are exercised is variable in both sexes. In the female the period is usually about thirty years—from puberty, at fifteen years, to the "change of life," at forty-five years. In the males it is somewhat longer—generally from forty-five to fifty years, or from the fifteenth year of age to the sixtieth or seventieth year. There are many instances where the virile powers of the male have been retained even to a much more lengthened period—to the eightieth, ninetieth, or hundredth year. In the celebrated case of "Old *Parr*," it continued unimpaired until he reached one hundred and thirty years of age, *Masinissa*, king of Numidia, after he was eighty-six years old, begot *Methynate*. *Wadalas*, king of Poland, had two children after his ninetieth year. The Hon. *Jeremiah Smith* of New Hampshire became the father of a child when he was eighty. The author is acquainted with a gentleman who married for the first time when he was seventy-five and had two sons by a young wife. There are some cases on record of females menstruating the second time and bearing children at seventy or eighty years of age. I am cognizant of the case of a lady of Philadelphia who commenced menstruating at nearly eighty years of age, and conceived.

### SEXUAL FEELINGS.

In all animals where the distinction of sex exists, there are instinctive feelings experienced to a greater or less extent. This feeling depends upon the temperament of the body and the condition of the mind. In animals the impulse is concomitant more upon a peculiar state of the genital organs, which is manifested at a particular season of the year, known as the "breeding" or "rutting" period. In the female, at this time, a peculiar secretion takes place in the genital organs, the odor of which excites the sexual functions of the male.

In the human species a similar feeling exists, but which is capable of being placed under intellectual and moral control. When not so governed, this passion is productive of the most revolting obscenity and prostitution.* Hence the necessity of legislative enactments to restrain licentiousness and concubinage.

The sexual passion is modified very much in some temperaments. For instance, the sanguine being more voluptuous, love amorous preludes. The bilious are under an erotic fury, which is as great as it is quickly exhausted. The melancholic burn with a secret and

* See work entitled "Boyhood's Perils and Manhood's Curse." by the author of the present volume. Chap. i., Part 2, and Appendix.

more constant flame, while the phlegmatic are cold and insensible.

The temperaments should be more understood than they are by those selecting a partner for life. That happiness which is so desirable in wedlock, is seldom found where the temperaments, sentiments and sexual feelings of the husband and wife are of opposite or antagonistic character. Among the lower classes this incompatibility of impulses or "unequal yoking," as St. Paul expresses it, often leads to adultery, separation, and other domestic discomforts and miseries.

The brain appears to exert considerable influence over the sexual organs. The sexual feelings are more or less under the control of the mental faculties, in the same manner that the action of the heart, digestive process, respiration, secretion, and, in fact, all the functions of the body, are subject to the operations of the intellectual apparatus. It is also a fact that the genital organs excite mental desires.

Phrenologists maintain that the *cerebellum* (or lower brain, back of the head) presides over the sexual feelings, or rather that such impulses belong to that organ, and that it is from thence all sexual desires emanate. It is found that those who have the back of the head and neck large, have the sexual passions more strongly developed than is the case in those persons where such prominence does not exist. The same fact has been observed in animals; while it has been proven by observation that diseases of the cerebellum, such as inflammation, and injuries from gun-shot and other wounds, impair or destroy sexual desires. Also, it is known that if the cerebellum be stimulated in any manner the sexual desires are increased in accordance with such stimulation.

*Carpenter* mentions several instances of this kind. One of these cases was that of a man whose sexual proclivities had always been strongly manifested through life, although they were entirely under the control of the will, until about three months previous to his death, when such erotic impulses increased in a most extraordinary degree. A post-mortem examination after death, revealed a tumor on the *Pons varolii.* The other case was that of a young officer, who, on the eve of marriage, received a blow on the occiput by falling from a horse. He became impotent, without any other derangement of his bodily or mental powers. In distress upon this discovery of his imperfection he committed suicide on the morning fixed for his wedding.

There are many other instances on record of this character, going to substantiate the phrenological theory that the cerebellum, (or lower brain) is the seat of the amorous or voluptuous passions.

## FECUNDATION.

It has been already stated, when speaking of the office of the Fallopian tubes, that impregnation is accomplished by the union of the male spermatozoa and the ovum of the female, during the passage of the latter through these tubes toward the uterus, while the change which takes place in the ovum after the union occurs, has also been explained. (See *Figs.* 20, 21, 22, 23, 24). If the spermatozoa do not come in contact with the ova, these changes do not take place, but the eggs pass out into the uterus and are lost. It has also been stated that menstruation is a process preparatory to impregnation. In other words, that during the menstrual phenomenon an ovum is ripened and expelled from the ovary; that it is then taken up by the fimbriated extremities of the tube, drawn into its channel and forced, (by a series of contractions or certain peristaltic action, with the assistance of the *ciliary* lining of the tube,) toward the uterus, which is the receptacle for the further development of the egg or embryo.

As has been remarked, the office of the uterus is to receive the seminal fluid and conduct it into the Fallopian tubes. The neck of the uterus does not, as many suppose, receive the male semen, when it is first ejected from the male intromittent instrument; but it is thrown into a pouch-like receptacle at the upper portion of the vagina, surrounding the mouth of the womb and formed by dilation of that organ. The uterus is suspended in the axis of the pelvis, and in such a position to the vagina that the mouth of the womb is maintained in the very centre of this pouch, (See *Fig.* 3) and thus affording a facility for the semen to pass into the neck of the uterus.

*Blundell** describes a peculiar movement which he observed in the vagina of the rabbit, that very clearly explains the manner of the introduction of the semen into the uterus. "This canal," (the vagina, says he,) "during the heat is never at rest. It shortens—it

* Researches Phys. and Pathol., p. 55, 1825.

lengthens—it changes continually in its circular dimensions, and when irritated especially will sometimes contract to one-third of its quiescent diameter. In addition to this action the vagina performs another," which "consists in the falling down, as it were, of that part of the vagina which lies in the vicinity of the womb; so that it every now and then lays itself as flatly over its orifice, as we should apply the hand over the mouth in an endeavor to stop it. How well adapted the whole of this curious movement is for the introduction of the semen at the opening, it is needless to explain."

The cervical canal is traversed by a large number of furrows, (*see Fig.* 4, *c*, *c*,) and (*Fig.* 29, *B*,) which assist in conducting the semen into the body of the uterus. It is not likely that the ejaculatory act of the male is sufficient to throw the semen beyond the pouch and against the *os* or head of the womb, inasmuch as the close approximation of the walls of the cervix would prevent it passing further. It is not certainly known in what way the spermatozoa are assisted in their passage through the womb into the Fallopian tubes. It is, however, supposed that the ciliæ which line the cervix or neck of the womb, in conjunction with the approximation of the walls of the uterus, afford the requisite facility for such purpose. The close approximation of the walls of the uterus would naturally facilitate the rise of the semen, the same as water placed between two pieces of glass will rise so as to cover the internal surface of both.

The movement of the spermatozoa is most likely the principal power that is used for their propulsion upward. Indeed, it would appear that it is only by such movements that they can penetrate and pass up the Fallopian tubes toward the ovaries, inasmuch as the cilia that line the cavity of these tubes would rather retard than promote their ascension, for the simple reason that their (the cilia's) wave-like motion is in the reverse direction, or *toward* the womb from the fimbriated extremities of the tubes. There is further proof that the movement of the spermatozoa is the principal agent in their ascension, in the fact of their possessing sufficient power to pass into the egg or ovum on coming in contact with it.

Having thus shown the process by which the semen is received into the vagina, and given some idea of the manner of the passage of the spermatozoa into the Fallopian tubes, it will now be proper to investigate a very important part of the subject of Generation, as included in the question as to—

## WHEN DOES IMPREGNATION TAKE PLACE?

The *precise* period at which impregnation takes place in the human female, unfortunately cannot be definitely determined. From observations, however, that have been made in a large number of cases, it would seem *certain* that it must occur during the *first half* of the *menstrual interval,* most probably during the *first week* after the cessation of the discharge. In sixteen cases observed by *Raciboski*, conception only occurred as late as the tenth day. Notwithstanding the occurrence of impregnation is perhaps ninety-nine per cent. of cases within ten or twelve days after the cessation of the catemenial flux, the other case may occur at any time subsequent to the last and prior to the next menstrual period.

There is no evidence to support the theory that impregnation may occur at any time during each month, by the rupture of an ovasac, as a consequence of sexual excitement. Nor is it likely that the ovum is retained in the Fallopian tubes from one menstrual period to another. Indeed, the contrary is proven by examination made on animals. It has been already stated in this work, that the ovum is usually from six to eight days in passing through the Fallopian tubes of the bitch. In the Guinea pig, the time is from two to three days. In the rabbit it does not extend beyond the fourth day. Therefore, if the theory just mentioned cannot be maintained, the second hypothesis would seem inevitable, viz.: that an ovum, after it is ejected from the ovary, is from six to fourteen days in passing the tubes, and that impregnation must take place during that time. M. *Pouchet* is quite positive that the period is not beyond fourteen days. If the views of this distinguished physiologist be correct, it follows, as a matter of course, that there is a *period after the cessation of the menstrual discharge during which woman is incapable of conception*, which idea *Pouchet* himself adopts as logically philosophical.*

* *Théorie Positive.*—M. Pouchet believes that a slender decidua is always formed at the decline of each menstruation, which, together with the unimpregnated ovum, is cast off from the uterus, between the tenth and fourteenth day; and after *this event every woman remains incapable of conception until the next menstrual period*, when the detachment of another ovum from the ovary renews her capacity for impregnation.—Also, A. Farre Cyclop. Anat. et Phys., p. 668.

No doubt such is the fact, as a general rule, but it may be necessary to account for the occasional mishap, or exceptional case, out of the two hundred that have been named. This is explained by M. *Coste*, who holds the same views with M. Pouchet in regard to *the time* in which conception takes place after the cessation of the menstrual flow.

Coste supposes that when a chance impregnation takes place after the fourteen days, that it is owing to the Graafian vesicle having failed to expel the ripened ovum, or the one that came to maturity at the last menstrual period, while sexual commerce occurring after this period is sufficient (on account of the excitement attending it) to rupture the follicle and liberate the imprisoned ovum, and thus insure impregnation. To prove this he has presented a number of experiments which he made upon animals.* One of these cases is that of a rabbit which during heat manifested great desire for the male, but was not permitted conjunction. Forty-eight hours afterward it was killed, when the genital organs were found very much congested with blood. Six follicles in one ovary and two in the other were ready to burst, but no rupture had yet taken place.

Another experiment also was upon a rabbit, which remained in heat three days, manifesting great ardor. On the fifth day it was killed, when the ovaries were found greatly congested, but without rupture of the follicles. Coste attributes the absence of rupture to the prevention of coitus.

* Histoire du Développement, 1847.

These experiments seem to favor the old theory of conception, viz.: that the ova are detached conjointly with fecundation, and that conception may take place at any time during the interval of menstruation.

Other experiments, however, which have been more recently made, and which have already been presented in this work, set aside this theory as incorrect. It is well known that the ova are ripening during menstruation, and that when this ceases they are no longer eliminated or thrown out of the ovaries. An occasional retention should not overturn a theory that has the whole chain of proof upon its side, with the exception of one link, which deficiency is satisfactorily explained by M. Coste.

In summary of established facts, then, a recapitulation of the most plausible and rational theory now entertained, may be presented as follows:

*It is during the menstrual period that the ova are ripened. They are then received into the Fallopian tubes, and occupy from six to fourteen days in their passage to the uterus. If impregnation occur, it must be from the union of the spermatozoon with the ovum, before the latter has passed out of the tube. Should there be no impregnation, the ovum passes into the uterus and is lost.* If five days be allowed for menstruation and fourteen days more for the passage of the ova (though twelve are accounted sufficient), there is accordingly a period of *nine days during which impregnation cannot take place* except in rare cases, say once in one hundred times or, indeed, in five hundred times.

## PREVENTION OF CONCEPTION.

The question is often asked, "*Can Conception be prevented at all times?*" Certainly, this is possible; but such an interference with Nature's laws is inadmissible, and perhaps never to be justified in any case whatever.

During the past few years hundreds of works have been written, and many circulars distributed, to the females of the land, holding forth the idea that *new* remedies had been discovered for the prevention of conception. It is needless to state that such asseverations are impudent and wicked fabrications, and that the volumes and pamphlets are mere catch-penny devices, intended to deceive the public and enrich the pockets of miserable and unprincipled charlatans and impostors.

The *truth* is, there is no medicine *taken internally* capable of preventing conception, and the person who asserts to the contrary, not only speaks falsely, but is both a knave and a fool. It is true enough that remedies may be taken to produce *abortion* after conception occurs; but those who prescribe and those who resort to such desperate expedients, can only be placed in the category of lunatics and assassins!

The only way that Conception may be prevented, is by abstinence from sexual commerce during the first fourteen days after the cessation of the menstrual discharge; or else by the destruction of the vitality of the spermatozoa, while in the vagina, or before they pass up through the uterus and come in contact with the ova in the Fallopian tubes, while on their passage toward the womb.

Many plans have been devised by the French for the prevention of Conception, but the most rational and certain means is to dissolve the spermatozoa while in the vagina, and before they pass into the womb. As this subject is treated of in another part of this work, it will be unnecessary to say more at the present time on this point. (See page 132.)

I have noticed a work recently published in Philadelphia, of considerable circulation, that professes to inform parents how they may have male or female children at their pleasure. It is scarcely necessary to remark that such opinion is absurd and erroneous. The ideas advanced are that the right testicle of the male secretes male semen, and the left testicle female semen. This supposition is equally ridiculous with that of the ancient physiologists, who imagined that the spermatozoa were miniature men and women.

There is not a particle of truth in such speculations. It is well known that men with only one testicle have been known to have had both male and female children. While upon this subject, it may be appropriate to mention certain vague and loose hypotheses that have recently been advanced.

Dr. *Silas Wright,* of New Hampshire, in a paper published in the *Buffalo Medical Journal,* of April. 1850,* maintains that males are conceived a short time prior to the menstrual discharge, and females shortly after its cessation. In other words, if the

* Also, see "Gardner on Sterility," p. 19.

ovum be impregnated before the appearance of the "courses," it will generally grow to be a male; if after the menses, a female child will result.

Again, in regard to the production of the sex, it has been stated that the right ovary produces male ova, and the left female ova.

There is not a particle of proof in favor of either of these theories. On the contrary, there is abundant evidence against their probability.

There are some other miscellaneous matters in reference to Generation that may be appropriately presented in the present chapter.

## SUPERFŒTATION.

SUPERFŒTATION is literally the impregnation of a woman already pregnant. About the time the ovum arrives in the uterus, and even before, or about the time of conception, the uterus undergoes a change to prepare for the ovum. There is a sort of a lymph that forms on the outer surface of the lining membrane of that organ, of a flaky or velvety character, which is usually called the bed for the egg. This viscid mucus also blocks up the passage into the mouth of the womb, thus presenting subsequent conception.

Among the lower animals, and in some few cases of the human female, there appears to be *Superfœtation.* It is known that puppies of a bitch will resemble more than one dog with which she has had connection during the period of heat, which time may embrace ten or twelve days.

A mare which had been covered by a stallion was five days afterward covered by an ass, and bore twins —one being a horse, the other a mule.

There are similar cases on record in regard to the human female. Women have borne children of different colors at the same parturition. In one of these instances, the mother acknowledged having admitted the embraces of a black servant a few hours after conjunction with her husband, who was white.

*Eisenmann** mentions the case of a woman bearing a full-grown male child, and neither milk nor lochia (a uterine discharge that takes place after delivery) occurring after birth. In one hundred and thirty-nine days afterward she gave birth to a fine female child when the milk and discharge came naturally. It was supposed that this woman had a double uterus, (see *Fig.* 2) which, however, was not the case, as was verified by an examination after death.

*Desgranges* mentions a case of a woman who bore two girls, at an interval of one hundred and sixty-eight days between them. *Fourneir* speaks of two girls born at an interval of five months. *Starke* instances a case of two children whose births were one hundred and nine days apart, while *Velpeau* relates that Mad. Bigaux had two living children at an interval of four and half months between the first and second birth.

Dr. *Mason* published an account of a woman who was delivered of a full-grown infant, and in three calendar months afterward of another, apparently at full time.

* Cyclop. Anat. et Phys. † Trans. Coll. Phys., Vol. IV.

A woman was delivered at Strasburg, the 30th of April, 1748, at ten in the morning; in a month afterward, M. *Leriche* discovered a second fœtus, and on the 16th of September, at five o'clock in the morning, the woman was delivered of a healthy full-grown infant.*

*Buffon* related a case of a woman in South Carolina, who brought forth a white and black infant; and on inquiry it was discovered that a negro had entered her apartment after the departure of her husband, and threatened to murder her unless she complied with his wishes. *Moseley*, *Gardien*, and *Valentin*, relate similar cases of black and white children born of intercourse with a white and black man on the same night, and the woman having children of different colors at the same parturition.

As has been stated, each male dog will produce a distinct puppy; this no one can deny. The offspring will resemble the males that fecundate the bitch in succession. This is the case with the mare, conjoined to the stallion and ass in succession, and likewise with other animals. Hence, reasoning from analogy, if a number of healthy vigorous men were to have intercourse in succession, immediately after the first conception, it is quite probable and very possible that similar fœtation should happen. Dr. *Elliotson* advocates superfœtation, and explains Buffon's case in this way. *Magendie* is of the same opinion. Medical men, and others, should bear in mind that women have had three, four, and five, and even six and

* Manuel Complet de Med. Leg., per Briand.

seven children at one birth, while various cases of infants of different sizes being expelled in succession are recorded in our own Medical journals.*

Professor *Velpeau*, of Paris, speaking of Superfœtation, says:—

"In according all possible authenticity to these observations, regarding their exactitude as demonstrated, the idea which prevails in physiology on generation, permits an easy explanation. Two ovules can be fecundated one after the other, in a woman who accords her favors to two or more men, the same day, or in two or three days afterward; that is to say, to the moment when the excitation of the first coition causes the effusion of coagulable lymph into the uterus, to form the caducous membrane (decidua). These ovules may not descend through the uterine tube at the same time, and may be differently developed."

*Velpeau*, however, thinks superfœtation impossible *after the decidua is formed.* According to *Dewees*, the closure of the os uteri after conception, does not *take place for some days, weeks, or months.*

Admitting superfœtation to be possible, (says *Ryan*) and it cannot be denied in the early weeks of generation, we cannot decide paternity, unless when one infant is black or brown, and the other white, but if both fathers were of the same color the decision might be difficult, unless some physical mark on the infant existed in one of them."

Some writers maintain that superfœtation is pos-

* Medical and Physical Journal, Vol. XXII., p. 27; Vol. XXIV. p. 232. Medico Chirurgical Transactions, Vol. IX.; Philos. Transact., Vol. LX. Ryan's Medical Jurisprudence.

sible during the *two first months* of pregnancy. The majority, however, hold it possible during the first few days after conception, before the uterine tubes are closed by the decidua. This is the received opinion, though there are cases on record which justified *Zacchias* and other jurists to conclude that superfœtation might occur until the sixtieth day, or even later.

## INFLUENCE EXERTED BY PARENTS ON OFFSPRING.

One of the most important laws of the reproductive functions, is the preservation of distinct species for an undeviating succession of generations, preventing the extinction of the species by being blended and lost in others.

Most persons are familiar with the resemblance that subsists between families from generation to generation, while it is well known that offspring inherit many of the qualities and peculiarities of the parents. Hereditary resemblance, however, is seldom ever complete—numerous differences being almost always observed in the features and other characteristics of the same family. Male and female children seldom perfectly resemble either the father or the mother, but a blending of the characteristics of both are readily recognizable in the offspring.

It might be supposed that as the mother furnishes the egg and its nourishment after conception, that the offspring would partake more of her peculiarities than of the father's. This, however, is not the fact. There will be quite as much resemblance to the father as to the mother, if such phenomenon be not in favor of the former.

The influence of the father must be imparted to the offspring at the time of the mingling of the spermatozoon and ovum, which is only momentarily. This being the case, it is reasonable to suppose that the greater proportion of the resemblance of the mother is imparted to the egg previous to conception; although it cannot be doubted that the mother exerts more or less physical and mental influence during the whole peried of utero-gestation.

In some animals the male parent seems to exert the greatest influence in the formation of the physical frame. This is particularly the case with dogs, horses, fowls, etc. It is known that the bantam cock will cause a common hen to lay a small egg, and a common cock a bantam hen to lay a large egg.

As a general rule it cannot be said that either the male or female in the human species exerts more influence than the other in the physical and intellectual conformations or peculiarities of the offspring. In some families the children will most resemble the father; in others, the mother's traits are the more predominant.

Dr. *Walker*, in an Essay lately published, states that the upper and back part of the head usually resembles the mother's; while the face from the eyes downward most frequently resemble that of the father.

The transmission of color seems to be better marked than other peculiarities. Two persons of different color cohabiting, and producing offspring, will produce a mulatto. In regard to color the preponderance seems to be on the side of the father. A dark man cohabiting with a white woman will produce a darker child than a dark mother conjoining with a white father.

In some animals the color of both parents seems to be equally preserved. This is the case with piebald horses. In some breeds of horses it has been found that as many as two hundred and five of the offspring or product of two hundred and sixteen pair of horses, the color of the parents was equally preserved.

The qualities of the mind are perhaps as much liable to hereditary transmission as bodily configuration. Memory, judgment, imagination, passions, diseases, and what is usually called *genius*, are often markedly traced in the offspring.

I have known mental impressions forcibly impressed upon offspring at the time of conception, as concomitant of some peculiar eccentricity, idiosyncracy, waywardness, irritability, morbidness, or proclivity of either or both parents. I recollect the case of a female who was quite a coquette before her marriage. She married against her parents' will, and went West with her husband. Having failed in his business, he was compelled to locate in his wife's neighborhood, and among her friends. This so humbled her pride that she excluded herself from society, and occupied the most of her time in reading the Scriptures and singing psalms, which seemed the only gratification for her mind. She conceived, and gave birth to a daughter while laboring under this religious melancholy or mental peculiarity. The child, as soon as it was old enough to notice any thing, exhibited a singular fondness for the Bible, and was constantly humming psalms.

I know a man whose mind was so much troubled in consequence of the cares of his business that he became extremely excitable and irritable of temper. His wife bore him a child while this mental disturbance continued. Before its birth, he remarked that its mind would be on the "high-pressure principle." This prediction some years afterward was fully verified.

There can be no doubt that the peculiar mental characteristics of a parent are often repeated in the offspring. In estimating mental and physical inheritances, however, it should be remembered that much will depend upon education, pursuits, and modes of life, as all have a strong tendency to overcome hereditary influence.

The transmission of disease from parent to offspring, is often markedly noticed. Almost all forms of mental derangements are hereditary—one of the parents, or near relation, being afflicted. Physical or bodily weakness is often hereditary, such as scrofula, gout, rheumatism, rickets, consumption, apoplexy, hernia, urinary calculi, hemorrhoids or piles, cataract, etc In fact, all physical weakness if ingrafted in either parent, are transmitted from parents to offspring, and are often more strongly marked in the latter than in the former.

Where both parents are affected with the same disease, the children will have the hereditary transmission more prominently developed than where only one parent is diseased. From observations made in upward of two hundred cases of consumption in 1855–6, I discovered that the child, which most resembled the parent that was consumptive almost invariably contracted the disease and died with it before they had arrived at the middle period of life.

In order to be more perfectly understood, a supposed case may be presented. The father is predisposed to consumption and the mother to nervous affections. They have six children—three of them resemble the father in temperament and other physical and mental peculiarities—while the other three have equally as strong a resemblance for those of the mother. Those that partake of the traits of the father are most liable to consumption and to die of that disease, while those resembling the mother will inherit her infirmities. The children in whose organization are blended the peculiarities of both parents are usually liable to their respective idiosyncracies and ailments.

This law I have found invariably correct. Taking facts like these into consideration, how very important is it for persons before selecting partners for life, to deliberately weigh every element and circumstance of this nature, if they would ensure a felicitous union, and not entail upon their posterity, disease, misery and despair. Alas! in too many instances matrimony is made a *matter of money*, while all earthly joys are sacrificed upon the accursed altars of lust and mammon. The chapter on "LOVE, COURTSHIP and MARRIAGE," in this work, will afford some wholesome suggestions in regard to this important subject to

13

newly-married persons and those contemplating entering upon the connubial union.

### MARKS AND DEFORMITIES.

Marks and deformities are also transmissible from parents to offspring, equally with diseases and peculiar proclivities. Among such blemishes may be mentioned moles, hair-lips, deficient or supernumerary fingers, toes, and other characteristics. It is also asserted that dogs and cats that have accidentally lost their tails, bring forth young similarly deformed. *Blumenbach* tells of a man who had lost his little finger having children with the same deformity. Injuries of the iris and deformities of fingers from whitlow are said to have been transmitted from parents to offspring. Such freaks of nature are possible, yet all such statements of peculiar anomalies are to be regarded with distrust, since it is well known that many maimed and malformed persons are the parents of children without such imperfections of physical appearance.

A belief is entertained that the frequent breeding in the same family has a tendency to deteriorate a race. This rule appears to be applicable also to the animal kingdom. In the human such deterioration seems to be both mentally and physically manifested. The marriage of *first* cousins, although recognized in this country by law, is strongly denounced by many physiologists as extremely inimical to the perpetuation of a pure-blooded and vigorous race. The intermarriage of different nations of the same *type*, as that of a Caucasian branch with another branch of the same; or an African with another branch Ethiopian stock, will tend to the mental and physical vigor of the offspring of either type; but *admixture* of the *Caucasian* with the *Ethiopian*, will *deteriorate* the type of the former race.

An example of the admixture of one Caucasian race with other of the same order of genus, being productive of signal advantage is afforded in the Persian race by their intermarriage with the most beautiful Circassian and Georgian woman. The same may be noticed in all civilized nations. The blending of the Saxon with the Celtic races, for instance, has an important bearing upon the temperament, mental qualities and physical conformations of the intermediate stock or issue. There seems to be an advantageous union of the respective elements of each, increasing physical stamina and intellectual attributes, as well as adding to the symmetry, grace, beauty and manliness of both nations. The union of the mercurial, fiery, and impulsive with the cool and phlegmatic, tends to promote that medium and balance of temperaments which is desirable as the chief characteristic of a proud, noble and perfect man or women, or even of a nation or people.

The peculiar features, idiosyncracies, or other peculiarities of the Jewish or Hebrew race, are strikingly identical wherever these people are found, in all parts of the world—from the simple fact that they rarely ever marry or mix their blood with other than Jewish people, or with other races, whether of the same Caucasian *type* or not. Were these "peculiar people" to amalgamate more largely with other Caucasian branches of the human family, no doubt the Jewish physiognomy would soon become greatly altered, or modified at least, if not much *improved.*

The *law* of *Nature* appears to be immutable in respect to procreation or reproduction. The more vigorous the races and types that commingle, the more certain it is that the product will be of an improved and exalted character. The breeders of fine cattle and other animals are cognizant of this principle of Nature, and accordingly select the purest breeds in order to ensure the finest possible progeny. The same law is applicable in husbandry, horticulture, floriculture, etc. The choicest fruits, flowers and vegetables, are the result of a proper selection of the procreative elements and a strict observance of Nature's mandates and requirements. So with the human family. It is doubtless capable of wonderful improvement and exaltation, were there a judicious blending of the highest physical and mental attributes of the male and female progenitors of the species. The *purer* the parent stock, the *more perfect* will be the progeny, and the nearer will they approximate to the original or *primitive type* of excellence, or of organism.

The *stronger* principle very naturally will drive out the *weaker.* Good and bad qualities will not *permanently* coalesce and produce any thing perfect. There will be a *tendency* either to *good* or *evil.* If the good element be the strongest, it will finally eradicate the evil element. If the evil principle be paramount, that which is intrinsically good must succumb before its dominant power. There is evidently a tendency in every thing to return to the original type.*

We have examples of this in the mixture of the black and white races—or rather *types*—of mankind. Whatever may be said of the *unity* of the human race, it would seem that these *types* are entirely *distinct*, and by consequence, could not have sprung from the same original parent stock.

According to the most reliable physiological and other data, there are at least *four* distinct *types* of man, as embraced under the terms Caucasian or *white;* the Ethiopian, or *black;* the Mongolian or *yellow;* and the Indian, or *red,* however varied or multiplied the branches of each may appear. They are perhaps as distinct in essential elements as the rat and the mouse are distinct, or the monkey and baboon, or the lion and the cat, and were never intended to intermix, nor will they ever *coalesce* if allowed to remain in their normal or natural condition. The very *location* in which these respective types of man are found, favor this theory. The *negro* is as much *indigenous* to Africa, or its latitudes and climates, as is the lion and boa-constrictor to the same regions of the globe; so with the other types of men to their native or specific latitudes. The banana is not found growing in the North, nor the apple in the South. So with flowers, fauna, and other objects of the animal and vegetable kingdoms. All have ther *fitting* places, or *locations,* most adapted or suitable for their development, procreation or reproduction. The tiger does not thrive in a northern clime, nor will the bear or hog flourish

* See "Primordial Philosophy," etc., p. 51 of this work.

in the torrid zone. The birds and fowls of a warm climate are different from those of a colder one, however they may resemble each other in many respects, or even when ranked in the same class, or of the same genus or species. These facts are self-apparent, and will require no special argument for their verification.

Take, for example, the crossing of the black and white races of man. The offspring of each successive generation becomes more nearly allied to the *purest* breed of the two—which is that of the *white* or Caucasian type. The progeny become *whiter* and *whiter* until the *dark* or negro element is entirely obliterated.* On the contrary, by no process or alchemy of Nature can you ever convert the progeny of a *black* man by a *white* woman to the dark color of the African father. The vis vitæ of the two distinct races seem antagonistical and inharmonious, and therefore cannot equally commingle. That of the Caucasian being more highly endowed, overcomes that of the African. The latter after several successive generations becomes completely extinct or absorbed by the former. This is illustrated by analogy, in the fact that the rat of Norway, imported into England and America, has totally driven out the original common rat of these countries. This seems to be a universal law of Nature, intended to protect and preserve distinct types—to save the weaker from the stronger. This truth is confirmed in the fact that *hybrids* rarely *propagate*, or if they do, it is only for a limited and definite period. The dominant principle must always prevail. Hence

* See Combe's "Constitution of Man."

it is easy to believe in hereditary predisposition, or in the transmission of diseases or peculiarities from parents to offspring. Not only is this the fact, but such abnormal peculiarities may extend through several successive generations. Sometimes they are intermitted, or lost in one immediate generation to appear in a subsequent or later one, even to the third or fourth remove from the original malformed or diseased parental stock, agreeably to the text of Scripture, that the "*sins* (or infirmities) of the parents are visited upon the children to the third and fourth generation."

Mr. *Gross* has attempted to arrange a family table exhibiting family peculiarities and resemblances through a series of results from the grandparent to the grandchild. Thus, a grandchild may resemble the grandparent of the same sex; that is to say, a grandson whose father is like *his* (the father's mother) will resemble most the grandfather, as in the following table:

| | | | | |
|---|---|---|---|---|
| 1 Generation. | Grandf. | Grandm. | Grandf. | Grandm. |
| 2 " | ——— | Father. | Mother. | ——— |
| 3 " | Son. | Daughter. | Son. | Daughter. |

It becomes a matter of wonder when we come to inquire into the peculiarities of hereditary transmission, that two microscopic specks, such as the egg of the female and the spermatozoon of the male are capable of transmitting during three or four subsequent generations, all the weaknesses and imperfections of parents. This law, however, even becomes the more surprising, when we come to inquire into the influence exerted by the minds of the parents upon these microscopic atoms at the time of conception, which is to unfold them into the future human being.*

We have already given several cases in corroboration of the influence exerted by parents upon posterity, even in the most rudimental or incipient form of embryotic existence. *Combe,* in his great work on the "Constitution of Man," sustains similar views in an admirable manner. The celebrated *Darwin*, though he indulged in many chimerical notions, among others that man was originally developed from a *tadpole*—held views respecting the influence of the parent's mental qualities upon the offspring at the time of conception, that appear to be based upon the clearest facts and the highest philosophical deductions. Both of these authors demonstrate, that children conceived during or after drunkenness or debauchery, are liable not only to a predisposition to intemperance, but to a debility, both of mind and body, amounting in many instances to idiotcy itself. The same is proved of the venerous or amorous impulses. In short, according to the predominance of any propensity or frame of mind, the offspring may be a genius or a dolt, a sentimental swain or an unfeeling brute, a thief, a robber, or a murderer.

These notions are corroborated in too many instances to gainsay their verity, yet I am constrained to think that more importance is attached to them than they deserve, in view of the power of *secondary* causes that

* See the portion of the present work which treats of "Primordial Philosophy."

may be brought to bear for the correction, amelioration, or eradication of such inherent proclivities. Such influences, no doubt, are capable of being materially controlled by the mother, not only during the embryotic and fœtal life of the offspring, but in its physical and mental training in a subsequent period, after it arrives at a proper age, or years of intelligence and reflection. "Just as the twig is bent the tree's inclined," is an axiom as applicable to the human creature as to the tree or shrub. Hence the necessity of having mothers properly educated and fitted to mould the minds and mollify any physical and mental defect in their offspring, in the earlier stages of their existence, as well as having them to understand those laws which are calculated to ensure the rarest beauty and vigor of their progeny, as concomitant of a wise and judicious wedded union of the sexes, and those adjuncts of health and happiness flowing out of pure habits and a rational dietetic and hygienic system compatible with the *vis medicatrix naturæ* of the general organism. As the potter moulds his clay into beautiful and fantastic devises, so it is largely in the power of woman to *assist* Nature in forming the most perfect and glorious of human intellectual and physical developments and conformations. She should ever strive for her own *perfection*, and should never think of marriage until she can possess the proper mental and physical qualifications to become a *mother!* Indeed, the very name of *mother* is significant of every thing that is pure and beautiful and lofty. The *model* men—the great and wise and good men—in all ages of the world, owe their exaltation to the pure minds, noble hearts, and heavenly virtues of beautiful and adorable MOTHERS!

The effect of the imagination of mothers upon their progeny, at the time of conception and after, has been doubted and ridiculed by many physiologists. Doubts and sneers and ridicule, however, are the weapons of ignorance and imbecility, and can never be used as *arguments* to overthrow palpable and irrefragable *facts.* Besides what has been advanced in the foregoing pages, there is a great abundance of evidence still at hand, to substantiate all that has been affirmed in that regard. The same influence will hold good not only in the human being, but perhaps in *all* of the lower orders of the animal kingdom.

It is related* that when a stallion is about to cover a mare, and the color of the stallion be objectionable to the groom, if he will place before the mare during the time of sexual conjunction, a stallion of the desired color, it will have the effect upon the mare to produce the required color in the foal, or a color different from that of its sire. This method has been repeatedly tried with unvarying success.

The tyrant *Dionysius* supposed that handsome pictures and other objects influenced the minds of females during pregnancy so as to have a bearing upon the intellectual and physical attributes of their offspring. Hence, he was in the habit of hanging beautiful paintings in his wife's chamber, in order to improve the appearance of his children. *Walker*, in his work on "Beauty," supports a similar hypothesis.†

* Combe's Constitution of Man; also, Cyclop. of Anat. et Phys.

† See "Primordial Philosophy," in present volume.

The sacred Scriptures speak of Jacob placing the peeled black and willow rods before the ewes as they went to drink, and the consequence in the ring-streaked, speckled and spotted colors of the off-spring.*

The mother of Napoleon the Great, before he was born, followed her husband in his campaigns, and was subject to all the dangers and vicissitudes of a military life. To the influeuce of the mind of the mother, during utero-gestation, has been attributed the military skill and ambition of the illustrious Emperor of France. On the other hand, the murder of *David Rizzio*, in the presence of *Queen Mary*, was the deathblow to the courage of *King James*, and caused his strong dislike to edged tools, which dislike was a peculiar characteristic of that crafty and pedantic monarch.

It is well known that some contagious diseases are readily transmitted from mother to offspring during utero-gestation; such as syphilis, small-pox, measles, etc. Violence and severe affections of the mother are known to destroy the fœtal child, and expel it from the uterus. Poisons have exerted the same influence when taken by the mother during pregnancy. This is easily explained and understood in the fact that poisons enter into the circulation, and that the same blood that circulates in the mother also supplies the fœtal child with nourishment. By the same philosophy it is comprehended how a cancer may be made to grow on the breast of a female, by the concentra-

* Genesis, chap. xxx.

tion of her mind on the idea or possibility of such a result, or that cancers may be also cured through a similar force or influence of the imagination upon the fact. Dr. *Warren* of Boston, instances a case of this kind. Jet black hair has been changed to white, as a result of some violent emotion, fear, etc. The milk of mothers has been rendered poisonous, so as speedily to destroy the offspring, through the influence of passion or other cerebral disturbance. For some remarkable cases of this kind see chapter on "LACTATION," in the present work. Such phenomena are explained on the principle that nutrition, secretion, excretion, assimilation, and in fact, every function of the animal organism is controlled by the nervous system—that the force generated in that system, called the "nerve force," is to the physical system what steam is to the machinery. It is by deranging this force that we have disease—*first* of functional character, which if not removed, soon causes a change in the structure of the organ. A cancerous tumor is a change in the nutrition of the part by an interference in some way with the function of the sympathetic nervous system, either by causing a change in the blood by interfering with digestion or assimilation, or by causing a direct change in the nutrition of the part.

In further proof that the condition of mind of the mother can and does exercise a powerful and wonderful influence upon fœtal existence or offspring, a few remarkable and well-authenticated examples may be here presented.*

* "Burdach's Physiologie," B. 11; and "Refutations of the Doctrines of Imaginationists, by Dr. Blundell," of London. Also, Cyclop. Anat. et Phys.

1. A cow killed by a blow of a hatchet was found pregnant with a bruise on the same place of the forehead of the fœtus.

2. A woman bitten on the vulva by a dog, bore a child having a similar wound on the glans penis. The boy suffered from epilepsy, and when the fit came on, or during sleep, was frequently heard to cry out "The dog bites me!"

3. A woman who was cut for rupture in the groin during pregnancy, bore a boy having a similar scar in the same region.

4. A pregnant woman who was suddenly alarmed from seeing her husband come home with one side of his face swollen and distorted by a blow, bore a girl with a purple swelling upon the same side of the face.

5. A mother seeing a criminal broken upon a wheel, gave birth to an idiot child, the bones of which were similarly broken.

6. A woman seeing a person in an epileptic fit, brought forth a child which was subject to epilepsy.

7. A lady who was frightened by a beggar presenting the stump of an arm to her, bore a child wanting a hand.

8. A child was born pierced through the head, in consequence of its mother seeing a man run through the body with a sword.

9. A woman who was forced to be present at the opening of a calf by a butcher, bore a child with all its bowels protruding from the abdomen. She was aware at the time of something going on within the womb.

10. A similar misfortune occurred with a woman who witnessed the opening of the abdomen of a pig.

11. A woman absent from home became alarmed by seeing a great fire in the direction of her own house, bore a child with a distinct mark of the flame up its forehead.

12. A pregnant woman who became frightened at herhusb and pursuing her with a drawn sword, bore a child with a large wound in its forehead.

13. A man who had personated a devil, went to bed in an assumed dress. His wife bore a child that had cloven feet, horns, etc.

14. A pregnant woman fell into a violent passion at not being able to procure a particular piece of meat of a butcher; she bled at the nose, and wiping the blood from her lips, bore a child wanting a lip.

15. A pregnant woman became frightened at a lizard jumping into her bosom; she bore a child with a fleshy excrescence exactly resembling a lizard, growing from the breast, adhering by the head and neck.

16. A woman gave birth to a child covered with hair and having the claws of a bear. This was attributed to her beholding the images and pictures of bears hung up in the palace of the Ursini family, to which she belonged.

17. Two girls (twins) were born with their bodies joined together; the mother had contemplated some sacred images similarly placed while pregnant.

18. A woman who had longed for a lobster brought forth a child resembling one of these animals.

19. Another woman had a female child, the head

of which looked like a shell-fish, (a bivalve that opens and shut its mouth,) which was caused by the mother having a strong desire for mussels during pregnancy.

20. A pregnant woman had a longing desire to bite the shoulder of a baker of her acquaintance. The husband wishing to gratify this morbid fancy of his wife, hired the man to submit to the operation. The woman made two bites, and so severe, that he would not allow her try again. She gave birth to three children—one dead and two living. In this case it seemed to require a bite for each child to remove the morbid disease of the mind. Two bites being granted, and the third refused, the refusal no doubt caused the third child to fall a victim to the morbid mind of the mother.

21. A woman who had borne healthy children, became frightened by a beggar with a wooden leg and a stumped arm, who threatened to embrace her. Her next child had one stump leg and two stump arms.

22. A woman frightened in her first pregnancy by a sight of a child with a hair lip, had a child with a deformity of the same kind. Her second child had a deep slit, and the third a mark of a similar character, or modified hair lips. In this instance the morbid mind of the mother affected several successive issues of her body.

23. A lady is mentioned by some medical writer, on whose back, between the shoulders, is the perfect impression of a mouse, hair and all, flattened down to the surface of the skin. Several months before her birth her mother was frightened by a mouse, which

got between her clothes and her person at that particular part.

Many more cases might be quoted were it deemed necessary to show the influence of the mind upon uterine gestation. It is proper to add, however, that women are often violently affected in many ways, without leaving evidence of any abnormal peculiarities in the mental or physical characteristics of their offspring. The mysteries of Nature are often inexplicable, but it is certainly a wise philosophy never to interfere improperly with her regular course of operations. The giving way to passions, freaks and whims, is always more or less productive of mischief, not only to mothers, but the offspring is liable to be affected by them. An unnatural propensity should be curbed, if practicable. A passive, cheerful mind, agreeable society, suitable amusements, recreations, and exercise, with a careful attention to food and clothing, etc., all have a wonderful efficacy in dispelling megrims, moping melancholy, and other abnormal influences, quieting nervous irritability, purifying the blood, and inducing joyous bounding health, with intellectual strength and physical beauty, and the highest bliss and happiness possibly incident to a terrestrial state of existence.

*Truths* of such importance as detailed in the foregoing pages are certainly worthy of the serious consideration of every married lady, or females of marriageable age, not only as a guide to save them multiform diseases and miseries, but as a means for the attainment of the highest and intellectual perfection compatible with the organism of woman, in the present state of existence.

# CHAPTER XI.

## NATURE'S INSTITUTES FOR THE PROCREATION AND PERPETUATION OF THE HUMAN SPECIES.

MORAL LOVE AND SEXUAL PASSION—COURTSHIP—MARRIAGE—EFFECTS OF CONTINENCE—CELIBACY CONTRARY TO NATURE—PHILOPROGENITIVENESS, OR PARENTAL LOVE AND CARE OF OFFSPRING—WHEN AND WHOM TO MARRY—SUMMARY OF THE ECONOMY OF HUMAN LIFE.

### A. MORAL LOVE AND SEXUAL PASSION.

MANY persons talk without either knowing what they say, or whereof they affirm. Nothing is more commonly spoken of, or so little considered as the subjects that head this chapter. Let us not waste words in showing how often these important matters are misunderstood and misapplied by the light and the trifling, the gay and the thoughtless, or the vicious and the ensnaring; but trace them at once through all their mazes to a satisfactory solution of their purport.

What then is *Love!* Delightful emotion that binds the mother to her offspring—dear daughter of desire and parent of tender sensibility, heaver of the throbbing heart, and sweet exciter of the maiden's blush, how—how shall we describe thee? Indescribable art thou: a beautiful and pure, as well as an all-conquering passion! No poet can adequately define thee, nor painter portray thee, lovely and all refining, spotless and heavenly as thou art! Yet, all-pervading as thou art, who has not felt the delicious witchery of thy power!

The ancient Greeks represented LOVE under a two-fold aspect. The one was a love for the good and beautiful, the excellent or desirable, in the abstract. The other, besides these qualities, included the love of the sexes for one another. 'Ερως, EROS, meant passion, desire, affection or kindness; and the Greek Eros was similar to the Latin CUPIDO*, or *Cupid*, the fabled son of *Venus*, who is said to have inflamed mortals, and even the inhabitants of Olympus with arrows from his subduing quiver. Αγάπη, *Agapæ*, signifies love, friendship, affection, charity, etc., and also, (as employed in the Sacred Volume) the love of God to man.

*Moral love* is the kind which must first claim our cog-

* Cupido, a celebrated deity among the ancients—god of love, and love itself. There are, according to the more received opinions, two Cupids—one of whom is a lively ingenious youth, son of Jupiter and Venus; while the other, son of Nox and Erebus, is distinguished by his debauchery and riotous disposition. Cupid is represented as a winged infant, naked, with a bow and a quiver full of arrows. On gems, and all other pieces of antiquity, he is represented as amusing himself with some childish diversion. His power was generally known by his riding on the back of a lion, or on a dolphin, or breaking to pieces the thunderbolts of Jupiter. Among the ancients he was worshipped with the same solemnity as his mother Venus.—*Lempriere's Classical Dictionary.*

nizance. This sort implies that affection which persons of different sexes feel toward one another. On analysis, we find it to consist in ideas attached in part to matter and in part to mind. Love is pure. It is not what the sensualist imagines it to be. The voluptuary does not know the meaning of the word. The vicious know it not. These follow but a vain shadow—a low, vile passion; not the ennobling, sublimating, soul-refining delights known only to the virtuous, as attached to the idea comprehended in the word *Love.* For instance, two individuals, different in character and pursuits, meet a young lady at an evening party. She is arrived at blooming seventeen. Her form is a fit model for *Phidias* or *Praxiteles.* Her lips are like rubies, her teeth like ivory, her eye like the gazelle's. Her countenance is angelic, and realizes the *beau ideal* of poetic beauty. As she moves in the gay circle of the dance, her whole deportment combines all that is agile with all that is graceful; and as the waving jetty curls flow down her fair neck, the eye rests for a moment on the *embonpoint* of her heaving breast; and the two individuals thus viewing her—the one from the gaming-table and the haunts of vice and debauchery—the other from an unpolluted home, the abode of a loving mother and an affectionate sister—these two individuals see the fair girl at the same moment, and she inspires the one with *passion* —the other with *love.*

Thus both gaze on her—and while the one would only plot how to rob her of the pearl of virtue, and gratify a transitory passion by sacrificing her purity and happiness to his ungovernable lust—the other, inspired by a heavenly sentiment, grows deathly pale, his lips quiver, his voice trembles, and filled with inexpressible tenderness and purest emotions, he views her as the fair star of his destiny, the beacon light of his future; and studying her interests and felicity, no less than his own, he desires to devote his life to the pleasing task of making her happy, and that in the holy state of matrimony.

This is *pure* love, and undefiled. In like manner, a tender maiden sees a man who is the object of her esteem. His comely proportions, his exalted character, his noble disposition, all tend to impress her favorably, and scarce known to herself, she thinks of him when he is absent, blushes in his presence betrays some little tender emotions, and already her heart is his own—she *loves!* Thrilling and delightful emotion in the pure heart of woman! For woman's heart is kind and is not made of rock: on the contrary, it is more like the wax which is pliable and can easily be impressed.

> "What thing is Love which nought can countervail!
> Nought save itself, even such a thing is love;
> And worldly wealth in worth as far doth fail,
> As lowest earth doth yield to Heaven above.
> Divine is Love, and scorneth worldly pelf,
> And can be bought with nothing but with self."

There is thus in the sexes an adaptation to one another. Each without the other, is imperfect. The coarseness of the man, his hardness and asperity, are refined and softened and smoothed down, by the gentle influences of woman. They have a mutual attraction for each other, like the opposite poles of a powerful magnet. The woman may be called the negative pole. She is passive as it were. The motive and exciting power must come from man. Nature has made all creatures perfect, and endowed woman with *static*—man with the *dynamic* force. Thus man and woman but fulfill their destiny when they mate and unite for life, and "multiply and replenish the earth."

Among animals the *sexual instinct*, is perhaps purely *physical*—at least there is no *reasoning* faculty in them to guide and control and limit such instinct or passion They have their certain seasons of sexual conjunction —a burning heat consumes them—they are occupied with their desires alone. Scarcely, indeed, do they think of their personal safety during their erotic agitation or excitement. We find as a general rule that animals cohabit at fixed periods and certain times of the year, and afterward seem to lose all sexual passion in their desire to satisfy their other wants, as of food, etc. On the contrary, man is not subject to the influence of the seasons in the exercise of his genital functions. Man alone has sexual intercourse at all times, and impregnates the female under every latitude and in every clime.*

* *Roubaud* thinks that venereal desires are instinctive in animals at the rutting season, as well as in young men at puberty, after long periods of continence, or after leading a quiet country life. Later in life, however, when the first ardor of instinct has been calmed down, their desire only answers or responds to the voice of imagination or sensation. At puberty "life is in excess: the blood boils, the desires are impetuous and

*Moral love* in man has the same principle with *physical love* among animals. The only difference between them is, the animal seeks directly to satisfy his wants, while reason and moral circumstances prevent man from obeying the mere animal instincts of Nature.

To accomplish the purposes of love, as *Rousseau* has well remarked, men ought to attack—woman to defend. In other words, man should woo, and woman surrender, when she can discover in the prudent and mild guidance of their mutual pleasures, a supporter, a defender, a friend, lover, husband, a beloved companion for life.

As a distinguished writer on "Kalogynomia, or the Laws of Female Beauty," well expresses it:—

"If there existed no other than physical love, there would be no difference between the individuals of an opposite sex as is the case with some of the lower animals. Anthony would have found other women as beautiful as Cleopatra; and yet for her he abandoned life and the empire of the world. With regard to beauty, if there existed no *moral love*, every woman, beautiful or ugly, would be equal: there would be no reason for preferring one to another."

It is *moral* love, then, which is the foundation of all that is beautiful in the tender passion, and of all the interest which erotic writers have thrown around this peculiar sentiment or feeling. Pure affection is not based on mere sexual instinct, but a holier and

tormenting—Nature is almost an accomplice. Yet man is, or ought to be, a reasoning being, and thus capable of subduing his passions and directing his feelings in the direction of moderation and chastity."

diviner impulse, although sexual conjunction is not irrelevant to its blissful fruition.

In regard to the mere animal propensity, there may be sensual love without *affection*. At the period of puberty, especially, in both sexes the sexual instinct —as if by a spontaneous internal voice of Nature—at first excites, and then renders man, now in the flower of his life, more prone to the venereal embrace. At this peculiar erotic period, the agitation and disorder of the senses give birth to a new sense, in which man alone seems to receive his existence—in which every thing becomes animated and embellished, and in which all around him appear to burn with the same flame by which he is so deliciously consumed. Nor is the influence of animal love, or the sexual instinct, confined to man alone. It extends to the whole of Nature, as is shown in the following lines of *Darwin*, which are so exquisitely beautiful, that we cannot refrain from quoting them in this place:—

"Now young Desires, on purple pinions borne,
Mount the warm gales of manhood's rising morn,
With softer fires through virgin bosoms dart
Flush the pale cheek and goad the tender heart,
Ere the weak powers of transient life decay,
And Heaven's etherial image melts away;
Love with nice touch renews the organic frame,
Forms a young Ens, another and the same;
Gives from his rosy lips the vital breath,
And parries with his hand the shafts of death;
While Beauty broods with angel wings unfurled
O'er nascent life, and saves the sinking world.

"Here on green leaves the sexual pleasures dwell,
And Loves and Beauties crowd the blossoms' bell;

The wakeful Anther in his silken bed
O'er the pleased stigma bows his waxen head;
With meeting lips and mingling smiles they sup
Ambrosial dewdrops from the nectar'd cup;
Or buoy'd in air the plumy Lover springs,
And seeks his panting bride on Hymen's wings.

"The Stamen males, with appetencies just,
Produce a formative prolific dust;
With apt propensities, the Styles recluse
Secrete a formative prolific juice:
These in the pericarp erewhile arrive,
Rush to each other, and embrace alive.
—Formed by new powers progressive parts succeed,
Join in one whole, and swell into a seed.

"So in fond swarms the living Anthers shine
Of bright Pallisner on the wavy Rhine;
Break from their stems, and on the liquid glass
Surround the admiring Stigmas as they pass;
The love-sick Beauties lift their essenced brows,
Sigh to the Cyprian queen their secret vows,
Like watchful Hero* feel their soft alarms,
And clasp their floating lovers in their arms.

"Hence the male Ants their gauzy wings unfold,
And young Lampyris waves his plumes of gold;

* According to "Classical History," *Hero* was a beautiful priestess of Venus at Sestos, greatly enamored of *Leander*, a youth of Abydos. These two lovers were so faithful to one another, that Leander in the night escaped from the vigilance of his family, and swam across the Hellespont, while Hero in Sestos directed his course by holding a burning torch on the top of a high tower. After many interviews of mutual affection and tenderness, Leander was drowned in a tempestuous night as he attempted his usual course, and Hero in despair threw herself down from her tower and perished in the sea.

The Glow-worm* sparkles with impassion'd light
On each green bank, and charms the eye of night;
While new desires the painted Snail† perplex,
And two-fold love unites the double sex.

"Hence, when the Morus in Italia's lands
To Spring's warm beam its timid leaf expands;
The Silkworm broods in countless tribes above,
Crops the green treasure, uninform'd of love;
Ere while the changeful worm with circling head
Weaves the nice curtains of his silken bed;
Web within web involves his larva form,
Alike secured from sunshine and from storm.

* The Glow-worm (*Lampyris noctiluca*) is an animal resembling a caterpillar; its light proceeds from a pale-colored patch that terminates the underside of the abdomen. This is the perfect female of a winged beetle, from which it is altogether so different that nothing but actual observation could have inferred the fact of their being the sexes of the same insect. The object of the light appears to be to attract the male, since it is most brilliant in the female—in some species, if not all, present only in the season when the sexes are destined to meet, and strikingly more vivid at the moment when the meeting takes place. Besides the above uses, it is most probably intended to conduct the sexes to each other. The torch which the wingless female, doomed to crawl upon the grass, lights up at the approach of night, is a beacon which unerringly guides the vagrant male to her "lone, illumined form," however obscure the place of her abode. The cause of this light is doubtless phosphorus, which, we have reason to suppose is extended to a great extent in the act of copulation.—(See *Acton on the "Reproductive Organs,"* p. 12; also, *Kirby* and *Spence*, Vol. II., p. 420.)

† There is a class of animals called Hermaphrodite, which, in one and the same animal, have perfect male and female organs, yet are not self-impregnating, but, as in the leech, require for fecundation the sexual congress of two animals. This same peculiarity is found in snails. The manner in which snails copulate

"For twelve long days he dreams of blossom'd groves
Untasted honey, and ideal loves;
Wakes from his trance, alarm'd with young Desire,
Finds his new sex, and feels ecstatic fire;
From flower to flower with honied lip he springs,
And seeks his velvet loves on silver wings.

"The dèmon Jealousy, with Gorgon frown,
Blasts the sweet flowers of Pleasure not his own;
Rolls his wild eyes, and through the shuddering grove
Pursues the steps of unsuspecting Love:
Or drives o'er rattling plains his iron car,
Flings his red torch, and lights the flames of war.

"Here Cocks* heroic burn with rival rage,
And Quails with quails in doubtful fight engage;
Of armed heels and bristling plumage proud,
They sound the insulting clarion shrill and loud,
With rustling pinions meet, and swelling chests,
And seize with closing beaks their bleeding crests;
Rise on quick wings above the struggling foe
And aim in air the death-devoting blow.

"There the hoarse Stag† his croaking rival scorns,
And butts and parries with his branching horns;

is not a little curious, their union being accompanied by preparatory blandishments of a very extraordinary kind, that to a spectator would seem rather like a combat between mortal foes than the tender advances of the lovers. Each of the two snails, by inserting its penis into the vagina or aperture of the other, impregnates its partner, and is itself impregnated at the same time.—(See *Rymer Jones'* "*Natural History,*" and *Acton on the* "*Reproductive Organs.*")

* In farm-yards, the cock must show his prowess, and *win his spurs* before he is allowed, by the more powerful birds, to tread the hens.

† Young bucks are driven away by the older and stronger ones.

Contending Boars with tusk enamell'd strike,
And guard with shoulder-shield the blow oblique;
While female bands attend in mute surprise,
And view the victor with admiring eyes.

"So knight on knight, recorded in romance,
Urged the proud steed, and couch'd the extended lance!
He whose dread prowess with resistless force,
O'erthrew the opposing warrior and his horse,
Bless'd as the golden guerdon of his toils,
Bow'd to the Beauty, and received her smiles.

"So when fair HELEN* with ill-fated charms,
By PARIS woo'd, provoked the world to arms,

* *Helen* or *Helena*, was the most beautiful woman of her age. She was the daughter of *Leda* and *Jupiter*. Jupiter, to enjoy the favor of Leda, transformed himself into a swan, and she brought forth two eggs, from one of which sprang *Pollux* and *Helena*, and from the other *Castor* and *Clytemnestra*. HELENA'S beauty was universally admired, and her hand eagerly sought after by all the princes of Greece. *Tyndaris*, who had married Leda, (the mother of TYNDARIS, a patronymic of Helen) and was at the time king of Lacedæmon, was rather alarmed than pleased at the sight of such a number of illustrious suitors. He knew that he could not prefer one without displeasing all the rest, and from this perplexity he was drawn by the artifices of Ulysses. This prince advised the king to bind by a solemn oath all the suitors, that they would approve of the uninfluenced choice which Helen should make of one of them; and engage them to unite together to defend her person and character if ever any attempts were made to ravish her from her husband. The advice of Ulysses was followed, and Helen fixed her choice on *Menelaus* (a king of Sparta) and married him, when he also became king of Lacedæmon, by the resignation of the throne by *Tyndarus* in his favor. *Hermione* was the only fruit of this union, which continued for three years with mutual happiness. After this, *Paris*, son of *Priam*, king of Troy, came to Lacedæmon, on pretense of sacrificing to Apollo. He was kindly received by

Left her vindictive lord to sigh in vain
For broken vows, lost love, and cold disdain;
Fired at his wrongs, associate to destroy
The realms unjust of proud adulterous Troy,
Unnumbered heroes braved the dubious fight,
And sunk lamented to the shades of night.*

"Now vows connubial chain the plighted pair,
And join paternal with maternal care;
The married birds with nice selection cull
Soft thistle down, grey moss, and scattered wool,
Line the secluded nest with feathery rings,
Meet with fond bills, and woo with fluttering wings.
Week after week, regardless of her food,
The incumbent Linnet warms her future brood;
Each spotted egg with ivory lips she turns,
Day after day with fond expectance burns,
Hears the young prisoner chirping in his cell,
And breaks in hemispheres the obdurate shell.
Loud trills sweet Philomel his tender strain,
Charms his fond bride, and wakes his infant train;

Menelaus, but shamefully abused his favors, and in his absence in Crete he corrupted the fidelity of his wife Helen, and persuaded her to follow him to Troy, B. C. 1198. At his return, Menelaus, highly sensible of the injury he had received, assembled the princes, and reminded them of their solemn promises. They resolved to make war against the Trojans; and soon their combined forces assembled and sailed for the coast of Asia. The behavior of Helen during the Trojan war, is not clearly known. When Paris was killed in the ninth year of the war, she voluntarily married Deiphobus, one of Priam's sons, and brother of her paramour Paris; but when Troy was taken, she made no scruple to betray him and introduce the Greeks into his chamber, to ingratiate herself with Menelaus. She returned to Lacedæmon, and the love of Menelaus forgave the errors which she had committed.—*Lempriere's* Classical Dictionary.

* For a very interesting love story, or romantic history of Paris, see also *Lempriere's* Classical Dictionary.

Perch'd on the circling moss, the listening throng
Wave their young wings and whisper to the song.

"The Lion-king forgets his savage pride,
And courts with playful paws his tawny bride;
The listening Tiger hears with kindling flame
The love-lorn night-call of his brindled dame;
Despotic LOVE dissolves the bestial war,
Bends their proud necks, and joins them to his car;
Shakes o'er the obedient pairs his silken throng,
And goads the humble, or restrains the strong."

The above picture is glowing in the extreme, but none the less *true* and *faithful to nature.* Sexual love or sexual instincts are vividly portrayed, as well in their physical as their moral aspects. We see everywhere the law of sexual union exemplified, and its result in mating or marriage, and progeny.

## B. COURTSHIP.

We have in the preceding pages presented some general ideas in respect to what should be understood in regard to the difference between *moral love*, or the mere *sensual* or *physical passion,* as developed in the human creature, especially. We may next in order, give some views relative to what is meant by COURTSHIP, and show the moral and natural relations of the sexes toward one another, in this regard.

Courtship, in which the gentleman does the agreeable, is a very pleasant thing. It is so delightful in itself that many persons never go further. It consists in much billing and cooing, in serenading, and in walks by the lonely lake, or unfrequented path in the moonlight stroll upon the lawn, or the whispered conversation in the recess of the window, in interchange of love and eternal fidelity, etc. Love makes all harmonize. The coy maiden, it is true, will be very shy for a while, and "faint heart never gained fair lady," but, for all that, if not preoccupied—

> "Who listens once will listen twice,
> For sure her heart is not of ice,
> And one refusal no rebuff."

Yes, a certain brisk confidence must be assumed, for a lady delights in an ardent lover, and many such have triumphed when all others have failed.

For this cause, perhaps, successful villains, who have much practice in the wiles that gain woman's heart, are more likely to gain their ends than he who truly loves, but is by bashfulness deterred; while, in many cases, woman has loved "not wisely but too well." Yea, under the fairest pretenses, women have been deceived, and under a promise of marriage have permitted the familiarities which prudence, virtue and custom alike reserve for the marriage state. Thus, many a fair confiding girl is lost to virtue, society and happiness, and robbed by a heartless villain of the pearl of virginity, fills up a degraded and miserable segment in the circle of life, while she might have shone as a star in the galaxy of beauty.

Courtship is a perilous period, inasmuch as human nature is not altogether perfect. Many there are who have begun well. They have continued to do so for days and months, or perhaps for years; but at length giving way to a momentary impulse, the saddest of all accidents has eventuated, and such as cannot easily be repaired. Let no one think that we exaggerate. Courtship is but a thorny state after all. It has three stages. The first when the parties meet, and ogling, interchange of glances, and a few hurried words take place. The second, when the whole frame thrills with the exquisitely delicious and melting emotion of the *first kiss!*

> "Humid seal of soft affection,
> Tend'rest pledge of future bliss,
> Dearest tie of young connection,
> Love's first snow-drop—virgin kiss!"*

* Kissing was an act of religion in ancient Rome. The nearest friend of a dying person performed the rite of receiving his soul by a kiss, supposing that it escaped through his lips at the moment of expiration. *Spenser*, in his "Pastoral Elegy on the Death of Sir Philip Sidney," mentions it as a circumstance which renders the loss of his illustrious friend more to be lamented, that—

> "None was nigh his eyelids up to close,
> And *kiss his lips.*"

A little after he introduces the lady, "the dearest love" of the deceased, weeping over him—

> "She with sweet kisses sucked the wasting breath
> Out of his lips, like lilies pale and soft."

The sacredness of the kiss was inviolable among the Romans for a long time. At length it was degraded into a current form of salutation. Among the early Christians, the kiss of peace was a sacred ceremony, observed upon their most solemn occasions. It was called *signaculum orationis*—the seal of prayer—and was a symbol of that mutual forgiveness and reconciliation which the Church required, as an essential condition, before any one was admitted to the sacraments. At length, the Roman civil-

The third, is that in which "the consummation so devoutly to be wished," is anticipated by plighted

ians took the kiss under their protection. Their code defined, with exquisite accuracy, the nature, limits, incidents, &c., of the rite of kissing, etc. The kiss had all the virtue of a bond, granted as a seal to the ceremony of betrothing; and if the husband elect broke the engagement, repenting of what he had done, he surrendered a moiety of the presents received in the ceremony of betrothing, in consequence of the violence done to the modesty of the lady by a kiss.

In much later times, the kiss was esteemed to be a ceremony of particular obligation, as could be shown in a thousand instances. The gentle Julia, in the "Two Gentlemen of Verona," after exchanging a ring with her lover, completes the contract with a kiss—

"And seal the bargain with a *holy* kiss."

The same lady seems to entertain a high opinion of the efficacy of a kiss, for in the throes of her remorse, a little before, for having torn into fragments the love-letter of Proteus, she hits upon the following expedient:—

"I'll kiss each separate paper for amends."

Not satisfied, however, with this act of compunction, and opining that a kiss is the "sovereignest thing on earth for an inward bruise," she thus apostrophizes her absent lover:—

"My bosom as a bed,
Shall lodge thee till thy wound be thoroughly healed,
And thus I search it with a sovereign kiss."

It would be a piece of useless industry to collect the thousand elaborate and ingenious things which poets, old and young, and modern, have wrought into a description of a kiss. The choice of all the sweet-scented flowers, and the most approved juices, whether for their gratefulness to the taste or the smell, have been from time to time defrauded of their exquisite proportion lovers who long for the sweets of dear felicitous love in the marriage state.

The first two stages are attended with many hours of pain and few moments of pleasure—many restless nights and heaving sighs. The third stage is not without danger, and should be pushed on to a conclusion as rapidly as rationally proper.

In courtship, there should be a great degree of respect paid to each other by the affianced parties, about one day to become man and wife. They should "look before they leap," count all the cost, and have their minds fully made up, to all the consequences and responsibilities which the married state involves. They naturally will think that all is to be joy and gladness, peace and "bliss—exquisite bliss," in the possession of each other. Experience, however, has proved to too many, that happiness is not a plant of earthly growth, and many who might have averted it, with prudent foresight, have had to lament an ill-assorted marriage ere the "honey-moon" had waned. Otherwise, and upon the whole, perhaps Courtship is a state of much felicity, and one which the wedded pair will look back upon with delight, if in it they have had mutual respect and esteem, and still maintain the integrity of such true sentiments and fidelity.

in favor of some particular class of kisses, to which the following one, we suppose, belongs :—

"'Tis every aromatic breeze
Wafted from Afric's spicy trees;
'Tis honey from the fragrant hive,
Which chemist bees with care derive
From all the newly-opened flowers."

Thus the enjoyment of reciprocal love is full of bliss on the threshold of matrimony which is yet an unexplored region.

This constitutes Courtship. Hence, the first step must be made by the male, for that the initiative should be taken by the fair lady, is, if not indelicate, at least unusual, or unnatural, except in Leap Year! The male must woo, while the lady must be wooed in order to be won. Madame de Staël, speaking of Courtship, says:—

"How enchanting is the first gleam of intelligence with her we love! Before memory comes in to share with hope, before words have expressed the sentiments, before eloquence has been able to paint what we feel, there is in these first moments a certain kind of tumult and mystery in the imagination, more transitory than happiness, but still more heavenly."

This made the immortal *Shakspeare* dictate the following unrivalled passages, in which Cressida first confesses to Troilus that she loves him.

*Cressida.*—Boldness comes to me now, and brings me heart!
Prince Troilus, I have loved you night and day,
For many weary months.
*Troilus.*—Why was my Cressid then so hard to win?
*Cressida.*—Hard to seem won; but I was won, my lord,
With the first glance that ever—Pardon me,
If I confess much, you will play the tyrant.
I love you now; but not, till now, so much
But I might master it:—in faith, I lie;
My thoughts were like unbridled children, grown
Too headstrong for their mother:—See, we fools!
Why have I blabb'd? Who shall be true to us,
When we are so unsecret to ourselves?

But, though I loved you well, I woo'd you not;
And yet, good faith, I wished myself a man;
Or that we women had men's privilege
Of speaking first.—Sweet, bid me hold my tongue;
For in this rapture I shall surely speak
The thing I shall repent.—See, see, your silence,
Cunning in dumbness, from my weakness draws
My very soul of counsel.—Stop my mouth.

On this passage, how true are *Godwin's* reflections!

"What charming ingenuousness, what exquisite *naivete*, what ravishing confusion of soul, are expressed in these words! We seem to perceive in them every fleeting thought as it rises in the mind of Cressida, at the same time that they delineate with equal skill all the beautiful timidity and innocent artifice which grace and consummate the feminine character."

Aristotle well sayeth, "No man loves but he that was first delighted with comeliness and beauty, the graces of mind and the impulses of a pure and generous heart."

### C. MARRIAGE.

The parties are wedded. The priest has pronounced as one those hearts that before beat in unison with each other. The assembled guests congratulate the happy pair. The fair bride has left her dear mother bedewed with tears and sobbing just as if her heart would break, and as if the happy bridegroom was leading her away captive against her will. They enter the carriage. It drives off on the wedding tour, and his arm encircles the yielding waist of her now all his own, while her head reclines on the breast of the man of her choice. If she be young and has married an old man, she will be sad. If she has married for a home, or position, or wealth, a pang will shoot across her fair bosom. If she has married without due consideration, or on too slight an acquaintance, it will be her sorrow before long. But, if loving and beloved, she has united her destiny with a worthy man, she will rejoice, and on her journey feel a glow of satisfaction and delight unfelt before, and which will be often renewed, and daily prove as the living waters from some perennial spring.

Happiness then attends the well-mated and congenial pair, who in the morning of life—he in the robust grace of ripened manhood, and she in her youthful beauty and guilelessness of heart—are thus united and on their wedding tour. We will not draw the veil that hides them for a while from the gaze even of their most intimate friends. They are happy each revolving day in the society of one another.

They return from their bridal tour, and are visited by their friends. Congratulations again are poured in, and all goes on in sweetest harmony, like some exquisite piece of music.

"Each is to each other a dearer self."

Anon, the fair bride is indisposed. She has hues unusual in her radiant face. She grows faint at times. She nauseates. Her health seems far from robust, and several changes have taken place that have arrested her attention at first and seemed to her a new and curious mystery. She consults her physician. It is as she expected. She is in that delicate situation that "ladies wish to be who love their lords." In short, her rotundity of person, the areola of the nipples, the enlargement of the breast, and other indications, neither few nor unmarked, proclaim her *enceinte*. After a due period of gestation, she becomes a—*mother*—and sheds tears of joy over her new-born child.

This is then the fruit of marriage. She is bound to her husband with a more powerful chain. Their love is proportionably augmented, and increasing years adds to the number of their smiling offspring—a glorious and healthy progeny.

Some have contended that marriage is not a *natural* institution; that the selection of one sexual mate is not a law of our being. This proposition we think, untenable as it is debasing. For a true interpretation of the law of God, or Nature, we have only to appeal to the voice of God as revealed in the best developed of the lower animals. For instance, the lion, whose voice makes all other animals, and even man, tremble, might assert and maintain his right to *indiscriminate love* without restraint or opposition; yet he selects his companion for life, and lives faithfully attached to that one object of choice and affection all his natural days. The eagle, too, the lord of all that wings the air, quietly chooses his life companion, and lives in the bonds of faithful wedlock; and for half a century both labor to feed and rear their young. Do kings and priests make the marriage laws of lions, eagles, geese, and robins? Is their marriage institution an imposition, a burden, a yoke of bondage? If so, why do they not assert their freedom in some great "free convention," or set up a "free-love" community for themselves? As man is an epitome embodiment in himself of all the capabilities and propensities of all the lower animals, we find, among other faculties that of *mating* a predominant disposition. Man is therefore a marrying being, while the instinct or faculty of *union for life* is the basis of marriage and of the laws and customs which recognize the life-choice of one woman for one man. Friendship, it is true, often exists between a man and woman before any other love element is awakened; but a look, or word, or other slight incident awakens between them the connubial impulse, and in a moment their views of each other and of their relations for life are entirely changed. Before they were friends, as two men or two women could be—nothing more; now they are lovers, and henceforth their hopes, aspirations, and joys, run in the same channel. Hence *mating*, or matrimony, is the result, and progeny the natural and legitimate fruit, agreeably to the laws or ordinances of God and Nature.

### D.—EFFECTS OF CONTINENCE.—CELIBACY CONTRARY TO NATURE.

It is not *continence* but CHASTITY, which is at once prescribed by Nature and the laws of Society. It is indeed easy to show that the passion of sexual love is, in a moral point of view, almost as obligatory as the appetite for food.

As remarked in another place, Nature has destined man to attack, and woman to defend. In other words, she has implanted in the breast of man passions which are less easy of control, than those which she has given to woman. Nature herself has rendered woman less physically able to indulge in sexual love than man, even were she morally so disposed. The periods of menstruation, pregnancy and suckling, are accompanied by more or less of the same indisposition on the part of woman, and leaves the passions with which man is blessed and cursed, in a state of ungratified desperation, if the erotic fury is not capable of being controlled by cool reflection inducing continence and virtue. It is, however, a great mistake to suppose that reasonable abstinence from sexual congress would prove injurious to the virile stamina of the male. The vigor of the Athletæ of ancient Greece is proof sufficient on this point.* The marriage state, however, with moderate indulgence of sexual love, is best calculated for securing the health and happiness of the *genus homo*—man and woman. This truth is established in the simple fact that the number of the unmarried insane of both sexes in the Asylums of the land, is about double the number of those who are married. *Absolute continence*, however, has very different effects, according to the sex and disposition of the individual. Among women its effects are not the same as among men. In general, they bear more easily both the excesses and privations of sexual love; yet, when these privations are not voluntary on their

* See Acton's "Functions and Disorders of the Reproductive Organs."

part, they have generally for women, especially those who are solitary and unemployed, inconveniences and miseries unknown to the nature of man.

It often happens, that an unmarried woman, under the influence, or, we may say, the domination, of an organ in which the gratifications of love do not temperate the vital energy, drags on a languid existence, and is a prey to hysteric and nervous affections. On the other hand, if she fulfill her destiny, and discharge the duty common to all living beings, of reproducing her species, the symptoms of destruction disappear, and the torch of life, formerly on the point of expiring, resumes new light and sparkles with new fires. Is ever a married woman phthisical or epileptic? Is she exposed to convulsions and to a hundred dangerous or mortal ills? Impregnation and pregnancy cure them all, or at least suspend their course. All seem to respect the sacred state of maternity. Nature watches over the young being with a solicitude truly maternal.

Hence, men and women who, from religious zeal, devote themselves to an eternal chastity, often contract an obligation which is above human power to fulfill. Nature rejects it: and the vital action produces the singular phenomena of *priapomania* (or satyriasis) or of nymphomania; the first causing sexual frenzy in males, and the other the use of horrible means of sexual gratification on the part of females. Frequently this erotic fury is communicated by sight, or by a recital, to very irritable persons who are similarly circumstanced, and is propagated like an epidemic disease. It gives origin to hysteric convulsions and to exstacies of passion which cannot be subjected to the laws of modesty. *Buffon* indeed relates that even birds when separated from their mates often die of epilepsy. The nuns of Flanders, in the scandalous scenes of their erotomania, and amidst their attitudes of lascivious rage, are said to have bit each other. The young men who secretly introduced themselves into the convent, cured this sort of malady, which spread through Germany and Holland in the fifteenth century, and prevailed in Rome in 1535. Who, moreover, knows not the history of the erotic convulsionaries of St. Medard, of the Ursulines of Louden, etc. Love, indeed, often punishes with death those who satisfy not this law of Nature. Hence it is, that *Rachel* says to Jacob, "*Give me children, or else I die!*"

In truth, Cenobites are more exposed than others to cancers of the breast and the uterus.

It is thus that we perceive that MORAL LOVE and the union of the sexes by the bonds of marriage, are adapted to, and expressive of a primary *Institute of Nature*—THE PERPETUATION OF THE HUMAN RACE.

## E. PHILOPROGENITIVENESS—PARENTAL LOVE AND CARE OF OFFSPRING.

PHILOPROGENTIVENESS, phrenologically speaking, expresses the relations of parents to children. All forms of life are feeble in their inception, are easily destroyed, and need special care and protection. Without such care all that is born would inevitably die, and all the provisions of earth for the happiness of her creatures would be forestalled by the infantile death of all her young. But Nature *must not* lose her races. Especially must she pre-provide for the perpetuity of the *human* family. Nature has made this provision by creating that *strong love* which every parental animal and human being experiences for its *own* young. Why *own* young? Why not *all* adults care for *all* children? Because Nature must *apportion* her work to see that it is done. To make *sure* work, she specifies that all parents shall take the express and special care of their *own* young. She effects this by *parental love*, by creating in all parents a *special* love for their *own* young. Parental love both rears its own children and makes the parent inexpressibly happy in its own delightful task.

Fouriere and many Socialists and "Free-lovers" contend that the *community* should care for the children of the community in gross. If this system were best for man, it would be best, for the same reason, for animals. Why should not all cows suckle all calves in general, and none in particular? Why not all hens scratch for and brood over all chickens in general—nay, cluck and scratch for all ducklings, goslings, hawklings, etc.? Why not the lions rear lambs, lion-whelps, pigs, jackals, or the elephant rear horses, dromedaries, etc.? Why not make a "happy family" of all animals, man included, and let them herd in promiscuous intercourse, and in support of one another, and of the entire bestial social arrangement?* See into what absurdities Fourierism and

* Those who bend any one of Nature's straight lines, must bend a thousand others also.

Free-love proclivities would lead us! Nature, however, is not so ridiculous. She has not fitted the elephant to nurse the chicken, or any other animal any creature not of its own begetting. The natural function of Philoprogenitiveness is love of our *own* young. This is proven by the entire natural history of the parental sentiment all throughout the entire animal kingdom. The maternal hen will scratch and cluck all day, and brood and purr tenderly and patiently all night over her *own* young, but turn another chicken into her flock, and she will peck its pate instantly, even if she has but a single chick of her own. This shows why stepmothers are more partial to their own children than those of their husband's first wife. Now this fondness for our *own* young, and the requisition for rearing them, implies and requires that we *know* them. Hence the necessity of the marriage relation, and that men and women should be *faithful* in wedlock. Marriage is thus a divine and natural institution—opposed to celibacy, concubinage, harlotry, adultery, and promiscuous sexual intercourse. The fact is, nature has her own laws, and they must not be violated. *Love* thus implies both mating and fidelity, and interdicts free-love and amatory promiscuosity in any form. Sexual conjunction, accordingly, is only proper after reciprocal love has eventuated in marriage. But marriage itself is not desirable unless it eventuate in its natural product—*children*—which *both* parents can *together* bring up—*all* as *their own* mutual children, begotten in wedlock. This is *true* love. Hence the *Family state*, or the connubial connection, is the sublimest of

Nature's Institutes for the well-being and happiness of man.

## F. WHEN AND WHOM TO MARRY

The desire for *sexual union* is rarely indicated until the male and female have arrived at *Puberty*. This is a period of life, when childhood is passing from a stage of immaturity of the sexual organs to a full development of their functions. In other words, Puberty is that combination of circumstances in which the passion of love originates. Sex, climate, and manner of living, however, have a great influence on the earlier or later appearance of the phenomena of puberty. Woman attains to this state a year or two sooner than man, and the inhabitants of southern, before those of northern countries. In the hotter climes of Africa, Asia, and America, girls are marriageable as early as ten years of age; in the temperate zones, the period of puberty is from twelve to fifteen; while in the colder regions of Russia, Sweden, Denmark, England, the northern parts of the United States and Canada, menstruation, the most characteristic sign of puberty, is frequently delayed to the seventeenth year. As a general rule, however, in this country, women are pubeses at fifteen and young men at about sixteen.

It will not be necessary, in this chapter to present specially all the indications of puberty. We may say, in a word, that it marks itself by certain physical aspects too palpable to the sight and senses to be misunderstood. It manifest itself by the increase of strength and of animal heat, by the impetuosity of the vital motions, and by the fire which sparkles in the eyes.

*Early* marriage, in fact, is a primary law of human nature, and, whatever the doctrines of *Malthus* and *Franklin* in respect to over-increase of population, &c., should be consummated while the parties are in the first flush of ripened life, when the affections are pure, and every sentiment refined and ennobling, when man and woman are congenially associated in every element of physical health. A woman at eighteen would not be unequally yoked to a man of twenty-five or twenty-eight; but any greater disparity of ages is seldom ever productive of benefits or felicity. If marriage be delayed too long in either sex, say from thirty to forty-five, the offspring will be puny, and more liable to insanity, idiotcy, and other maladies concomitant to the increasing debility of the parties. On the contrary, if she be fully organized and glows with joyous, bounding health and vitality, the early age of "sweet sixteen" may not be an inappropriate season to enter upon the marriage relation, provided her deliberate reason and judgment have sanctioned the object of her affections, and that the man of her choice be equally developed in every manly attribute, and whose age does not greatly exceed her own. Women, likewise, who are too early married, are speedily enervated; and if this takes place before their full growth, they remain always of diminished stature, weak, pale, emaciated and miserable. The proper age for a woman to marry in this country, is, perhaps, about eighteen, but not *then* if she be immaturely developed, suffer from ill health, labor under any malformation, or is liable to hereditary affections of any kind whatever.

We must not, however, always judge of the advancement of the young man by the early appearance of the beard; for it is known that those who abandon themselves early to sexual indulgence have an earlier beard. Hence, *Martial* says,

> " Inde tragus celeres, pili, mirandaque matiri,
> Barba. . . . . ."

But if manhood be premature; death, fatal death is premature also.

But who is fitted to enter upon the important state of matrimony? Who is there that weighs its fearful responsibilities, and measures its chances for enduring felicity or irremedial misery? Surely, in forming the conjugal union, the health and constitution of the parties should be critically regarded. We have no natural or moral right to perpetuate unhealthy constitutions. We have no right to poison the *morals*, or cramp and mislead the minds of children; and we do them and the race, a serious wrong in multiplying the number of hereditary invalids. A whole family of children fall before some hereditary malady into an untimely grave. These misfortunes are generally regarded as the inscrutable providence of God, as "severe trials," and " sore afflictions," without dreaming of the *true* causes which produce them.

In the language of Mrs. *Sigourney*, we ask of—

"Mothers, is there any thing we can do to acquire for our daughters a good constitution? Is there truth in the sentiment sometimes repeated, that the female sex is becoming more effeminate? Are our daughters as capable of enduring hardships as were their grandmothers? Have our daughters as much stamina of constitution, as much aptitude as we (their mothers) possess? These questions affect the welfare of the community; for the ability or inability of woman to discharge what the Almighty has committed to her, touches the equilibrium of society and the hidden springs of existence."

Truly, "*First make the tree good, then shall the fruit be good also.*"

It is notorious all over the civilized world that American females are unhealthy, and that the tendency to disease and infirmity is constantly increasing. The daughters, as a general rule, are more infirm than their mothers, as their mothers compare unfavorably with their grandmothers. There can be no question that the *vitality* of our females is running down. This painful fact is evidenced, even in very many young women and *girls*, in the exhibition of delicate nerves, tender stomachs, falling hair, decaying teeth, and spinal irritation. Even the Medical journals and the ordinary daily and weekly papers of the land, are frequently comparing the health and stamina of American females with those of Great Britain, Germany, etc., and always to the disadvantage of the former. Our young men cannot be ignorant of these things, and hence CELIBACY or "single blessedness," (as it is not probably, under the circumstances, inappropriately termed) is alarmingly on the increase. Young men are, and must be fond of the society of young ladies, and reason and custom incline them to marry, but with the thought of every thing except beds of roses and domestic joys, they refuse to take the lead. So far as courting goes, all is pleasant enough; but with marriage is associated the idea of doctors, nurses, and a constant monologue about pains, aches, bad feelings, morbid sensations, as the prevailing music of the fireside. The young man knows that the chances are against him of marrying a *patient* to take care of, instead of a wife to enjoy. Young men are just as selfish as women—perhaps more so. The young lady who supposes that any young man on the face of the earth wishes to marry her for the sake of nursing her through life makes a very great mistake. Young men will play court where they cannot think of marrying. Whenever they find their attentions are beginning to be taken in earnest, they will seek other society. They will not of course give the reason for this, and the young ladies will of course wonder "why don't the men propose?" Make proposals of marriage, indeed! Surely they will not, when they see the sad evidences of infirmity, which false hair, artificial teeth and expansive skirts are unable to conceal! Nay, they rather avoid all approaches to intimacy, and often abandon the society of those who could be healthy and make good wives, and seek amusement in less respectable society and more debasing associations. Hence the increase of *celibacy*, profligacy, and sensualism in every form. Facts like these are of fearful interest to generations yet to come. It requires no extraordinary reach of thought to comprehend that the natural and inevitable result must be, sooner or later, the general demoralization of both male and female, and the utter disorganization of human society. Without the maintenance of these domestic associations and duties, which are known only where the marriage institution is made sacred, no society ever did, never can exist above barbarism or savageism.

The young women of America have it in their power to arrest entirely this growing evil. Let them make themselves healthy, and prove their capacity to be useful as well as ornamental, and they will not be long in the matrimonial market. Let them snap their fingers at the fashions of London and the follies of Paris, and act like sensible human beings: otherwise, they are neither fit for wives nor mothers.

A *true* union must be based on an organic law. Oil and water will not mingle. A lion will not lie down quietly with a lamb, nor can ill-assorted marriages be productive of aught but discord.

The choice of a husband requires the coolest judgment and most vigilant sagacity. As a sensible poet well advises:—

"Select that man
Whose blood and bones and muscle, are so well joined,
That they are not pipes for *disease's* finger
To sound its horrid discord."

Another bard suggests—

"Let the woman take
An elder than herself, so wears she to him—
So sways she rules in her husband's heart."

While another poet sagely remarks that—

> "Marriage is a matter of more worth,
> Than to be dealt with by attorneyship."

For—husband and wife—

> "Are they not *one?* Are they not joined by Heaven?
> Each interwoven by the other's fate?"

Love and virginity and beauty are the jewels of women, yet are not to be selfishly hoarded, but prudently dispensed and shared with some noble, manly heart and bosom. Then—

> "List, lady, be not coy, and be not cozened
> With that same vaunted name virginity;
> Beauty is nature's coin, must not be hoarded
> But must be current, and the good thereof
> Consist in the enjoyment of itself.
> If you let slip the time, like a neglected rose
> It withers on the stock with languishing head."

The author of the "Seasons," speaking of the influence of love, thus beautifully sings:—

> "Oh happy they, the happiest of their kind!
> Whom gentle stars unite, and in one fate
> Their hearts, their fortunes, and their beings blend.
> 'Tis not alone the tie of *human* laws
> That binds their peace—but *harmony* itself,
> Attuning all their passions into *love;*
> Thought meeting thought, and will pervading will,
> With boundless confidence—for nought but love
> Can answer love and render bliss secure."

## G. A SUMMARY OF THE ECONOMY OF HUMAN LIFE IN RESPECT TO MEN AND WOMEN AND THEIR PROGENY.

The foregoing may be regarded as the ordinary economy of human life—the romance and misery of "love, courtship, and marriage," as viewed and considered by the masses of mankind. There are, however, other points connected with the peculiar theme which deserve to be scanned in the light of sound morals, health and beauty, as physiologically and philosophically confirmed and established, to secure the physical perfection, happiness and glory of every human creature.

First then let us descant upon the *moral* relations of the subject—reveal the power of desire and love—show the true relationship between man and woman—husband, wife and children—and give such caution and advice, as may tend to the highest exaltation and beatitude of the great human family. We adopt accordingly the quaint and judicious words of an ancient Brahmin, as translated from an Indian Manuscript, entitled the "Economy of Human Life."

### DESIRE AND LOVE.

We quote from the Brahmin:

"Beware, young man! Beware of the allurements of wantonness, and let not the harlot tempt thee to excess in her delights.

"The madness of desire shall defeat its own pursuits; from the blindness of its rage, thou shalt rush upon destruction.

"Therefore, give not thy heart to her sweet enticements, neither suffer thy soul to be ensnared by her enchanting delusions

"The fountain of health, which must supply the stream of pleasure, shall be quickly dried up, and every spring of joy shall be exhausted.

"In the prime of thy life, old age shall overtake thee: Thy sun shall decline in the morning of thy days.

"But when virtue and modesty enlighten her charms, the lustre of a beautiful woman is brighter than the stars of heaven, and the influence of her power it is in vain to resist.

"The whiteness of her bosom transcendeth the lily; her smiles are more delicious than a garden of roses.

"The innocence of her eye is like that of the turtle-dove; simplicity and truth dwell in her heart.

"The kisses of her mouth are sweeter than honey; the perfumes of Arabia breathe from her lips.

"Shut not thy bosom to the tenderness of love; the purity of its flame shall ennoble thy heart, and soften it to receive the fairest impressions."

## WOMAN—WIFE—MOTHER.

"Give ear, fair daughter of love! to the instructions of prudence, and let the precepts of truth sink deep in thy heart: So shall the charm of thy mind add elegance to thy form; and thy beauty, like the rose it resembleth, shall retain its sweetness when its bloom is withered.

"In the spring of thy youth, in the morning of thy days, when the eyes of men gaze on thee with delight, and nature whispereth to thine ear the meaning of their looks: Ah! hear with caution their seducing words, guard well thy heart, nor listen to their soft persuasions.

"Remember thou art made man's reasonable companion, not the slave of his passion; the end of thy being is not merely to gratify his loose desire, but to assist him in the toils of life, to soothe him with thy tenderness, and recompense his care with soft endearments.

"Who is she that winneth the heart of a man, that subdueth him to love, and reigneth in his breast?

"Lo! yonder she walketh in maiden sweetness, with innocence in her mind, and modesty upon her cheeks.

"Her hand seeketh employment, her foot delighteth not in gadding abroad.

"She is clothed with neatness, she is fed with temperance; humility and meekness are as a crown of glory circling her head.

"On her tongue dwelleth music, the sweetness of honey floweth from her lips.

"Decency is in all her words, in her answers are mildness and truth.

"Submission and obedience are the lessons of her life, and peace and happiness are her reward.

"Before her steps walketh prudence, and virtue attendeth at her right hand.

"Her eye speaketh softness and love; but discretion with a sceptre sitteth on her brow.

"The tongue of the licentious is dumb in her presence, the awe of her virtue keepeth him silent.

"When scandal is busy, and the fame of her neighbor is tossed from tongue to tongue; if charity and good-nature open not her mouth, the finger of silence resteth on her lip.

"Her breast is the mansion of goodness, and therefore she suspecteth no evil in others.

"Happy is the man that shall make her his wife; happy is the child that shall call her mother.

"She presideth in the house, and there is peace; she commandeth with judgment, and is obeyed.

"She ariseth in the morning, she considereth her affairs, and appointeth to every one their proper business.

"The care of her family is her whole delight; to that alone she applieth her study, and elegance with frugality is seen in her mansion.

"The prudence of her management is an honor to her husband, and he heareth her praise with a secret delight.

"She informeth the minds of her children with wisdom, she fashioneth their manners from the example of her own goodness.

"The word of her mouth is the law of their youth, the motion of her eye commandeth their obedience.

"She speaketh, and her servants fly; she pointeth, and the thing is done.

"For the law of love is in their hearts, and her kindness addeth wings to their feet.

'In prosperity she is not puffed up; in adversity she healeth the wounds of fortune with patience.

"The troubles of her husband are alleviated by her counsels, and sweetened by her endearments; he putteth his heart in her bosom, and receiveth comfort.

"Happy the man that has made her his wife; happy the child that calleth her mother."

## HUSBAND.

"Take unto thyself a wife, and obey the ordinance of God. Take unto thyself a wife, and become a faithful member of society.

"But examine with care, and fix not suddenly. On thy present choice, depends thy future happiness. If much of her time is destroyed in dress and adornments; if she is enamored of her own beauty, and delighted with her own praise; if she laugheth much, and talketh loud; if her foot abideth not in her father's house, and her eyes with boldness rove on the faces of men; though her beauty were as the sun in the firmament of Heaven, turn thy eyes from her charms, turn thy feet from her paths, and suffer not thy soul to be ensnared by the allurements of imagination.

"But when thou findest sensibility of heart, joined with softness of manners; an accomplished mind, with a form agreeable to thy fancy; take her to thine house; she is worthy to be thy friend, thy companion in life, the wife of thy bosom.

"O cherish her as a blessing sent thee from Heaven.

Let the kindness of thy behavior endear thee to her heart.

"She is the mistress of thy house; treat her therefore with respect, that thy servants may obey her.

"Oppose not her inclination without cause; she is the partner of thy cares, make her also the companion of thy pleasures.

"Reprove her faults with gentleness, exact not her obedience with rigor.

"Trust thy secrets in her breast; her counsels are sincere, thou shalt not be deceived.

"Be faithful to her bed; for she is the mother of thy children.

"When pain and sickness assault her, let thy tenderness soothe her afflictions; a look from thee, of pity and love, shall alleviate her grief, or mitigate her pain, and be of more avail than many physicians.

"Consider the tenderness of her sex, the delicacy of her frame; and be not severe to her weakness, but remember thine own imperfections."

---

Truly there is abundance of wisdom, truth, love and justice, in the terse and epigrammatic sentences of the Oriental Brahmin! Are not these sage maxims worthy the thoughtful consideration of every man and woman contemplating marriage, and of those already united in its indissoluble bonds? What purity and bliss, health and beauty, would flow from an observance of these moral obligations and physical restraints, could they be generally enforced and maintained through all the ramifications of human society!

# CHAPTER XII.

## PREGNANCY OR GESTATION.

PREGNANCY is divided into uterine and extra-uterine. Extra-uterine pregnancy is divided into three kinds—Fallopian pregnancy, Ovarian pregnancy, and Abdominal pregnancy. In extra-uterine pregnancy, the product of conception seldom reaches its full growth, and if it should, cannot be expelled, and its destruction is an inevitable consequence of Nature's error. The fœtus usually dies about the second or third month and putrefies.

In natural pregnancy the product of conception is deposited in the uterus, and is there developed. There is sometimes false uterine pregnancy, which will deceive the most experienced practitioner.

### A.—NATURAL OR UTERINE PREGNANCY.

Natural gestation or pregnancy may be said to commence the moment the ovum is penetrated by the spermatozoa in the Fallopian tube, and is subsesequently received in the uterine cavity, where it is nourished by the female parent. If the male sperm does not come in contact with the ovum in the Fallopian tube, no change takes place in it, except a slight alteration while on its passage along the Fallopian tube, being received into the uterine cavity where it is ultimately lost or decomposed. After impregnation a series of remarkable changes take place in the uterus, whereby it becomes fitted for the protection and development of the ovum during a period of nine months or forty weeks. The uterus meantime undergoes a new state of growth or development, which is occasioned by the stimulus of impregnation and the growth of the ovum. The ratio of increase of the uterus during gestation is subject to great variation. The enlargement, in ordinary cases, is expressed by the following table. The size of the gravid (a fully developed uterus) has already been given in another chapter.

*Rate of Increase of the Gravid Uterus according to Months.**

| | Length. | Breadth. |
|---|---|---|
| End of 3 months..... | 4½ to 5 inches..... | 4 inches. |
| " 4 " .... | 5½ to 6 " .... | 5 " |
| " 5 " .... | 6 to 7 " .... | 5½ " |
| " 6 " .... | 8 to 9 " .... | 6½ " |
| " 7 " .... | 10 " .... | 7½ " |
| " 8 " .... | 11 " .... | 8 " |
| " 9 " .... | 12 " .... | 9 " |

There is considerable change in the form of the uterus during the first four months of pregnancy, without any apparent difference in the figure of the female. From the fourth month there is a rapid bodily enlargement. There is, however, no increase in the thickness of the walls of the uterus. On the contrary, they become gradually thinner, up to the period of nine months. The neck of the womb commences

* Cyclop. Anat. et Phys. No. 49–50.

to shorten about the fifth month; at the end of nine months it is obliterated, which is occasioned by the lateral extension and expansion of the uterus.

It is now necessary again to trace the ovum from the time it is expelled from the ovary and received into the Fallopian tube. It has been stated that no apparent change occurs unless it is impregnated by the male sperm, which impregnation usually takes place in the middle and lower third of the tube. When the ovum or egg is expelled from the Graafian vesicle, it has attached to its surface a portion of the membrana granulosa. (*Fig.* 20.) As the egg passes along the upper third of the tube, this layer of cells becomes divested. (*Fig.* 21.) Should it now meet the male sperm, material changes take place. The spermatozoa readily penetrate 'the soft covering of the yelk. There is next a cleverage of the yelk substance, (*Fig.* 22,) which continues dividing and subdividing until it is broken up into a granular mass. As the egg passes the latter third of the tube another change is observed —that of a deposit of albumen around the *zona pellucida*, or outer covering of the egg. (*Fig.* 24.) On the outer surface of this albuminous deposit are developed villi. The addition of these villi form what is called the chorion, which becomes very vascular. These villi project, forming a bulbous expansion (*Fig.* 29, C,) which serves as an absorbing point, and thus affords the channel through which the embryo is nourished, until a more perfect communication is established.

Having thus traced the ovum in its passage to the uterus, it is now proper to speak of the changes which take place in that organ—(changes not from the presence of the ovum, but in consequence of conception.) One of these is the formation of the *membrana decidua*, as it is called, from the fact of its being thrown off at each parturition. This is not a new membrane formed within the uterus, as formerly supposed. The observations of Dr. *Sharpey*, and others, prove that it is merely composed of the inner portion of the lining membrane of the uterus, undergone considerable change in its character. This lining membrane is tubular. (*Fig.* 42.) These tubes become thickened

FIG. 42.

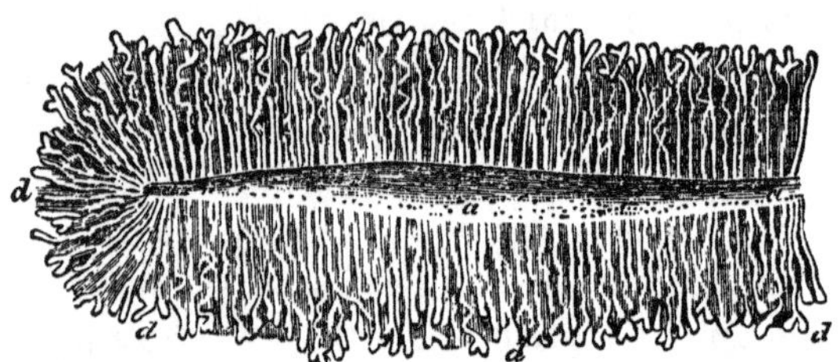


SECTION OF THE LINING MEMBRANE OF THE HUMAN UTERUS AT THE PERIOD OF COMMENCING PREGNANCY.—(*After E. H. Weber.*)

*d, d, d,* shows the arrangement and other peculiarities of the glands, with these orifices, *a, a, a,* on the internal surface of the organ. Twice the natural size.*

a short time after conception, and are lined by an epithelium similar to the lining of the gastric follicles or tubes of the stomach. After the thickening of these tubes, a fluid is poured out from them, which fills up the cavity of the uterus. Into this secretion the ovum is imbedded. The villi of the chorion receive nourishment from this secretion, or from the tubes direct. In

* Carpenter's "Human Physiology."

Fig. 44.

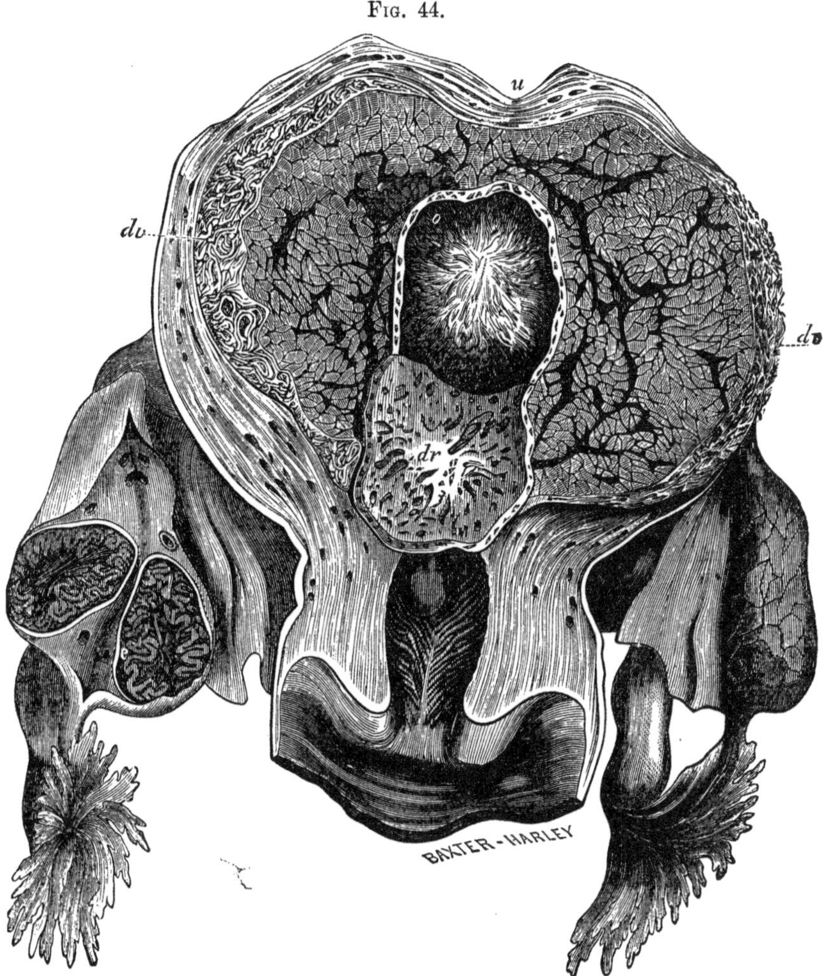


UTERUS IN THE FIRST MONTH OF GESTATION; SHOWING THE FORMATION OF THE FŒTAL CHAMBER BY THE MEMBRANÆ DECIDUA. (*After Coste.*)

*u*, uterine walls traversed by numerous blood-vessels; *d v*, decidua vera, or developed lining membrane of the uterus, the uterine glands or canals being much enlarged; *d r*, decidua reflexa, in which lies the ovum *o*, which is still at this stage unattached; *c*, corpus luteum.

the dog, the villi have been found piercing the mouth of their tubes and drawing nourishment from them. The secretion that fills the cavity of the uterus, and in which the ovum is imbedded, grows up around it, and forms the membrana decidua. (*Fig.* 29, *c*, and *Fig.* 43.) This continues until it has completely enveloped the ovum, and forms the decidua reflexa. The uterus,

FIG. 43.

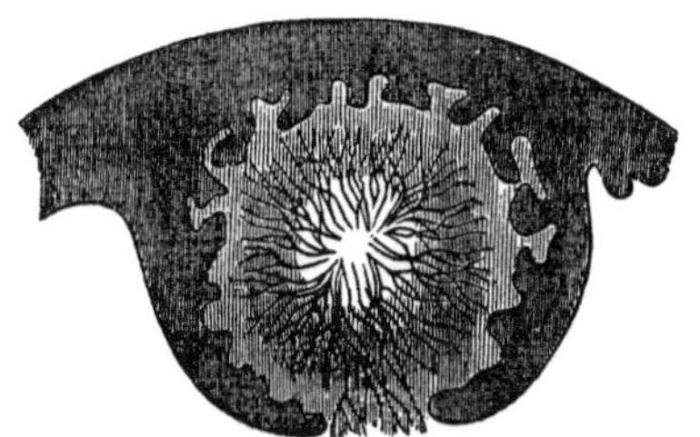

ADVANCED STAGE OF THE DECIDUA REFLEXA AROUND THE OVUM.

or womb, is also lined by a decidua, called *decidua vera.* As the ovum grows, the space between these decidua is diminished, and they ultimately come together. This junction occurs about the third month. (*Fig.* 44.) At this period they can scarcely be distinguished as two distinct membranes. It was formerly supposed a decidua vera lined the uterus previous to the passage of the ovum into that receptacle. This would naturally force the membrane before it, and make a double membrane, from which it has derived its name. This view is incorrect, as has been demonstrated by M. *Coste*, whose views have been sustained by other eminent physiologists, as already described.

In the early state of development of the chorion, it contains no blood-vessels, but receives its nourishment by drawing in fluid through its villi or tufts. In this way the embryo* is nourished until the placenta is formed. The placenta is formed by the prolongation or extension of the tufts of the chorion, which seem to prolong or develop upon one side of the chorion, forming one side of the placenta, properly called the fœtal side of the placenta. While the fœtal portion is thus being formed by the extension of the tufts of the chorion, the blood-vessels of the decidua also enlarge, so as to form sinuses or canals. (*Fig.* 45, *b*,

Fig. 45.

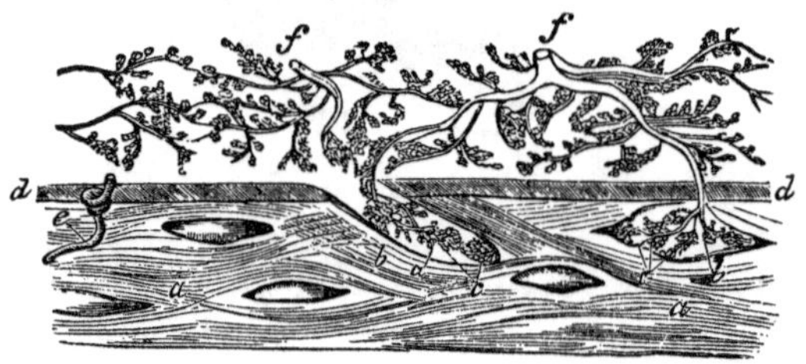

DIAGRAM OF THE STRUCTURE OF THE PLACENTA.—(*From Carpenter.*)

*a*, substance of the uterus; *b*, the cavity of a sinus; *c*, *c*, fœtal tufts dipping down into the sinuses; *d*, *d*, the decidual lining of the uterus; *e*, curling arteries of the uterus; *f*, *f*, branches of fœtal tufts forming the umbilical vessels.

and *Fig.* 46, *b*.) Into these sinuses the villi of the chorion penetrate and are completely bound in. (*Fig.* 45, *c*, and *Fig.* 46, *d*.) In this way the placental cavities or sinuses are intersected by numerous tufts and

* We use the term embryo after the ovum has passed into the uterus. After four months, embryotic life ceases, when fœtal life commences and continues till close of pregnancy.

FIG. 46.

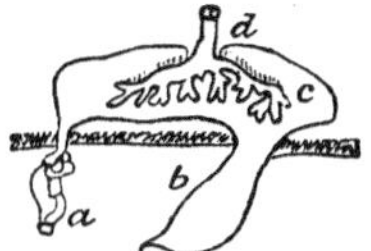


DIAGRAM OF THE PLACENTAL CAVITY.—(*After Dr. Reid.*)

*a*, curling artery of the uterus; *b*, sinus of uterus; *c*, cavity of the placenta; *d*, fœtal tuft imbedded in it, and held there by reflection of its walls.

bound down by the delicate membrane forming the walls of the deciduum. (*Fig.* 45, *d, d.*) The placenta thus formed is supplied by "curling arteries of the uterus" (*Fig.* 45, *e*), and the blood returned to large veins called sinuses or canals. (*Fig.* 45, *b.*) The extremities of the fœtal vessels being retained in their sinuses are bathed in the blood of these canals, receiving oxygen from the maternal blood and parting with its carbonic acid. These tufts may be compared to the rootlets of plants, imbedded in the ground, and absorbing moisture and nutrition from the soil.

The excrementitious substances of the fœtus are most likely passed off to the mother in this way. By the same process, poisons, and various constitutional diseases of parents, may be conveyed to the child. This is the only direct communication between the mother and child, viz.: the bathing of the fœtal tufts in the venous sinuses of the mother. The placenta begins to form about the latter part of the second month, and is sufficiently developed during the third month to supply the fœtus with nourishment; and continues to develop or increase with the growth of the embryo.

The blood-vessels of the uterus, particularly the part to which the placenta is attached, also undergo great enlargement. The blood flowing through them produces a peculiar sound, and is the most positive sign of pregnancy. This sound is described by Dr. Montgomery as "the placental bruit," and resembles that produced by gently blowing over the lip of a wide-mouth vial, being "accompanied by a slight rushing noise."

It should have been stated that while the chorion is being developed, the amnion is likewise formed by two folds of serous laminæ. These are the lining membranes of the chorion; they gradually approach one another, and finally meeting enclose the embryo, thus forming an additional investment to the embryo. It is not known at what period of embryotic life this membrane is formed. It takes place in the chicken on the third day. It is this membrane that encloses the *liquor amnion.* This fluid consists of water, holding in solution a small quantity of albumen and salts, and resembles dilute serum of the blood. The amnion not only encloses the liquor amnii, but secretes it. In some females previous to labor it amounts to several quarts. If there be a large quantity of water, the labor will be lingering; which is owing to the great distension of the uterus. Sometimes this distension is so great that it becomes necessary to let off the water previous to labor, in order to overcome the difficulty of breathing, and the influence which the distension has over the function of the stomach and other vital organs.

## B. GROWTH OF THE EMBRYO.

Before the seventh day there is nothing in the uterus to indicate a new being; probably the ovum has not yet passed from the Fallopian tube. On the tenth day, a semi-transparent grayish substance of no definite form is observed. From the twelfth to the fourteenth day there is perceived a vesicle of the size of a pea. This contains a thick fluid, in the midst of which is found an opaque spot, being the first evidence of a new being, and bearing the name of an embryo, surrounded by the chorion and amnion. The weight at this period is about one grain. (*Fig.* 47.) At twenty-one days it resembles in form a large ant, and is about the third of an inch in length, and

FIG 47.

EMBRYO OF TWELVE TO FOURTEEN DAYS LAID OPEN.

FIG. 48.

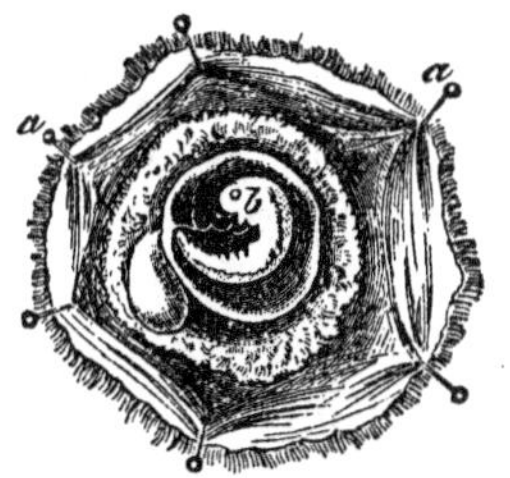


EMBRYO OF TWENTY-ONE DAYS LAID OPEN.
*a*, *a*, *a*, chorion laid open and secured by pins; *b*, the embryo with amnion laid open.

weighs about four grains. (*Fig.* 48.) At this period cartilage, which subsequently becomes bones, is forming. On the thirtieth day the embryo is about the size of a horse-fly, and looks something like a worm

Fig. 49.

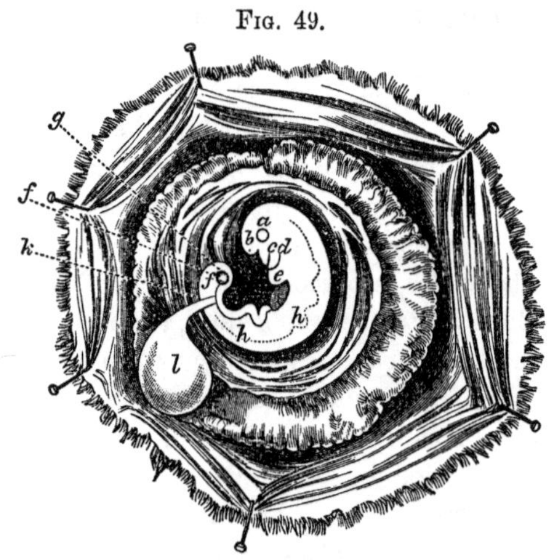


EMBRYO OF THIRTY DAYS.

*a*, Head of embryo; *b*, the eyes; *c*, the mouth; *d*, the neck; *e*, the thorax; *f*, the abdomen; *g*, the extremity of spine; *h h*, the spinal arch; *k*, neck of umbilical vesicle; *l*, the vesicle.

that is bent. A faint outline of organs is now perceived—the head appearing larger than the body, while there are spots indicating eyes. The embryo is about one inch in length and weighs twelve grains. (*Fig.* 49.)

At the forty-fifth day the body of the embryo is lengthened, while the eyes, mouth and nose are strongly marked. The length is over an inch, and the weight about sixty grains. (*Fig.* 50.)

At sixty days, or two months, the eyes are enlarged, and the eyelids are visible; also the external part of the ear; the nose is slightly prominent, the mouth clearly defined, the heart partially developed, while the soft and pulpy substance of the brain is being developed. (*Fig.* 51.)

Fig. 50.

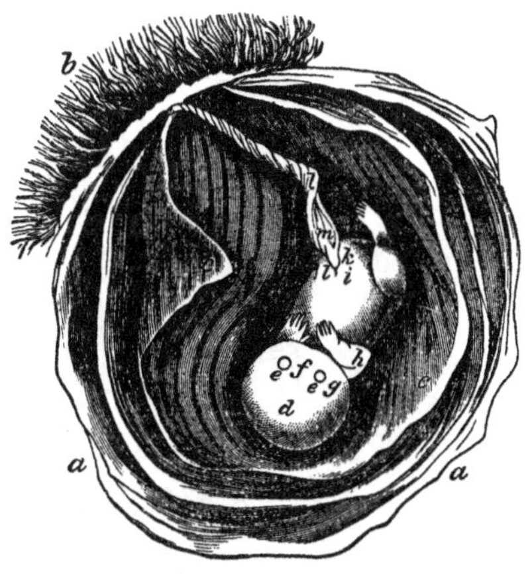


EMBRYO OF FORTY-FIVE DAYS.

*a, a, a*, chorion; *b*, villiosities of placenta; *c, c*, amnion; *d*, head of embryo *e, e*, temples; *f*, interval between eyes or root of nose; *h*, the arms; *i*, the abdomen; *k*, the sexual organs; *l, l*, umbilical cord; *m*, the internal portion of cord.

At ninety days, or three months, the embryo is better defined; the eye-lids are well-formed and closely shut; the organs of generation, in either sex,

Fig. 51.

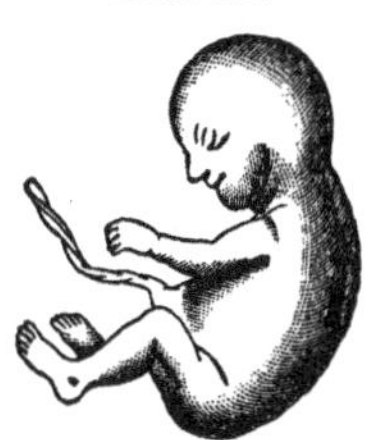

EMBRYO OF SIXTY DAYS OR TWO MONTHS.

are prominent; the heart is plainly seen, and beats with force, the vessels carrying red blood; the fin-

FIG. 52.

EMBRYO OF THREE MONTHS ENCLOSED IN THE AMNION.

gers and toes are well defined. The length of the embryo is now about four inches, and its weight two ounces and a half. (*Fig.* 52.)

At four months the embryo is perfect. After this period it is called the fœtus. From this time, the head and liver, instead of increasing, decrease in size; the brain and spinal marrow become more consistent, while a small quantity of meconium collects in the bowels. The muscular system also is now quite distinct, and the fœtus perceptibly moves. Length about eight inches; weight from seven to eight ounces. (*Fig.* 53.)

FIG. 53.

FŒTUS AT THE AGE OF FOUR MONTHS.

At five months, or one hundred and fifty days, the muscular system is well marked and the movements of the child can no longer be doubted. The lungs

FIG. 54.

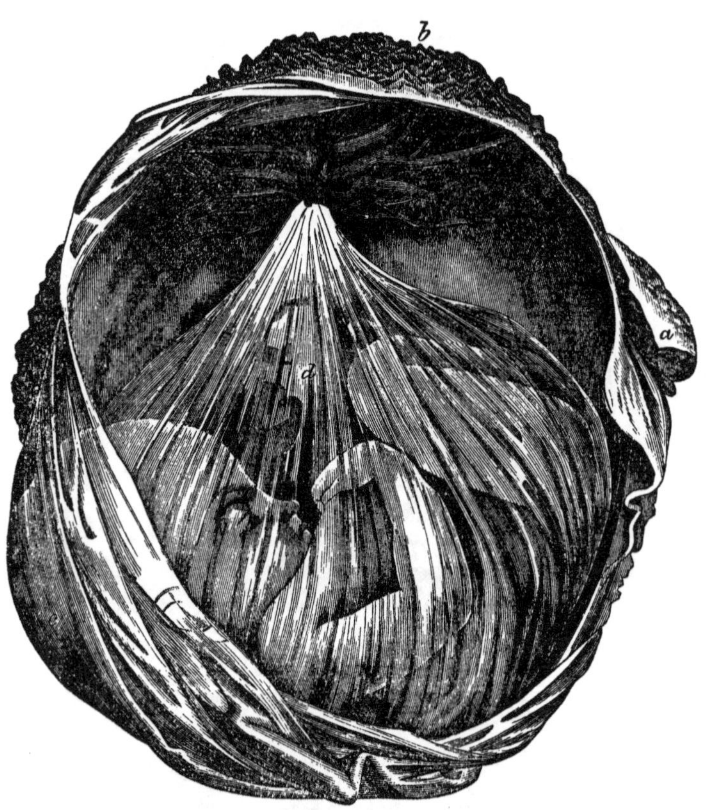


Fœtus at the age of five months, with the placenta and membranes. The chorion is laid open to exhibit the fœtus enclosed in the amnion. The amnion is attached to the centre of the internal surface of the placenta, through which the cord passes. The external surface of the placenta is seen covered by the chorion and decidua.

are developed and may be distended to a certain extent. The meconium passes through the greater portion of the intestinal canal. The whole form of the child is now perfectly distinct; length ten inches; weight one pound. No evidence yet of the intellectual functions. (*Fig.* 54.)

At the sixth month, or one hundred and eighty days, down makes its appearance upon the head, and the nails are distinguishable. The whole form of the child is more distinct; length twelve inches, weight two pounds.

At the seventh month, or two hundred and ten days, the nails are formed; hair is seen on the head; the testicles descend into the scrotum; bones are completely formed, and the features well developed. A child born at this period can cry, breathe and suck. The intellectual functions are still undeveloped, but the senses are susceptible of slight impressions. Length fourteen inches; weight three pounds. (*Fig.* 55.)

At eight months the fœtus gains strength and volume; the form of each part is being more fully perfected. Length sixteen inches; weight four pounds. Intellectual faculties still undeveloped, but the senses are more acute.

Nine months or forty weeks is the natural period of gestation, involving the birth of a healthy child. The organs, at this period, have acquired the growth that is necessary to support life. The motions of the child are lively and quick; the heart pulsates rapidly, and the blood circulates freely; the blood is rich and abundant: the alimentary canal, which has had heretofore no perceptible action, now contracts upon the meconium, and causes it to escape by the anus,

FIG. 55.

FŒTUS OF SEVEN MONTHS.

The length is eighteen inches; weight six to eight pounds. Intellectual faculties still in abeyance; senses quite acute. The child is sensible to pain, and

Fig. 56.

FŒTUS AT THE AGE OF NINE MONTHS, OR THE FULL PERIOD OF GESTATION

cries from hunger and cold; while warmth, nursing, and gentle rocking, puts it to sleep. (*Fig.* 56.)

## C. THE PLACENTA.

The formation of the placenta and its attachment to the walls of the uterus, have been already described. It is by such union that the child obtains its nourishment from the mother.

In pregnancy, the placenta is a spongy, cellular, vascular mass—generally circular with flattened sides. It is about one inch in thickness, and from seven to eight inches broad; its weight, with the cord, from twelve to fourteen ounces. The uterine face of the placenta adheres to the walls of the uterus during the whole of pregnancy, generally to the fundus, though in rare instances it is found attached over the mouth of the womb. When the latter is the case, the placenta will be delivered before the child. If labor is slow, the child cannot survive, from the fact that the connection with the mother is cast off. There is also great danger of hemorrhage. When the placenta presents, death may result from it, especially if the labor is prolonged. The umbilical cord is generally inserted near the centre of the placenta. (*Fig.* 61.) The color of the cord is dark red, while it, (the cord) is composed principally of blood-vessels and fibrous tissue—the latter uniting the blood-vessels in a compact mass. Every fœtus has a placenta; if there be twins, there will be two placentas united by their edges. There will also be two cords in such cases. Should there be six or eight children—there being such instances on record—there will be a placenta for each. So with every number of children. In this way the circulation of each child is distinct.

## D. THE UMBILICAL CORD.

The umbilical cord is very short at the beginning of pregnancy, and is composed of the umbilical arteries and veins. The length at parturition is from eighteen to twenty-four inches. It extends from the umbilicus of the child to the placenta, and is divided at birth. (*Fig.* 61.)

## E. NUTRITION AND CIRCULATION OF THE FŒTUS.

It is no longer doubted that the fœtus is nourished by the fluids of the mother, through the placenta and umbilical cord.

It has been frequently asserted that the infant is nourished by sucking the fluids that inclose it, and that these, on entering the stomach, are subject to the laws of digestion and assimilation, and thus become elements of nutrition to the fœtus. This hypothesis is not well sustained. From analysis of the liquid amnii, it is found that it does not possess the elements necessary for nutrition. At the end of pregnancy, they are often turbid and purulent. Sometimes the membranes are ruptured for several weeks before labor, and the water eliminated. Such being the case, the child could not live, which fact would go to overthrow the theory heretofore entertained, as stated in the present connection.

It has also been supposed that the fœtus is nourished by absorption through the skin. As the waters have not the necessary qualities of nutrition, this cannot be correct.

We should look upon the fœtus during pregnancy as an offshoot of the parent, and nourished as such through the medium of the blood of the mother. When it arrives at maturity, it is thrown off, and is in a condition to subsist without this connection or union. Yet it still depends, in a measure, upon the mother for support or nourishment.

The circulation of the fœtus before birth being different in several respects from what it is afterward, it will not be uninteresting to give a brief description of it here.

The lungs of the fœtus cannot perform their office—which is the elimination of carbonic acid and the reception of the oxygen of the air. Neither can the digestive and assimilating organs perform their office. Therefore the mother must furnish the necessary fluids for nutrition. This is done through the umbilical vein. This vein arises in the placenta and passes direct to the umbilicus, without communicating with the umbilical artery. It then penetrates into the abdomen, and passes directly into the great fissure of the liver, where it gives off two twigs, one for the right lobe and the other for the left lobe of that organ. Another portion of the blood is carried through the ductus venosus to the ascending vena cava. The blood that passes through the liver is also conveyed to the ascending vena cava, through the hepatic veins. The ascending vena cava conveys the blood into the right auricle of the heart, where it becomes mixed with the blood from the descending vena cava, which collects the blood from the head, neck and upper extremities.

The blood from the ascending vena cava is directed through the foramen ovale into the left auricle, while the blood of the descending vena cava is directed into the right ventrical. When the ventricles of the heart centract, the arterial blood which the left contains is propelled into the ascending aorta, and supplies the branches that proceed to the head and upper extremities before it undergoes any admixture; whilst the venous blood contained in the right ventricle is forced through the pulmonary artery and ductus arteriosus into the descending aorta, mingling with the arterial current which that vessel previously contained, and thus passing to the trunk and lower extremities. Hence the head and superior extremities, whose development is required to be in advance of that of the lower, are supplied with blood, nearly as pure as that which returns from the placenta; whilst the rest of the body receives a mixture of this with what has previously circulated through the system, and of this mixture a portion is transmitted to the placenta through the umbilical artery, to be removed by coming into relation with the maternal blood. (*Fig.* 61.)

After birth, a most remarkable change takes place in the circulation of the child. As soon as the air enters the lungs, respiration is established—the blood which was before black now becoming red and light. The blood returns for the first time through the pulmonary veins into the left auricle, depressing the valve of the foramen ovale, and thus preventing the blood from passing through into the right auricle. It is carried from the left auricle into the left ventricle, and thence into the aorta to be distributed to the whole system.

During pregnancy, the blood at the lower part of the aorta, at its bifurcation, proceeded through the umbilical arteries. After birth, instead of passing through these, (which have become obliterated), it is sent into the iliac arteries, and abundantly distributed to the lower extremities. The blueness of children after birth is occasioned by the opening of the foramina ovale not being closed, causing a mingling of the venous and arterial blood. When this is obliterated, the blueness disappears.

It has been already stated that the weight of a full-grown child at birth is from six to eight pounds. When the weight is less than five pounds, the child is considered delicate, feeble, or sickly, and will be raised with difficulty. If the weight be above eight pounds, the child is considered large, which causes labor to be slow and sometimes difficult, requiring artificial assistance.

## F. SIGNS OF PREGNANCY.

Pregnancy begins immediately after conception, and terminates by delivery of the fœtus at parturition.

The duration of pregnancy is nine months, or forty weeks. The period may be retarded or advanced some days. Births may occur at the thirty-sixth week, or the period of gestation may be extended to

FIG. 57.

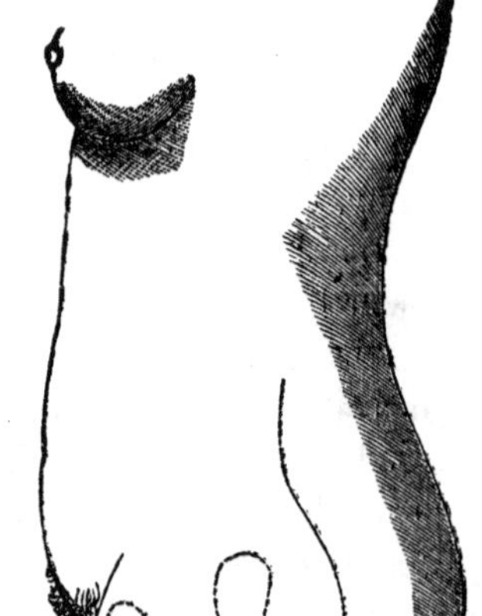

POSITION AND SIZE OF THE UNIMPREGNATED UTERUS.

the *forty-fifth* week. There are cases of the kind on record, and been subject of medico-legal investigation and proof.

The signs of pregnancy are usually divided into the *presumptive*, or rational, and the *positive*, or sensible.

The presumptive or rational signs are those that lead to a suspicion that a female is pregnant. These are numerous, the principal ones being as follows:—Suppression of the menses, discolorations of the areola of the breast, its brownish appearance, swelling of the breast, and dribblings from the nipple, peculiar tastes

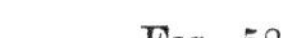

FIG. 58.

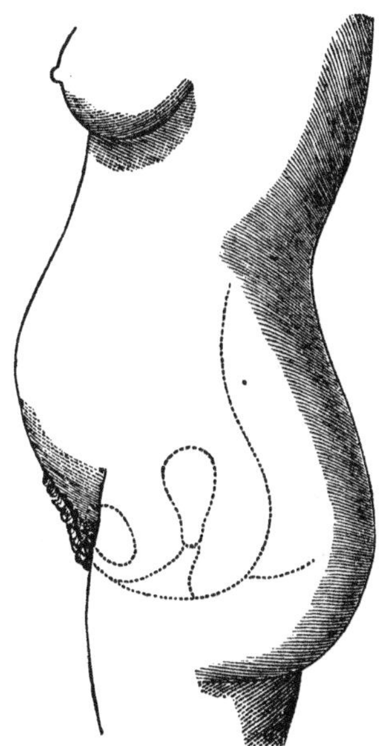

POSITION AND SIZE OF THE IMPREGNATED UTERUS, OF THE PERIOD OF THREE MONTHS.

and inclinations, paleness of countenance (which is peculiar to some women), sickness of stomach, particularly on rising in the morning. All of these are symptoms of pregnancy, but are not *positive*, as they occur from other causes.

The *positive* or sensible signs of pregnancy, are change of the abdomen, and quickening, which takes place about the fourth month. At the third month, the abdomen is slightly enlarged, by the uterus pressing back the intestines. At the fourth month the uterus rises some two or three fingers above the rim of the pelvis, while, at times, the motion of the child

Fig. 59.

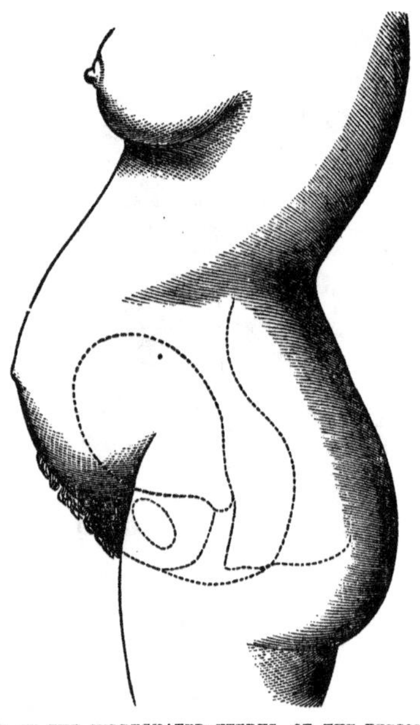

POSITION AND SIZE OF THE IMPREGNATED UTERUS, OF THE PERIOD OF SIX MONTHS.

may be felt. At this period an examination per vagina may detect the child in the womb. At the end of the fifth month there are signs that settle all doubt. The base of the uterus is now found within two fingers of the umbilicus. At the end of six months it is two inches above the umbilicus; the head of the child may be felt without difficulty, as well as the action of the heart. At the end of the seventh month the uterus is still higher, and entered the epigastric region. During the eighth month it occupies very nearly the whole of this location. At the close of the ninth month, instead of being still higher up, as

FIG. 60.

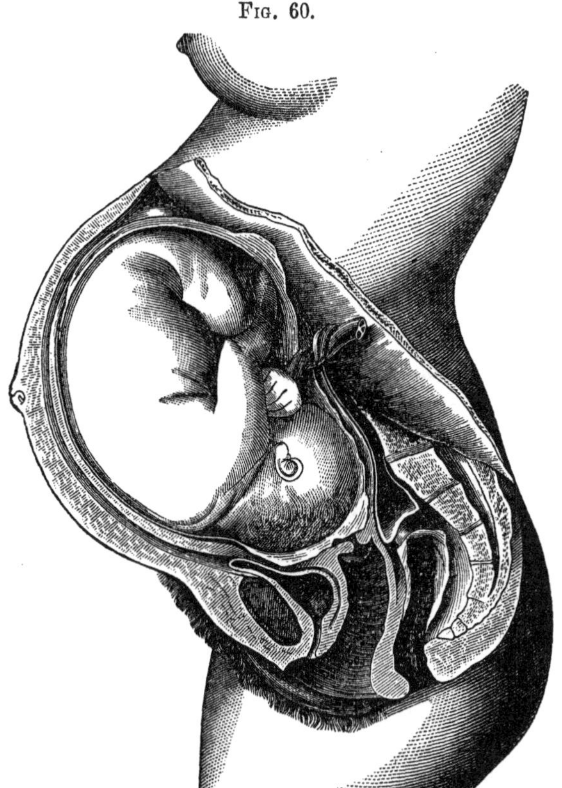

PERIOD OF NINE MONTHS, WITH THE NATURAL POSITION OF THE CHILD.

might be naturally expected, it is found depressed to near the umbilical region. The child's head becoming heavier it is carried down into the pelvis. For a more tangible idea of the size and position of the womb during the various months of gestation, the reader is referred to *Figs.* 57, 58, 59 and 60.

# CHAPTER XIII.

## OF LABOR.

Labor is divided according to the period in which it occurs.

If it takes place before the fifteenth day, it is called *afflux*. Before the seventh month, *abortion*. From the seventh to the ninth month, *premature labor*. At nine months, it is *natural labor*.

### A.—SYMPTOMS OF LABOR.

These are divided into two heads:

1. Those symptoms which indicate labor.
2. Those when the process of labor has commenced.

*a.* Symptoms of Approaching Labor.—About the middle of the eighth month, the uterus has attained its height in the abdomen. Two weeks later it has decreased or fallen back or down to where it was at the beginning of the eighth month. Sometimes this diminution is sudden, occurring in one or two nights, so that the female is surprised to find herself so much smaller on rising in the morning. This diminution is occasioned by the slow and passive contraction of the uterus, and is regarded as a favorable symptom. It is common for females to remark, under such circumstances, that they feel much lighter and more active than for several weeks previous.

Another evidence of the approach of labor, is a relaxation of the vagina and external organs of generation, with an increased moisture in and about the parts. These symptoms are favorable, and indicate that Nature is preparing for the process of parturition.

A strong indication of approaching labor, also, is anxiety and fidgetiness. This is strikingly manifested in the lower animals. In the cat there is observed great distress one or two days previous to the time; but such uneasiness does not arise from pain. Women, however, has her intellect to fortify her, and religion to soothe and comfort her, and to quiet all needless alarm or apprehension of danger.

*b.*—SYMPTOMS THAT LABOR HAS COMMENCED.—There is frequent inclination to pass urine and fæces, owing to the irritation of the bladder and rectum, as a result of a sympathy between them by their nervous connections. Sometimes the desire to urinate occurs every ten or fifteen minutes. This cannot be obviated by remedies. When the neck of the uterus, however, is sufficiently dilated for the head to occupy the cavity of the pelvis, these symptoms subside. If labor be slow and the symptoms distressing, an enema of laudanum and starch may be used. Take from forty to sixty drops of laudanum and half a pint of thin starch—inject per rectum and retain as long as possible.

Nausea and vomiting are also symptoms of the commencement of labor. They are to be regarded as highly favorable. Labor may be prolonged several hours owing to a tense os uteri.

If sickness and vomiting occur, or be induced by the physician, the os becomes relaxed and there is no further retardation. In ordinary cases the vomiting should not be checked. If it be distressing to the patient, and is not necessary for relaxation, or continue after delivery, it will be proper to ameliorate the same. The annexed formula will generally accomplish the purpose:—

℞ Tinct. aconite, *fol*....f ʒ ssj.
Tinct. opii.......... ʒ ij.
Tint. camphora..... ʒ iij.
Simple syrup....... ℥ iv.

Take one teaspoonful every one or two hours, so long as the nausea continues. If the vomiting be severe, repeat the dose every half hour till partially relieved; then every one or two hours afterward. Laudanum injection by the rectum may also be used: sixty drops to one pint of starch. The sickness being occasioned by the sympathy of the womb, the laudanum will annul the sympathy and relieve the sickness. If there be much prostration and weakness at pit of the stomach from the effects of vomiting, a mustard plaster may be applied to the stomach, and some port wine made into a sangaree taken as a drink.

Vomiting is of great benefit in many cases. In fact it would be difficult in many instances of protracted labor, to relax the os uteri without such provision of Nature. If allowed, however, to progress too far, it may result in great injury. Therefore great discrimination will be required on the part of the attendants. The pulse should be watched and the matter vomited be inspected. Such matter is often a good guide. In unfavorable cases, it is fœtid, dark-colored, of a greenish cast, or resembling what is thrown up in the latter stage of typhus fever, having the appearance of coffee-grounds.

Sometimes at the commencement of labor, there will be a chilliness sufficient to cause the teeth to chatter and the bed to shake. This is also occasioned by the dilation of the os uteri. When this is accomplished, the chilliness subsides. All that is necessary to be done is to add a blanket or two to the body or bed.

Another symptom is a discharge of a glazy substance from the vagina, called by nurses the *show.* This discharge is a mixture of the mucos secretions of the neck of the uterus and the lining membrane of the vagina with a little blood that exudes from the vessels of the os uteri. It may make its appearance either with or without pain.

The most prominent symptoms of labor are the appearance of labor-pains which are occasioned by the contraction of the muscular tissue of the uterus. The fœtus, after it has matured and become fitted for an independent existence, may be viewed as a ripe fruit upon the stem. As such it is placed in the position of a foreign body to the uterus, or as food to the alimentary canal. In the same manner as food is propelled outward by peristaltic action, so is the fœtus ejected by a series of peristaltic contractions of the muscular tissues of the uterus.

The pain is occasioned by the sensitiveness of the uterus—increased by the contraction and pressure of the child against the resisting os uteri and by the dilatation or enlargement of the vagina during the passage of the child. The pain is proportionate to the tonicity or resistance of the uterus. In some intances, it is so enlarged, that the child is nearly born before labor pains are experienced. In other cases the pain is from the commencement to the termination of labor. In the first instances, only a slight contraction is necessary to overcome the relaxation of the os uteri; while a series of powerful contractions are requisite in the latter.

Labor pains may be readily modified by the administration of opiates, either by the medium of the stomach or injections into the rectum, and by inhalations of ether or chloroform, without retarding labor. There is no objection to the use of ether or chloroform, provided they are not pushed too far, or where there is no organic disease of the lungs or heart.

Labor pains are different from ordinary pains. They are of a *grinding* or *cutting* character, and responded to by a moaning or grumbling noise on the part of the patient. During the pain the female supports herself in some way, and bears down with some degree of force. On the dilatation of the os uteri, and when a portion of the child is passed into the vagina; the pains become of a more *forcing* character causing the patient to hold her breath and assist in the effort for its expulsion. When the child's head is pressing forcibly against the perineum, and is about to be delivered, the bearing down and pain is so strong and acute, as to cause the patient to give a loud shriek or wild cry.

*Spurious Pains.*—Toward the latter end of gestation there are pains in the loins and bowels, resembling labor pains, but not connected with uterine action. These are called false or spurious pains. They are occasioned by spasmodic action of the diaphragm and abdominal muscle, causing the female to bear down and imagine that she has labor pains.

Sometimes during these pains there is considerable discharge from the glands of the os uteri or vagina; or there may be a sudden gush of urine, causing the female to think the membranes have bursted and that the liquor amnii has been discharged.

Spurious pains may continue at intervals for weeks before the commencement of labor. They generally occur at night, and thus annoy the patient and prevent sleep. It is important to be able to distinguish spurious pains and arrest them.

*Diagnosis of False Pains.*—They are irregular in their return and duration, and usually confined to the abdomen and the muscles of the back; while *true* pains commence in the lower part of the loins and extend to the abdomen and thighs. False pains continually shift from the back to the sides or some part of the abdomen. True pains, at the commencement of labor, are weak, of short duration, and the intervals long between; they increase in frequency as labor progresses. True pains may also be distinguished by placing the hand over the abdomen. The structure will then become firmer, harder and denser with every pain. This will not always be the case; for the contraction of the uterine walls may be so slow and gradual as not to be felt by the hand. All doubts, however, may be settled by an examination *per vaginam.* If the examination be made, and the os uteri be found slightly open; or if the edges are stretched like a cord, or the membranes are tense and pressed down during each pain, and again relax after the pain subside, all this will be a sure indication of true labor-pains.

On the contrary, if the os uteri be completely closed and remain so during the pain and bearing down, it will indicate false pains.

If there be any doubt in the matter, it may be settled by an examination of the abdomen and os uteri. If this be not done, unnecessary trouble, watching, and loss of rest, may exhaust the patience and strength of the patient.

Spurious pains frequently mislead the physician, and cause him a large amount of unnecessary delay and trouble. When he can decide that they are spurious, he should at once set about removing them, in order to prevent the strength of the patient becoming exhausted by them.

*Treatment.*—The position that is most comfortable should be taken. If the bowels are constipated, they should be opened by purgative medicine, or ar enemata prepared as follows:—

℞ Water, lukewarm,....................1 pint.
Common salt,......................2 teaspoonsful.
Common molasses,...................2 tablespoonsful.

Mix together and inject. After the bowels are

opened, an opiate should be administered by the stomach or the rectum.

If by the stomach, a small teaspoonful of paregoric may be given, and repeated every two hours, if relief is not afforded. Or the prescription on page 276 may be substituted.

It should be borne in mind, that, in case of constipation, if the bowels are not freely moved, the opiates may produce more injury than good—particularly if the bowels are the cause of the difficulty. Should the pains be confined to the back, thighs, and abdomen, a liniment may be applied with the hand—care being taken in rubbing it over the abdomen, as friction over the uterus tends to bring on contraction.

The following is one of the best liniments for this purpose:—

℞ Aqua ammonia, } *a*........................℥ij.
Tinct. opii., }
Soap liniment,.............................℥j.

Keep well corked, and shake before using.

## B. LABOR.

Labor is usually divided into several classes, each class being again divided. The most simple classification that can be given is the following:—

*a*. Natural.—This is when the child's head presents, and delivery is effected in twenty-four hours from the commencement of labor.

*b*. Difficult.—The head also presents, but the time is extended. In some cases instruments will be required to deliver the child.

*c*. Preternatural.—This form of labor includes

those cases where some part of the body presents, and not the head. The presentation may be feet, knees, breech, back, belly, side, shoulder, arm, or hand.

*d.* Complex.—This class of labor embraces all of the foregoing presentations, or where there are complicated and embarrassing circumstances, such as hemorrhage, convulsions, fainting, rupture of the bladder, or uterus, etc.

It is not the object of this work to instruct in all the details of labor—neither would it be necessary, if space permitted. The female should always employ some skillful physician, during the latter part of gestation, to guarantee a safe and easy delivery.

There are some cases, however, where labor is so speedy, that there is no time to procure a physician. All that will be necessary in such an emergency, is for the person in attendance to support the perineum when the child's head presses forcibly against it, and when it has passed, to sustain it until the rest of the body is delivered, which may be after or one more strong pains or efforts at expulsion. It should also be observed that the cord is not around the child's neck, otherwise it might retard labor and jeopardize the life of the child.

When the babe is born, it should be removed five or six inches from the mother, or to the length of the cord, without stretching it or tearing it away from its attachments, or inverting the uterus. The cord should now be tied with nine or ten strands of thread of sufficient thickness not to break, or to cut the cord in tying. If the thread be too thick, it may not compress the artery sufficient to prevent hemorrhage after the cord is cut. Two ligatures should be used—one to be tied about two inches, or three fingers breadth, from the child's navel, and secured by a double knot; the other about four inches from the child, and secured in the same way by a double knot.

The ligature is sometimes placed too near the umbilicus, which may enclose a portion of the intestine, as it sometimes protrudes in such a way. Occasionally it may be necessary to throw a second ligature around the cord, on account of the first not being drawn sufficiently tight. Having thus secured the cord in two places with two strong ligatures, the next thing to be done is to cut the cord with a pair of sharp scissors between the ligatures. (*Fig.* 61.) Care must be observed not to cut off any of the child's fingers or toes, as has been done by parties calling themselves, or considered, skillful physicians!

One point especially is to be observed before the cord is tied. The child should breathe or cry. This will be evidence that the functions have commenced action, and that the child is capable of subsisting independent of the placental relation that existed during fœtal life.

Sometimes the child at birth shows no signs of life, and it may be difficult to determine whether it be dead or not. Such condition of the child may depend on pressure on the head or on the cord during labor, or it may result from loss of blood by the mother during travail or parturition. To ascertain if the babe be dead or not, place the hand over the heart; if a tremulous sensation is observed in the organ, there is a possibility of saving the child. Sometimes a few small smacks upon its buttocks are sufficient

FIG. 61.

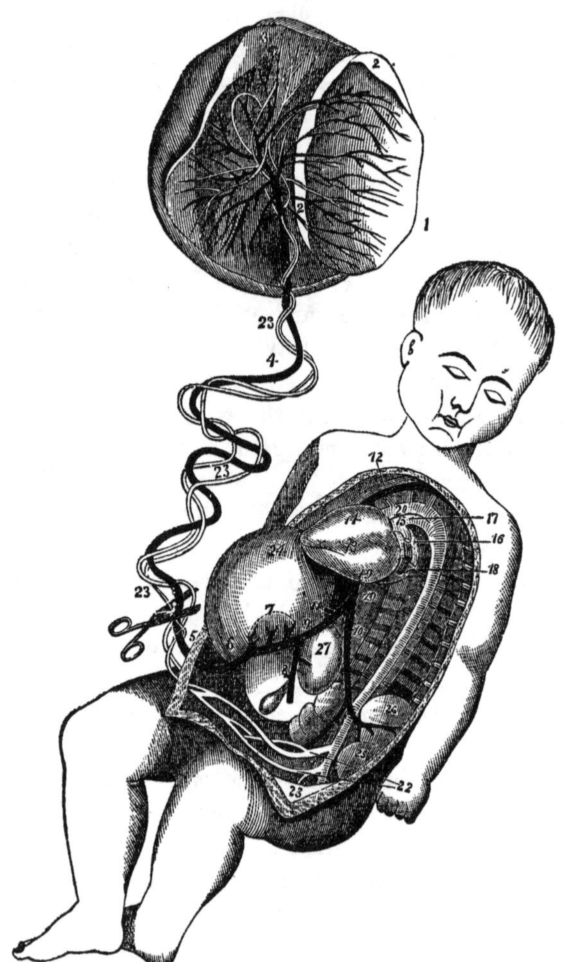


PLAN OF FŒTAL CIRCULATION. (*From Morton.*)

1, placenta; 2, amnion; 3, chorion; 4, 5, umbilical vein; 6, its passage through the liver; 7, its hepatic branches; 8, vena portarum; 9, ductus venosus; 10, ascending vena cava; 11, hepatic vein; 12, descending vena cava; 13, heart turned upon its anterior side; 14, right ventricle; 15, pulmonary artery; 16, left pulmonary artery; 17, ductus arteriosus; 18, left pulmonary veins, opening to left auricle; 19, left ventricle; 20, arch of the aorta; 21, descending aorta; 22, primitive iliac arteries; 23, umbilical arteries; 24, liver, turned up; 25, kidney; 26, renal capsule; 27, lobulus spigelii.

to bring forth a sob, which will end in a cry. If this should not be effectual, it should be at once placed in warm water, at the temperature of blood heat, or 98°. This is often sufficient to rouse the animation of the child.

After the child has been in the water a few minutes without reviving, or if the heart seems to be growing weaker, it should immediately be taken from the warm bath, wiped dry, placed in a warm flannel or blanket, and artificial respiration attempted. The *modus operandi* of this is as follows:—Press the thumb and fore-finger upon the nostril so as to close them; then place your lips to those of the child and blow the breath into its mouth and lungs. The chest is also to be compressed to expel the air thus introduced. Keep up this artificial respiration for some time, provided there be any evidence of vitality. By way of cleanliness, a piece of flannel may be spread over the child's mouth, and the breathing performed through it. If life manifests itself very slowly, the child should be rubbed with alcohol or whiskey made luke-warm. A drop or two of the liquor may also be applied to the back part of the throat or glottis with the finger. So long as there is action of the heart, we should persevere to save the child. Sometimes a dash of cold water in the face, or a slight irritant to the nostrils, will arouse the child when other more apparently vigorous means have failed. When the stupor or torpidity is overcome, a proper disposition must be made of the bantling.

*Removal of the Placenta.*—As a slight mismanagement in the removal of the placenta may result in injury, it will be best to leave it to the judgment of the physician. If he be not at hand, nor likely soon to be present, the hand of the nurse, or other person, should be passed over the patient's abdomen, to ascertain if there be a second child. This being done, a reasonable time should be allowed for the uterus to expel the placenta, and not pull and jerk at it, as is too often done by the attending physician. In order to promote contraction and facilitate the expulsion of the placenta, slight friction should be made over the abdomen, particularly if there be much hemorrhage or flooding. A slight twisting of the cord and gentle traction of it, may be sufficient to bring it away from the vagina; but this must not be attempted so long as it remains in the womb, for fear of hemorrhage.

Should the placenta not come away soon after the delivery of the child, the wet cloths and napkins must be removed, and warm ones placed under the nips, while a blanket or something of the kind should be thrown over the patient to prevent a "creep" or chill, after the profuse perspiration usually concomitant of delivery. The attention of the nurse should be directed solely to the mother until the placenta is removed; nor should the physician, under any circumstance, leave the house until this is effected, and the condition of the patient ascertained.

Should the patient be weak, and there be symptoms of faintness, a little warm wine and water or cordial may be administered—not otherwise. When the placenta has been removed, one or two warm napkins must be gently laid under the hips and between the thighs, in order to collect the sanguineous discharge, while the patient should be placed in a proper position in bed and made comfortable.

*After Treatment.*—When the flooding has entirely subsided, the woman's garments must be quickly changed, and herself be placed in some comfortable position, in a darkened room, to induce sleep, and kept from being disturbed by her anxious friends. The nurse, or some one accustomed to do such things, should apply a bandage to brace the bowels and give support to the abdominal muscles, in order to prevent the distress and faintiness usually attendant upon the removal of the pressure of the child. The bandage also assists in stimulating the uterus to contract and prevent hemorrhage. It should extend from the pubes to the ensiform cartilage, or to the bottom of the ribs.

It is customary to administer some medicine after delivery, with a view to quiet the nervous system and induce sleep. Some physicians are in the habit of giving large doses of laudanum. This must act injuriously by preventing the contractions of the uterus, which are necessary, in order to restore it to its former condition and to prevent hemorrhage. A small dose of laudanum, say five to eight drops, with a few drops of camphor, every two or three hours, is not objectionable. The following formula is one of the best that can be used, allaying inflammation and preventing fever.

℞ Tinct. Aconite, *fol*,............gtt. xxx.
Camphor water,....................℥j.
Laudanum,.........................ʒj.
Simple syrup,.....................℥j.

Dose—One teaspoonful in a wine-glass of sweetened water every two hours.

*Diet.*—The diet of the patient for three or four days should be of the plainest kind—such as tea, toast, or farinaceous food. On the third day, more nourishing aliment, as beef-tea or chicken broth, may be allowed, provided the bowels have been freely opened and no unfavorable symptoms have intervened. From this time the diet may be increased gradually to more substantial food.

The horizontal position should be strictly maintained for the first week. During this time she may be changed from one side of the bed to the other, in order to relieve her and adjust the couch; but she must not sit up while the bed is being made. After a week or nine days she may be up and down, as it suits her feelings, care being observed not to remain up until fatigued. In the course of two weeks or two weeks and a half, the uterus will regain its former unpregnated size, when the patient may go out of her room, still observing care not to expose herself.

## C. INFANT AFTER BIRTH.

It is presumed that there are always females in attendance in labor, who know what should be done with the child after delivery. It will not be necessary, therefore, to go into detail in this regard. It will be sufficient to say that care should be taken to remove the secretions from the mouth and nostrils, if they are sufficient to obstruct its breathing.

## CHAPTER XIV.

### LACTATION.

WHEN delivery takes place, the functions of the genital organs cease, and the lively irritation that existed in them is transferred to the mammæ for the preservation of the child. To accomplish this, a saccharine and very nutritious fluid is secreted by the mammæ, which escapes by a slight suction of the child or by a slight titilation of the organ. This is called *Lactation.*

### A. STRUCTURE OF MAMMÆ.

At puberty in the female, the mammæ, or breasts, increase rapidly in size, and assume a firmness and plumpness, that disappear in those who have borne children and nursed their offspring.

The mammæ are composed of a number of glands with their ducts, in the centre of which they terminate in a prominence called the nipple, which is surrounded by an areolar, or a small, red or brown circle. In young females it is usually of a delicate red, but in females who have borne children it is of a brown color The whole is covered with a thin, tender and soft skin.

If we divide the mammæ of a female lately confined through the centre of the nipple, we will find the structure arranged in a very simple manner. The secreting portions consists of minute cells, which, when distended with milk, are no larger than the smallest pin's head, and are scarcely visible to the naked eye. They are collected into groups, from which the milk tubes arise. These tubes increase in size as they approach the nipple, by the addition of other glands, whose minute ducts terminate in them. (*Fig.* 62.) These ducts, as they approach the nipple, terminate in some fifteen or twenty larger ducts, and are so contracted at their orifice as only to admit a small-sized bristle. The function of these glands is to secrete milk from the blood. According to *Simon*, the lacteal secretion is composed of the following ingredients :—

| | |
|---|---|
| Water, | 88.06 |
| Caseine, | 3.70 |
| Sugar, | 4.54 |
| Butter, | 3.40 |
| Salts, etc., | 0.30 |
| | 100.00 |

The milk which is secreted the first few days after child-birth is called *Colostrum*, being very different from ordinary milk, and possessing purgative properties. It is of a yellow color and viscous consistency It contains a large amount of milk globules, which give a thick layer of cream on top if allowed to stand a short time. The milk, from day to day, undergoes change, and at the end of twenty-four days nas passed from the condition of colostrum to milk of the ordinary character.

FIG. 62

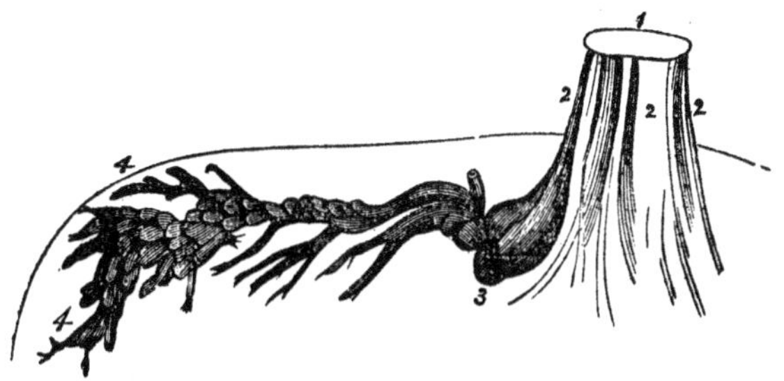


LACTIFEROUS MAMMARY GLANDS. (*From Sir A. Cooper.*)

1, Orifice of the nipple; 2, 2, 2, terminal extremity of lactiferous ducts of the nipple; 3, dilatation of the ducts at the base of the nipple; 4, 4, origin of the ducts in the substance of the gland.

The colostrum does not uniformly disappear in this time — in some it is earlier, and in others later. *Nasse* states that it disappears sooner in women who have borne many children than in those who have had but a single child. The persistence of the colostrum may continue in the milk without exhibiting any outward appearance, and can only be detected by the microscope and by the influence which it has upon the child, impairing its health and strength.

When the milk of the mother does not seem to agree with the child, or it fails in its health and strength without any visible cause, the milk should be examined with a microscope, and if colostrum be detected, a wet-nurse should be immediately obtained. It has been observed by *Donne* that milk may entirely lose the character of colostrum and again pass into that state at any time during lactation. He has also discovered that one breast may secrete colostrum, and the other be entirely free from it. When such is the case the mother should cease nursing, as it indicates a diseased condition of the mammary glands, or a vitiated condition of her blood.

It has also been discovered that if milk be allowed to remain too long in the breasts, it becomes thin and watery. This fact is important in some cases —as when the milk is too rich, it may be allowed to remain in the breast until it becomes more adapted to the requirements of the child.

In some females, during menstruation, the milk undergoes a change by increasing the colostrum, which subsides on the cessation of the catamenial flow.

Milk is frequently found in the breasts of unmarried females, and always in pregnant women before confinement. In all these cases it contains a large quantity of colostrum, similar to what it is after delivery. Not only is milk found in young unmarried females, but in infants and young children of both sexes. In such cases it presents all the appearance of ordinary milk with some colostrum.

### B. SIGNS OF GOOD MILK.

The richness and goodness of milk will depend upon the amount of globules it contains. As these globules are not distinctly visible to the naked eye, the use of the microscope will best detect the quality of the milk. The opacity of the milk will indicate, in some degree, to the naked eye, the quantity of globules. Thus milk that is white and opaque is rich in globules; that which is watery and transparent is of poor quality.

The milk of the ass may be known by its watery aspect, and by its bluish tint. That of the goat by its opacity and richness. The following is an analysis of the milk of woman, the cow, the goat, and the ass :—*

| | *Woman.* | *Cow.* | *Goat* | *Ass.* |
|---|---|---|---|---|
| Butter, | 8.97 | 2.68 | 4.56 | 1.29 |
| Sugar, | 1.20 | 5.68 | 9.12 | 6.29 |
| Caseine, | 1.93 | 8.95 | 4.38 | 1.95 |
| Water, | 87.90 | 84.69 | 81.94 | 90.98 |
| | 100 | 100 | 100 | 100 |

It will be seen that the milk of woman is richest in butter, while that of the ass contains the least. Butter is considered the principal ingredient of milk, which may vary very much in different females and animals. The milk of the goat is next to that of woman's in respect to its nourishing qualities. This is important to be known, as goat's milk is a good substitute for the impoverished milk of a mother. It answers better than cow's milk, in containing less caseine, which disagrees with some children. A good substitute for a mother's milk, is one-third of good cream and two-thirds of cow's milk boiled together This answers exceedingly well in marasmus, especially if a few drops of good Port wine in water be given three or four times a day to the child. In such cases, also, the child should be bathed night and morning with luke-warm whiskey.

The relative proportions of the ingredients of milk will vary very much with diet. Hence females who

* Cours de Microscopie of Donne.

are nursing and have poor milk, should live on rich food, and take a glass of good beer or porter two or three times a day. Milk is sometimes wonderfully enriched by the use of chocolate and coffee, particularly the former.

Should cow's milk be selected, it should always be from the same cow, and boiled before given to the child. It should be pure and unadulterated. The milk of commerce is often sophisticated in order to give it color and opacity. The substances used for such purpose, are chalk, flour, starch, the brains of sheep and water—the latter very commonly.

A substitute for milk, that does not disagree with a babe, is a preparation recommended by Dr. Meigs of Philadelphia, namely:—To a piece of gelatine two inches square, add one pint of cold water, and let it soak for half an hour. Then add two teaspoonsful of arrow-root, three tablespoonsful of cow's milk and two of cream, with a small lump of white sugar, and let the whole come to a gentle boil. As the child increases in age and strength, the milk may be increased.

*Occurrences of Medicines, Poisons, etc. in Milk.*—From the rapidity with which milk is secreted from the blood, it is not surprising that chemical matters existing in the circulation of the mother should have an influence on the lacteal secretion. Medicines and various articles of food have been detected in the milk a few minutes after they had been taken into the stomach. Coloring matter, turpentine, garlic, nitrate of potash, and other salts, have been thus discovered. It is of the utmost importance for mothers and nurses to know this fact—for a purgative or narcotic is apt to affect the child more powerfully than the mother. There are many cases on record, showing that powerful doses of medicines taken by the mother have either jeopardized or destroyed the life of the child.

## C.—INFLUENCE OF MIND ON THE SECRETIONS OF MILK.

All glandular secretions are influenced by emotions of the mind. This is noticed in the flow of saliva on thinking of food, particularly that of a savory character, or in the flow of lachrymal secretions, as in crying from excitement of the emotions, whether of joy or grief.

It is well known that the secretion of milk is increased by the mind dwelling on the offspring, and also at the sight of the infant. Strong desire to furnish milk will cause an increased flow of blood to the glands. Milk has been known to be secreted in old women, young girls, and even men, by such causes. In fact, there is no secretion of the body so easily influenced. The following case is recorded by Sir A. Cooper in his excellent work on the Breast.

"This case occurred in a robust, sanguine soldier, twenty-two years old. At the age of eighteen, he often felt a pricking sensation in his breasts, and slight periodic colic. About a year later, he observed after each occurrence of such symptoms, a slight swelling of, and a milky discharge from, the mammæ; and during work, his shirt was several times bewetted with the fluid. When in the hospital for acute rheumatism, a considerable quantity of milk was found to be secreted. On examining the breasts and nipples, the latter was found highly red, erectile, somewhat cracked at the apices, and much higher than in man generally, and surrounded by a somewhat darker areola, through which a subjacent vascular net-work could be seen. On pressing the papillæ, two or three fine streams of milk would jet out of the minute orifices; it had a bluish-white color and a very sweet taste. The secretion was consistent, but increased at various periods, especially at night, producing somewhat painful sensations till it was evacuated. The usual quantity was from half an ounce to an ounce daily, but sometimes not more than two or three drachms daily. On one occasion a wine glassful was drawn off, and for the fortnight that he was under observation, ten or eleven ounces were secreted. After the evacuation of it, he always said he had headache, faintiness, and sometimes pain in the abdomen. Diet had no material influence over the secretion. Collected in a glass and left to stand quiet, cream soon separated, and sometimes the milk at once coagulated. After some hours' standing, the butter separated and floated at the top in yellow drops. The milk had a slightly alkaline reaction. Its specific weight was 1.024, and it contained, according to analyses of *Mayer*, "fat, alcoholic extract, water, and insoluble compound."

Dr. *Louis Young*, of the West Indies, reports a similar case, which is also published in *Sir A. Cooper's* work on the Breast, viz.:—

"Although I have never witnessed an instance in

which the (male) gland secreted milk, yet I have heard related a well-authenticated case which occurred at Barbadoes, in which the man was known to take the care of one of his grandchildren, to tend, nurse and suckle it as a mother, which it had lost soon after birth. The account is that the child obtained nourishment from his breasts, lived and did well."

Speaking of such secretions, *Sir A. Cooper* remarks:

"The secretion of milk proceeds from a *tranquil state of the mind.* With a cheerful temper, the milk is regularly abundant and agrees well with the child. On the contrary, a *fretful temper* lessens the quantity of milk, makes it thin and serous, and causes it to disturb the child's bowels, producing intestinal fevers and much griping. *Fits of anger* produce a very irritating milk, followed by griping in the infant, with green stools. *Grief* has a great influence on lactation, and consequently upon the child. The loss of a near and dear relative, or change of fortune, will often so much diminish the secretion of milk as to render adventitious aid necessary for the support of the child, *Anxiety of mind* diminishes the quantity and alters the quality of the milk. The reception of a letter which leaves the mind in anxious suspense, lessens the draught, and the breasts become empty. If the child be ill, and the mother is anxious respecting it, she complains to her medical attendant that she has little milk, and that her infant is griped, and has frequent green and frothy stools. *Fear* has a powerful influence on the secretion of milk. I am informed by a medical man who practices much among the poor, that the apprehension of the brutal conduct of a drunken husband, will put a stop for a time to the secretion of milk. When this happens, the breasts feel knotted and hard, flaccid from the absence of milk, and that which is secreted is highly irritating, and some time elapses before a healthy secretion returns. *Terror* which is sudden, and great fear, instantly stops the secretion. A nurse was hired, and in the morning she had abundance of milk, but having to go fifty miles to the place at which the parents of the child resided, in a common diligence, the horses proved restive and the passengers were in much danger. When the nurse, who had been greatly terrified, arrived at her place, at the end of the journey, the milk had entirely disappeared, and the secretion could not be reproduced, although she was stimulated by spirits, medicines, and by the best local applications a medical man could suggest. A lady in excellent health and a good nurse, was overturned in her pony-chaise, and when she returned home and greatly alarmed, she had no milk; nor did it return, and she was obliged to wean her child."

A female, a patient of the author of the present work, in 1856, was nursing a child two months old, and had more milk than the child could consume. An older child took sick, and her anxiety for it caused the milk to decrease, and in the course of a week to disappear altogether, so that she was compelled to wean her babe.

The influence of mental excitement may be so great as to actually poison the mammary secretions. "A carpenter fell into a quarrel with a soldier, billetted in his house, and was set upon by the latter with his drawn sword. The wife of the carpenter at first trembled from fear and terror, and then suddenly threw herself between the combatants, wrested the sword from the soldier's hand, broke it in pieces and threw it away. During the tumult, some neighbors came in and separated the men. While in this state of strong excitement, the mother took up her child from the cradle, where it lay playing and in the most perfect health, never having had a moment's illness. She gave it the breast, and in so doing sealed its fate. In a few minutes the infant left off suckling, became restless, panted and sank dead upon its mother's bosom. The physician who was instantly called in, found the child lying in the cradle, as if asleep, with its features undisturbed; but all his resources were fruitless. It was irrecoverably gone."*

*Carpenter*, in a note, page 945, gives similar cases. Two are mentioned by Mr. *Wardrop* in the London *Lancet*, No. 516. Having removed a small tumor from behind the ear of a mother, all went well, until she fell into a violent passion, and the child being suckled soon afterward, died in convulsions. Dr. Wardrop was sent for hastily to see another child in convulsions after taking the breast of a nurse who had just been seriously reprimanded. *Sir Richard Croft* states that he has seen similar instances. Several cases are given by *Burdach*. One was that of an infant affected with convulsions on the right side and hemiplegia on the left, from sucking immediately after its mother had

* Dr. Von Ammon in his treatise "Die ersten Mutterpplichten und die erste Rurderpflegi," quoted by Dr. Combe in his work on the "Management of Infants."

met with a distressing occurrence. Another case was of a puppy seized with epileptic convulsions on sucking its mother after a fit of rage.

*Carpenter*, in his valuable work on Physiology, mentions two cases quite as striking as those already related, which should serve as a salutary warning to mothers not to indulge either in the exciting or depressing passions. He states in substance that a lady had several children, none of whom had ever exhibited any tendency to cerebral disease. The youngest was a healthy infant of a few months, when she heard of the death of a child of a neighbor from acute hydrocephalus. The circumstance made a strong impression on her mind. Soon after she nursed her child, when it was seized with convulsions and died. He relates another instance, where a lady who had lost several children by convulsive disorders, who had an infant that seemed perfectly healthy in every respect. One day, in a moody frame of mind, she dwelt on the fear of losing her last infant in the way the rest had been taken away. She nursed the child while laboring under such morbid feelings, and transferred it to the arms of an attendant. Soon after it was seized with convulsions, and died almost instantly.

There may have been a predisposing cause in this latter case, but there is no doubt the immediate or *exciting* cause is referable to the mother's anxiety.

My advice to mothers has always been never to nurse a child while under the influence of mental excitements of any kind, particularly when they have lost children while nursing. I have long been satisfied that a chief cause of the excessive mortality of children under two years, is owing to the mental emotions of the mother—even more so than in that of teething, usually considered the main cause of infantile mortality, I will suppose a case:—

A mother of very susceptible disposition is nursing her child, and it is taken sick from teething or other exciting cause, the anxiety of the mother must naturally be as great an exciting cause as the one producing the disease. In this way we have fuel added to the flame, as it were, or two exciting causes operating to make "assurance doubly sure" in the death of the child, inasmuch as either is often sufficient to cause the dissolution of the offspring.

This hypothesis is sustained by the fact that sick and delicate children taken from a mother while laboring under great anxiety or mental disturbance, and given to a wet nurse, very often recover from diseases that would have otherwise proved fatal.

The recovery, in such cases, is usually attributed to the quality of the milk. I believe it may be more reasonably attributed to the removal of the influence of the mother's mind from the infant, in the change of the nurse.

## D. NURSING.

Nursing may be divided into *natural* and *artificial.*—Natural is the direct application of the infant's mouth to the nipple from which it draws or derives its nourishment, by the act of sucking. Artificial, is the furnishing of food to the child by artificial means.

Fig. 63.

A MOTHER NURSING HER CHILD.

*a.* NATURAL NURSING (*Fig.* 63).—Nursing by the

mother requires but little teaching of the child. All that is necessary is to present the breast; the child will grasp it, and instantly there is a copious flow of milk. There is a sort of sympathy between the mo ther and the child—the one seeking what the other desires to give.

Some women have a great distaste for nursing, and positively refuse to do so, on account of the trouble and confinement imposed.

There is no question that it is the duty of the mother to allow her offspring to partake of the nourishment Nature has provided by the maternal font, provided her health and strength permit, and the child is not injured by the nature of the lacteal aliment. The process is equally advantageous to mother and child, in a healthy condition. It is Nature's food for the infant, and designed expressly for its further development and strength, while, as respects the mother, the drawing away of the fluid will prevent inflammation and ulceration of the glands of the breast, and drain from the pelvic and abdominal viscera the congestion usually attendant upon pregnancy. In this way many serious organic diseases are avoided, which would be inevitably concomitant of any other course of procedure than the natural nursing of the babe by its mother.

*Ramsbotham*, speaking on this subject, well remarks that "Mothers should forego the pleasures of society, give up the necessity of appearing in public, and waive even the etiquette of court, if these pleasures or that etiquette interfere in any material degree with her duties to her infant. I cannot allow that a physician would be honestly and conscientiously fulfilling the trust reposed in him, who did not, even in the highest grade of society, point out the dangers that may spring from this most natural and engaging employment being abandoned; and I would always think better of a woman's feeling, both toward her husband and her infant, who gave it the advantage of her own breast."

As before intimated, there may be circumstances which should exempt the mother from nursing her offspring. The preservation of her own health and that of her child should have paramount consideration. It is also improper to nurse during pregnancy, as is often done among women in the humbler walks of society. Many a woman nurses her child till within two or three months of a new confinement. This must not only undermine the strength of the female, but be extremely prejudicial both to the living and the yet unborn child.

The weaning of a child should be decided upon by its mother, after it has reached the twelfth or fourteenth month of its age. This is the period that Nature seems to indicate for the cessation of lactation. The milk begins about this time to diminish in quantity and deteriorate in quality; hence the child will require other nourishment besides that afforded by the maternal parent.

It is necessary sometimes to employ a stranger or wet-nurse. Great caution should be exercised in such selection—having in view what has been already said in regard to the influence of mind on the secretion of milk—the transmission of medicines and poisons as well as constitutional vices to the child, by the nurse. We should inquire particularly about her antecedents, habits, mode of living, general health, etc. Her breast should be examined and found full and plump; while her milk should be thoroughly analyzed by some competent person, to insure its proper purity and richness, etc.

*b.* Artificial Nursing.—This should resemble natural nursing as much as possible. For this purpose a glass bottle should be used, with an artificial nipple attached. One of the most convenient nursing bottles I have seen, is an invention by *Mrs. Bailey.* It consists of a glass bottle, in the top of which is a screw fitting into a stopper, that has attached to it a caoutchouc, (or Indian rubber) nipple or mouth-piece. The same movements of the child's lips, tongue and gums, are required to draw the milk from the bottle as from the mammæ or mother's breasts. Pure cow's milk, boiled, as already stated, or other equally good substitute, should supply the place of the natural secretion.

## E. DISEASES OF BREAST DURING LACTATION.

The breast may become diseased from various causes, and assume various forms. It will be proper here to speak only of those disorders or difficulties of the breast which are concomitant of lactation.

*a.* Sore Nipples.—A sore nipple generally commences in a chap or crack, while the action of the child's mouth has a tendency to remove the skin and keep up an irritation, that will soon put on some form of ulceration and lay the foundation of a mammary abscess.

*Treatment.*—There are two points to be observed in treating sore nipples. One is to induce the healing process, and the other to protect them while healing.

To accomplish the former some astringent wash may be used—as alum, borax, sulphate of zinc or copper, dissolved in rose-water or combined in the form of an ointment. One of the very best ointments I have ever seen employed for this purpose is that prepared by Mr. Stackhouse, called the "*Oleate of Roses.*"* I know the constituents of this ointment, and have had opportunities of judging of its effects upon all chafed and chapped surfaces. It is a valuable preparation, and should be in the possession of every mother. If the nipple is washed off once a day with warm water and Castile soap, and the ointment applied two or three times a day, it will be all that is necessary to heal the abrasure or soreness, except protecting the nipple. This may be effectually accomplished by *Neadham's* "Nipple Shield," which is capable of meeting every indication. It is a good plan to bathe the nipple a few weeks before delivery, with alum, borax, or tanic acid dissolved in rose water. It will harden the skin that covers the nipple and prevent it cracking so easily after commencing to nurse.

*b.* Retracted Nipple.—In such cases the nipple is flattened on the breast, or so compressed as to produce a cup-like depression in the breast. It is gene-

* This may be procured at Mr. Stackhouse's, S. E. corner of Eighth and Green streets, Phila.

rally occasioned by the foolish habit of lacing the chest when young. This practice is yet too much indulged by young ladies, for the purpose of having a small waist.

*Treatment.*—At birth, or before, when we find the retracted nipple, it should be drawn out by the breast pump, before the mammæ fill with milk. Otherwise the depression may be increased. Frequent application of the breast-pump prior to labor, will tend to obviate all difficulties, and enable the child to grasp the nipple. In England, there are females who hire themselves, as a special business, to suck the breast several times a day, in order to elongate the nipple, or draw it out from its retracted position.

*c.* INFLAMMATION OF THE BREAST.—This is a very common occurrence during lactation. It may be confined at first to a single gland, or it may attack the whole cellular structure of the breast. If the inflammation be allowed to continue a short time, there will be ulceration and deposit of pus.

*Symptoms* usually commence with fever and chills, and darting and shooting pains in the mammæ, which increase on pressure. The breast feels hard on pressure, and as the swelling increases, the skin assumes a dusky-red color. There is a throbbing which increases as the breast enlarges. This is evidence that deep-seated suppuration is taking place. This is most apt to occur in delicate females and those of a scrofulous diathesis. After a time there is an evacuation of pus, after which the pain and inflammation gradually subsides. Inflammation of the breast is not a fatal disease, although in delicate females, where there is much and long-continued discharges of pus, it reduces the system very rapidly. As a matter of course, if the strength is not maintained, the patient may soon sink from the general debility of the system.

*Causes.*—The most common cause is the accumulation of milk in the lactiferous ducts—frequently induced by the mother absenting herself from her child in visiting places of amusement, etc., and not allowing the milk to be drawn off, as frequently as Nature would require to be done. It, however, may result from cold or a blow upon the breast, or from mental emotion.

*Treatment.*—Inflammation will seldom occur unless the lactiferous ducts be allowed to become distended with milk. When any part of the glands feel hard or knotty, or painful to the touch, no time should be lost in drawing off the milk, either by applying the child to the breast or by the use of a breast-pump. No mother who is nursing should be without a good breast-pump. Sometimes in the middle of night-time the breasts may fill up and become painful, so as to require to be drawn off at once, and thus save the suffering which would otherwise have to be endured till morning. In such emergencies, and to prevent suppuration which might arise from delay in drawing off the fluid, the Neadham apparatus is a capital contrivance. It works with a bellows, so that any amount of suction or drawing may be produced. When using this pump, the hard and painful parts of the glands should be gently pressed so as to assist in forcing the milk from the duct which has become much distended. The gland should be well bathed with the following wash, and the pump frequently applied until the swelling is reduced:—

℞ Tinct. belladonna,......................℥i.
Tinct. camphor,........................℥i.
Mix, and rub the part three or four times a day.

Should the swelling not be reduced by the above means, warm vinegar must be freely applied, and persevered in for at least twenty-four hours, if necessary. Leeches also, at the same time, may be applied below the breast, so as not to interfere with the application of the vinegar.

If this will not be sufficient to lessen the swelling and pain, a warm poultice made of hops should be applied, and the following taken by the stomach:—

℞ Tinct. aconite, *fol*......................f ʒij.
Morphæ acetate,.................... grs. ij.
Sweet spirits nitre,......................℥j.
Water,..................................℥iij.
Mix, and take one teaspoonful every hour until the fever and pain subside. Afterward every two or three hours.

As soon as the abscess points, it should be lanced, or the accumulated pus may break down a large portion of the gland. At the same time it relieves the pain by removing the pressure upon the nerves.

The breast should be supported during the whole process of the disease. This may be done by adhesive strips carried below and around the gland. When the gland has opened, poultices should be continued, or what will answer equally well, and be less cumbersome, is patent lint saturated with hot water, applied, and covered up with oiled silk.

The discharge may be so great as to require the system to be supported by tonics, and a nourishing diet. Sweet wine, beer, or porter, may also be given Should it require an alterative, as is sometimes the case when there is a scrofulous diathesis, the following formula may be used:—

℞ Comp. stillingæ syrup,...............℥viij.
Iodide potash,......................ʒij.
Fowler's solution,..................fʒjss.
Take two teaspoonsful three times a day in water.

If the ulcer does not incline to heal, a solution of sulphate of zinc or nitrate of silver may be injected. If the ulcer is superficial, oxyde of zinc ointment may be applied. Should there be a want of healthy granulation, *Meyers'* ointment may be used, or the following:—

℞ Iodide plumbi (lead),..................℈j.
Glycerine,...........................ʒj.
Simple cerate,.......................℥ij.
Mix, and apply night and morning to ulcer.

*d.* SHOULD THE CHILD BE NURSED FROM THE DISEASED BREAST?—In order to prevent ulceration of the breast, the first point is to relieve the distended glands of the milk, according to the means or methods already indicated in the foregoing pages. After suppuration has commenced, or is likely to be extensive, or continue long, so as to affect the health of the mother, the child should not be allowed to feed even from the healthy breast, but either be given to a hired nurse or weaned. The drain of milk from one breast, and the suppurative discharge from the other, is more than the generality of mothers can bear. Due circumspection must be exercised in all cases, as may be best to promote the health and comfort of both the parent and the child.

# CHAPTER XV.

## OVER-PRODUCTIVENESS.

## RELATIVE PROPORTION OF THE MALE AND FEMALE .SEXES.

THE more simple the organization of animals, the more fruitful or prolific they are. In some of the Entozoa and Mollusca, millions of ova are found. The *Aphides*, or plant lice, furnish a remarkable instance of fecundation. A single intercourse is sufficient to impregnate not only the female parent, but all her progeny down to the ninth generation. At the fifth generation a single *aphis* might be the great grandmother of 5,900,000,000 young ones. The progeny of three flesh-flies would consume a dead ox as quickly as would a lion. Nine millions of ova have been calculated to be spawned by a single codfish.

In the warm-blooded animals, the necessity of incubation or utero-gestation, places a limit to the number of animals. In the human fèmale, the number of children is limited by reason of the time necessary for a woman to travail with each child, and the comparatively few years during which she is capable of bear ing children. Many women bear children every twenty months. In some the interval is from twelve to fifteen months. Such fecundation, however, depends upon lactation, which generally prevents conception. Women usually bear a single child at a time. The proportion of twins to single children according to *Burdach*, is one to seventy or eighty The proportion of triplets is one to six or seven thou sand. Occasionally, five or six children are born at one birth.

The production of so many children at a birth, is evidence of a strong constitution in the female, and great activity in the ovaries. There must be as many ova eliminated at the monthly period as there are children born at a birth. Over-productiveness does not depend so much on the supply of spermatozoa furnished by the male, as upon the prolific condition of the ovaries, in throwing off ova at each monthly period. It is supposed that a single spermatozoon is sufficient to impregnate each ovum or egg. If so, man, at each sexual conjunction, would be capable of impregnating many thousands of ova. Over-productiveness, therefore, when it occurs, may be attributed more to the female than to the male.

Men have been known to beget seventy to eighty children at two or more marriages. A healthy woman bearing all the time allowed her, say thirty years, and having one child every twenty months, might, accordingly, become the mother of twenty children at least. Many women have had fifteen or sixteen children—some seventeen or eighteen, or even more, as the following remarkable and well-authenticated cases will verify:—

Ambrose Paré tells of a woman who had eighteen children at six births. Another authority mentions a woman who was the mother of *forty-four* children—

thirty by the first husband and fourteen by the second. Another more extraordinary instance, (as related by *Fournier*,) is of a woman who had fifty-three children in one marriage. Eighteen times the births were single; five times they were twins; four times triplets; once six at a birth; and seven at another.* A case is also recorded in "Good's Study of Medicine," of a woman who had fifty-seven children.

The following is a more extraordinary case than either of those above related. It occurred in Russia, and is recorded in a Russian journal. A peasant by the name of *Ririlow*, with his wife, was presented to the Empress. He was married for the second time, at seventy years of age. His first wife was confined twenty-one times. Four times there were quadruplets, seven times triplets, and ten times twins, or in all fifty-seven, and all alive. His second wife was confined seven times—once of triplets, and six times of twins—in all fifteen children; making the husband the father of seventy-two children, fifteen of whom were born to him after he was seventy years of age.

Such over-productiveness is said to be quite common among the peasantry of Russia. If so, it speaks well for the vigor of the people of that country.

The most remarkable case upon record of over-productiveness is that of the Countess Henneberg, recorded on a marble tablet, which is still to be seen in the church of Lousdunen, near Leyden. The history of the case is taken from Ramsbotham's Midwifery, p.

* See Fournier, Dict. des Scien. Med. Com. 10.

626. On the monument is found the following inscription:

> "En tibi monstrosum et memorabile factum,
> Quale nec a mundi conditione datum,
> Ostendam."

After these lines there is a prose account of the miracle, with her pedigree for many generations:

"That Margaret, wife of Harman, Earl of Henneberg, and daughter of Florence, the fourth Earl of Holland and Zealand; being about forty years old, upon Easter-day, 1276, at 9 A. M., was brought to bed of 365 chlldren, all of which were baptized in two brazen basins by Guido, the suffragan of Utrecht. The males, how many soever there were of them, were christened John, all the daughters Elizabeth; who all, together with their mother, died on the same day, and with their mother lie buried in this church of Lousdunen." This supernatural infliction is accounted for on the principle of retributive justice, for we are informed that the Countess, being solicited for alms by a poor woman who was carrying twins, shook her off with contempt, declaring that she could not have them by one father; whereupon the poor woman prayed to God to send her as many children as there were days in the whole year; "which came to pass, as is briefly recorded in this table, for perpetual recollection, testified as well by ancient manuscript as by many printed chronicles." (For a brief notice of this "fact" "upon unquestionable record," see *Evelyn's Discourse on Medals*, fol. 1697, p. 267.)

AVERAGE OF MALE AND FEMALE BIRTHS.—According to *Burdach*, the proportion of children born in each marriage in England is 5–7; in Italy, 2–3; France, 4–5; Germany, 6–8. Out of every fifty marriages one is unfruitful. There is on an average one birth for every twenty-five of the population of a place. Taking the population of the world at six hundred and thirty-three millions, about fifty children are born every second.* In all countries where observation has extended, in the average number of births, the males exceed the females from four to twenty in one hundred. It has also been observed by *Burdach*, that the first children of a marriage consist of a greater number of females than males in the proportion of one hundred females to fifty-three males. An effort has been made to establish a data in explanation of the formation of male and female offspring; but no satisfactory law can be given in this regard. In some families, the offspring are all females, in others all males. In some, only one female and the rest males, and *vice versa;* and similar results running through several generations.

Some suppose the right testicle of the male and right ovary of the female furnish a male child, and the left, or reverse, the female. Upon this idea was founded the celebrated advice of Hippocrates: "*Ubi femellem generare volet (pater) cœat, ac dextram testem obliget, quantum id tolerare poteret, sed si marem generare appetat, sinister testis obligandus erit.*"

The wishes of parents have also been supposed to

* Cyclop. Anat. et Phys.

exert an influence at the time of conception. The character of the food used by the female at pregnancy, the use of charms, medicine, magical receipts, etc., have been supposed to exert an influence in the production of either a male or female child.

According to *Giron*, *Hofacker*, *Turingen* and *Saddler*, when the husband is considerably younger than the wife, the proportion is ninety sons to one hundred daughters. If the husband is considerably older than the wife, the proportion is from one hundred and fifty to one hundred and sixty sons to one hundred daughters. Intermediate ages have been found to give a proportionate scale.

*Burdach* states that very fruitful females bear more boys than girls, as for example:*

| | | | | *Boys.* | *Girls.* |
|---|---|---|---|---|---|
| 1st | woman | bore | | 26 | 6 |
| 2d | " | " | in first marriage | 27 | 3 |
| " | " | " | in second marriage | 14 | 0 |
| 3d | " | " | | 38 | 15 |

With our present knowledge of embryotic development, no rules can be laid down to insure offspring definitely of either sex. It, however, may be here stated, that in the earlier stages of embryotic life, the sexes are perfectly alike in structure, and it is impossible to say whether the young embryo will unfold in a male or female child. The type of the sexual organs in the early part of utero-gestation is not double, as generally supposed. The influence which is exerted

* Cyclop. Anat. et Phys.

to develop the male or female child out of a single or common type, is yet an unfathomed mystery of Nature.

From the single type of the genital organs, it may be perceived how one side of the embryo may have the male organs developed, and on the other side those of the female. Such cases have already been given in the chapter on Hermaphrodism in the present volume. There may be also a blending of the male and female species in what is called the "Free-martin" calf—which occurs in a cow bearing two calves, one of which is a male, and the other resembling a female in respect to its external reproductive organs, while the internal apparatus is imperfect—and hence its name of hermaphrodite or "free martin."

In the reproduction of the human being, and indeed in all organized creatures of the animal or vegetable kingdoms, there is found a wonderful uniformity in Nature, in providing a relative proportion of the male and female elements of pro-creation. Every creature or thing has its mate or fellow, while it is not in the power of man to set limits to the relative amount of the male and female forces, concomitant of fecundation or the law of increase.

## CHAPTER XVI.

### EXTRA-UTERINE PREGNANCY.

EXTRA-UTERINE PREGNANCY is divided into three varieties—*Ovarian*, *Fallopian* and *Abdominal.*

*a.* OVARIAN PREGNANCY.—This is when the spermatozoa passes along the Fallopian tube, and impregnates the ovum before it has been grasped by the fimbriated portion of the tube and allowed the ova or ovum to become regularly impregnated after being detached from the ovary. The gland or ovary is thus converted into a sac, in which the ovum is imbedded and developed. *Fig.* 64 shows an embryo three or four months old imbedded in such manner in the ovary.

*b.* ABDOMINAL PREGNANCY.—In this form of pregnancy, the ovum has become impregnated after it has been received into the fimbriated extremity of the Fallopian tube, prior to being dropped into the abdominal cavity, where a vascular sac surrounds it, and it undergoes development.

*c.* FALLOPIAN PREGNANCY.—In this species of pregnancy, the ovum, after it has become impregnated, is obstructed in its translation toward the uterus, and retained in the tube.

In either of these forms of pregnancy, the uterus will take on the same forms of preparation as if the

Fig. 64.

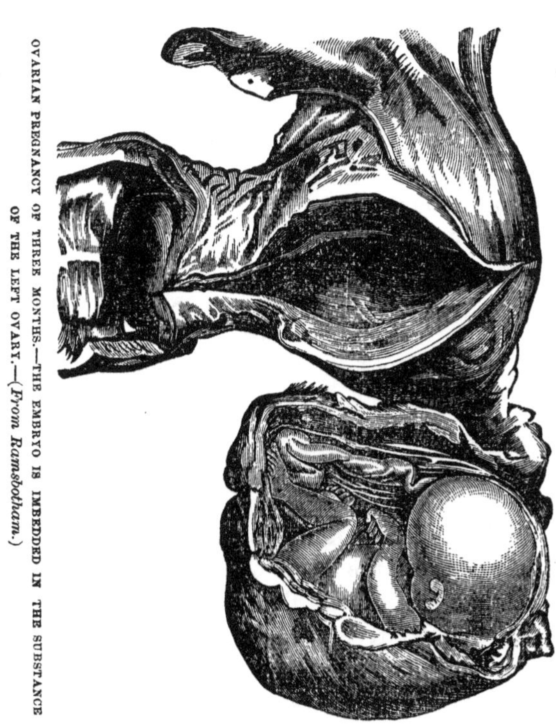

OVARIAN PREGNANCY OF THREE MONTHS.—THE EMBRYO IS IMBEDDED IN THE SUBSTANCE OF THE LEFT OVARY.—(*From Ramsbotham.*)

pregnancy was natural. The deciduous membrane will form within the uterine cavity; a mucus secreted by the glands at the neck of the womb, will close the neck; while the uterus itself will sometimes increase or enlarge to two or three times its natural size.

While these extra-uterine pregnancies exist, natural pregnancy may occur from an ovum, which has passed through the tube on the opposite side of the body into the womb.

Extra-uterine pregnancy is frequently arrested before the period of nine months. The fœtus will either decompose and pass away by ulceration, or else remain for years imbedded in the part in which it is deposited. There are many instances on record where the fœtus has thus remained for a number of years in abeyance, while in the interval the female has given birth to several healthy children.

The following are examples in point:—

In *Baubine's* Latin translation of Roussel, 1601, there is a history of a fœtus that had remained in the abdomen of a female twenty-eight years, and become converted into a hard earthy mass. This female died at sixty-eight.* Another case is given in the *Hist. de l'Academie Royal des Sciences,* An. 1778, in which the fœtus remained in the abdomen for nine years. In the same publication there is another account of a fœtus, weighing eight pounds, that had remained in the abdominal cavity thirty-five years, the woman dying of pulmonary disease. Also, still another case, where a woman conceived at forty-six and died at ninety-four, in whose abdomen was found an ossified fœtus which she must have carried for forty-eight years.

In the *Medico-Chirurgical Transactions*, Vol. v., p. 104, a case is reported of a fœtus that had remained in a woman's body for fifty-two years. In the *Edinburgh Medical and Surgical Journal*, Vol. II., p. 22, there are two similar cases presented—the one being

* Ramsbotham's Midwifery.

retained twenty-six years and the other between thirty and forty years.

*Campbell* (Memoir, p. 45) mentions a case where the fœtus had been retained fifty-five years. In the *Philosophical Transactions*, there are a number of cases given. One of these is of a woman, who died at eighty-four having carried a fœtus twenty-six years, that weighed eight pounds. Another woman carried a fœtus twenty-eight years, during which time she gave birth to two healthy children. Dr. *Campbell*, in his researches, presents seventy-five cases, where the fœtus had been retained for periods varying from three months to fifty-six years.*

It has been observed that at the end of nine months in extra-uterine gestation, the uterus will take on its expulsive action; all the symptoms of labor and parturition will continue for several days, and terminate in the expulsion of the deciduous membrane. The same action of the uterus will occur should the fœtus die before the natural period of gestation.

The fœtus in all of these cases, where it has remained in the cavity of the abdomen for a length of time, has been converted either into a substance resembling adipocere,† or coated with a bony or earthy crust—thus preserving it for an indefinite period, and causing no inconvenience, except its weight and bulk, to the female.

* See Note—Ramsbotham's Midwifery, p. 472.

† Adipocére (*adeps*, fat; *cera*, wax). A fatty, spermaceti-like substance into which flesh is converted, after being a long time immersed in water, or buried in the earth.

The cause has been attributed to fright during the sexual congress. This idea, however, is not sanctioned by the physiologists of the present age. It rarely occurs in married females—mostly in the unmarried, or those of irregular habits and immoral character.

# CHAPTER XVII.

## TERMATOLOGY; OR, CONGENITAL DEFORMITIES.

## DISEASES OF CHILDREN PREVIOUS TO BIRTH.

FROM observation there is reason to believe that the child previous to birth may take on certain diseases existing at the time-being, in the mother, communicaied through some infection or other cause, or from the father to the mother and afterward by her to the child. In this way syphilis, scrofula, small-pox, and other diseases may be communicated to the unborn child. Malformations may also result from some strong mental impression, (as befere intimated), or may arise from falls, blows, concussions, pressure, etc.

The investigation of this subject is not only interesting, but important, as calculated to benefit both mother and child, by pointing out the causes that produce them and the means by which they may be obviated. Were mothers made acquainted with the diseases liable to affect their children during uterine gestation, they would be enabled to avoid them, and thus save much suffering both to themselves and offspring.

The fœtus is liable to arrest and change in the formative process, in the early stages of utero-gestation, through excessive action of such process; or it may result from the arrest of natural development, or from some change in parts after natural development has commenced—more generally, however, in the former than in the latter instance.

The ovum before it becomes fecundated with the male sperm, may have communicated to it some morbid taint by the mother, and hence malformation results as a consequence. It may occur from adhesion of two germs or ova, and thus give rise to anomalies, like such as is witnessed in the "Siamese twins;" or in the more remarkable case, of which a sketch is given (*Fig.* 65), of two children born a few years ago

Fig. 65.

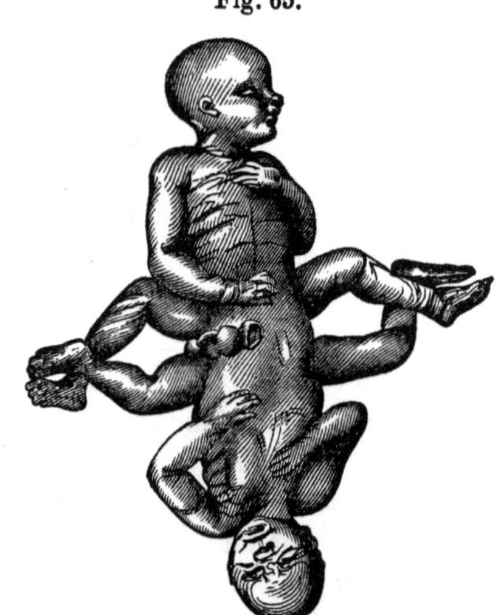

CONGENITAL-MALFORMATION OF TWO FŒTUSES.—(*From Cyclop. Anat. et Physiol.*)

at Boyle, in the county Roscommon, Ireland. Theso were born alive and lived more than a week. After death they were procured by the College of Surgeons, Dublin.

Sir E. *Home* gives an account of a case where there were two heads joined together. *Ramsbotham*, also, in his excellent work on "Midwifery," gives two cases where the children were joined together by the back, sternum, abdomen, and sides, both of which subjects are preserved in the London Hospital Museum. (*See Figs.* 66 and 67.)

In some instances, such individuals live a long time. A case of this kind is that of the celebrated "Hungarian Sisters," who were exhibited in Europe during the last century. These sisters had double viscera, although but one anus. They had two vaginæ. One girl was more delicate than the other, and while one suffered convulsions the other was well. One slept while the other was awake. When one was hungry the other was not. They died at the same instant, aged twenty-two.

The Siamese twins is another example. They are connected at the lower part of the sternum by a band of only four inches long and ten inches in circumference. Their systems seem to act in unison. One cannot sleep without the other does. They awake from sleep at the same moment; both hunger alike and desire the same food; in short, all the functions of the duplex organisms are performed simultaneously, as if they were the functions of a single being. They married sisters, have children, and now reside on their plantation in the State of Georgia.

There are a number of cases recorded in which the body of one was only slightly developed while the

Fig. 66.

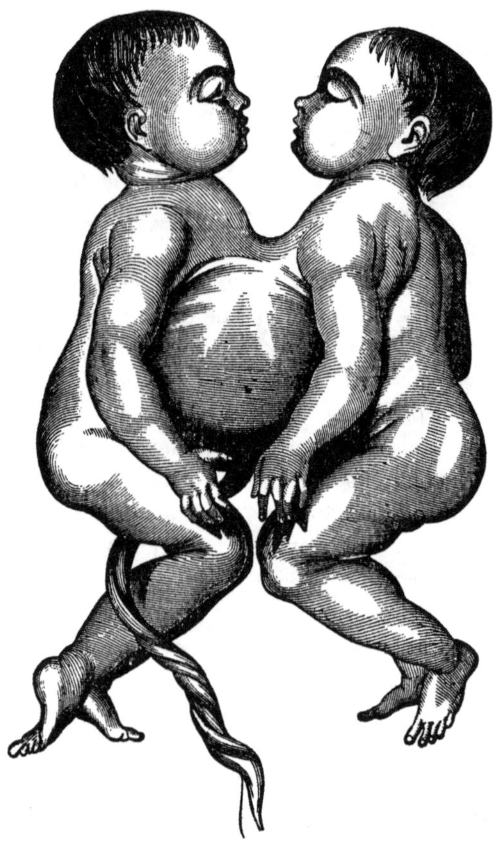

CONGENITAL MALFORMATION OF TWO FŒTUSES. (*From Ramsbotham.*)
The union occurs at the abdomen.

other was fully formed. The Chinese boy A-KE is an example. He had the loins, upper and lower ex

FIG. 67.

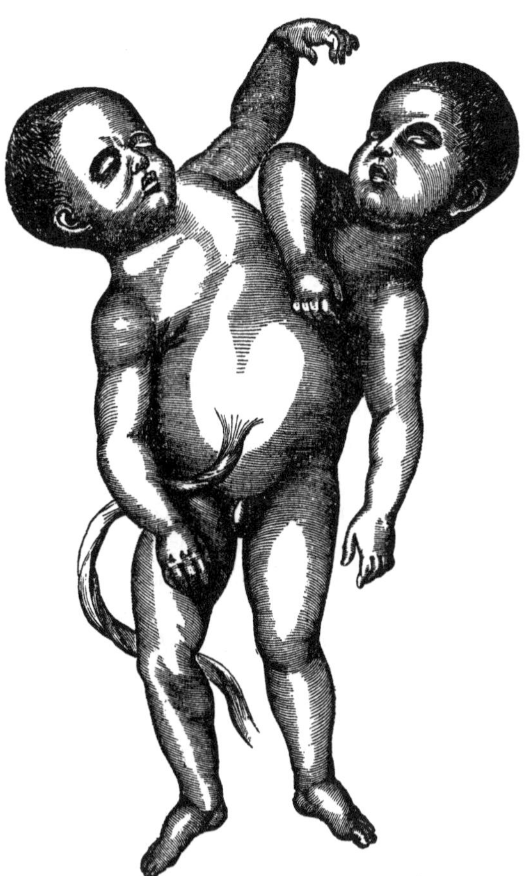

CONGENITAL MALFORMATION OF TWO FŒTUSES. (*From Ramsbotham.*)
The union occurs at the sternum, sides, back and abdomen.

tremities of a brother attached to his umbilicus and sternum.

*Ambrose Paré* relates a case which was exhibited in 1550 in Paris. The individual was forty years old. He had growing upon his abdomen, a small body perfect in all its parts, excepting its head and shoulders, which were wanting.

*Zacchias* tells of a well-formed man named *Lazarus Colloredo*, aged twenty-eight, who had a twin brother, *John*, hanging from his chest. John had a larger head than Lazarus, two arms, and the fingers on each hand, and was sustained by the food taken by Lazarus.

Many curious cases of malformation come under the notice of the hospitals and clinics connected with the various medical schools of Philadelphia. A recent instance, as reported in the "Medical and Surgical Reporter," of Philadelphia, for March 5, 1859, which received the service of Dr. *Pancoast*, at the Hospital of the Jefferson College, is of too remarkable a character to be omitted in this chapter. It was perhaps the most unique case of monstrosity on record, in modern times. It was termed "*Herteradelphia*," and the operation was by the "*écraseur*." It first came under the notice of the Professor and class on the 12th of February, 1859, the subject being brought from the western part of Pennsylvania. It was a child seven months old, having appended to its left cheek a large mass, growing more rapidly than the child itself, and containing the materials of an imperfectly formed child. Fingers were seen, and a portion of a rudimentary forearm. At birth, the tumor was about the size of an apple; at seven months, (or time when it was presented to the clinique,) it was nearly a foot long. The intestines, then covered with skin, were at birth distinctly visible. Below the mass of the intestines was a sort of *cloaque*, which, however, had no communication with the bowels. There was a prominence resembling a penis. A corpus cavernosum was also felt by the finger. There was pulsation in the mass numbering from forty to one hundred beats in a minute, although they were not synchronous with the beat of the heart of the perfect child. An abscess was found in one portion of the mass, and the rosy color of the tumor, as well as the presence of a large artery, showed that it was largely supplied with blood. The buccinator muscle of the child was drawn into the mass, so that when the finger of the surgeon was passed into its mouth it passed into a tube. A peculiar caul-like membrane, pierced with holes, separated the primary child from the parasite; but its nature or office was not determined. The mass, likewise, had a liver, which was disproportionate to the size of the child. The child suffered greatly from *erythema intertrigo*, from the constant friction to which it was subjected from the parasite, although the mother afforded a constant support to the tumor with her hand.

Dr. Pancoast explained the nature of the formation of monsters, as owing to excess or defect; gave his views of cases of inclusion in which a fœtus was contained within another, *fœtus in fœtu*, and detailed much important information in regard to double monsters in general. On the 19th of February an operation was decided upon, the parents having been informed of the great danger likely to be the consequence of the removal of the tumor. Dr. *Pancoast* believed with Dr. *Dunglison*, that the operation by the knife would be attended with an amount of hemorrhage that would probably be fatal before the child could be removed from the table. It was hence agreed to use the *écraseur*, which, by forcing down the skin and bruising the vessels thoroughly before the chain of the instrument cuts through the mass, prevents hemorrhage.

"The application of ether as an anæsthetic agent," says the *Reporter*, "to the perfect child had the effect at once to put a stop to the pulsations going on in the parasite. Four needles were passed through the caul-like membrane, so as to get as much skin as possible from the outside of the buccinator muscle, and several threads were passed around them. The instrument was applied, and the chain rapidly worked at first until the parts were well compressed, and then very slowly. After about fifteen minutes, the tumor came away with the instrument, the chain having worked through, with scarcely a drop of blood following the removal, and but one small vessel requiring ligation. The surface left was about ten inches by about an inch and three quarters. The tumor weighed nearly two pounds and a half."

A dissection of the mass confirmed all the facts of its being a case of *fœtus in fœtu*. The child from which it was taken was doing very well, a week after the operation; the space left in the cheek was healing up by granulation very satisfactorily, the patient being well enough to be returned to the home of his parents in the west.

This intus-susception or adhesion of one germ with another, has been frequently met with in the hen's egg, and the eggs of various animals.

The ancients attributed such malformations to Divine vengeance, witchcraft, or the influence of the devil. These opinions answered in the dark ages, but are now entirely exploded. The light of science enables modern pathologists and physiologists to explain many of the causes of such remarkable abnormal phenomena.

It is important to know that the same species of deformity may be produced in successive progression, in the same female. The first child will be the most deformed, the next less so, and finally the deformity will entirely disappear. It not unfrequently happens that the deformity of the mother is communicated to her offspring. Likewise that of the father, though these cases are less frequent than those affecting the mother.

*Ramsbotham* gives two cases of this kind, in his work on "Midwifery." In the year 1831, two children were born twins. One of them had a supernumerary finger on each hand and toe on each foot; while the other had an extra finger on the right hand. The mother of these twins had similar supernumerary fingers and toes. She was the mother of twenty-one children. All the girls except one were born with extra fingers and toes; but only one of the boys was so affected. This woman's mother and sister had similar deformities.

*Meckle*, in his Pathological Anatomy, presents a variety of such singular freaks of Nature.

In the article on *Generation*, in the present work, a

number of cases of defects and malformations are presented, as concomitant of the mother's mental impressions during pregnancy. These remarkable statements should be received with considerable caution. There can be no doubt, that the mother does exert more or less influence upon her child during utero-gestation, as a result of the operations of her mind or mental feelings. The influence of the mind in producing diseases, and in removing them, is sufficiently well established, and it is only reasonable to suppose that similar influences might, and do, extend to the offspring while being nourished in its embryotic or fœtal state.

*Tiedemann* attributes all malformations to some defect in the vascular or nervous system. He states that the hare-lip is owing to the absence of olfactory nerves; and malformations of the eyes to some defect in the optic nerves. Recent observations, however, do not confirm his views.

The *causes* of malformation, no doubt, are as various as are the abnormal developments, and it is scarcely possible that they can all ever be ascertained. With many of them, however, modern physiologists are sufficiently familiar, to found a rational hypothesis as a basis for the whole, from the curious facts which have already been detailed.

There is abundant evidence from the cases on record, that many diseases and malformations of children are directly attributable to physical and mental defects and peculiarities of the parents, particularly as manifested in the abnormal conditions of the mother.

For instance, ulcerations of the bowels of children

at birth, have often been noticed, whose mother's had been troubled with inflammation of that organ during the period of gestation. Cancers and other diseases of liver have often been observed. Tubercles of the lungs are common even with still-born children, one or other of the parents having been similarly afflicted The author of this work, a short time since, delivered a consumptive woman of child, who died subsequently from the disease. The child also died soon after birth, when an examination revealed its lungs studded with tubercles, while in some places ulcerations had commenced.

*Montgomery* gives a number of cases where tubercles were found in the lungs of children at birth, and in nearly every instance the mother labored under consumption at the time.

*Dropsy* is quite as common as consumption in infants previous to birth, as a resultant of the mother's infirmity in this regard. Obstetricians of extensive practice report many such instances.

*Skin diseases* may also occur. *Vogel* and *Rosen* mention two cases of children born with measles, the mothers having been afflicted with the disease prior to the birth of their offspring. *Guersent* reports similar instances of children born with the same disease, as a probable resultant of the parent's affliction with the disorder.

*Montgomery* tells of a child that had the *scarlatina* at birth, whose mother shortly before had recovered from scarlet fever.

*Small-pox* is another disease which sometimes occurs to the fœtus. *Mead* mentions a remarkable case

22

of a child born at full time, that presented a most horrible sight, being covered with small-pox pustules, of which it died previous to birth. The child contracted the disorder from the mother, who had nursed her husband with the distemper, a short time before her confinement. *Billard* mentions a case of a six months' fœtus that had contracted the affection from the mother, at an early stage of her pregnancy *Pemphigus, Lobstein, Joerg,* and *Siebold,* detail similar instances.

*Syphilis* is another disease that is apt to be manifest in the child, if either parents had it at the time of conception. It is more apt to occur, however, a few weeks or months after birth. Cases have occurred where the child has been completely putrid from this disease at birth. *Cruveilhier, Collins,* and others, detail many such instances. The author has seen two cases of the kind—the disorder making its appearance some time after birth, and traceable to the father, who had contracted the disease, and been imperfectly cured of it several years before.*

A volume might be filled with instances of fœtal diseases, concomitant of parental infirmities, were it necessary, to more fully substantiate what has already been detailed in regard to such peculiarities. The few cases now presented, should be sufficient to caution mothers of the liability of diseases and peculiarities being entailed upon their offspring.

* See "Boyhood's Perils and Manhood's Curse," by S. Pancoast, M. D., for a full account of these cases.

## CHAPTER XVIII.

### WOMAN'S SPHERE OF ACTION.

THERE are many weighty facts and majestic truths, which, amid the conventionalities of a strained or artificial state of society, do not receive the philosophical consideration which their immutable irrefragability demands. Among these are those which comprehend "Woman's Sphere of Action"—the amelioration of her present condition—and her advancement toward her proper and *natural* position in the scale of elevated humanity. With the elements and principles involved in Woman's greatest perfection and happiness, the public mind cannot become too familiar.

When we speak of "Woman's Rights" and "Woman's Sphere of Action," we do not wish to be placed in the category of those Modern Pseudo-Reformers who would have Women *unsex* themselves by running into those wild vagaries and excesses of a Political and Social nature which have of late years brought odium on the glorious cause of Woman's perfect emancipation from the condition of the Servant and Mistress of Man. We go for her advancement in every attribute consistent with her normal organism, and the attainment of every exaltation that will render her fully the *equal* of man in all the moral and social relations of general society. Woman was never designed to be ranked as the "mere beast of burden," nor to be the despised creature of man's sensualities, or, at best, the idol and plaything of the sudden generosities and caprices of his lordly nature. She was created to be his "Helpmeet"—his companion and coequal—an indispensable half of himself—without whose conjunction the *homo genus* could not exist.

Much has been said of late years of Woman's *potentiality*, in respect to the position which she *naturally* holds to man. This potentiality is self-apparent, and cannot be fairly denied or contemned. There is a *parallelism* between the two sexes—man and woman—which cannot be obliterated. Woman is the *equal* of man—nothing more, nothing less. By consequence, there is no such thing as a "Sphere of Woman," except as the phrase is applicable to the well-being of general humanity. Surely it is not for man to set bounds to what Nature has not, in determining, as such, the *sphere* of any human being. There is no such thing as either "man's rights" or "woman's rights," in a distinctive sense. There is, however, such a thing as *human* rights, in the assertion and maintenance of which, both men and women are equally concerned. Woman's true orbit, especially, is the broadest enlargement of general humanity. As already asserted, the sexes are not only equal before God, but really and substantially so before the law and the world. Man may war against the laws of Nature, but he can never alter them. Then why should it be feared that woman at *liberty* would deviate from her *true orbit*, or transcend her natural mission? Is it not palpable, then, that whatever interferes with Woman's making the most of the powers which Omnipotence has given her, is a gross violation of her inherent rights—a grievous wrong and injustice not only to Woman herself but to humanity at large? Surely none can gainsay propositions so glaringly self-evident as these. Fools may cavil about such points, but the wise must admit them, and push them forward to their ultimate and legitimate fruition.

In all ages of the world, Woman has ever been practically either the slave or mistress of man. She is so virtually *now*, even in our day of boasted civilization, refinement and intelligence, to a very large extent; yet her *present* condition is most gloriously advanced beyond her *status* of the more primordial times. If we institute a research of history, we will find that Woman's position vibrates between that of legal servitude and forced homage.

There was a time, indeed, when women were deemed not only an "inferior race," but doubts were entertained *whether they really belonged to the* HUMAN RACE.* Not only was woman refused to be acknowledged as a *human* creature, but she has often been sold and transferred from one master to another, as sheep and asses and cattle are sold, as well by heathen as enlightened nations. The husband had the right among the Athenians to bequeath his wife, like a part of his

* St. *Foix* quotes Gregory of Tours, to prove that at the Council of Macon, the question whether women were not *human* beings was hotly disputed. After much division of sentiment, it was at last solemnly decreed in council that women did actually constitute a part of the human race. See *Holcoft's* "Travels in Holland and France."

estate, to any man whom he chose for his successor. The mother of *Demosthenes* was so bequeathed and left by will to *Apnobus*, among other personal property and real estate.* Not many years ago, there was a law in England which prohibited the New Testament to be read by women.† At this very day, it is stated as a fact, that an old law remains on the Statute Books of Great Britain, which permits a man to beat his wife with a stick of the thickness of his thumb, while there have been recent instances where a husband has led his wife, by a halter around her neck, and sold her to another man, as he would a shote or a sheep. In Scotland, only a few years ago, women were not admitted as witnesses in civil cases. In Germany and France, women, are, to this day, frequently seen working in harness with oxen and asses, and performing the most menial and degrading drudgeries in the open fields and streets. In Turkey and Eastern lands Women have been denied to posess an immortal *soul*, while their highest elevation has been to fill the harems and seraglios of sensual lords and masters.

Happily, however, this brutal and shameful degradation of women is being rapidly ameliorated, while there is a strong inclination felt among all truly refined and intelligent nations to recognize the indefeasible rights of Woman, and admit her to the *status* which is incontestibly her privilege as the equal of man before Immaculate Heaven and the world. Even in Turkey, *Polygamy* is rapidly losing its odious

* *Jones' Translation* of the "Speeches of Isæus."

† Lord Kame's "History of Man."

features. The Sultan himself has only seven wives, called "Kadines," who have the privilege of producing an heir to the throne. An American author,* writing from Constantinople, says the "Sultan has great difficulty in managing his wives. He has become worried and teased and *caudled* into a shadow of a man by them. His heart is soft, his nature is kind, and they give him a world of trouble. They run him in debt, and though he forbids it, and swears he won't pay, yet pay he must, almost to his ruin!"

The earnest manner in which the journalists of the United States are discussing the condition of women, shows *thought* for her welfare has been at length awakened—that agitation is begun in the *right* quarter, with a view to the eradication not only of the musty errors of the past but of the many complicated social evils which still exist as affecting women's welfare and glory. Such movements would indicate that woman's emancipation from unnatural and unhallowed thraldom is not far remote.

It is indeed a happy sign to observe that many of the Legislatures of the States of America are yielding many essential points for the advantage of women. No sensible man can ever disparage laws of this wholesome description. The laws of divorce are amended for the better, as a general rule; while married women have now the right to the disposition of their own legitimate earnings, and receive suitable protection from the brutality of sottish husbands, who would reduce them to beggary and drive them into

* The senior *Brooks* of the New York Daily Express.

the pathways of shame and crime. The right of suffrage has been asked for women in certain quarters, but, perhaps, wisely withheld. Surely, no woman having a proper appreciation of her own sensitive, delicate and peculiar organism, would ever wish to unsex herself and degrade the very name of woman, by an association with all the disgusting elements of discord now surrounding the political machinery of party warfare? The denial of the right of suffrage, in sooth, should be regarded as a decided compliment to woman's better nature. Indeed, so far as our knowledge goes, few women care to have extended to them the right of suffrage. They almost invariably object to be placed in a condition which would involve them in the politics of their times. Woman is unfitted by nature to mingle in cabals and caucuses; yet American ladies can exert and do exert a powerful influence upon the political history and destiny of their land. Their influence is of that quiet and silent kind which falls, as the snow-flakes fall, pure and genial, and more potential than the sword or ballot-box, for the general well-being of humanity. As mothers, wives, sisters, lovers and companions, they virtually make the laws of the land, though arrogant and self-sufficient man imagines that his will alone is sovereign and efficient for the happiness of the race.

Though I have referred to the degradation and inferiority of woman, in the abstract, under barbarous and unnatural laws and restraints, in every clime, yet there are many instances, recorded in history, where woman has had her fullest rights acknowledged, and where her exercise of them has resulted in signal advantage to general humanity. For instance, the reign of *Elizabeth* of England, was distinguished as an era of glory and renown. She left behind her a name at which political infidelity, even at this late period, turns away in discomfiture and dishonor. *Catherine* of Russia was the most splendid monarch of her times. Her career, though marked with crime, in some instances, was one which the world must ever applaud. Many other illustrious examples might be cited, were it necessary, to prove the *capacity* of woman to fill any position of life, or society, equally with man. In *France,* the *salique* law predominates, and no woman can ascend the throne; but in England, Queen Victoria rules her people with a dignity and justice equal to that of any monarch that has ever wielded the sceptre of a mighty empire.

It may be emphatically asserted that most of the women, of the present day, who have been *properly educated,* are quite as well fitted for all the social and business relations of society, as men. When thrown upon their own resources, they acquit themselves in a manner well calculated to make many of the "lords of creation" blush at their own positive *inferiority,* in every quality essential for success in life, in comparison with them.

In the United States they have been educated in theology, medicine, law, in sculpture, painting, and many of the other noble and elevated pursuits and professions, and have found themselves fully equal to the duties and responsibilities involved in their respective spheres of action. The Rev. Antoinette *Brown,* Miss *Blackburn,* Lucy *Stone,* Mrs. *Spencer,* Miss *Hosmer,* are illustrious names among the theological, legal and artistic professions, while in the literary fields the women who have won the amaranthine laurels, are *legion!*

The public schools of all the great cities of America are now under the management of thoroughly-educated and accomplished female teachers. Our dry-goods stores are filled with female clerks, while they are found employed in many of the lighter pursuits of trade and industry, and everywhere having the preference over men for their steadiness of habits and industrious qualities.

As a further example of woman's industrial and artistic proficiency, it may be mentioned that many of the pictorial illustrations of the present volume have been achieved by women and girls. Who will say that they are not fully equal to any drawings and wood engravings ever executed by the sterner sex? The pictorials of the best illustrated journals of England and the United States are now the work of women. Their fields of labor are being gradually extended, and many find remunerating wages for their dainty skill and faithful toil. The time is coming when men will be driven from all the lighter pursuits of in-door occupations, and forced to seek those of the rougher toils of the open fields, as more compatible with the coarser elements of their normal organism.

Though we thus perceive that a reform is gradually creeping forward, calculated for extensive blessings to woman, still there are yet too many thousand females in servile bondage and shameful degradation. The poor needle-women who make men's shirts at six cents apiece, and vests and pants, and other clothing, at "starvation prices," are in this deplorable category, not to speak of those females compelled to subsist by other means equally precarious. In Philadelphia, especially, there are a number of palatial Halls and Towers, peering up among the very clouds, devoted to the sale of clothing, whose avaricious proprietors have grown wealthy and insolent upon the excessive toil, tears and sufferings, of the needle-women employed by them. Would it be credited that there are many men in Philadelphia engaged in the *un*manly employment of making dresses for ladies?

*Hood's* affecting "Song of the Shirt," however, is reaching the hearts of many philanthropists and humanitarians, and will ultimately secure the amelioration of all the oppressed female industrials of the land, notwithstanding mercenary "bards" may be employed to write execrable doggrel advertisements in perpetuation of the gross swindlings and robberies of women by pampered and profligate employers. Surely those who seek to aggrandize themselves on the sufferings and oppressions of women, will but sow the wind to reap the whirlwind of popular scorn and engulfment in the final *denouement.*

May we not also hope that the day is at hand when women and girls will not be forced into the brothels of all the great cities, as the only alternative of starvation and death? Statistics show that the large amount of prostitution in London, New York, Philadelphia and other large cities, is chiefly owing to the miserable wages paid to women. We may talk about licensing the so-called "necessary evil," and putting restraints upon vice and crime; but there will never be a decrease of such fearful horrors until women can have full employment and adequate remuneration for services in all the honorable and decent walks of life and occupations. The innate modesty and virtue of the sex, cause them to shrink with loathing from entering upon the "paths which take hold on hell;" but life is sweet and precious, and even insult, injustice and frightful degradation, are preferable to poverty, despair and death.*

The truth is, as an eloquent writer expresses it, "The woman who does not labor—rich and honored though she be—bears on her head the inevitable curse of heaven. The curse works in her failing health—in her fading beauty—in her fretful temper—in her days devoured by ennui. Let her not even dare to think that because she has no domestic circle to care for, she is free from the law meant to be universal."

*Labor*, however, does not consist in servile and exhausting drudgery, but in a moderate and rational exercise of every function of the mental and physical organism.

God Almighty, we again affirm, only intended woman to be a "helpmeet" for man, but "man has sought out many inventions," and prefers as a general rule, even in this enlightened age, that woman shall be degraded to the condition of a servant or a harlot. It was the intention of the wise Ruler of the universe that men should take women for their wives, and that

* See "Acton on Prostitution."

women should have the care of their households, and should rear and educate their children and make them useful and pleasant to their parents and society; but instead of this, in our day, in this glorious land of liberty, we drive women into the streets to feed on garbage and to become a nuisance and disgrace to society.

There is no more manifest indication of the growing depravity of the times, than may be seen in the large and increasing number of men who do not marry. Every man who remains in celibacy deprives a woman of support, and aids in driving her to despair and degradation; and why is it that men refuse to marry, and thus deprive themselves of the comforts of a home? Because they see that most of those who do marry condemn themselves to poverty and embarrassment. Honest, virtuous and useful conduct is not esteemed; but heartless avarice grows rich, and is honored and courted, while obscure worth is despised.

We see many articles in the public prints, speaking of the uselessness and extravagance of American women, giving that as a *cause* for young men remaining single. But why are there so many useless, fashionable ladies? What is the cause of so much extravagance and indolence? In the the first place, women's principal pleasure is to please the men. A wife's greatest pleasure is, or should be, to please her husband. If you ask a married lady why she follows every foolish, frivolous fashion, she will be apt to answer, "Oh, we are compelled to fix up to make our husbands love us." Of course, they have been taught that the only way to please their husbands and retain their love, is to adorn their persons; and surely no one should blame them for the exercise of such a laudable ambition. But why do young ladies spend so much time in preparing for company, attending balls, parties, the opera, and even the church? Go to the ball-room and watch the company, and you will soon see why it is that women are so fond of display, and take such pains to make fools of themselves. See that plain, but neatly-dressed lady; she wears but few ornaments, arranged with taste and simplicity. Her countenance is the index to a mind stored with useful knowledge—she can hold a sensible conversation on any subject; on her hands are visible the marks of the broom or smoothing-iron; she can tell you how to make a pudding, bake a loaf of bread, or roast a fowl. But these are not the qualities to please the gentlemen—the dashing beaux and gallants. They may extend to her the compliments of the evening, but they will quickly pass on to prattle and flirt with some more dressy, though less sensible girl. See that delicate, fragile-looking lady, colorless, except a spot on each cheek, her delicate person almost loaded with jewelry and costly apparel, her hands soft and tender, a languid smile plays about her face; as for cooking, she never thinks of such a vulgarity—that would be robbing servants; she can talk as much nonsense as any fashionable lady, while she can smile and sing fashionably besides. She is surrounded by admirers, all eager to confer a favor, and so much obliged to her for that smile if she happens to cast one in that direction. Young men make choice of ladies raised and educated in this manner, and then expect them to be perfect domestic wives! Where is the philosophy of that? Or, if their better judgment tells them their limited means will not permit of their marrying a fashionable lady, they remain single—for the most of young ladies belong to that class—because young men show a decided preference for ladies raised and educated in that manner. So long as fashionable airs and costly apparel receive more attention and respect than intelligence, simplicity and domestic accomplishment, uselessness, extravagance and profligacy will increase, and society become more and more degenerate. In sooth, it is not "charity" but "*money*" which covers a multitude of sins. Love of *show* and *splendor*, especially, now enter more largely into the marriage ceremony than *true conjugal affection*. The overstrained attentions which men pay to women, in fashionable circles, may well leave a sensible man in doubt as to which of the two, the man or the woman, has the better right to the appellation of the "*softer* sex." Truly every thing is silly and absurd that is not in accordance with the simple edicts of immaculate Nature.

It is palpably obvious that the proper way to find the *true* sphere of woman, is to educate her up to her fullest capacity. Why should not woman's *work* flow spontaneously from woman's nature? Would not this be the case were she left unrestrained to develop her real mission on earth? She should have a training worthy of her inheritance and the object of her creation, as the primal font of man's existence and happiness. From the very peculiarities of her organization, Woman's first and noblest place is the fulfilling of the duties of *Home!* We should have no fear that any freedom given to woman would ever estrange her from the place which God has so peculiarly fitted her to occupy. Woman can only be properly esteemed at *Home*. Here her sway is supreme, whether as mother, wife, sister, friend or companion of man. Who can adequately define the heavenly qualities of a woman's love? The love of a true mother, a true wife, and a true woman is the most estimable blessing that can possibly be given to fallen and sinful man. He who would degrade the sex, and reduce her to the *slave* of his whims and lusts, is the unworthy, paltry wretch, whom it were an insult to Deity to denominate by the name of—*man!*

Every young lady is taught to consider marriage as the great and ultimate end of her life. It is that to which she looks forward for happiness. The female heart is naturally kind and generous—it feels its own weakness and its inability to encounter singly the snares and troubles of life; in short, that it must lean upon another in order to enjoy the delights most congenial to its natural feelings, and the emanation of those tender affections, in the exercise of which, the enjoyments of the female mind chiefly consist. It is thus that the heart of many young women become by degrees irrevocably fixed on those whom they were wont to regard with the utmost indifference, if not with contempt; merely from the latent principle of generosity existing in the original frame of their nature, a principle which is absolutely necessary toward the proper balancing of our respective rights and pleasures, as well as the regulation of the conduct of either sex to the other. Yea, a good wife is man's best safeguard against crime; and a baby in the cradle has often paid more than its milk score by putting many cheery thoughts in its father's heart, and inducing him to save his earnings for a rainy day.

Truly woman's sphere is *Home*. The *family* is conceded to be the most important of the divinely ordained institutions upon which the whole superstructure of society is based, and on which the happiness and moral welfare of all races and nations depend. It is this which constitutes the moral sanctity of all our earthly existence, and upon which God's first and earliest blessing rested, and is all that is left to us of that once blissful paradise which our first parents occupied—the only blessing in fact which survived the fall. Around it clusters all our hopes of earthly happiness, and all the soul-connecting links that seemingly bind us to heaven. It is from this source that emanate all the strong and holy influences of a mother's love, all the sacred ties of parental affection and regard, all the filial and fraternal relations, obligations and duties of life, upon which not only the well-being, but the very existence of society itself depends. It is through the sacred privileges and immunities of the family that, according to the Divine dispensation, the race itself is to be perpetuated—not merely brought into existence, but nurtured, protected, educated, reared up to man's estate. How supremely glorious, then, is woman's mission! Who will deny that she possesses rights equal with man? Who would desecrate the rights and immunities of the family? Who would betray and deceive his offspring? Who would flaunt vice in the presence of innocence and purity? Who would esteem woman as the mere mistress and servant of despotic and brutalized man? Every principle of justice and humanity condemns the debasing inequalities of conventional society, and demands the highest happiness and perfection of WOMAN!

In conclusion, we may observe that wherever we find Woman exercising good sense, modesty and discretion, we will find her filling a sphere of real usefulness and nobly assisting to work out the great and mysterious problem concomitant of man's ultimate exaltation and felicity on earth.

## CHAPTER XIX.

### PHYSICAL PERFECTION—KALYGYNOMIAL PATHOLOGY

### ELEMENTS OF FEMALE BEAUTY.

### IMPORTANCE OF UNDERSTANDING THE SUBJECT OF HUMAN BEAUTY.

> " Oh, who can call this earth a wilderness
> Who feels the power of BEAUTY's charm to bless !"

DR. PRITCHARD has well expressed a great truth in his observation that the "idea of beauty of person is synonymous with that of *health* and *perfect organization.*"

In fact, the perception of human beauty is the chief principle in every country which directs men in their marriages.

Sir *Anthony Carlile* thinks that "a taste for beauty is worthy of being cultivated." "Man," he remarks, "dwells with felicity even on *ideal* female attributes, and in imagination discovers beauties and perfections which solace his wearied hours, far beyond any other resource within the scope of human life. It cannot, therefore, be unwise to cultivate and refine this natural tendency, and to enhance, if possible, these charms of life."

*Horne*, in his "Elements of Criticism," observes, "that a perception of beauty in external objects is requisite to attach us to them; that it greatly promotes industry, by promoting a desire to possess things that are beautiful."

Undoubtedly, we would say, that the *possession* of "beauty" and "worth" constitute not only the *bond* of attraction, but the *very life of* the social union.

The body is as much a desirable part of the human being as the mind. It is the medium by which *all* our senses are discernible. By the body do we communicate hopes, fears, affections and love, and receive them. Why should we, therefore, contemn as a piece of common clay, that which is the only emblem of our existence? God created the body, not only for usefulness, but with loveliness. Then, what he has made so pleasing shall we disesteem, and refuse to apply our knowledge to its admirable destination?

The very approving and innocent complacency we all feel in the contemplation of beauty, whether it be that of a landscape or of a flower, is a sufficient witness that the pleasure which pervades our hearts at the sight of human beauty was planted there by the Great Framer of all things, as a principle of delight and attraction. To this end we are called to the study of the principles of human beauty and perpetuation.

## ANATOMICAL AND PHYSIOLOGICAL PRINCIPLES OF BEAUTY.

> "To *him*, who, in the love of Nature, holds
> Communion with her *visible* form, she speaks
> A various language; for his gayer hours
> She has a voice of gladness, and a smile
> And eloquence of Beauty."

To acquire a knowledge of external beauty, some little physiological information as well as anatomical is desirable. The human body is composed of *parts*, each part contributes a separate economy depending on the *whole*, and the whole is sustained by its *parts*. Internally there is a strong framework of bones, called

### THE SKELETON,

Upon which the superstructure rests. The bones consist of a mixture of earthy and animal matter. The earthy part gives them solidity and strength, while the animal part endows them with vitality. The active and industrious person, whose digestion is good, and lungs healthy and well-developed, will have generally well-formed limbs.

Sir *Charles Bell*, in his "Animal Mechanics," thus describes the beauty of the human framework, as exhibited in the spinal construction:

"The spine consists of twenty-four bones, each bending a little and making a joint with its fellow—all yielding in a slight degree, and permitting, in its whole line, that degree of flexibility which is necessary to the motions of the body. Between these bones or vertebræ there is an elastic, gristly substance, which permits them to approach and play a little in the actions of the body. Whenever there is a weight upon the head, this gristle yields; and the moment it is removed, the gristle regains its place, and the bones resume their position. The spine, which is in the form of an italic *f*, yields, recoils, and forms the most perfect spring, calculated to carry the head without jar or injury. The spine rests on what is called the pelvis, a circle of bones, of which the haunches are the extreme parts."

Connected with the framework comes.

### THE MUSCULAR SYSTEM.

Over the bones is laid a thick bed of muscular flesh, in regular layers, composed of long, slender fibres, that usually run parallel with each other, and are fastened, by a strong, whitish-looking substance, into bundles. They constitute the bulk of the limbs, and much of the back and neck. Each of these layers acts like a pulley, rising and depressing the bones at the will of the individual.

### THE NUTRITIVE SYSTEM,

Or nutritive apparatus, comes next. This embraces the stomach, heart, lungs, liver, pancreas, blood, viscera, etc. The general office of these organs is to digest the food, convert it into chyme, absorb the chyle, and convey it through the body by muscular action, and eject the refuse from the system. The blood is kept pure by the lungs. It is a law of nature, that each of these organs is excited to healthy action by its appropriate stimulus. Accordingly, food that is *adapted* to the wants of the system imparts a healthy stimulus to the salivary glands during the process of mastication. Food well *masticated*, and blended with a *proper* amount of saliva, will induce a healthy action in the stomach, as this *is its* appropriate stimulus. Well prepared *chyme* is the natural stimulus of the duodenum, liver and lungs. If the process of *mastication* and *insalivation* are defective, the whole machinery is wrong, and danger and death are not very remote. When these organs are sound and healthy, they give the human form that beautiful, full and rounded outline, so desirable in preference to sharp points and angles.

## THE NERVOUS SYSTEM

Constitutes the grand medium through which we have communication with every part of the body and the external world. The former systems or functions refer to *organic* life or structure. The nervous system, which is the central and governing apparatus of life, consists of the brain, the spinal cord and the nerves. The brain is in the head, the spinal cord is enclosed in the channel of the backbone, and the nerves are distributed to all the organs and parts of the body. As our astronomical system is called the solar system, because the sun is in the centre watching over our planets, so of these nerves, whose centre is the brain and spinal marrow, but whose smaller departments communicate with every part of our miniature universe.

## THE RELATIVE BEAUTY OF THE MALE AND FEMALE FORMS.

It is only by carefully regarding the admirable models of the ancients that we can gain correct notions of manly beauty and female loveliness.

Both should be proportionally developed in their separate systems. The female should have the nutritive elements predominating, while the male should excel in the nervous or mental and locomotive.

Weak haunches in the male indicate lumbar weak ness, and overgrowth in the procreant functions. On the contrary, wide haunches are a beauty to the female, proving that the reproductive organs are well-developed.

A well-formed man should have his shoulders wider and more prominent than his hips. A well-formed woman should be the reverse.

He should taper from the shoulders up and down —she should taper up and down from the abdomen and hips.

The female should have shoulders and chest small but compact, arms and limbs relatively short; her hips apart and elevated, her abdomen large, and her thigh voluminous. The male should be large about the chest, to indicate expansive lungs; small around the hips to imply locomotive power and vigor.

The length of the neck should be proportionably

less in man than woman, because the dependence of the mental system on the nutritive is connected with the shorter distance of the vessels of the neck.

The back of woman should be more hollow than that of man, to give sufficient depth for parturition. The loins of woman should be more extended at the expense of the superior and inferior parts, than in man, to allow easy gestation. The surface of the whole female form should be characterized by plumpness, elasticity, delicacy and smoothness, because this is not only essential to beauty in woman, but is necessary for the gradual and easy expansion of her person during gestation and delivery. Man should be muscular and wiry, as indicative of strength and energy.

The principal object of a true man's discourse should be what is useful; that of a true woman's that which is agreeable. There should be nothing in common in their discourse but truth—nothing in their feelings but mutual affection. As the poet has beautifully expressed it,—

> "Man is the proud and lofty pine
>   That frowns on many a wave-beat shore;
> Woman, the young and tender vine,
> Whose curling tendrils round it twine,
>   And deck its rough bark o'er."

The most perfect model of the human female ever created by Grecian art, is that of the celebrated piece of sculptuary known as

THE VENUS DE MEDICI.

It was not only the favorite of the Greeks and Romans, but has been the admiration of every intelligent traveler and artist who has seen it. A copy of it should adorn the houses of all who would wish to accustom themselves to the highest conceptions of the human form. The whole figure displays profound physiological and physiognomical knowledge, even in the minutest detail, and is worthy of careful study by the lover of the beauty of his species. Well might Byron say of it:

> "We gaze and turn away, and know not where
> Dazzled and drunk with beauty, till the heart
> Reels with its fullness."

Sir *James Clark* says that young ladies should take the Venus de Medici as the example of what a female figure should be. Every man of true taste, also, should look upon every female as approaching perfection in the proportion as she approaches either the figure of the "Venus de Medici," or the celebrated piece of sculptuary by *Hiram Powers* known as the "*Greek Slave.*"

# PART II.

## DISEASES OF FEMALES AND CHILDREN.

### CHAPTER I.

#### SOME OF THE PRINCIPAL DISEASES OCCURRING FROM INFANCY TO PUBERTY.

In a work of the present limits it will be impossible to speak of all the ailments incident to women and children; therefore reference will only be made to those of the most important and intractable character—the leading features of which will be succinctly and faithfully presented. It is, however, not expected that females uneducated in medicine will be enabled to treat of all the forms of disease mentioned in this volume. Diseases not unfrequently assume a very severe form, both in children and those of pubescent persons; hence the attention of some skillful practitioner will be promptly required, in order to maintain the *vis vitæ* of the organism from the ravages of the maladies.

The diseases of which this work shall treat, will generally yield to the treatment and remedies suggested, and therefore, in most cases, may be regarded as eminently reliable for their curative effects.

Before entering upon the subject of special diseases, it will be necessary to treat of *Irritation*, as it is a condition frequently occurring in children, and sometimes mistaken for inflammation.

## A. IRRITATION AND SYMPATHY.

IRRITATION, from *irrito*, to excite, is produced from some exciting cause operating on some part of the system, and thence extending to other organs or parts, through a law of *sympathy*. The younger and more delicate the child, the more susceptible is its constitution to irritating causes. For instance, the slightest pressure of the teeth against the dental cartilage or gum in an infant, is sufficient to produce the most alarming symptoms, such as convulsions, and other cerebral derangements. Again, irritation of the bowels, liver, etc., will cause bilious derangements, diarrhœa, or cholera infantum, and a long train of other maladies. It is thus perceived that it is highly important to possess a correct idea of irritation, before attempting to combat either its effects or the diseases concomitant of its influence.

As a celebrated writer has well remarked, a knowledge of this influence is as essential to the medical practitioner as the compass is to the mariner. It is a guide to him in the detection of disease, and enables him to use proper remedies for its removal, which he could not otherwise command. It will also prevent, in many instances, the use of depleting means with a view of allaying inflammation, when the system, in fact, is only under the influence of some morbid excitement or irritation. Unfortunately for patients, many acute diseases are treated as the result of some inflammatory action or organic lesion, and, accordingly, the system is reduced by blood-letting and other antiphlogistic treatment, when the disorder is nothing more than simple irritation.

Many children, with naturally strong constitutions, are compelled to struggle through a course of treatment based upon inflammatory action. Thus it is that a large majority sink under such treatment. The bills of infantile mortality most abundantly attest this fact. It is palpable that nearly all the diseases of children arise from irritation and not from inflammation; hence the barbarous system of depletion, in such cases, cannot be too severely condemned. It but adds injury to injury, or fuel to the flame, in order to extinguish it!

Dr. *Copeland*, speaking of the Pathology of Irritation, observes, that if an irritant or stimulus acts upon a living tissue or organ, certain changes are produced. If the digestive organ be acted upon by an irritant, certain actions are increased or modified; while if the irritant be increased, the irritation is increased and extended to other parts. Any function of a part may be more or less modified by the application of an irritant, or be so disordered as to be completely overturned. If a portion of the intestinal canal be irritated by mechanical or chemical stimuli, its contractility is augmented—the secretion and circulation of the canal more or less accelerated, and the sensibility increased, causing pain, in more or less degree or acuteness. In addition to these local changes, if the irritatives be increased, the influence is extended to different parts, through the medium of the nervous system.

In this way one organ is made to sympathize with other and more remote organs. Hence, an irritant applied to the stomach may extend to the intestines and produce colic pains; or to the liver, causing an increased flow of bile; or to the lungs, heart or brain and excite morbid action and distress.

Again, if an irritant be applied to the kidneys, it may produce not only symptoms of inflammation in them, but the irritation may extend to the stomach, through the nervous connection, and cause vomiting; or it may extend to the genital organs, and greatly excite and injure them.

Similar sympathy may arise from teething, and produce vomiting, purging, griping, with green bilious discharges, as the result of the irritation extending to the stomach, liver and intestinal canal; or it may extend to the brain and spinal cord, producing convulsions and coma. Improper food taken into the stomach, or worms in the intestinal canal, produce similar symptoms.

External impressions, such as fear, etc., may produce convulsions, and symptoms of apoplexy, in children. *Hood*, in his work on diseases of children, gives two striking cases in this regard. A nobleman having anxiously desired a son to be born to him, in order to inherit his fortune and title, his wishes at length were gratified. Preparations were made on a grand scale for the infant's christening, which cere mony was to take place at night, in a brilliantly lighted room. When the child was brought in for such purpose, the sudden flare of light caused instantaneous convulsions, from which the infant soon after died. The other was a case, also, where the first-born son of a noble family was to be christened. The bishop had arrived to perform the sacred rite, when the servants knocked so loudly at the door, that the child was frightened, and died of convulsions in consequence.

Irritation when slight may be confined to the part, but cannot exist long without other organs experiencing the same disorder through the sympathetic and cerebro-spinal nervous system.

The more susceptible the nervous system, the more readily are these symptoms between the different organs set up. This is well illustrated in the delicate female laboring under uterine irritation. The sympathy will extend from the uterus to the stomach, and produce derangement of that organ; to the heart, and cause palpitation; to the head, and produce neuralgia; or to other parts of the system, and thus excite the symptoms of a variety of other diseases. Flatulence in the stomach is a very common exciting cause of palpitation of the heart. So will deranged liver and stomach produce the same result. Hence, a physician should have a full knowledge of the laws of sympathy before attempting to treat or remove disease from the organism.

In all organized beings, there is a natural or normal susceptibility, called by some a normal irritability, peculiar to the nervous system. This susceptibility is increased by debility of the nervous system, which makes the whole organism more susceptible to irritating causes. This is seen in a child with its health impaired by teething. It is then more liable to cold from exposure, particularly of the lungs. Mothers, accordingly, should never expose the tender infant's neck and arms, when their own systems would revolt at such unnatural treatment. Thousands of children are annually sacrificed by this foolish and cruel habit alone.

As children advance in age, the susceptibility diminishes, and there is less liability to irritability from exciting causes. We may compare the infant, by way of analogy, to the delicate shoot from the parent plant or shrub. It will wither and die from the slightest frost, while the parent tree or plant is not materially affected by the winter's blasts.

There are some temperaments more liable to irritating influences than others. Children of the nervous and sanguine are more susceptible to irritabilities than those of the bilious or phlegmatic temperaments. The nervous and sanguine are characterized by light eyes and hair, and fair skin; the bilious and phlegmatic have dark hair, eyes and skin. The former are much more susceptible to medicines than the latter. The temperaments are sometimes mixed—the nervous and sanguine uniting, or the nervous and bilious, in the same individual. It is necessary that the temperaments of children be studied as well as their physiognomy. The latter is of the most importance to the medical practitioner. In fact, no physician can be successful in the treatment of children, unless he can diagnose from the physiognomy of the child.

It is said of the celebrated physician *Andral*, that he had such a knowledge of physiognomical presentations of diseases, that he could, by surveying the features of a patient, detect the disease lurking in the system, and point it out without questioning the patient.

The illustrious *Haller* expresses himself thus: "It is the will of God, the great Author of society, that the affections of the mind should express themselves by the voice, the gesture, but especially by the countenance. Nor is this species of language wholly denied even to the brute creation. They, too, by signs, express their love of kind, social friendship, maternal affection, or rage, joy, grief, fear, and all the more violent emotions. A dog easily discovers whether you be angry with him, by your face and tone of voice."

The physiognomy of countenance has been ably treated by *Lavater*, who asks:—

"Does the human face—the mirror of the Deity—that masterpiece of the visible creation, present no appearance of cause and effect; no relation between the external and the internal, the visible and the invisible, and the cause which produces?" As to physicians, he remarks:—

"The physiognomy of the patient frequently instructs him better than all the verbal information he can receive from the invalid. It is astonishing how far some physicians can carry their sagacity in this respect."

The author of the present volume was called, not long since, to see the son of a physician, who labored under a disorder that seemed to baffle all the remedies applied. The lad was about twelve years of age, of a sanguine temperament. The writer found him in a comatose state, in which he had lain for twelve hours. The remedies had been used without any effect, from a belief that the cause of disorder was confined to the brain. When the author saw the expression of his countenance, he came to the conclusion that the stomach was at fault. This proved the fact on examination. A few cups and a blister to the stomach cured the lad before morning, to the astonishment of the father, who had looked upon the case as hopeless. An emetic would have afforded relief much sooner, but it could not be readily given owing to the coma.

Another case, equally striking, may be mentioned. I was called in haste by a physician, to consult with him in a severe case of cerebritis, or inflammation of the brain. The patient was a powerful muscular man, mate of one of the Liverpool packets sailing out of the port of Philadelphia. He was over six feet in height and weighed about two hundred and twenty pounds. He lay insensible in the bed, bedewed with a cold perspiration, his clothes as effectually saturated as if he had been dipped in a pool of water. His pulse was about sixty, and very weak. His countenance indicated gastric derangement; on examination, my suspicions were verified. He was accordingly cupped over the stomach and consciousness speedily returned, and the next day he was well, except feeling a little weak.

Here are two striking cases, showing that an irritation of a local part had the power to affect the brain through a sympathetical influence alone. They will illustrate the importance of studying physiognomy in diagonising diseases.

From an inspection of a child's countenance, much information may be gained. If a child looks heavy about the eyes, has a pale face, and moves and rolls its head from side to side, and cries frequently, it is an evidence that it suffers from headache. If it frowns and dislikes the light, it shows some derangement in the circulation of the brain. If the pupil is dilated and remains so on exposure to light, we may rest assured there is congestion of the brain. Should the pupil contract powerfully on exposing the eye to the light, it is evidence of irritation of the brain. If the features seem pinched, (the muscles of the forehead contracted,) and if there be bluishness around the upper lip, the edges of the nose and angles of the mouth, or if the legs be drawn up and the child screams and starts—if there be any or all of these appearances—they will present evidence of griping, from flatulence or acidity of stomach or bowels.

If the lips, tongue and mouth are dry, and there is a throwing of the hands back of the ear, it is an evidence of pain in the gums from teething.

If the child's flesh feels soft and flabby, blue veins appearing upon the forehead and between the eyes, and its features are pale, with little life or animation, it is evidence that the child has impoverished blood.

In such children, according to Dr. *Hood*, there is danger of that alarming and fatal disease, usually called laryngismus stridulus or crowing respiration of infants.

The skin is also a guide. If it be bluish-white and "pasty" it is an evidence of the impurity of the blood. If of a "dirty yellow," it indicates deranged liver. If the skin is dark and dry, it is an evidence of irritation in some of the vital organs.

The position of the child is also a guide to the physician. If it seems to be lying naturally, with its arms folded, and thighs drawn up toward its belly, and lying on its side, it is a sign that the child is doing well, and not suffering from any great amount of irritation or derangement of the system.

These facts and views cannot be too attentively considered by physicians and mothers, when treating the diseases to which children are subject.

## B. DENTITION OR TEETHING.

For a description of the formation and development of the teeth, the reader is referred to Part III. of this work.

The protrusion of the tooth through the gum takes place at different periods in different children. As a general rule, they commence six months after birth, and end at two and a half years. The first are called deciduous teeth, and are twenty in number, ten upon the upper and ten upon the under jaw. They usually appear in the following order:—

1st. Two lower incisors or front teeth.

2d. Two upper incisors. These usually appear from the sixth to the eighth month.

3rd. The first lower molars or jaw teeth.

4th. The first upper molars. These usually appear from the twelfth to the sixteenth month.

5th. Lower canine or stomach teeth.

6th. Upper canine or eye-teeth. These usually appear from the fourteenth to the twentieth month.

7th. The four last molars or jaw teeth. These usually appear from the twenty-fourth to the thirtieth month.

Some children are very irregular in cutting their teeth. In a few instances they are born with their front teeth already cut. Sometimes the lower teeth appear before the upper ones; while some children do not commence cutting them until they are nearly eighteen months old.

*Meckel* mentions a case where there was but a single tooth to each jaw; and another case where there was none. It is more common, however, to meet with an excess than deficiency.

The cutting of the teeth may produce functional derangement in almost every organ of the body, through the irritation and pain occasioned by the pressure of the tooth against the sensitive dental nerves. The brain, stomach, lungs, liver, bowels, and, in fact, every organ and function may, separately or combined, become affected through this cause.

The mother, in most cases, is aware that the child is cutting its teeth, and familiar with the fact that its delicate system is liable to receive a severe shock from such cause. Hence the dread that mothers have for the second summer, which induces many to nurse longer than they otherwise would.

During dentition, the child becomes restless and peevish; the mouth is hot any dry; sometimes there is a free flow of saliva; frequent putting the fingers in the mouth; throwing the hands back of the ears; wakefulness and restlessness at night, etc. The irritation may affect other parts of the system sympathetically. This is more apt to be the case in weak and delicate children, because the system in such cases, is more susceptible to irritation than in those of robust constitutions. With some children the brain and spinal-nervous system particularly sympathize, causing convulsions, spasmodic twitchings, etc. Sometimes the irritation extends to the lungs, producing obstinate and protracted cough; or to the stomach and bowels, causing sickness, vomiting, and looseness of the bowels. If the looseness of bowels is only moderate, it acts favorably by relieving the brain. Sometimes the irritation extends to the skin, inducing eruptions which may continue during dentition. The eruption is more apt to make its appearance behind the ears or upon the face.

*Treatment.*—If the bowels are inclined to be costive, they should be opened with some mild purgative.

I have found that a fourth or half drop of the tincture of nux vomica, administered two or three times a day, in a little water, to answer better in overcoming constipation than any other remedy.

Purgatives are always objectionable in constipation, where there is a predisposition that way, as they are apt to render the constipation more obstinate than be fore. If purgatives seem necessary, magnesia or castor oil may answer the purpose.

If there be much fever, with hot gums, the follow ing may be administered :—

℞ Tinct. aconite, *fol.*....................f ʒj
Tinct. balladonna,....................ʒss.
Sweet spirits nitre,....................℥ss.
Water,.............................℥vj.
Dose, teaspoonful every hour.

The child should frequently be offered cold drinks, and its gums bathed with cold water. This may be done by saturating a rag with ice-water, and placing it frequently on the gums.

Looseness of the bowels should not be checked unless it is such as to reduce the strength of the child; nor should eruptions be interfered with, for their appearance is often the salvation of the child. Dr. *Parrish* was in the habit of imitating Nature by blistering behind the ears, and keeping up a discharge, to the great relief of the child.

If the gum is hot, too sore, or too highly inflamed, the child should be induced to chew upon some hard substance, such as ivory or bone. When the gum is highly inflamed, and the tooth well advanced, the gum may be divided with a lance or sharp knife. The incision should be made through the gum. If the tooth is not well advanced, it is best not to lance, on account of the edges uniting and forming a hard cicatrix, which makes it more difficult for the penetration of the teeth afterward.

If alarming symptoms should occur, such as convulsions and incessant drainings from the bowels, attended with vomiting, there should be no hesitation in lancing the gums. It will often give immediate relief, by unloading the congestive capillaries of the gum and lessen the irritation. Sometimes it is necessary to lance after a portion of the tooth has protruded through the gum, in order to relieve it from pressing against the sharp edges of the tooth. This is the case with the eye, stomach, and front teeth.

If the bowels should be too loose, they should be moderately checked. For such purpose, the following is one of the best remedies that can be used:—

℞ Tinct. aconite,........................ʒj.
Acetate morphine, .....................½ gr.
Water, ...............................℥vj.

Dose, one teaspoonful every one or two hours, until partially checked.

If there should be sickness of stomach, two or three drops of camphor may be added to each dose, and a spice plaster applied to the stomach.

If the discharge from the bowels continue, or the sickness at the stomach, from the irritation of the gum, a small blister behind the ear may afford some relief, providing the discharge is kept up.

Some physicians recommend the administration of calomel for the green discharges from the bowels, believing it to be owing to some serious derangement of the liver. They should remember that the same sympathetic cause which affects the bowels and stomach, is extended to the liver, causing an increased secretion of that organ. Hence the bilious discharges. Morphine and aconite will generally break up this sympathy, and in that way diminish the discharge, which cannot be done by the administration of mercury.

Should there be convulsions the child should be set in warm water with a little mustard dissolved in it. The mere placing the feet in warm water will not answer. The lower part of its body and limbs should be immersed, and cold applications made to the head by saturating cloths with ice-water. The tooth should also be lanced at once, provided the gum is swollen and inflamed. It is surprising to find what instantaneous relief is sometimes afforded by lancing the gum. This process relieves the pressure on the dental nerves, and removes the bulk of irritation. After the convulsions subside, the prescription on page 372 should be given, and repeated every one or two hours. At the same time the bowels must be kept open.

Sponging the child's head and face several times a day with cold water, will afford great relief, when there is much fever and hot skin. In weak and delicate children, fresh country air will afford more relief and tend to keep down the irritation than all the medicine that can be administered. If the child cannot be taken into the country, it should be carried early in the morning into the open air, with its body well protected from exposure. It should be kept from the night air, while its sleeping chamber should be well ventilated.

Sometimes the submaxillary glands, which are located on the inner and lower surface of the lower jaw, will enlarge and suppurate if they do not receive attention. I have found that an emetic administered every three or four days, has a powerful tendency to promote the absorbents and reduce the swelling. Ipecac is the mildest and best emetic that can be used. From five to six grains in powder at a dose is sufficient to produce free vomiting. If the glands should continue to enlarge, the ointment of Iodide of potash may be applied:

℞ Iodide potash,......................ʒj.
Simple cerate,.........................℥j.

Mix.

Rub a piece about the size of a chestnut night and morning into and around the tumor.

The child's diet should receive strict attention. If the mother's milk agrees with it, it will require no other nourishment. If it is not nursed, the milk from the same cow should be given, after being boiled. If the bowels incline to be loose, a cracker soaked in the milk and it sweetened with loaf sugar, with a little nutmeg added, may be used. If the child is much debilitated, a little good Port wine may be added to the cracker victuals; or cream half diluted with milk may be given, and occasionally a few drops of wine with water and nutmeg.

### B. CHOLERA INFANTUM, OR SUMMER COMPLAINT.

This is one of the most fatal diseases of children. It usually occurs during the first or second summer — frequently from the irritation attendant upon dentition.

Another frequent cause is improper diet and the bad ventilation of the apartments in which the children, especially of the poorer classes of society, are compelled to lived.

SYMPTOMS.—The attack of Summer complaint is usually preceded by diarrhœa, existing in some cases, for some time previously with the patient. Sometimes the attack will be instantaneous, commencing with violent vomiting and purging. At times the stomach is so irritable as to eject every thing taken into it, even a mouthful of cold water, at the same time there is spasmodic pains in the stomach and bowels. The features become shrunken, the skin cool and clammy, the eyes half closed, while there is partial insensibility and twitchings and starting. Insensibility may continue until it amounts to coma and death.

The disease may commence and terminate with these symptoms in two or three days, or a shorter period. In those fatal cases, attended with insensibility, there is a morbid condition of the brain. The attacks are attended usually with fever and quick pulse; the pulse is also weak or corded; the mouth is hot and dry; tongue furred; extremities cool, while the surface of the body and head is hot. If the attack is very severe, the child weakens rapidly; the eyes become sunken; the surface cool and pale, harsh and dry.

In some of the very severe cases, the mucous membrane of the mouth and tongue takes on an aphthous or inflamed condition, the whole surface becoming covered with white ulcers or sloughs. Sometimes they present a dark-brownish appearance, which is indicative of great debility or prostration. Frequently an eruption appears upon the body, resembling flea-bites, catled *petechiæ*. The skin, also, presents a dirty, dull hue, the eyes are blood-shotten, while the emaciation is in the extreme.

The discharges from the bowels are as various as are the symptoms. At first they seem to consist principally of undigested food, such as curdled milk, and other coagulated liquids. As they become more copious and frequent, they consist of yellow or yellowish-white secretion; or they may be green and slimy. During the disease they seldom present the natural fecal odor. The matter vomited is sour, slimy, and sometimes a yellowish-green liquid. The disease may continue for weeks or months, providing the exciting cause is not removed.

CAUSES.—Unwholesome food, dentition, ill-ventilated apartments, and the increasing temperature of the weather, are the most prominent causes of the complaint.

TREATMENT.—The first step in the treatment is to remove the causes that keep up the irritation. The second is to allay the irritation. If it be the heated and impure atmosphere, the child should be removed to the country, if practicable. If this cannot be accomplished, it should be kept as much as may be deemed advisable in the open air, during the day, by airings in the parks, excursions on the water, or in drives about the suburbs of towns and cities. I have known a day's trip on the river to arrest the most alarming symptoms, when all other curative means had failed. I have also known one day's confinement in a crowded and heated apartment, to bring back the symptoms in their fullest virulence and force. Sometimes the mother's milk will disagree with the child. This it is sure to do, if it contains cholostrum. The mother's anxiety of mind may also act as a secondary cause to render the lacteal fluid unfit for the child. For full information on this point, see the article on LACTATION, in another part of this volume. If the exciting cause be dentition, the treatment recommended in that article should be employed. If the mother's milk or her mental anxiety be the cause of the child's illness, a wet nurse should be procured, or a resort be had to artificial nursing.

If the teeth press against the dental nerve, and it be inflamed and reddened, the gum should be lanced, and the prescription on page 372 be given every hour or every two hours; or the following may be taken at intervals of an hour, or an hour and a half, or two hours:—

No. 1. ℞ Tinct. Aconite, *fol*,................f ʒjss.
Acetate morphia..................gr. j.
Tinct. Veratria *alba*,...............f ʒj.
Camphor water,...................℥v.
One teaspoonful every three hours.

Or,

No. 2. ℞ Corrosive chloride mercury,........gr. ½
Tinct. aconite, *fol*.,...............f ʒjss.
Water,.........................℥vj.
One teaspoonful every three hours, alternating with the one above.

For sickness of stomach, a spice plaster should be applied over the entire abdomen. I have known the spice plaster to act like a charm in allaying sickness and restlessness. If the disease assumes an intermittent form, the following powder may be given two or three times a day, and No. 1 prescription on page 377 given every three hours until the discharges diminish, when it need not be repeated so frequently.

℞ Sulph. Quinnia, }
Tannic acid, } *a a*, ....................gr. v.
Pulv. sugar...............................ʒj.

Mix, and make into twelve powders, and give as above directed.

The powders may also be given if there is much weakness or debility without the periodicity. The child's strength must be kept up with wine or brandy, until a change takes place.

The foregoing treatment will answer in most cases where medicine will prove of any avail. There are cases in which all treatment fails. The child's salvation will then depend upon country air, in conjunction with the remedies presented. As a general rule, the gentler the child is treated, and the less medicine that is given, the better, to insure its recovery to health. Thousands of children are annually virtually slaughtered by over-dosing with medicine, instead of allowing Nature an opportunity of exerting her recuperative power in overcoming the difficulty.

### C. SCARLET FEVER.

This is a disease of fearful mortality among children, in some seasons, leaving its desolating effects in many families, whether the affluent or humble.

There are three varieties of Scarlet. Fever—*Scarlatina Simple, Scarlatina Anginosa*, and *Scarlatina Maligna* —usually described by writers. We present another form, frequently met with, called by some, *Scarlatina without eruption.*

All these forms are one and the same, only manifesting different degrees of severity. In some cases, they are so intimately blended that it is almost impossible to designate to which division they belong.

The first and last divisions are attended with but little danger and usually run their course in four or five days.

The other two forms, if not treated early, will terminate in gangrene, sloughing and fatal disorganization of the throat and larynx.

Scarlet fever is more prevalent in the Fall and Winter, and usually occurs in children after dentition and before puberty.

Scarlet fever is often mistaken for other Febrile diseases, particularly Measles. It may be distinguished from Measles by the absence of the catarrhal symptoms, which always accompany the latter. The rash occurs earlier in Scarlet Fever than in the Measles. In the first, it makes its appearance on the second day; in the other, usually about the fourth day. Scarlet Fever is also accompanied with sore throat and redness of the fauces. In Scarlet Fever, the eruption makes its appearance in a small rash, which runs together in patches. In Measles, the eruption consists in small circular dots like flea-bites, that cluster to gether. The rash in Measles is not near so red as in Scarlet Fever.

*a.* SCARLATINA SIMPLEX.—Chilly sensations, or shiverings, succeeded by frequent pulse, headache, nausea, and slight soreness of the throat. In about two days or forty-eight hours, the eruption makes its appearance upon the face and neck, and gradully extends to the body and extremities. The eruption consists of fine red pimples which seem to run together and extend over the whole surface of the body. After the eruption makes its appearance the unpleasant symptoms, such as nausea and oppression at the stomach, subside. On the fourth or fifth day, the eruption has run its course, when the skin desquamates and convalescence occurs.

*b.* SCARLATINA ANGINOSA.—*Symptoms.*—In this variety the symptoms are more strongly marked than in the foregoing. The chilliness is greater, the pulse stronger, there is more nausea and vomiting, the throat is very sore and deglutition or swallowing difficult and painful. The tongue is covered with a white or yellowish fur; the fauces, throat and tonsils are swollen, inflamed, and ulcerated; the voice thick and hoarse, with difficult breathing and slight cough. There is severe headache, the eyes are swollen and injected, while there is stiffness of the neck and tenderness of the abdomen and stomach.

The eruption does not usually make its appearance so soon as in *Scarlatina Simplex;* but occur from the second to the fifth day, and are uniformly diffused over the whole body, or in blotches. If the disease terminates favorably, the eruptions commence subsiding about the sixth or eighth day, and gradually convalescence is established.

Should the eruptions extend down into the stomach and bronchi instead of extending out under the skin, all the symptoms become more aggravated; inflammation of the stomach, bronchi, and brain supervene, which, if not speedily arrested, terminate fatally In this disease the inflammation ranges higher than in most other febrile diseases, with a strong, bounding pulse.

*c.* SCARLATINA MALIGNA.—This is one of the most dangerous diseases the physician has to contend against. It usually commences with the ordinary train of symptoms, as indicated in the last form, but very soon gives way to those of a typhoid character, producing great prostration of the system. The pulse becomes less frequent, and weak; the skin, instead of assuming a bright red appearance, is pale; the heat subsides below the healthy standard; the eye becomes dull and suffused; the throat covered with ulcers of a pale ash color; the fauces and larynx become swollen and inflamed, as well as the bronchi; an acrid discharge passes from the nostrils, and the tongue becomes dry and of a dark mahogany hue, followed by diarrhœa and hemorrhage.

The disease may also extend to the brain, as well as the abdominal viscera, causing coma and death.

The ulcers of the throat often slough, destroying or involving the soft part and cartilages of the larynx.

In some cases of scarlatina maligna, the eruption does not make its appearance upon the surface of the body. In others, a few blotches make their appearance and disappear. In another class of cases, most alarming symptoms occur, as it were, all at once, overwhelming the *vis vitæ* of the system in a few hours, and causing death.

*d.* SCARLATINA WITHOUT ERUPTION.—During the prevalence of scarlet fever, there are cases of fever and sore throat, which seem to run the exact course of the disease. These are said to be capable of imparting scarlet fever.

*Cause.*—Scarlet fever no doubt results from a morbific contagion. This contagion is no doubt diffused through the atmosphere, occurring in some sections of country an epidemic. Persons of all ages are liable to the disease—adult females more than adult males, and children more than either of the other two. It is, however, more fatal to males after puberty than to females after menstruation. There is only small liability to the disease after the age of fifty.

Without doubt, scarlet fever, like measles, depends upon an infusoria which locate in the mucous membranes of the fauces, and either follows the course of the mucous membrane into the stomach and air passages, or travels out under the epidermis or outer layer of the skin.

The idea of the rash striking in after it makes its appearance, is an absurdity. The basement membrane of the skin and mucous membrane is a matrix in which the infusoria seem to be rapidly nourished. Its usual course is outward, under the epidermis. In the malignant form of the disease, it follows the course of the mucous membrane, involving the stomach, bowels, and lungs, which being vital organs must produce disastrous effects upon the system.

In malignant forms the system is more susceptible to its influences. The rapid development of infusoria causes ulceration and sloughing of the mucous membrane of the throat, if such development be not speedily arrested. This may be readily done, if the proper means be adopted, as we shall presently show.

Scarlet fever is always worse in low, damp, and badly drained districts, which seem to favor the *Infusoria* theory of scarlet fever.

It has been noticed that feather beds, woolen bed clothes, etc., when not exposed to fresh air will retain for a long time the contagion.

Dr. *Withering*, in his work on "Scarlet Fever," states, in his opinion, that scarlet fever poison first lodges in the mucous membrane of the fauces. He accordingly recommends those who are exposed, to promote the discharge from the throat and mouth and frequently spit out the secretion. He also advises those who have imbibed the poison to take an emetic and frequently wash out the throat with soap-lye diluted with water.

Dr. *Hood*, in his work on "Scarlet Fever," states, that Dr. *Fuller* informed him, that when attending a case of a young man laboring under the malignant form of scarlet fever, he recommended his mother—who kept a boarding house that was full of boarders, who became greatly alarmed—to saturate towels dipped in chlorine water and hang them on backs of chairs, so that the air of the chambers might be thoroughly impregnated with its qualities. The result was that not one of the family contracted the disease. Strange to say, also, the young man whose throat was very painful, and attended with great difficulty in swallowing, was so much influenced in half an hour by the chlorine, that his throat became much better, and all his symptoms subsided.

Dr. *Hood* always employed chlorine after this in scarlet fever, with signal advantage. I have also used chlorine in the treatment of scarlet fever, with entire satisfaction in the worst forms of the disease.

## PREVENTIVES IN SCARLET FEVER.

Belladonna and chlorine are no doubt prophylactics in scarlet fever. My own experience fully satisfies me of this fact. I have always met with the happiest results from their employment. I have also noticed that where belladonna has been used, and the individual took the disease, it always assumed a very mild form.

My plan of administering belladonna is in three-drop doses, three times a day, having the house well ventilated and chlorine used to purify the air of the room. The plan I use for generating this disinfecting agent will be found detailed in page 387.

Treatment.—If there be difficulty in swallowing, if the throat and tonsils are inflamed and swollen, if the face be injected and there be suffusion of the eyes, with strong bounding pulse and dry skin, I administer an emetic and produce free vomiting. This will reduce all these symptoms and afford a more prompt action for other remedies.

The best emetic is pulverized Ipecacuanha alone, or combined with sulphate of zinc.

To a child of six years old. I would give the following:—

℞ Pulv. ipecac.,.................... x grs.
Sulphate zinc,.................. x grs.
Simple syrup,..................... ʒij.
Water,............................ ℥j.

The whole to be taken followed by a cup of warm water. The warm water may be repeated till vomiting occurs. When there is difficulty in inducing a child to take the above, I order one teaspoonful of the syrup of ipecac to be administered every fifteen minutes until vomiting is induced. After vomiting, the skin becomes moist, the bowels are relieved, and the child will say it feels much better, and complain of feeling hungry, which may be gratified by giving a little toast and tea.

Emetics may also be usefully employed during the course of the disease, if there be swelling of the throat and other urgent symptoms; or if there be evidence of insensibility or coma, or sickness of the stomach—thus relieving the brain, and eliminating the bilious and acid secretions, the one being the cause of coma and the other of the nausea, etc.

Sometimes emetics will fail to act, owing to too great a depression of the vital energies of the system. In such cases I usually combine with ipecac one grain of Cayenne pepper, or a teaspoonful of brandy may be administered; either of which will wonder fully assist the ipecac in producing free vomiting.

Emetics may be safely administered in the worst and lowest forms of the disease with brandy. Where the brain is affected and the bowels not relaxed, a mild purgative may be given. If the system is prostrated, a teaspoonful of brandy and water and castor oil may be administered.

After the stomach is freely evacuated and the bowels acted upon, take a solution of the chloride of lime, one ounce to the pint, and swab out the throat and mouth with it, provided the child is not too young to apply the gargle. The swab may be made by tieing a piece of rag around a stick. If a little of the solution should happen to be swallowed, it will be a benefit rather than a disadvantage to the patient. This swabbing should be repeated twice a day. The child's body should also be sponged night and morning with the same solution. This will destroy the infusoria, and thus relieve the throat and mucous membrane of the irritating cause. It will also deaden the eruption of the skin, which is also keeping up the irritation and promoting the fever.

The following is to be taken in teaspoonful doses, every hour, until the fever subsides:

℞ Tinct. aconite, *fol.*,..................ʒiss.
Tinct. belladona,..................ʒj.
Camphor water, }
Water, } *aa*,.............℥iij.

This treatment, with the wash of chloride of lime, is sufficient in ordinary cases, without the use of emetics. It is only for the relief of the throat and for the relaxation of the system, that I use the emetics.

The following may be used as a drink and disen

fecting agent:—To twenty grains of chloride of potash in a quart bottle, add one drachm of hydrochloric acid, and cork it tightly. Let the mixture stand about half an hour, and then add by degrees a quart of water. Shake well at every addition of the water, to make the water absorb the gas. After the water add three ounces of syrup of orange peel. This may be kept by the bedside of the patient, and will answer both as a disenfecting agent and a grateful drink.

There is one important point to be mentioned in connection with the treatment of the malignant forms of Scarlet Fever. When I find that there is a constant tendency to swelling of the throat and ulceration, I always administer an emetic, while if the bowels are inclined to constipation, I act gently on them. I afterward commence at once with quinine, in connection with the prescription mentioned at page 386, and the chloride of lime wash.

If there be an increase of pulse and fever while using quinine, I either reduce the dose of quinine, or continue it as before, in connection with another emetic. This plan will soon relieve the system.

For a child from six to eight years of age, I give one or two grains of quinine at a dose, first observing the degree of depression of the system.

I frequently give the quinine in the following form:—

℞ Sulphate quinine,............grs. xviii.
Comp. tinct. cinchona,........℥j.
Dilute sulphuric acid,........ʒj.
Syrup of orange peel,.........℥ij.
Water,....................℥ij.

Mix, and give two teaspoonsful to a child six years old, three times a day, in a wineglass of water.

There is sometimes difficulty in getting children to take this preparation. In such instances, the tincture of orange peel may be substituted for the tincture of cinchona.

With the treatment here presented, there will be no difficulty in curing the most malignant forms of Scarlet Fever, provided the treatment is commenced before the contagion has completely overwhelmed the *vis vitæ** of the system. In no case should bleeding be attempted. The physician might as well plunge a dagger into the heart of the child at once as take its blood by blood-letting.

## D. MEASLES, OR RUBEOLA.

This is an eruptive disease occurring in childhood. It sometimes attacks grown persons—and usually more severely than children. Like scarlatina, one attack will generally secure the individual against the same disease again.

*Symptoms.*—The symptoms at first are very similar to ordinary catarrh, commencing with chilliness, running of the nose, red and watery eyes, slight soreness of throat, cough, soreness and pain in chest, difficult breathing, great heat and thirst, nausea, headache and sneezing are the prominent precursory symptoms. These symptoms continue four or five days, after which the eruption makes its appearance. It commences generally upon the face, usually the forehead,

* See "Law of Life," in "Boyhood's Perils and Manhood's Curse."

and gradually extends downward to the neck, breast, back, and finally to the lower extremities.

The more profuse the eruption the higher the fever, which continues unabated until the eruption begins to subside; which is usually in four or five days. On the ninth day, they disappear, when bran-like scurf is cast off from the skin. During the course of the disease, the cough is troublesome, which is occasioned by the contagion attacking the air passages.

The eruption makes its appearance in small scattered red spots, in the centre of which spots we find a small pimple, looking like small flea-bites, about the size of a small millet-seed. These, as they grow, unite into red spots. They rise above the skin, and feel rough if the hand is rubbed over its surface.

Measles may occur at any time from three days to three weeks after the child has been exposed to the contagion. It, however, usually occurs from the seventh to the fourteenth day.

Measles may be mistaken for an eruption occurring in dentition, accompanied with the usual symptoms of cold, such as sneezing, running of nose, redness of eyes, etc. The eruption which resembles measles, usually makes its appearance on a different part of the body from measles, commencing first on the back and stomach. This eruption is of comparative little consequence, and depends on derangement of the stomach or bowels. With proper treatment and diet, it will disappear in twenty-four hours.

The difference between Scarlet Fever and Measles is well marked.

The primary symptoms of Measles are sneezing, running of nose, cough, hoarseness, red and watery eyes. These are wanting in Scarlet Fever.

The eruption from Measles appears in spots looking like flea-bites, which run together in patches of a semilunar shape, while Scarlatina-rash consists of minute pimples, diffused all over the body, producing a bright red color. There is also a roughness of the skin in Measles which is not observed in Scarlatina. The color of the eruption is also different—Measles being of a purplish or *dark scarlet*, while Scarlet-rash is of a *light* scarlet color. There is a form of Measles called *Rubeola Nigra* or Black-measles. They depend upon a low condition of the vital powers of the system. A similar condition of system is observed in Malignant Scarlet Fever.

*Cause.*—Like all other contagious diseases, Measles depends upon a species of Infusoria which locates in the air-passages, and are there nourished as in Scarlet Fever. They pass out under the epidemics as in Scarlet Fever, or they may pass into the air-passages and lungs, and thus produce inflammation, and plant the seeds of Consumption, particularly when they occur in grown persons with weak lungs.

If the vital powers of the system are low, they exert a greater influence, while the symptoms are likewise more violent.

*Treatment.*—Measles, in ordinary cases, require but little medical treatment. The only danger to be apprehended is from the damage which may be done to the lungs by the passage of the infusoria down into the air passages, instead of passing out under the epidermis.

The bowels should be kept regular, and the patient moderately warm. All warm drinks and emetics must be avoided, as their tendency is only to increase the fever and eruption, by favoring the development of the contagion.

I have found the same wash, which I recommended in Scarlet Fever, to answer remarkably well in cases where the eruption has been very profuse and the fever high. Under ordinary circumstances, however, it is unnecessary to make any application whatever to the skin.

If there be much fever, three drops of the Tincture Aconite *fol.* may be combined with five drops of the Tincture of Camphor and ten drops of Sweet Spirits of Nitre, and given every two or three hours in water. Should there be catarrhal symptoms, attended with distressing cough, the following may be given:—

℞ Tinct. aconite, *fol*........................ʒj.
Tinct. pulsatilla, ..........................ʒss.
Acetate morphia,.........................gr. j
Water, ..................................℥iv.

Dose for a child of six years, one teaspoonful every two hours.

Pulsatilla is especially adapted to Measles—as much so as Belladonna is to Scarlet Fever—and may be given to children that have not taken the measles in the same family where the disorder exists. If it does not prevent the occurrence of measles, it will make the symptoms much lighter than they would be otherwise.

After the eruption disappears in measles, the skin is often found to be harsh and dry. If a tepid bath be taken and the skin well rubbed, it will change its character and afford great relief to the patient.

When the eruption disappears and leaves a dry, hacking cough, it should be removed as speedily as practicable, otherwise it may induce obstinate bronchial inflammation and consumption.

## E. CROUP.

It is only within the present century that a distinction has been made between Hooping-cough, Asthma, Bronchitis and Croup. Formerly they were regarded as one and the same complaint. By the light of modern science, however, we are enabled to distinguish a marked difference between these varieties of disorders.

Under the old treatment of blood-letting and other depletions, Croup becomes a formidable disease. By the modern method it may be readily subdued and eradicated. It is a disease that seldom occurs after the age of eight years.

*Cause.*—Croup sometimes appears to be an epidemic. and is more prevalent in low, ill-drained localities Exposure to cold damp wind is a frequent cause. If a child is attacked once with the Croup it is apt to occur again. The attack seems to leave a susceptibility in the lining membrane of the larynx, trachia and bronchial tubes.

*Symptoms of Croup.*—Croup is usually divided into two forms—*Catarrhal Croup* and *Pseudo-membraneous or false membranous Croup.* These two forms may exist at the same time, and it is difficult to distinguish them in the commencement of the disease.

*a.* CATARRHAL CROUP—sometimes called *Spasmodic Croup*—usually develops itself suddenly. The child, on waking from sleep, gives utterance to a peculiar, shrill-sounding cough, somewhat similar to the crowing of a cock. Sometimes it is preceded with a dry cough and hoarseness for some days previous. There is considerable dyspnœa, or difficult breathing, which is very distressing. The voice is also rough and hoarse.

*b.* PSEUDO, OR FALSE MEMBRANOUS CROUP sometimes assumes this form from the commencement. At other times it is ushered in with the symptoms of Catarrhal Croup, and thus it is impossible to distinguish them until the false membrane has commenced forming, when the voice becomes whispering, and the cough changes from a ringing or sonorous to a husky sound.

Whenever the voice cannot be raised above a whisper and the fauces reveals white patches of exudation, we may be assured that it is the worst form of Croup. As the disease advances there is great difficulty in breathing, much anxiety of countenance, and an impossibility to raise the voice so as to be distinctly understood, with swelling of the throat.

*Treatment.*—As soon as Croup is detected, which is generally at night, about or little after midnight, the child should be immediately taken into a warm room and placed in a tub of warm water, about blood-heat, while a towel wet with cold water and wrung out, should be applied to the throat, and frequently repeated, giving at the same time the following:—

Tincture aconite, *fol.*,..........f ʒj.
Tinct. belladonna..............f ʒss.
Tartar emetic..................gr. ij.
Water .......................℥iv.

A teaspoonful should be given every ten or fifteen minutes until the child is relieved. After this it may be given every one or two hours.

Should the cough continue for several days, a spice plaster placed on the chest, will afford great relief. If the disease seems spasmodic, I keep the child nauseated with ipecac or tincture of lobelia, or pulverized lobelia mixed with syrup. When I find the foregoing preparation will not break up the attack, or the improvement is not as rapid as I desire, I give the following in place of it:—

℞ Tincture lobelia,.....................f ℥j.
Tinct. aconite, *fol.*,..................f ʒj.

Mix—Dose, ten to twenty drops every ten or fifteen minutes, until free vomiting is produced.

As a second attack generally occurs the succeeding night about the same time with more alarming symptoms, if the disease is not completely broken up, I usually administer one of the following powders after supper, at nine o'clock, and again about one hour before the time for the attack to occur, which will in nearly every instance prevent its occurrence.

℞ Sulphate quinine, .................gr. viij.
Pulv. ipecac,.....................gr. x.

Mix—Make into ten powders, and give as above indicated.

This treatment will seldom fail to be successful in catarrhal croup.

If a false membrane has formed the prognosis is not so favorable. The treatment already given should be persevered with and free vomiting produced in order to expel the membrane, and the following application be made to the throat, which has been highly extolled by some of the European journals.

℞ Extract belladonna,....................ʒij.
Mercurial ointment,...................ʒvi.
Mix together.

It is to be well rubbed in on the throat every two hours. It will act much more promptly if the surface be first blistered with ordinary blistering cerate.

*Spongia* is recommended by the Homeopathics, and claimed to be a *specific.* Its virtue probably rests in the iodine. If so, why not use the iodine at once? For this purpose, I would recommend one or two drops of *Lougal's* solution, in a little water, and given every half hour. Iodine acts powerfully upon the absorbents, and no doubt would be an efficacious remedy, in connection with the local application I have prescribed. I would, at least, recommend it to be tried in all apparently hopeless cases.

The best preventive of croup is to sponge the child's body daily with cold water, the year round, and rub it dry with a coarse towel. The child should be warmly clothed, especially its throat and neck protected from damp, chilly atmosphere. Its feet, also, must be kept warm and dry.

## F. HOOPING COUGH.

Writers generally recognize three distinct stages of hooping cough.

1st. *Forming Stage.*—The symptoms are similar to ordinary catarrh, such as sneezing, dry cough, watery eyes, headache, oppression in the chest, fever, etc., which continue two or three weeks, when the second stage commences. This is called—

2d. *Convulsive Stage.*—During this stage the cough is paroxysmal, of a convulsive and suffocative character. The peculiar hoop is caused by the spasmodic contraction of the glottis, giving rise to suffocation and difficult respiration during the paroxysm. The paroxysms of coughing usually continue from one to five minutes, at the termination of which there is usually vomiting and expectoration of ropy mucus. The convulsive stage generally lasts from five to six weeks, when the third stage commences, which is called the—

3d. *Declining Stage.*—At this stage the symptoms are less severe and the paroxysms less violent, and in the course of two or three weeks the disease disappears.

*Causes.*—The causes, like those of scarlet fever and measles, is dependent upon a peculiar miasma, that affects the individual but once in his life-time. The system is made susceptible to this influence by colds, diseases of the respiratory organs, debility, fatigue, etc. When the disease occurs at the latter end of the Spring, it usually runs its course with comparative mildness. When it commences at the latter end of Autumn, during the Winter, or beginning of Spring it is more trying to the patient—the Eastern and Northerly winds aggravating the cough and keeping up the irritation of the air passages.

*Treatment.*—In a majority of cases, I have found three drops of the tincture of hyosciamos, three times a day, for a child from three to six years of age, to answer remarkably well. In most cases it seems to act as *specifically* as belladonna does in the prevention of scarlet fever. It quiets the nervous system and cough, and seems to cut short the second stage of the disease. In more severe forms I have found that it acts more promptly when combined with hydrocyanic acid.

℞ Camphor water,......................℥ij.
Tincture hyosciamos,..................ʒj.
*Dilute* hydrocyanic acid, ..............v gtt.*

Dose for a child from three to six years old, one teaspoonful three times a day.

If the paroxysms are violent and cough troublesome, the dose may be gradually increased to two teaspoonsful three times a day. Should there be considerable irritation of the bronchial tubes and lungs, which is sometimes the case in severe forms, I use the following:—

℞ Tincture aconite, .....}
Tincture hyosciamos,..} *aa* ...........ʒi.
Tartar emetic, .......}
Morphia,............} *aa* ...........gr. j.
Simple syrup,.........................℥iv.

Dose for a child from three to six years of age one teaspoonful three or four times a day.

* Gtt. stands for drops. This preparation should be compounded by a druggist, as hydrocyanic acid is a dangerous remedy in unskillful hands.

This may be used in the third stage or after the paroxysms have subsided, (which will generally be relieved by the hyosciamos and hydrocyanic acid,) when the cough is troublesome and seems to be prolonged, depending upon irritation of the bronchæ and lungs. Where the paroxysms are very severe, the following may be applied along the spine with advantage;—

℞ Laudanum, ....}
Oil of amber, ..} *aa* ................℥j.
Alcohol, .......}
Sweet oil, .....} *aa* ..................℥ij.
Mix, and shake before it is used.

Sponging the chest and arms with salt and water, or vinegar and tepid water, followed by friction, will also be found of great service in shortening the disease. Change of air is an effectual remedy when there is debility.

## G. CATARRH IN CHILDREN.

This disease consists in inflammation of the mucous membrane of the lungs and bronchial tubes. It is a disease, liable, improperly treated by blood-letting and other reducing means, to terminate fatally.

*Symptoms.*—The disease generally commences in the nostrils, and gradually extends to the fauces, larynx, trachea, bronchæ, and in children, to the lungs, causing pneumonia and inflammation. It is generally at first attended with dry cough, sometimes difficult breathing, and suffocation when it extends to the lungs. Most mothers are so familiar with the symptoms of ordinary catarrh, that a further description of them will not be necessary.

*Treatment.*—When the disease first commences the feet should be soaked in warm water, and the following remedy given:—

℞ Tinct. aconite,........................ʒi.
Tartar emetic,⎫
Morphia,..... ⎭ *aa*....................gr. j.
Water, or simple syrup,................℥iv.

If the head and throat should be much affected, the same quantity of belladonna as of the aconite may be added to this mixture, and the same dose given.

Dose, for a child from one to three years of age, half a teaspoonful three or four times a day; from three to six years, one teaspoonful three or four times a day.

If the cough be severe with difficult breathing, a spice plaster should be applied, so as to cover the entire breast, and allowed to remain until the symptoms subside; or the following may be spread thin upon a linen rag about the size of the hand and applied over the bronchial tubes.

℞ Cantharides cerate,...................ʒij.
Simple cerate,........................ʒvj.
Mix well together and use as directed.

It should be examined after being on three or four hours; and if much irritation of the skin has taken place it should be removed, and a rag saturated with sweet oil applied over the irritated surface. The plaster may be repeated in three or four days if the inflammatory symptoms do not subside.

# CHAPTER II.

## DISEASES OF FEMALES UNATTENDED WITH PREGNANCY.

WITHOUT a thorough acquaintance with the structure and functions of the reproductive organs, it will be impossible to comprehend and properly treat the many diseases or complications of derangements to which they are liable. These have been very clearly explained, and further elucidated by numerous engravings, in the preceding pages of this work, so that any female of ordinary intelligence and judgment will be able to readily master a majority of the complaints incident to the sex, without the special assistance of a medical practitioner.

## DIVISION I.

### DISEASES OF THE EXTERNAL ORGANS OF GENERATION.

*a.* DISEASES OF THE LABIA.—The labia are liable to inflammation from acrid discharges, syphilis, gonorrhœa, etc.

*Symptoms.*—Where there is much inflammation there is heat, swelling and throbbing, attended by fever. From the looseness and vascularity of the texture, the progress of inflammation is generally rapid, soon terminating in suppuration.

*Treatment.*—As the movement of the parts causes pain, the female should confine herself to bed. Leeches are then to be applied; if these cannot be obtained, poultices must be used.

For pain and fever the following should be taken:—

℞ Tincture aconite, *fol*..................ʒij.
Morphine,..........................grs. iij.
Water,..............................℥iv.

Take a teaspoonful three times a day in water; oftener if the pain is severe.

If the bowels are constipated, they should be opened by injections. Where there is a tendency to suppuration, the abscess should be opened on the inside of the lips and the pus pressed out.

Should the parts not incline to heal, a solution of sesqui-carbonate potassa, one drachm to four ounces of water may be used, injected into the abscess.

Abscesses of the labia sometimes terminate in fistulas. In such cases the advice of some skillful physician will be necessary.

*b.* Irritation and Inflammation of the Vulva in children.—Children are liable to an irritation of the lips of the pudendum or vulva. This will terminate in inflammation and give much trouble, if not promptly rectified.

*Symptoms.*—Stinging and burning sensation, redness of the lining membrane of the external labia and vulva, with a white discharge—leucorrhæa or "whites." Urination increases the soreness and smarting, causing the child to cry and retain the urine.

*Treatment.*—Wash the parts well with Castile soap and water two or three times a day, wiping dry.

Afterward apply freely the oxyde of zinc ointment, or a solution of sulphate of zinc, five grains to an ounce of water, to the irritated surface. This may be done after each washing, if necessary.

*c.* PRURITUS, OR ITCHING OF THE VULVA.—This attends inflammation and other disorders of the vulva. It may occur from pregnancy, from disease of the neck of the womb, from leucorrhœa, and diseases of the bladder and rectum. It may also occur from seat-worms, and from diseases of the roots of the hair on the external labia.

*Symptoms.*—Tormenting irritation of the vulva, extending into the vagina and meatus urinarius. The itching is increased by the warmth of the bed, fatigue from walking, stimulating food and drinks. If the parts be examined there will be found small, slightly-elevated pimples. These being scratched with the nails, causes a slight acrid bloody discharge from them, and the surrounding parts to be highly inflamed. Sometimes the irritation is so great as to excite the venerous or erotic passion to a degree that cannot be restrained, amounting to mania. The health will soon give way under the inflammation and swelling, the constant irritation, the loss of sleep and appetite, watchfulness, etc.

*Treatment.*—First ascertain the cause and then seek to remove it. The cause may depend on some morbid condition of the bladder and rectum, or of the vagina.

The following local application, as recommended by Drs. *Meigs* and *Dewees*, will generally answer the purpose to allay the irritation:—

℞ Borate of soda,......................℥ss.
Sulphate morphia,....................grs. ij.
Rose water,..........................℥iv.

Mix—Apply twice a day with a piece of sponge, first washing the surface with soap and water, wiping dry

Should there be any abrasion of the mucous membrane of the vulva, the ointment of oxyde of zinc may be applied night and morning.

When the general health has suffered, tonics will be requisite, such as iron, cinchona, etc., accompanied with a nourishing diet, avoiding stimulating food and drinks, and keeping the parts strictly clean.

There are many other diseases of the external organs of generation, together with various forms of morbid growth, but as they will require the aid of an experienced physician, it is unnecessary to present them in this volume.

## DIVISION II.

### DISEASES OF THE VAGINA.

*a.* Imperforate Hymen.—The existence of an imperforate hymen is not generally noticed until the age of puberty. At this time the female may have all the symptoms which accompany menstruation without the discharge. There will then be a sense of weight and fullness in the vagina and an enlargement at the lower part of the abdomen, just above the pubis. When these indications are observed, an examination will readily detect whether they are occasioned by an imperforated hymen or otherwise.

*Treatment.*—The hymen must be divided or an aperture made. This operation is not attended with pain. The vagina should then be syringed with tepid water, and the recumbent position observed until the right position of the organ be regained.

*b.* VAGINETIS, OR INFLAMMATION OF THE VAGINA.—Inflammation of this organ may be confined to the lining membrane, or it may extend to the subcutaneous tissue.

*Symptoms.*—Sensation of weight and fullness in the vaginal canal; pain and redness of the part. The speculum will reveal redness and swelling of the lining membrane, which is tender to the touch. At first there is no discharge. After a few days there is a thin serous secretion, which finally becomes yellowish, or greenish, or purulent. It is difficult to detect this discharge from that of gonorrhœa. It is very important, however, to do so, in order to protect the character for chastity of the individual afflicted. The discharge of gonorrhœa can only be detected from that of vaginetis by the aid of the microscope. No physician should dare pronounce the discharge gonorrhœal without such microscopic examination.*

*Causes.*—It may result from cold, excessive sexual indulgence, child-bearing, stimulating food and drink, gonorrhœal virus, etc.

*Treatment.*—Warm hip-bath and injection of cold water into the vagina. If the discharge is excessive, procure a solution of five grains of sulphate of zinc to

* For appearance of gonorrhœal matter under microscope, see "Boyhood's Peril," etc., by S. Pancoast, M. D. Plate opposite page 58.

an ounce of water; two ounces to be injected three times a day. The bowels are to be kept regular. If there be frequent desire to urinate, with some scalding, the following may be given:—

℞ Sweet spirits nitre,................℥j.
Tincture Aconite, *fol.*,.............ʒij.
Water,.........................℥iij.
One teaspoonful three times a day in sweetened water.

When the vaginal discharge has ceased, cleanliness must be maintained, using frequent injections of cold water, mixing occasionally a little Castile soap with it.

*c.* LEUCORRHŒA, OR WHITES.—After the age of puberty this is one of the most frequent complaints of females. It is a dischage from the cervical glands, and the follicles of the uterus, and vaginal and lining membrane, of a white, yellow, greenish or purulent character, the result of inflammation.

*Symptoms.*—The general symptoms in connection with the discharge are as follows:—The face assumes a pale and yellow or sallow color; the eyes are surrounded by dark, leaden-colored circles; a dragging and weary sensation in the left side; dull pains in back and loins; nausea and loss of appetite, with more or less distention of stomach, palpitation of the heart, difficulty of breathing at times, loss of sexual desire; pain in the head, located generally on top or back part; lassitude, general debility, etc.

There are two distinct forms of leucorrhœa, each requiring a distinct treatment. The first is called *cervical leucorrhœa*, the discharge taking place from the glands and follicles of the cervix of the uterus The other is called *vaginal leucorrhœa*, the secretions flowing from the lining membrane of the vagina.

1. *Cervical Leucorrhœa.*—The discharge from the cervix is a clear transparent mucus, of an alkaline reaction when it comes in contact with the secretion of the vagina, which is acid. It is coagulable and resembles curdled milk. Sometimes it is mixed with pus and becomes purulent; or it may be mixed with blood, from the bleeding of the mouth of the womb, resembling menstrual secretion, and as often mistaken for such. Frequently the discharge is so great as to cause a drain upon the system and undermine the constitution.

2. VAGINAL LEUCORRHŒA.—The discharge is entirely from the vagina. Sometimes it will affect the glands of the cervix sympathetically, thus combining the two forms in one. In vaginal leucorrhœa the discharge consists of an acrid mucus, with patches and threads of epithelium or lining membrane. These patches are occasionally as large as a walnut rolled up. The organ will be found covered with a white coating, which may be removed with the forceps.

The cervical discharges produce an abrasion of the neck and mouth of the womb, stripping off the entire surface of the villi or lining coat, causing it to present a red, inflamed and velvety appearance, often mistaken for ulceration of the os uteri or head of the womb. On the advance of the disease, there will be a granular condition and ulceration finally. Cervical ulceration, in cervical leucorrhœa, is always occasioned by the cervical discharge.

*Taylor Smith* lays it down as a rule that cervical

leucorrhœa can rarely exist without inducing disorder of the os uteri. Accordingly the only plan of treating such cases successfully is to suppress the cervical discharge.

The secretion from the cervix may also cause the vagina to present a similar condition of a red velvety appearance and a pealing off of the lining membrane. This may extend the whole length of the vagina—give great pain in sexual intercourse, and suffering in walking and during menstruation. What is called irritable uterus is no doubt caused by leucorrhœa, attended with a neuralgic condition of the cervix and os uteri.

The symptoms of both are the same, as nausea, constant dyspepsia, and pain in the back, left side of the chest, groin, extending down to the thighs, etc.

Leuçorrhœal discharges have a very slight fetid odor, unless there be considerable purulent discharge from deep-seated abscesses. In cancer, the discharges are so fetid as to scent the whole room in which the patient is confined.

It is a very difficult matter sometimes to detect secondary syphilitic ulceration from ulcerations produced by long-continued cervical discharges. Such is also the case in gonorrhœal discharges from the cervix. The treatment for leucorrhœa will not have any effect upon either syphilis or gonorrhœa. Should the treatment for leucorrhœa fail, it would be well to have the advice of some regularly qualified physician.

Leucorrhœal discharges, it is proper to remark, will sometimes cause *Balanitis*, or irritation of the glans penis, as well as urethral irritation and a secretion resembling gonorrhœa, which discharge from the male urethra coming in contact with the healthy mucous membrane of the vagina, may also cause severe gonorrhœa in the female.

This form of disorder in the male has been denominated *abortive gonorrhœa.* It is a question whether gonorrhœa is not often communicated or propagated in this way. I have seen and treated cases which seem to confirm this view. Such cases yield more readily to treatment than those of a confirmed character.

Cervical leucorrhœa interferes with menstruation, and causes abortions. Both the vaginal and cervical leucorrhœa, likewise, will produce sterility—the acrid and purulent secretion of the female killing the spermatozoa of the male as soon as they are brought in contact with them.

CAUSES OF LEUCORRHŒA.—Pregnancy, over-sexual excitement and sexual intercourse, decline of life in plethoric persons or those of full habits; debility is a frequent cause; also depressing emotions, long fatiguing walk, indigestion, cold, etc. A common cause is lactation, or nursing, occurring with some females every time the child is nursed. Scrofulous and consumptive persons are liable to it. Residence in warm climates, by relaxing the system, will cause some of the worst forms of leucorrhœa, while piles and constipation often induce the complaint. Leucorrhœa is also hereditary. Children are liable where the mother has suffered long from the disorder.

*Treatment.*—First discover the cause, before com

mencing to remove the difficulty. Next seek to improve the general system, by a tonic treatment. Iron is one of the best tonics that can be given. The best preparation is the ammoniated iron alum. I usually prescribe it in the following form:—

℞ Tinct. conii, ........................f ℥j.
Tinct. aconite, *fol.* ..................f ʒiij.
Ammo. iron alum, ....................ʒiij.
Simple syrup,.........................℥viij

Mix—Dose, one teaspoonful three times a day in water, after meals.

Should there be constipation attended with piles, give one or two of the following pills at bed-time:—

℞ Suphus. loti,.........................ʒj.
Alcoholic extract nux vomica,..........grs. x.

Make into thirty pills. Dose, one pill night and morning.

*Injections.*—Before injecting, it is of the utmost importance to have a proper syringe. The ordinary glass or metallic syringes are of little use. The syringe should be so constructed that a large quantity of liquid may be thrown up the vagina at a time. There are various forms of gutta percha and India-rubber syringes which answer admirably. The kind which I have used and recommended for several years past, is so constructed that a constant stream may be injected without removing the syringe. It is the best kind I have seen employed.*

In profuse cervical leucorrhœa, the vagina should be well syringed with cold water, and the following preparation injected:—

* This form of syringe may be obtained of the author. Price varying from $1.50 to $2.50.

℞ Tannic acid,........................ʒj
Alum pulverized,......................℥ss.
Water,..................................1 qt.

Inject half night and morning.

By this method the most satisfactory results may be obtained in two or three weeks.

In severe forms of leucorrhœa, injections cannot be dispensed with. They not only arrest the discharge, but give tone to the uterine walls and cervix uteri, removing at the same time much of the depressed feelings of the patient.

In cases attended with pain, the following injection will be found of great benefit:—

℞ Laudanum,........................ fʒij.
Solution sub-acetate of lead,....... fʒi.
Water,............................ pint i.

Inject half night and morning.

In ulceration, nitrate of silver injections have been recommended. I would not advise this. If nitrate of silver seem advisable, it should be applied through the speculum, by a skillful physician, with a certainty of cure.

Iodine is also a valuable remedy in chronic indurations or enlargement of the os uteri. Like the nitrate of silver, it should be used with the speculum only in the hands of an experienced physician.

VAGINAL LEUCORRHŒA.—The constitutional treatment of vaginal leucorrhœa is similar to that of the cervical.

The injections, instead of being acid, should be alkaline, on account of the discharges being of an acid character.

Copious injections of cold water will prove of great avail in allaying irritation, removing the acid secretions, and in giving tone to the walls of the vagina.

Where the vaginal leucorrhœa has existed a long time, the parts will become so much relaxed as to cause prolapsus or falling of the womb. In such instances, cold injections will overcome the relaxation and give tonicity to the parts.

The injection I generally use is the following:—

℞ Bi-carbonate soda, ..................℥ss.
Bi-carbonate potash, ................℥ss.
Water, ............................1 quart.

Inject half night and morning.

Or

℞ Solution of sub-acetate lead,..........ʒij.
Water, ............................1 quart.

Inject half night and morning. Or the two may be alternated with daily.

When the vaginal secretions will not yield to the preparations already given, the following may be tried:—

℞ Fowler's solution,..................fʒij.
Tincture conium,....................f℥ss
Tincture aconite, *fol.*..............fʒij.
Simple syrup,.......................f℥iv.
Mix.

Dose—One teaspoonful three times a day, on every other day. The prescription on page 409 may be taken the intermediate day and so alternated daily.

If the disease still proves obstinate, some vice of the system may be suspected. In such cases the following should be given:—

℞ Bin. Iodide mercury, ..............gr. i.
Iodide potash, ....................ʒ iij.
Simple syrup,......................℥ iv.
Dose—One teaspoonful three times a day, in water.

In connection with this treatment the patient will require a moderate amount of exercise in the open air, with a rich stimulating diet, while the cold and tepid hip-baths should not be neglected. Sexual intercourse must be strictly avoided, and only moderately indulged after the subsidence of the disease, or the same condition may be induced.

As leucorrhœa is a disorder that requires a nice discrimination in adopting a proper treatment, it might be well in all cases to apply to some skillful physician for preliminary advice, before undertaking its management.

## DIVISION III.

### DISEASES OF UTERUS AND FALLOPIAN TUBES.

*a.* PROLAPSUS, OR FALLING OF THE WOMB.—This is the most common form of displacement. By reference to the second Chapter of this work, the reader will find a succinct description of the four ligaments which are intended as partial support to the uterus in the pelvis. These are called round, broad, utero-sacral and utero-cervical ligaments. The uterus is also partially supported by the vagina, and the relaxation of its walls is always sufficient of itself to cause more or less prolapsus. Dr. *Ashwell* maintains that the ligaments afford but very little protection and support to the womb, for this organ may be drawn down without putting it on the stretch. He contends that the bladder, rectum, vagina and muscles lining the pelvis are the main supports to the uterus. (*Fig.* 68.)

*Symptoms.*—The symptoms will vary with the extent of displacement. There is usually a dull heavy pain

Fig. 68.

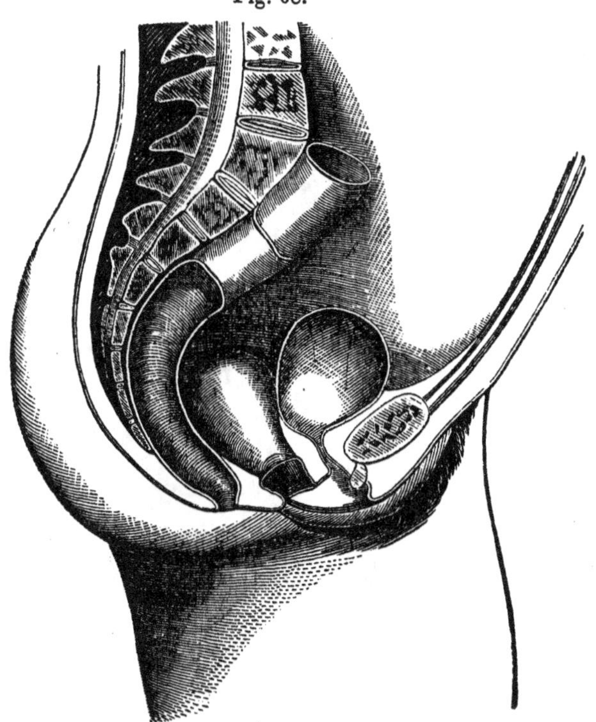

PROLAPSUS OR FALLING OF THE WOMB. (*From Scudder.*)

in the small of the back, and a dragging weight in the pelvis and at the lower part of the rectum. These

Fig. 69.

THE WELL-DEVELOPED, SYMMETRICAL AND HEALTHY FORM. *(From Banning.)*

Fig. 70.

APPEARANCE OF A FEMALE LABORING UNDER A FALLING OF THE WOMB AND DRAGGING CONDITION OF THE VISCERA. (*After Banning.*)

feelings are increased by exercise or by being long on the feet. These symptoms are relieved by lying down. When the prolapsus is very great, these indications are more prominently marked. There is also a pain and a feeling of distress in the groin, extending down the thighs, caused by pressure on the sacral nerves. The sensation of weight in the pelvis and groin, at times, is so great that the patient imagines "every thing is dropping through." There is frequent desire to urinate and evacuate the bowels. Sometimes the micturation is only a few drops, in consequence of the distressing irritation of the bladder. Other parts of the system besides those immediately surrounding the pelvis are sympathetically affected. Headache, a dejected and distressed expression of countenance, with an inclination to bend the body forward, are also characteristics of prolapsus. (See *Figs.* 68 and 70.) There is loss of appetite with dyspeptic symptoms. The distention of the stomach is so great that the female is compelled to loosen her dress. She expresses herself as being swelled. She has palpitation of the heart, pain in the left side, sometimes attended with a slight cough and leucorrhœa.

*Causes.*—If we glance a moment at the support of the uterus, we may readily perceive that so long as the parts are able to resist the constant action of the diaphragm and abdominal muscles, there cannot, as a general rule, be prolapsus. Whatever tends to relax and debilitate the general system may cause the complaint. The abdominal muscles which support the abdominal viscera are more or less relaxed by a debility of the system. By relaxation and withdrawing of support from the abdominal viscera, the bowels are allowed to press upon the pelvic viscera and tissue which support the uterus, and in consequence of this constant pressure it gives way. *Fig.* 71 shows the natural position of the viscera when there is no relaxation of the abdominal muscles, and *Fig.* 72 when there is relaxation and displacement of the womb. Another frequent cause is too early exercise after child bearing. Inflammation of womb, particularly of the cervix, increasing the bulk and weight of the organ, is also a common cause. It is likewise produced by dancing, leaping and jumping, particularly during the period of menstruation, when the organ is naturally increased in weight from the congestion concomitant of the catamenial flow.

*Treatment.*—First remove the cause. If the abdominal muscles are relaxed, an abdominal supporter is indispensable, in order to support the viscera and take the pressure from the pelvis. Supporters are strongly condemned by some practitioners. Unless they fit properly, they are worse than useless. If properly made, however, they afford great relief, and those accustomed to them cannot be induced to forego their employment.

Supporters have been recommended by manufacturers as applicable to all uterine diseases. Hence the abuse of them has led to their condemnation in toto. If we condemn all good and useful articles because they are liable to be abused, we would soon discover our error. I recommend the supporter in all cases of relaxation, and never engage to treat until one is procured. The supporter should be as uncomplicated

Fig. 71.

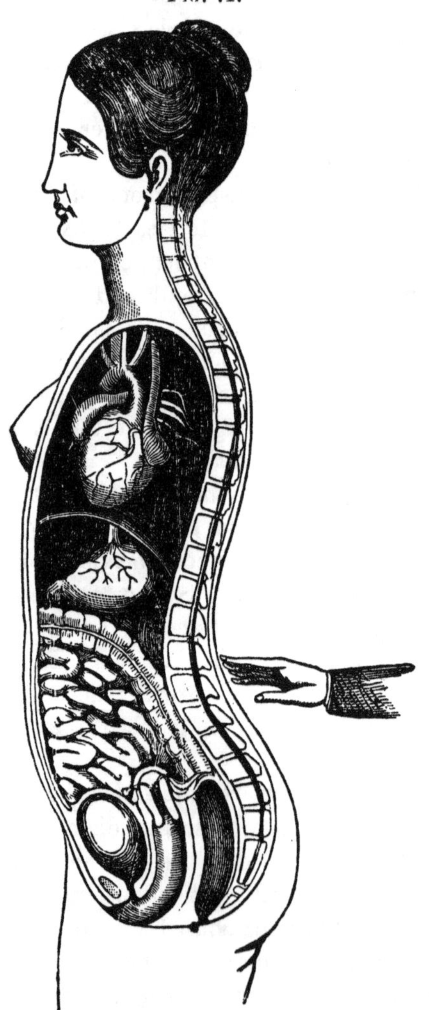

REPRESENTATION OF A HEALTHY, ERECT, AND WELL-PROPORTIONED FIGURE. THE SPINE HAS THE NATURAL CURVES, AND THE ABDOMINAL VISCERA IS PREVENTED FROM PRESSING UPON THE WOMB, RECTUM AND BLADDER BY THE ABDOMINAL MUSCLES. (*After Banning.*)

Fig. 72.

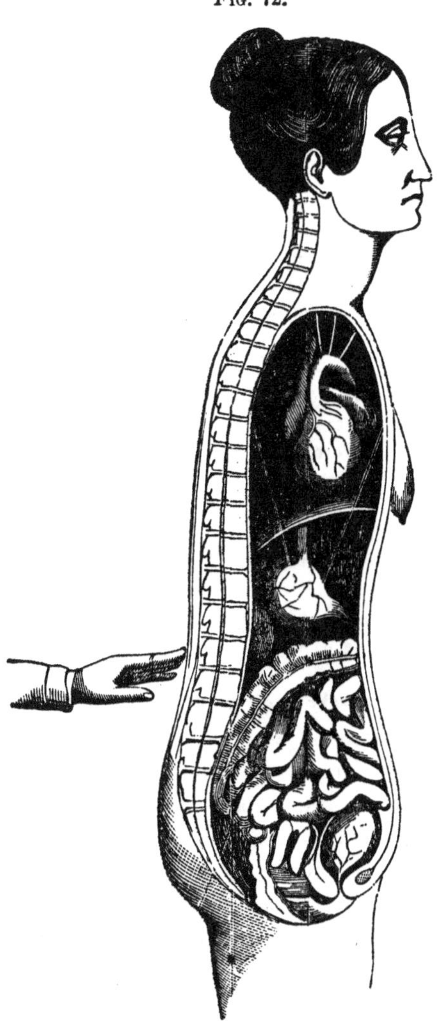

REPRESENTATION OF A RELAXED, DROOPING, AND BADLY-PROPORTIONED FIGURE, WITH THE LUNGS AND STOMACH DRAGGED, AND THE WOMB, BLADDER, RECTUM AND BLOOD-VESSELS OF THE PELVIS AND LEGS COMPRESSED BY THE FALLING OF THE BOWELS, FROM THE RELAXATION OF THE MUSCLES OF THE SPINE AND ABDOMEN. (*After Banning.*)

as possible, made of steel with front and back pads. Some are quilted and padded to such an extent as to be really injurious, by keeping up too great a warmth of the parts.

Tonics should be used to strengthen the general system. One of the following compounds may be used for this purpose:

℞ Sulphate cinchona,..........xxv grs.
Citrate iron, (soluable),......xxxv grs.

Make into twenty-four powders. Take one three times a day, after each meal, in sweet wine.

℞ Precip. carbonate iron,..........ʒv.
Extract coniam,..................ʒiv.
Balsam Peru,...................ʒj.
Simple syrup,...................℥viii.
Oil cinnamon,..................gtt. x.
Oil winter-green,...............gtt. x.
Pulv. gum Arabic,..............ʒij.

Mix.

Dose—two teaspoonsful three times a day, after meals To be well shaken before being used.

To give tone to the pelvic viscera, the cold hip-bath should be used once a day, followed by friction, while injections of cold water into the vagina must not be omitted. If there be any discharge, inject a solution of alum, one ounce to a pint of water. This will arrest the secretion, and at the same time harden and strengthen the vagina. Observe the recumbent position as much as possible, and avoid becoming fatigued. Cold bandages applied on going to bed and allowed to remain on all night, are also very efficacious.

The chief difficulty to overcome is the pressure around the waist by the use of corsets and wearing heavy skirts. Such pressure must be removed. The clothes should be loose and be suspended from the shoulders. Attention to this requirement cannot be too strongly impressed upon the mind of the patient.

The use of pessaries I utterly reprobate. They were used by the Egyptian, Greek, Roman and Arabian physicians, and are still recommended by some of the old-school practitioners of the present day. They are made of silver, gold, wood, cork, sponge and glass. Their use is merely palliative at best, while they often produce irritation and inflammation of the os-uteri and vagina, and, by consequence, lay the foundation of more formidable diseases, such as ulceration and cancer of the womb. The galvanic battery, in some cases, may be usefully employed, in connection with other treatment in prolapsus, especially if applied by or under the direction of an experienced practitioner.

*b*. RETROVERSION, OR RETROFLEXION OF UTERUS. —This is a displacement not so common as prolapsus. It may occur both in the pregnant and non-pregnant female. (*See Fig.* 73.) The uterus is here thrown back, the fundus resting against the rectum.

*Symptoms*.—If the retrocession is slight, there may be no well-marked symptoms. In other cases, the symptoms are dyspepsia and hysteria, and sometimes severe neuralgic pains in the breasts and along some portion of the spine; difficult breathing. Constipation is a common attendant; the uterus pressing against the rectum preventing the expulsion of the

FIG. 73.

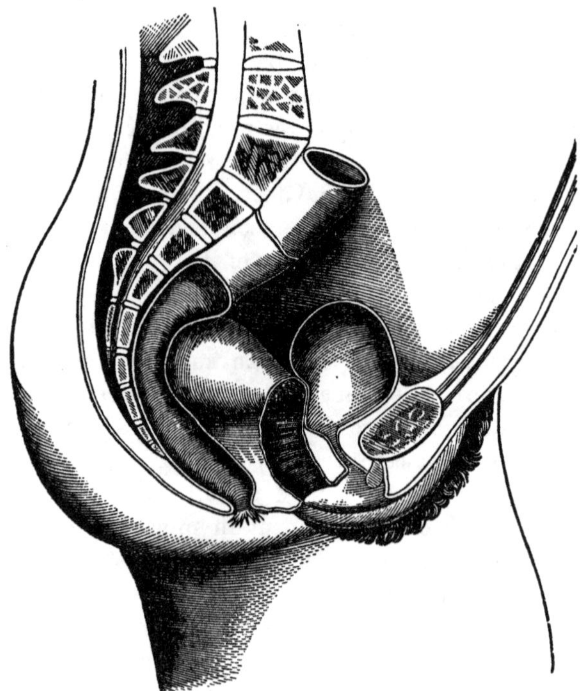

RETROVERSION, OR FALLING OF THE WOMB BACKWARD AGAINST THE RECTUM. (*After Scudder.*)

fœcal matter there accumulated. Sometimes there is a mucus discharge from the bowels, produced by the irritation, while the retention of urine is not unfrequent. There may also be pains in the loins, extending down the lower extremities, causing fatigue in walking or standing.

*Causes.*—Pregnancy, weakness of uterine support and increased weight of the fundus of the uterus, falls, sudden shocks, distended bladder, tumors in the uterus, such as polypi, which are usually attached to the fundus.

*Treatment.*—First restore the organ to its natural position. This may sometimes be done by passing two fingers up the vagina, and pressing between the cervix-uteri and rectum, at the same time drawing down the uterus with some instrument like the blade of a forceps.

Another plan is to pass a uterine sound into the uterus and turn the instrument so as to look toward the bladder. If used with care little or no pain will be produced. Before displacing the uterus the bladder should be emptied, either by natural means or by the catheter.

In cases of pregnancy the sound cannot be used. Draw off the urine and empty the rectum by an enema. Then pass one finger into the rectum so as to reach the fundus, and press up the canal of the intestines. By continuing gentle pressure, the uterus will suddenly emerge with a sort of jerk.

Sometimes it is necessary to have recourse to instruments. Dr. *Bond's* instrument answers a very good purpose. So does M. *Gariel's* Air Pessary, which distends the rectum, and by that means overcoming the displacement.

After the womb is replaced, the patient should maintain a horizontal position, the bladder must be kept emptied, while cold water injections in the vagina are not to be omitted, provided pregnancy does not exist, as this will give tone to and reduce the congestion of the organ, The cold bandages may also be worn, and if the system is much relaxed and debilitated, one of the iron mixtures mentioned in the pages on Prolapsus may be given.

*c.* ANTIVERSION OF THE UTERUS.—This displacement is quite the opposite to that just described—the fundus being against the bladder and the mouth toward the rectum. This form seldom occurs.

*Symptoms.*—Similar to those given of retroversion, though not so well marked. The most prominent symptom is a constant desire to urinate but difficulty in voiding the urine.

*Causes.*—Accumulations in the rectum, tumors attached to anterior wall of uterus, tilting it over, relaxation, a blow, fall, etc.

*Treatment.*—The displacement is much easier than in retroversion. The patient should lie on her back, with her hips considerably elevated, when the uterine sound is to be used, as in the last form of displacement. Prof. *Godfrey* recommends the patient to be placed on the side of the bed, with the head and hands on the floor, and the thighs and legs resting on the bed. In this position the intestines are drawn down toward the diaphragm, the pelvis becomes somewhat emptied, while the uterus being pressed upon assumes its natural position. When this is accomplished, the bladder should be kept partially distended for some time afterward.

The other treatment is similar to that in other forms of displacement.

*d.* INFLAMMATION OF OVARIES AND TUBES.—Diseases of the Fallopian tubes are said to be more common than inflammation of the ovaries. Where the tubes are much inflamed, thickening may occur, while there may also be a discharge similar to what is observed in inflammation of the uterus.

*Symptoms.*—Dull aching pain in one or both illiac regions, accompanied by sensations of weight and heat; pain and soreness on pressure in the region of the Ovaries, with some fever, which is almost always intermittent.

*Causes.*—Cold, blows in the region, over-sexual indulgence, suppression of menses, etc.

*Treatment.*—Counter-irritation in the region of the ovary, with the following:—

℞ Cantharides cerate,<br>
Simple cerate, } *aa*............℥ss.

Mix.

Spread on rag and apply until it causes a smarting sensation. Then remove it and substitute a greasy rag.

Give the following:—

℞ Tincture aconite, *fol.*, ...............ʒij.<br>
Morphine, .........................grs. ij.<br>
Water, ...........................℥iv.

Dose—One teaspoonful every two or three hours, in water.

*e.* AMENORRHŒA, OR OBSTRUCTION OF MENSES.—Two thirds of menstrual irregularities are included under this heading.

1. *Suppressed Menstruation.*—By this is understood those cases in which the menses have once occurred and been suppressed through some cause or other.

*Symptoms.*—They differ materially in different persons. With some there is slight headache, a feeling of weight about the pelvis, pain in back and loins.

In other cases these symptoms are more strongly marked; attended with quick pulse, hot skin, fever, inflammation of uterus, and frequently hysteria. Sometimes Nature relieves the system by the nose, lungs, stomach and bowels, eliminating blood, quite often in a profuse hemorrhage, or if not copious, lasting for several days. Blood has been known to be discharged in such cases from the axilla, ears, mouth, gums, fingers, toes and from ulcers upon the body Sometimes the discharge will not cease entirely, but become less in quantity and lighter in color at each succeeding monthly period, and generally preceded and followed by leucorrhœal discharges.

*Causes.*—One of the most common causes is cold during the menstrual period, from getting the feet wet, sitting on the damp ground, sleeping between wet sheets and wearing damp clothes, severe mental emotions just previous to the monthly occurrence, coitus during Menstruation, consumption, chronic liver derangement, general debility, etc.

*Treatment.*—As soon as the discharge has ceased, a warm sitz-bath will often bring them on. Should there be much inflammation of the uterus, the following may be given:—

℞ Tincture aconite, *fol.*, ............... ʒij.
Sweet spirits nitre, ............... f ℥j.
Simple syrup, ..................... f ℥iij.
Dose—One teaspoonful every two or three hours.

If there be hysterical symptoms, the following will generally afford immediate relief:—

℞ Tincture aconite, *fol.*,................ ʒij.
Tincture pulsatilla,.................. ʒj.
Water,.......................... ℥iv.

Dose—One teaspoonful every one or two hours until relief is afforded.

If the discharge cannot be re-established, the patient must wait until the next period. A day or two prior to the next term, the bowels should be freely opened and kept so until the period has arrived for the discharge. The pill of Aloes and Iron of the United States Dispensatory is one of the most useful that can be given, providing the patient is not troubled with piles. From one to three of these pills may be taken daily. There should also be taken before the period, the following:—

℞ Ætherial tincture of cantharides, from eight to ten drops, three times a day, in water.

Should this treatment not answer, and there be debility of the system, it must be improved before the function can be restored. This is particularly the case in consumption, scrofula, hepatic diseases, etc. If there be no apparent derangement of the system except that produced by the suppression, an examination should be made of the uterus, for inflammation and ulceration of the cervix will often cause suppression of the menses.

Should there be no assignable cause and the general health be good, the function should be forced, providing there is positive assurance that the female is not pregnant, and that her system is suffering from the suppression. For this purpose the following may be used:—

℞ Caulophyllin,..... ....................ʒi.
Extract aconite,........................grs. viij.
Aloes,..................................grs. xl.
Sulphate of iron,.......................grs. xl.

Make into forty pills. Two or three pills to be taken night and morning.

Or,

℞ Aloes,................................ʒj.
Myrrh,..................................ʒj.
Sulphate of iron,.......................ʒj.
Extract black hellebore,................ʒj.
Oil of savin............................ʒj.

Make into thirty pills. Dose, one pill from three to six times a day.

If the patient be troubled with piles, some other active cathartic should be substituted for the aloes.

Should there be much pain in the lower extremities and back, and sense of fullness in pelvis with the suppression, the following formula, recommended by Dr. *Dewees*, will be found of service:

℞ Pulv. G. guiaci orpt.,..................ʒiv.
Carb. sod. vel potass,..................ʒiss.
Pulv. pimento,..........................℥i.
Alcohol, dilute,........................℔. i.

Digest for a few days. Dose, one teaspoonful three or four times a day.

These remedies should always be taken a few days before the period arrives for the occurrence of the menses. It is much more difficult to bring on the discharge at any other time.

2. Absent Menstruation.—The usual period for menstruation is from the thirteenth to the sixteenth year, at which time the female is said to have arrived at puberty. In larger towns it occurs much sooner than in rural districts. Those brought up in luxury or sexual indulgence experience these changes sooner than those reared in hardihood and self-denial. Before or about the period of puberty, the organs of generation undergo a change. They increase considerably in size; the breasts enlarge, and other changes occur, the most striking being the catamenial flow.

Physicians acquainted with the functions of the reproductive organs never attempt to force the menses, providing their non-appearance causes no derangement of health, for there may be all the evidences of puberty with the exception of the discharge. This may be owing to some malformation similar to that spoken of in the chapter on Hermaphrodism. This, however, is not a frequent occurrence.

Amenorrhœa may be occasioned by an imperforated hymen, as spoken of in a previous part of this chapter. It may also be occasioned by some congenital malformation in the vagina or os uteri. This should be ascertained before the function is forced. Our purpose is only to speak of amenorrhœa existing with a fully developed body and sexual organs.

*Symptoms.*—Headache; weight, fullness and throbbing in the centre of the cranium and back part of the head; pain in back and loins; cold feet and hands, becoming sometimes very hot, skin harsh and dry, slow pulse, and not unfrequently attended with epilepsy.

*Treatment.*—About the period when the system is sympathizing the most, and there is evidence of its approach, the warm-hip bath should be taken twice a day, and cloths wrung out of warm water applied over the pubis or lower part of the abdomen. The bowels must be kept open by some gentle cathartic. Drastic purgatives should be avoided. During the menstrual discharge the following may be used, to relieve pain and fullness of head and promote discharge:—

℞ Tincture aconite, *fol.*,..................ʒii.
Tincture belladonna,..................ʒi.
Tincture cantharides,..................ʒj.
Morphia,............................grs. iij.
Simple syrup,........................℥iv.

Dose, one teaspoonful three times a day. If the pain is severe, it may be taken every two hours.

During the interval, if the system is not vigorous and robust, the following may be taken:—

℞ Precip. carbonate of iron,.............ʒv.
Extract conium,......................ʒij.
Balsam Peru,........................ʒi.
Alcohol,.............................℥iv.
Oil winter-green,.................... gtt. xx.
Simple syrup,........................℥viij.

Dose, two teaspoonfuls three times a day in water. The mixture should be well shaken before it is taken.

*b.* Dysmenorrhœa, or Painful Menstruation —This is of common occurrence in females of sanguineous and robust constitutions, and of ardent and animated temperament. The monthly discharge makes its appearance at the usual period, and in small quantity. It is often entirely suppressed for several hours.

Females troubled with dysmenorrhœa are subject to frequent headache, and rush of blood to the head during the interval of the catamenial periods.

*Symptoms.*—Severe bearing-down pain in the uterine region, resembling labor pains; aching in small of back, loins, and lower extremities; flatulence and cutting pains in the abdomen; scanty discharge, which is coagulated and contains shreds of fibrous structure, with the clots of dry blood, and not unfrequently severe attacks of hysteria.

*Causes.*—Inflammation or congestion of the blood-vessels of the uterus, and obstinate constipation; sedentary occupations; improper dressing; smallness of the mouth and neck of the womb, etc. Such females are almost always permanently relieved of the distressing symptoms after marriage.

*Treatment.*—When the attack commences, take a warm hip-bath; lie in bed and apply cloths wrung out of hot water to the lower part of the abdomen. Use the following:—

℞ Tincture of aconite, *fol.*, ................ ʒij.
Sweet spirits of nitre, ................ ℥i.
Morphia, .... ........................ grs. iij.
Simple syrup, ........................ ℥iv.
Dose, one teaspoonful every half hour, until relieved.

During the menstrual discharge the bowels must be kept open. In the intervals of the periods constipation should be overcome, while the body should be frictionized all over with a coarse crash towel once or twice a day. Take plenty of exercise in the open air. For the constipation one or two drops of the tincture of nux vomica may be taken three times a day, dropped on sugar.

This treatment will answer in a majority of cases. If it be occasioned by any mechanical obstruction, advice of a physician must be obtained. When the discharge is scanty and attended with pain and hysterical symptoms, I use in conbination with the prescription one drachm of the tincture of pulsatilla.

*g*. MENORRHAGIA, OR PROFUSE MENSTRUATION.—Profuse discharges may occur at any age from puberty to decline of the menstrual period, or turn of life. In some females the discharge is always profuse, without impairment of the general health.

*Symptoms.*—Exhaustion of the bodily powers; weakness and pain in back, extending to the hips, thighs, and across the loins; sallow and sunken features; headache; pains in stomach and bowels; neuralgic pains in face; sometimes there is diarrhœa and nervous debility, melancholy, epilepsy, etc.

*Treatment.*—Maintain a recumbent position, use plain diet, and abstain from all stimulating food and drinks. The feet must be soaked in warm water, and cold cloths applied to the lower parts of the abdomen The following may be given and is usually sufficient, if astringent remedies are required:—

℞ Acetate of lead,.................... grs. x.
Pulv. opium,..................... grs. vj.

Make into ten pills, and take one every two or three hours until the discharge diminishes.

I have used the oil of erigeron with considerable success. I employ it according to the following prescription:—

℞ Oil cinnamon, ........................ʒii.
Oil erigeron, ........................ʒij.
Water, ...............................℥iv.
Pulv. gum Arabic,.....................ʒj.

Dose, one or two teaspoonsful every two or three hours, in sweetened water.

I have found it necessary in some extreme cases to plug the uterus. Cases that will not yield to the above treatment will require the attention of a skillful physician.

During the interval of the periods, the system should be toned up and the blood enriched.

One of the best preparations for this purpose is the following:—

℞ Precip. carbonate iron,................ʒv.
Extract conium,.......................ʒij.
Balsam Peru...........................ʒj.
Oil cinnamon,.........................gtt. xx.
Simple syrup,.........................℥viij.
Pulv. gum Arabic,.....................ʒij.

Mix—Dose, two teaspoonsful three or four times a day, in water. Shaken before using.

Frictions on the surface of body daily, and exercise in the open air, should be observed.

*h.* Chlorosis, or Green Sickness.—This is a disease generally occurring in unmarried females of weak, delicate frame. Such as are so from birth, having feeble appetite and digestion. At puberty there is no menstrual discharge, or else it is very slight; there is an anæmia of system; the skin presents a yellowish dirty-green pallor. The disease sometimes attacks females advanced in life, and is generally preceded by eucorrhœa or menorrhagia.

This is purely a disease of the blood, and may occur in males as well as females; very seldom, however, in the former. The marked changes observed in the blood of chlorotic subjects is the diminution of the red corpuscles. The average normal amount of red corpuscles in one thousand parts is from one hundred and thirty to one hundred and forty parts. In chlorosis they are reduced to sixty, and, in some rare cases, twenty-six parts in one thousand.

We may readily understand what influence such a diminution of the corpuscles will have upon the general system, when we know that their office is to convey oxygen from the lungs to the different tissues and to convey carbonic acid out into the lungs to be eliminated. Assimilation, nutrition, combustion, and, in fact, no function of the animal economy can be performed without a supply of oxygen. It is the great sustaining principle of the *vis medicatrix*, or what the general is to the army when the battle is raging.

Without red corpuscles, the system cannot be supplied with oxygen; and without oxygen all the offices of the system must be impaired, or partially suspended. It is important to understand the nature of this disease, for it is considered a fatal one. Only a small percentage of patients are cured, which I have attributed to a want of knowledge of its true pathology. Many physicians will direct their remedies for the purpose of correcting the uterine function, which is no more suffering than the others. Such treatment is sure to destroy the patient.

*Symptoms.*—General debility, dislike to exercise, easily fatigued, dullness, listlessness, melancholy, de sire for solitude, frequent weeping without cause. poor appetite, loathing of food; desire for chalk, dirt, slate pencils, acids, pickles, etc. The breath is offensive, bowels constipated, quick pulse, palpitation of heart and more or less headache. Some split and bite their finger nails; hair loses its natural color and falls out, and there are an almost unlimited number of other indications which would be tedious to enumerate.

*Cause.*—Depressed vital powers, which derange all the functions of the body. The weakness is not unfrequently hereditary, the parents laboring under a similar condition, or has been brought about by the violation of some law of the animal economy, as by masturbation, etc.; living on unnutritious food, residence in ill-ventilated and damp apartments, etc.

*Treatment.*—If we take into consideration the pathology of the disease, the treatment will not be difficult. Exercise in the open air is very essential; the body should be protected from chilliness by warm clothing, and the patient should sleep on a mattrass, and in a well-ventilated room. The diet should be nutritious, not stimulating; game, where it agrees, may be freely eaten. The habits should be regular, the mind kept cheerful by pleasant society, amusements, etc. The surface of the body should be sponged night and morning with the following, and rubbed dry with a coarse towel, so as to produce action in the skin.

Common whiskey,..........one quart.
Cayenne pepper,............one teaspoonful.
Soap sufficient to make a lather.

In connection with this treatment, for it is all positively essential, the following formulæ may be given day about:

℞ Precip. carbonate of iron...........ʒv.
Extract conium...................ʒij.
Balsam Peru......................ʒi.
Oil cinnamon.....................gtt. xx.
Simple syrup.....................℥viij.
Pulverized gum Arabic............ʒij.

Mix. Dose, two teaspoonfuls three times every other day after meals. Shake before using.

℞ Tincture nux vomica,..................ʒi.
Syrup iodide of iron,..................℥j.
Simple syrup,.........................℥iv.

Dose, one teaspoonful three times every other day, in water, after meals.

*k.* Ovarian Dropsy.—By this disease is understood an accumulation of fluid in the Graafian follicles or cysts of the ovaries. The ovaries are capable of secreting an enormous quantity of fluid, but unlike other parts are incapable of reabsorbing the effused fluid, and therefore unlike general or abdominal dropsy. It matters not in ovarian dropsy how rapidly the kidneys may secrete, not the least influence is produced on the accumulation of fluid in the cysts. Although much attention has been paid to this subject of late years by the ablest American and European physicians, there is still much obscurity connected with the disease.

As there are too many forms of cystic disease to be spoken of in this volume, only the more important will receive consideration. These are the simple cysts, compound cysts, hydatic cysts, dermoid cysts, or those containing hair, teeth, bones, etc.

1. *Simple Cysts.*—The simple ovarian cyst is a simple sac, while the rest of the organ retains its normal condition. These cysts vary from the size of a pea to the bulk of the human head. This form is generally found hanging as an appendage to the ovarian ligament. The coats of the cysts become thickened, but not uniformly so, some parts being thicker than others. The outer coat consists of the peritoneum, which encloses the ovaries. The proper wall of the cyst becomes thickened, and consists of dense fibrous tissue. By this increase of thickness the cyst is prevented from rupturing. Sometimes the walls of these cysts become cartilaginous, and occasionally are found ossified or converted into bone. Upon the inner surface of this second coat there is a large number of blood-vessels, presenting a rectangular appearance, which are the carriers of the enormous quantity of blood secreted by the epithelium lining the sac. (*Fig.* 74.)

FIG. 74.

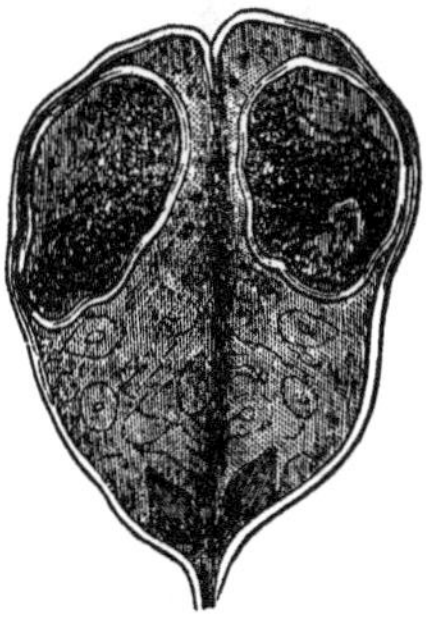

HUMAN OVARY CONTAINING A MORBIDLY DISTENDED GRAAFIAN FOLLICLE OR CYST, IN THE INCIPIENT STAGE—THE CYST HAS BEEN DIVIDED THROUGH THE CENTRE—THE BALANCE OF THE OVARY IS HEALTHY. (*Ad. Nat.*)

2. *Compouna Cysts.*—In this form there may be a number of cysts developed within the parent sac. (*Fig.* 75.) These forms of cysts are capable of great disten-

FIG. 75.

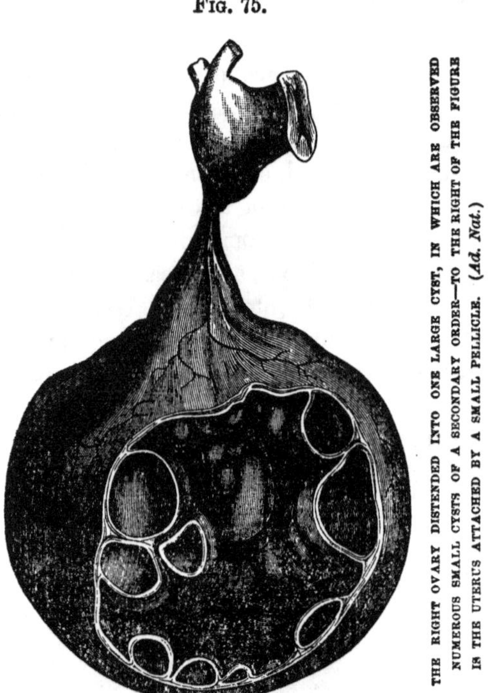

THE RIGHT OVARY DISTENDED INTO ONE LARGE CYST, IN WHICH ARE OBSERVED NUMEROUS SMALL CYSTS OF A SECONDARY ORDER—TO THE RIGHT OF THE FIGURE IS THE UTERUS ATTACHED BY A SMALL PELLICLE. (*Ad. Nat.*)

sion, and are usually found in ovarian dropsies. The smaller or secondary cysts are always attached to the superior or parent cyst, and are covered by the same membrane that covers the principal sac. The growth of these secondary cysts is very irregular, some enlarging rapidly, the walls becoming thin and rupturing, pour their contents into the parent cyst.

*Fluid Contents of Cysts.*—The thinnest fluid is generally obtained from the single cyst. The contents of the compound cyst are usually much more dense, of the consistency of the white of an egg, honey, or thin glue. Sometimes it is so dense that it is drawn off in long strings through the canula. Occasionally it is the color of coffee-grounds, at other times that of blood and pus mixed together.

*Quantity of Fluid.*—The quantity of fluid that has been taken from different persons is enormous. *Imhoff* gives a case where the right ovary contained forty-two pounds of fluid. *Daret*, a case of fifty pints. *Comper*, one where eighty pounds of serum were drawn off, and another is mentioned by *Muller* where there were one hundred and forty pounds in the two ovaries of a woman. The right ovary is twice as often affected as the left. Seldom both at one time. The number of tappings which they will bear is astonishing. *Pagenstecher* removed in thirty-eight tappings eleven hundred and thirty-two pounds. Dr. *Mead* tapped a patient sixty-seven times in five years and a half, and drew nineteen hundred and twenty pints. *Ford* punctured an ovary forty-nine times, and removed twenty-seven hundred and eighty-six pints. *Heidrich*, in eight years, punctured a woman two hundred and ninety-nine times, and removed nine thousand eight hundred and sixty-seven pounds. In another case, in eighty operations he drew six thousand six hundred and thirty-one pints, equal to thirteen hogsheads of fluid.

3. *Hydatids in Ovarian Cysts.*—This is a very rare form, few cases being on record. An interesting preparation is in the Pathological Museum of King's College, England. It consists of an aggregation of cysts, many of them filled with hydatids. They average in size a pigeon's egg, and possess the appearance of Acephalocysts (monsters without heads and hands).

4. *Dermoid Cysts.*—These consist of fatty matter, hair, teeth, bones, etc. They seldom grow to large size, and are not of frequent occurrence. *Figure* 76 illustrates a case where there is long tangled hair, mixed with hard sebaceous matter.

FIG. 76.

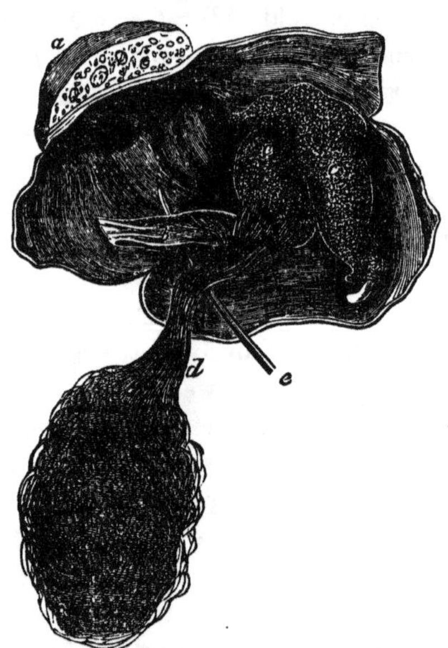


OVARIAN CYST CONTAINING HAIR, FATTY MATTER, SEBACEOUS GLANDS AND HAIR FOLLICLES. (*After Cuveilhier.*)

*Symptoms.*—In the commencement of the disease, there is a dull, heavy pain or soreness in the ovarian region; often the menses are suppressed, with a slight enlargement in the iliac region. As the cyst enlarges, the intestines are displaced, and the stomach, liver, spleen, and diaphragm are forced into the thorax. Sometimes there is hectic fever, more or less pain, vomiting and general emaciation. Occasionally the sac ruptures, and the contents are discharged into the abdominal cavity, Fallopian tubes or uterus. When emptied into the abdominal cavity, the fluid may be absorbed, or it may cause severe peritoneal inflammation and death.

*Cause.*—Falls are a frequent cause; blows, inflam mation, suppression of the menses, etc.

*Treatment.*—Had I space, I might present a large number of cases that have been successfully treated after having attained an enormous size and been frequently tapped.

The usual mode of affording relief after the cysts have attained a size to interfere with the functions of the viscera and impaired the general health, is by tapping. This is but temporary. The only successful treatment is the removal of the tumor, by some skillful physician.

The disease may be arrested if taken early. The following is the most rational means that can be adopted:—A pad should be applied to the tumor, secured by a bandage that will keep up a general pressure. Iodine should be applied by painting the surface of the skin, or by moistening the pad with it twice a day.

The following may be given by the stomach:—

℞ Syrup of iodide iron,....... ....℥iij.
Compound syrup of stillingia,....℥viii.
Dose—one teaspoonful three or four times a day.

After this has been given a couple of weeks, the following may be substituted for the same time:—

℞ Iodide potassium,...............ʒiij.
Fowler's solution,...............ʒj.
Simple syrup,..................℥viii.
Dose—one teaspoonful three times a day after meals.

The bowels should be opened once a day with cream of tartar and phodophylin.

In one case I treated, I found the inhalation of diluted oxygen gas prevented the tumor from enlarging for over two months, and greatly improved the patient's health. She stopped the treatment for the purpose of visiting the country, and during her absence it greatly enlarged. It was not afterward employed. It is certainly worthy of a more extensive trial.

HOW TO ARRANGE THE HAIR.

# PART III.

## TOILET.

---

## CHAPTER I.

### STRUCTURE OF THE SKIN.

THE skin consists of several distinct layers, and serves several important purposes in the animal economy.

1st. It affords a complete covering and protection to the sensitive nerves.

2nd. It affords a large exhalant surface for the elimination of effete fluids from the blood.

3rd. It possesses inhalant apparatus by which fluids may be absorbed.

4th. It prevents the too rapid evaporation of the fluids of the body.

The skin is usually divided into three distinct layers.

*A. Cutis vera, or sensitive skin.*—This forms the undermost layer, and consists of white and yellow fibrous tissue closely interwoven together. (*Fig.* 78.) It is usually divided into two parts. The lower, or inter-

FIG. 78.

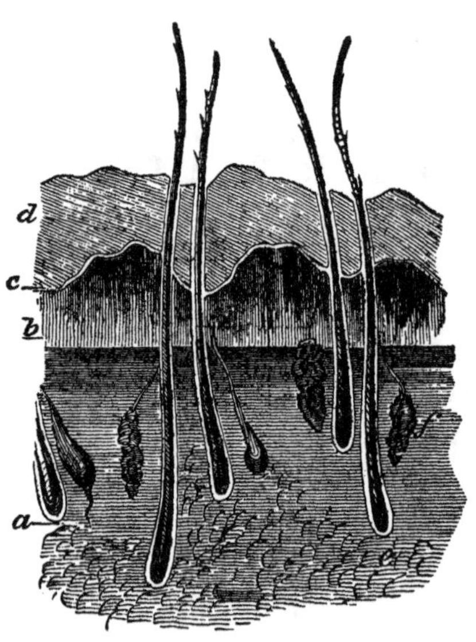


STRUCTURE OF THE SKIN.

*a*, Chorion; *b*, papillary portion of cutis vera; *c*, basement membrane, or rete mucosum; *d*, epidermis; *e*, hair bulb; *f*, sebaceous gland terminating in a hair follicle.

nal, is called the *chorion*, (*a*), and the upper or outer the *papillary body*, (*b*). The papillary surface possesses a distinct function, namely, that of touch. The sense of touch is dependent upon the sensitive nerves, which are arranged in loops in the papillary bodies of the skin. The papillæ are largely supplied with blood-vessels and lymphatics. They are more numerous when the skin is most sensitive, and contract on the approach of cold, which produces a roughness termed *cutis anserina, or goose-flesh.*

*B Basement Membrane*, or *Rete Mucosum*. (*Fig.* 78, *c*.)

This is the second layer of skin. It is the matrix of the epidermis or outer layer of the skin. It consists of a thin layer of homogeneous fluid derived from the blood-vessels, and contains the granules of cells which subsequently form the outer covering of the skin.

*C. Epidermis, or Cuticle.*—This is the outer layer of the skin, and invests the entire surface of the body. It consists of cells arranged in layers—those nearest the surface being dry and consisting of mere scales. It is insensible and unvascular, there being no nerves or blood-vessels found in it. It receives its nourishment from the basement membrane lying beneath. As new cells form, the others are pressed up and become dry and are thrown off in the form of scurf. Hence there is more or less scurf continually thrown off from the skin, which, if not eliminated, would clog up the pores of which the skin is supplied, and thus prevent the evaporation of effete matter from the blood. From this fact, we perceive the necessity of keeping the surface of the skin perfectly clean if we wish to maintain health and a healthy appearance of the body's surface.

The white and soap-like crust observed covering the skin of new-born children, consists of epidermic scales, with mucus and oil globules. This is called *vernix caseosa.*

In blistering, scalds and burns, the outer surface of the skin or epidermis is destroyed and stripped off, which leaves the sensitive surface, or *cutis vera*, exposed to the oxygen of the air, causing pain.

The main object in treating burns should be to form an artificial cuticle to protect this delicate surface.

One of the best remedies that can be applied, is by saturating raw cotton with one part of chloroform or ether, and two parts of sweet oil. The oil prevents the absorption of oxygen, while the chloroform or ether removes the pain. Flour mixed with water, in the form of paste, and applied, will also answer a good purpose. The white of eggs covered with oil-silk, will likewise afford an artificial cuticle. Carbonic acid applied to a burned surface, will immediately remove the pain.

The use of the epidermis is to protect the sensitive surface; to prevent a too rapid dissipation of caloric; and to prevent a too rapid evaporation of the fluids of the body.

The color of the different races is depending upon a pigment that is deposited in the second layer of the skin, which becomes mingled with the epidermic cells.

In the negro they are of a dark black color, while in the white races they are almost entirely wanting, excepting in freckles, when they are observed of a lightish hue.

By blistering the skin of a negro it becomes nearly the color of the white person, but the pigment soon forms again.

*D. Sudoriferous Glands.*—These are also called the sweat glands. They consist of tubes with open mouths upon the surface of the epidermis, and extend through the three layers of skin to the sub-cutaneous tissue below. (*Fig.* 79.)

According to Wilson, 2,800 of them are formed in a single square inch, and, when straightened, each tube is about a quarter of an inch in length.

The number of square inches in a man of ordinary stature is estimated at 2,500. Accordingly, the total number of pores must be 7,000,000, and the length of tubing 1,750,000 inches, or 145,833 feet, or 48,611 yards, or twenty-eight miles.

The fluid passing off from these glands is usually in the form of vapor, and is called *insensible perspiration.* When it is more profuse it appears in drops, and is then called *sensible perspiration.* It usually contains lactic acid, which gives the perspiration, when it is profuse, a sour smell. There are about twelve parts only in 1,000 of solid matter—the balance consists of water. The amount pass-

FIG. 79.

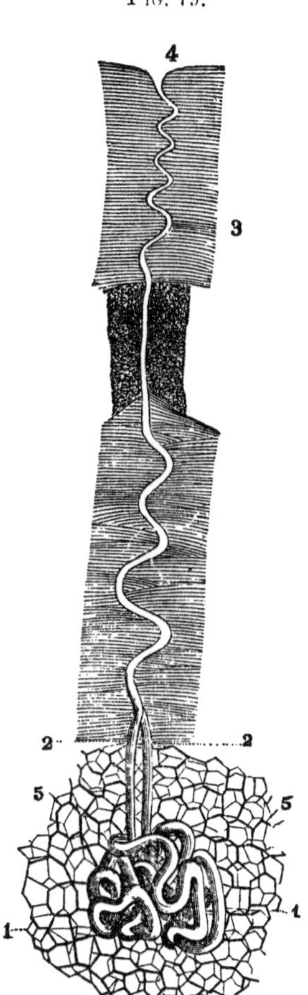


SUDORIFEROUS GLAND FROM THE PALM OF THE HAND—MAGNIFIED.

1, 1, Contorted tubes, composing the gland, which are united by two excretory ducts; 2, 2, which afterward unite into one spiral canal that passes through the epidermis at 3, and opens on its surface at 4; the gland is imbedded in fat-vesicles which are seen at 5, 5.

ing off in the shape of insensible perspiration, has been estimated at eleven grains per minute. Perspiration is wonderfully modified by the condition of the atmosphere. When the weather is dry and hot it is quite profuse; when it is warm and moist the perspiration is less, and when the weather is still colder the moisture of the skin is diminished in proportion to the degree of the thermal changes.

*E. Sebaceous Glands.*—These are distinct from the sudorific glands—the former being more abundant where the latter are the least abundant, and *vice versa.* They are absent on the soles of the feet and palms of hands, and numerous on the face, scalp, etc. They are little crypts or sacs, imbedded in the *cutis vera,* or true skin. (*Fig.* 78, *f*, and *Fig.* 80.) Sometimes there are several of these clustered around a duct, into which they open. Sometimes the ducts of *these* glands

Fig. 80.

REPRESENTATION OF THREE SEBACEOUS FOLLICLES TAKEN FROM THE NOSE, WITH AN ATTENDANT HAIR. THE DUCTS OF THE GLANDS OPEN IN THIS INSTANCE UPON THE SKIN. (*From S. G. Morton.*)

perform a double function, forming a sheath for the *hair*, and outlet for *their* glands.

These glands (the sebaceous) secrete an oleaginous substance, which serves to keep the skin smooth and pliable, and to prevent it from becoming dry and cracked by the action of heat, etc. The secretion is found more abundant in those who inhabit warm climates, and with those whose occupations subject them to high temperatures.

## CHAPTER II.

### FUNCTION OF THE SKIN AND THE BEST MEANS FOR ITS PRESERVATION.

THE function of the skin has already been explained, while the importance of keeping it clean and in a healthy condition, as an Element of Female Beauty, has likewise been demonstrated. It will, accordingly, only be necessary in this chapter to present some of the best cosmetics used in fashionable and refined society for preserving and beautifying the skin.

As I have already intimated, a bright, clear complexion, is only to be acquired by three things—*temperance, exercise, and cleanliness.* If these are not maintained, all the cosmetics in the world will be of no avail whatever. Were a young lady as fair as Hebe or charming as Venus, she will speedily mar the most exquisite and voluptuous loveliness by too high living and late hours. As to *diet*—strong coffee, hot cakes and butter; rich peppered soups; fish; sweetmeats, etc., have destroyed many a constitution, driven the roses from the cheeks and suffused the countenance with a saffron or bilious hue. There are a great many disorders induced by ignorance, as connected with fashion and habit. Besides these, the frequent changes of the weather, or the sudden transition from cold to heat, and heat to cold, have a sad effect upon the skin, roughening its texture, injuring its hue and deforming it with unseemly eruptions. The head and face, especially, need protection from the atmosphere. Nor should any lady ever go out into the hot sun without her veil, or without her having her head properly covered. Going out in the autumnal evening without a sufficient covering to the head, particularly, is exceedingly detrimental to the beauty of complexion. The custom of drying the perspiration from the face by powdering it, or cooling it when hot from exposure to sun or dancing, by washing with cold water, is most destructive to the softness and brilliancy of the complexion. The exercise of a little judgment would teach every lady that when she is over-heated, she ought to permit herself to cool gradually, and by all means to avoid going into the air, or allowing a draught through an open window or door to blow upon her when thus heated. Excessive heat is as bad as excessive cold for the com plexion. In the dingy face of the desert-wandering gypsy, may be seen the effects of exposure to alternate heats and colds. Let all young women, especially, attend to the few rules we have already laid down, and each will then be able to retain her health and beauty to the latest period of life.

## GENERAL RECEIPTS.

No. 1. WASH FOR THE SKIN AND COMPLEXION.—To remedy the rigidity of the muscles of the face, and to cure any roughness induced by daily exposure, the following *wash* may be applied, with almost certain relief, as we are assured by Madame LOLA MONTES, the celebrated *Countess of Landsfelt.*

Mix two pints of white brandy with one part of rose-water, and wash the face with it, night and morning.

The brandy keeps up a gentle action of the skin, which is so essential to its healthy appearance; also thoroughly cleanses its surface, while the rose-water counteracts the drying nature of the brandy, and leaves the skin in a natural, soft and flexible state.

No. 2. COMPLEXION PASTE.—The following is the receipt for the paste, by the use of which *Madame Vestris* is said to have preserved her beauty till very late in life. It is applied to the face on retiring for the night.

The white of four eggs boiled in rose-water, half an ounce of alum, half an ounce of oil of sweet almonds, beat the whole together till it assumes the consistence of a paste.

No. 3. A "REMARKABLE WASH," said to have been used by the Beauties of the Court of Charles II., is made of a simple tincture of benzoin precipitated in water. We quote:—

"This delightful wash seems to have the effect of calling the purple stream of the blood to the external fibres of the face, and gives the cheeks a beautiful rosy color. If left on the face to dry, it will render the skin clear and brilliant. It is an excellent remedy for spots, freckles, pimples and eruptions, if they have not been of long standing."

No. 4. TO REMOVE PIMPLES.—There are many

kinds of pimples, some of which partake almost of the nature of ulcers, which require medical treatment but the small red pimple, which is most common, may be removed by applying the following twice a day:—

| | | |
|---|---|---|
| Sulphur water, .................... | 1 | ounce. |
| Acetated liquor of ammonia, ........ | ½ | " |
| Solution of potassa, ................ | ½ | " |
| White-wine vinegar, ................ | 2 | " |
| Distilled water, .................... | 2 | " |

These pimples are sometimes cured by frequent washing in warm water and prolonged friction with a coarse towel. The cause of these pimples is obstruction of the skin and imperfect circulation.

No. 5. To Remove "Fleshworms."—Sometimes little black specks appear about the base of the nose, or on the forehead, or in the hollow of the chin, which are called "fleshworms;" are occasioned by coagulated secretion that obstructs the pores of the skin. They may be squeezed out by gentle pressing. They are permanently removed by washing with warm water, and severe friction with a towel, and then applying a little of the following preparation:—

| | | |
|---|---|---|
| Liquor of potassa, ..................... | 1 | ounce. |
| Cologne, ............................ | 2 | " |
| White brandy, ....................... | 4 | " |

The warm water and friction alone are sometimes sufficient.

No. 6. Queen Bess's Complexion Wash.—The following recipe has been handed down from the time of *Queen Elizabeth.* Its daily use preserved the beauty of her complexion to extreme old age.

Into a phial place one drachm of Benzoin gum in powder, the same quantity of grated nutmeg, and about six drops of the essence of orange blossoms; then fill up the bottle with a wineglassful of the finest Sherry. Shake the ingredients every day for a week, then mix the whole with a pint of orange-flower water; strain through fine muslin, and the "Lait Virginal," is finished. The face is to be bathed with it night and morning.

No. 7. AN EXCELLENT COSMETIC.—Take of blanched bitter almonds, two ounces; blanched sweet almonds, one ounce; beat to a paste, add distilled water, one quart; mix well, strain, put into a bottle, add corrosive sublimate, in powder, twenty grains, dissolve in two table-spoonsful of spirits of wine, and shake well. Used to impart a delightful softness to the skin, and also as a wash for obstinate, eruptive diseases. Wet the skin with it, either by means of the corner of a napkin, or the fingers dipped into it, and then gently wipe off with a dry cloth.

No. 8. LAVENDER WATER of a very excellent quality, may be prepared thus:—Rectified spirit, two quarts; rose water, one pint; English oil of lavender one ounce and a half; oil of cloves, half a drachm. Mix and distil the whole together so long as it comes over bright.

No. 9. ELDER-FLOWER WATER is frequently found serviceable in producing that enviable softness of the skin which the ladies so much admire; but the best way to begin is to attack the enemy in his strongest fortress, the stomach. Whilst trying cosmetics, it is an excellent plan to purify the blood with some gentle asperient; and the following simple preparation, which may be taken all through the spring, summer and autumn, will be found highly advantageous:—Put two ounces of Epsom salts, half an ounce of cream of tartar, and the half of a rind of lemon, into a quart of boiling water. When cold, decant it into a bottle, cork it close, and take a wineglassful every morning before breakfast. It will remove giddiness and headaches, besides operating as an admirable purifier.—*Elixir of Beauty.*

No. 10. Freckles.—Freckles are situated in the middle and outer membrane of the skin; and before any other application, it will be advisable to soften the surface by the use of some mild balsam or paste. The following is an excellent preparation:—Two ounces of fine honey, one ounce of purified wax, half an ounce of silver litharge, half an ounce of myrrh. Mix them well together over a slow fire, perfuming with oil of roses, eau-de-cologne, or any other agreeable perfume. Another: One ounce of bitter almonds, one ounce of barley-flour, mix a sufficient quantity of honey to make the whole into a smooth paste; with which the face, more particularly where the freckles are visible, is to be anointed at night, and the paste washed off in the morning.

No. 11. Freckle Paste.—The following is a good application, the surface of the skin having been previously softened by a little mild balsam or emollient paste:

One ounce of bitter almonds; one ounce of barley-flour. Mix with a sufficient quantity of honey to make the whole into a smooth paste, with which the face, particularly where the freckles appear, is to be anointed at night, and the paste washed off in the morning.

No. 12. FOR A WASH FOR FRECKLES, TAN, ETC.—Take two ounces of lemon juice, half a drachm of powdered borax, and one drachm of sugar. Mix them together and let them stand a few days in a glass bottle till the liquor is fit for use; rub it on the hands and face two or three times a day.

No. 13. FRECKLE COMPOUND. — The so-called "Unction de Maintenon," after the celebrated Madame de Maitnenon, mistress and wife of Louis XIV., is made as follows:—

| | |
|---|---|
| Venice soap,.............. | 1 ounce. |
| Lemon juice,.............. | ½ " |
| Oil of bitter almonds,...... | ¼ " |
| Deliquidated oil of tartar,... | ¼ " |
| Oil of rhodium,............ | 3 drops. |

No. 14. FRECKLE WASH.—One drachm of muriatic acid; half pint of rain water; half teaspoonful of spirit lavender. Mix them well together, and apply two or three times a day to the freckles, with a camel's-hair brush.

No. 15. LEMON CREAM FOR SUNBURNS, ETC.—Put two spoonsful of fresh cream into half a pint of new milk; squeeze into it the juice of a lemon, and half a glass of brandy, a little alum and loaf sugar; boil the whole, skim it well, and when cool it is fit for use.

No. 16. Preventive Wash for Sunburn.—Two drachms of borax; one drachm of Roman alum; one drachm of camphor; half ounce of sugar; one pound of ox-gall. Mix and stir well together, and repeat the stirring three or four times a day, until the mixture becomes transparent. Then strain it through filtering paper, and it is fit for use.

## CHAPTER III.

### THE HAIR.

#### POPULARLY AND PHYSIOLOGICALLY CONSIDERED.

In all ages of the world and among all nations, the hair has been regarded as one of the chief adornments of the person of the human family, while its healthy preservation and orderly arrangement have occupied much of the attention of the more cultivated and refined in every land. The hair is certainly one of the most important elements of that *ensemble* which constitutes the human being. Hence it is to the universal admission of this fact, that ingenuity has been put to the rack in every clime, with the view of discovering remedies capable of increasing, or of even creating the constituent characters of a fine head of hair, and also of ameliorating the defects of nature and of age. Notwithstanding all this, however, it is a matter of no little astonishment that comparatively so few artists of modern times have exercised their talents so as to demonstrate the advantage of taste, or taught a knowledge of the subject of arranging a lady's hair in a becoming and symmetrical manner. As an American writer* of considerable celebrity has well remarked, "There might be a hundred studies of the

* N. P. Willis.

various modifications of style, with an analysis of the meaning and expression of each one—the merry and the melancholy, the dignified and the playful, the firm and the yielding, the proud and the timid, the sainted and the coquettish, the practical and the poetical—each finding a picture of her own peculiar style, and guarded against stumbling ignorantly and unconsciously upon one which is entirely out of harmony with her character. It is a neglected chapter of the Arts. We admire woman too much to think that the propriety and fitness of beauty in the dressing of her head is a trifling matter. Science and art might well combine to give it some comprehensive system and redeem it from the present barbarous haphazard."

This is the right view to take of the matter, especially at a time like the present when the principles of Art are so much regarded, and when their influence on dress and personal decoration are so manifest in the highest quarters of refined and enlightened society. We therefore believe that it is not out of place in a volume of the present character, to add our efforts to extend their use by practical Illustrations, so that there may be no excuse hereafter for the monstrous mistakes which have been made by many ladies on this subject, through an ignorance of the right mode of adapting the Hair to the peculiarities of facial outlines so as to enable every one to render herself the

—"admired of all beholders,"

instead of repelling homage by a reckless and repeated outrage of the golden rules of propriety and good taste. My purpose, in the present chapter, accordingly is to treat of the structure of the hair, and to present the best means for its preservation, improvement and adornment, in connection with the various styles in which it is worn and decorated in all parts of the world. Until of late years a great paucity of materials has existed in respect to this subject. Of all the tissues of the human body the hair has claimed the least attention among scientific writers, while among the more popular authors it has remained a theme almost contemptuously ignored, notwithstanding the personal appearance is dependent on healthy vigor, and the great care bestowed on its culture and arrangement in all countries. It is true, the poets have sung the praises of the flowing hair through all times, perhaps, yet it has not been till the present century that any really valuable scientific work has appeared, treating of it in a physiological and popular manner. *Pope* was perhaps the first author who elevated the theme to the dignity of letter-press consideration. His poem, "Rape of the Lock," has received a world-wide fame, and brought into the field numerous writers among the medical profession, who have not only presented elaborate scientific essays, and many curious facts on the subject of the human hair, but extended their researches as to its historical characteristics, as a means of personal adornment among all the nations on the face of the globe. Thus, at the present day, we find that the gravest of *Quarterly Reviews* have not deemed it beneath their dignity to investigate and illustrate popularly the subject of the human hair, while the works of Drs. *Copeland, Hassel,*

*Cazenave*, *Erasmus Wilson*, and other eminent physiologists and philosophers, are likely ever to remain as standard authorities in this especial field of literature. It is perhaps needless to say that I have availed myself of all such materials of information, and that I expect to be pardoned for addressing myself to the task and giving to the world the collected result of my researches and experience in a matter of really very great importance to all classes of society, especially to the *belle sexe*. Besides showing the constitutional functions of the hair, and the best means of preserving it in a healthy condition, we shall show how to arrange the hair, and offer those golden rules which will serve to rectify all mistakes in respect to its use as a facial adornment.

Among the illustrations, the FRONTISPIECE TO PART THIRD is especially significant of the *improvement* in hair-dressing, which we are anxious to inaugurate. *Vide* BALZAC, passim. "The GNOMES and the SATYRS may be supposed, not inaptly, to have tortured the shining braids of the fair sex, in those Mediæval periods of barbarism, when it was drawn out forcibly to its utmost length, and twisted, and twisted over a cushion of preposterous height: but *now-a-days*, the Cupids, it is obvious, have the task entirely to themselves of moulding the tresses around a beautiful face into attractiveness and grace."

## B. THE STRUCTURE OF THE HAIR.

The whole body, except the palms of the hands and soles of the feet, is covered with hair, of a soft and downy character. The hair of the head is long and strong; sometimes it is of remarkable length; while it embraces every variety of color, as shades between the two primary ones of red and black. Hair consists of a *shaft*, covered or enveloped by a distinct structure, called the *corticle* substance, and may be compared to the outer bark of a tree.

*a.* Root of Hair.—The root of hair is first developed. It consists of two parts, *sheath* and *bulb*. The bulb is two or three times the diameter of the hair, and consists of granular cells. The cells form at the bottom of this follicle and gradually enlarge as they mount in the soft bulb, which owes its enlargment to the increase in the size of the cells. (*Fig.* 81.) The color of the hair is also developed in the bulb, which is diffused with the hair cells giving it color. In grey hair there is no coloring matter. The cells of the bulb as they ascend, become elongated and narrowed, which considerably diminishes the diameter of the shaft above the skin. These cells are so arranged together as to form the fibres of which the shaft consists. The corticle substance of the hair, (*Fig.* 81, *c*) consists of cells arranged like the tiles upon a house,

Fig. 81.

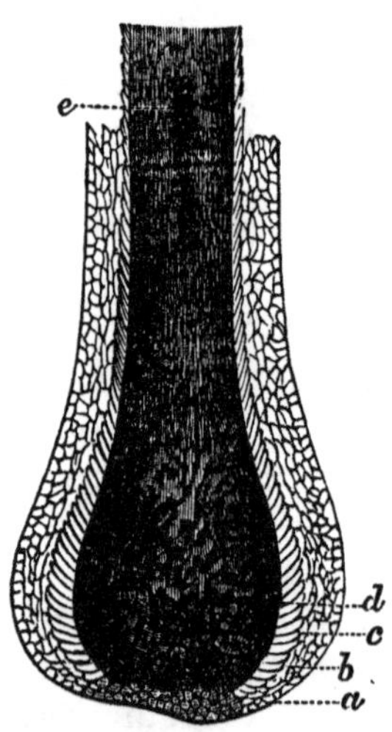


Representation of a Hair highly magnified. (*From S. G. Morton.*)

*a*, basement membrane of hair follicle; *b*, layer of cells resting upon it, which become more scaly as they approach *c*, and form the *cortex*. The medullary substance of the hair consists of cells at the base; at *d* they become elongated and finally fibrous; *e*, coloring matter of hair.

and they extend the whole length of the shaft. The hair follicle is lined by a reflection of the epidermis or outer covering of the skin, which dips down forming an envelop for the bulb of the hair. (*Fig.* 81, *b.*)

*b.* SHAFT.—The shaft is usually divided into the corticle, medullary, and fibrous portions. The corticle, as before remarked, consists of a layer of cells like the tiles upon the roof of a house. The fibrous portion consists of the aggregation of cells as they are formed in the bulb. It is colored with pigment, in young and healthy hairs. The medullary canal will be found in the centre of the hair, (*Fig.* 81, *e*) as is generally filled with coloring matter. In old and grey hairs the canal is nearly empty.

*c.* GROWTH OF HAIR.—The growth of all hairs take place at the root, (*Fig.* 81, *a*) which is largely supplied with blood-vessels. These vessels supply material for the cells of which the hairs are formed, and as the cells form they push the older ones up. In this way, additions are constantly being made to each hair. Hair is peculiarly susceptible of being affected by the conditions of health. If the system be debilitated from any cause, the hairs will either fall off spontaneously or by degrees. It is only the bulb that comes away and not the sheath and germ, and hence may be regenerated. When the sheath and germ has been destroyed, hair cannot be replaced.

## C. COLORS OF THE HAIR.

The COLOR of the hair is a point of considerable interest in its physiology. It was once believed that the coloring matter or fluid circulated in the centre of the hair, but this idea has been completely exploded by the researches of modern microscopists. According to *Bienvenu* there are really but *three* colors of hair—black, red and white—all the other varieties being only so many different shades of the same. According to *Cazenave* and *Grellier*, there are but *two* principal types of hair—red and black, to which belong the intermediate or decreasing shades, brown, chestnut, fair. Cazenave believes that white hair is the result of absence of coloring matter, as in the Albino, or of discoloration of the hair consequent of certain diseases. Grellier proves that the color of the hair varies according to climate. The nearer the north the fairer the hair of the inhabitants.

*Liebeg* gives the composition of the prevalent tints of hair, as follows:—

| | *Fair Hair.* | *Brown Hair.* | *Black Hair.* |
|---|---|---|---|
| Carbon, | 49.34 | 50.62 | 49.93 |
| Hydrogen, | 6.58 | 6.61 | 6.63 |
| Nitrogen, | 17.94 | 17.94 | 17.94 |
| Oxygen, | 26.14 | 24.83 | 25.50 |
| | 100. | | |

The brightness of the beautiful golden hair is attributable to the excess of sulphur and oxygen, with a deficiency of carbon. The coloring tint or pigment forms but one portion of the difference between the soft luxuriant tresses of the Saxon girl, and the coarse blue black locks of the North American squaw.

According to *Hassell* the depth of the color of the hair depends upon the development of pigmatory matter in other parts of the system, as in the eye and beneath the skin. The coloring of the lighter hairs, as the red and flaxen, depend less upon the depth of coloring of the pigment cells and granules than upon the presence of minute globules of a colored oil. In the hair of Albinos very little coloring matter is present; in grey hair the color matter has deserted the pigment cells and granules.

The constituents of different colored hair we thus see are by no means the same. All hair contains a certain portion of oily matter, some common salt, some phosphate of lime, a considerable portion of sulphur, various gases, and some manganese and iron. Fair hair contains least carbon and hydrogen; brown hair the most carbon and the smallest quantity of oxygen; red hair has the largest proportion of sulphur; grey hair the most phosphate of lime. All contain an equal amount of nitrogen.

## D. THE HAIR INDICATES RACES, COMPLEXION AND TEMPERAMENTS.

The color of the hair corresponds with that of the skin—being dark or black, with a dark complexion, and red or yellow with a fair skin. When a white skin is seen in conjunction with black hair, as among the women of Syria and Barbary, the apparent exception arises from protection from the sun's rays, and opposite colors are often found among people of one prevailing feature. Thus red-haired Jews are not uncommon, though the nation in general have dark complexion and hair.

Some writers suppose that there exists a certain relationship between the color of the hair and the moral temperaments. Thus the rapidity of circulation, love of change, vivacity of the imagination, and all other attributes of the sanguineous temperament, are associated with chestnut-colored hair. Black hair indicates athletic strength and vigor, energy and ambition, and the passions. Fair hair represents a soft and lax fibre, and is the emblem of mildness, tenderness and affection, blended with judgment; in short, all the qualities usually associated with a calm and mild temperament.

According to *Lavater*,* the hair affords a variety of indications of the temperament of an individual, of his powers, of his habit of thought, and consequently of his intellectual faculties. It corresponds with our physical constitution, as plants and fruits do to the soil which produced them. The diversity of the covering of the lower animals sufficiently indicates the expressive meaning conveyed by the different qualities and color of the human hair. Compare the wool of the sheep with the fur of the wolf; the hair of the rabbit with that of the hyena.

The fair-haired inhabitants of the earth are found north of the parallel of 48°; this line cutting off England, Belgium, the whole of North Germany and a great portion of Russia. Between the parallels of 48° and 45°, which includes northern France, Switzerland, and part of Piedmont, passes through Bohemia and Austria proper, and touches the Georgian and Circassian provinces of the Czar empire, dark brown hair

Vol. II. pp. 256--7.

is the predominant color. Below this line, Spain, Naples and Turkey, are found the genuine dark-haired races. Taking Europe broadly from North to South, its people present all gradations in the color of the hair; the light flaxen of the colder latitudes deepening by imperceptible degrees into the blue-black of the Mediterranean shores. The exceptions to this gradation are the dark tribes still lingering in England, the Celtic majority of the Irish, while even the modern Normans are included among the black-haired. On the contrary, Venice, which is in a southern latitude, has always been famed for the golden beauty of the hair of the people, beloved so of Titian and his school.

It would seem that race determines the color of the hair. Taking the parallel of 51° north and following it as it runs like a necklace around the world, we find a dozen nations threaded upon it like so many parti-colored beards.

The European portion of the necklace is light-haired; whereas the Tartars, Northern Mongols, and aboriginal American Indians have straight black hair. Canada breaks the chain once more with the blonde tresses of the Saxon.

## E. SUPERFLUOUS HAIR ON MEN AND WOMEN.

Partial excess of hair, or the growth of hair, in usual parts is very common. The Biblical story of *Sampson*, whose flowing locks were shorn by Delilah, is a striking instance of the kind. Such exuberance of hair is usually indicative of great physical vigor and strength in the male, but considered a misfortune in women. Many females have whiskers and beards such are usually sterile.

A man, named *Scapielione*, was exhibited in London and Paris, in 1841, as a modern Sampson. His hair resembled a mop, and stood out in a kind of Helmet, four feet and a half in circumference, requiring to be cut every week.

Dr. *Copeland* knew two persons whose entire bodies were thickly covered with dark brown hair. They were remarkable for strength and endurance.

*Hanno* brought two females to Europe from the Cape de Verde Islands, whose bodies were profusely covered with hair. Their skins were subsequently stuffed and suspended in the temple of Juno, at Carthage.

*Crawfurd*, in his "Mission to Ava," mentions a man who was covered all over with hair from four to eight inches long. He was married to a Burmese woman, and had two daughters, the youngest of whom was covered with hair like her father; it was fair hair, whereas her father's was jet black.

A year or two since a Mexican woman was exhibited in the United States, under the style of the "Bear woman." Her face and head resembled those of a bear, and she was covered all over with long black hair, resembling that animal. It was supposed that she was the result of an unnatural connection of a bear with an Indian woman. This is scarcely credible, and barely possible, among the freaks of Nature.

A bearded woman was exhibited at *Barnum's Museum*, in New York, a year or two since. Her whiskers and moustaches were full and symmetrical as ever seen on a modern dandy or "lady's man." She was married and the mother of several children.

A bearded woman was taken by the Prussians, at the battle of Pultowa, and presented to the Czar, Peter I., in 1724. Her beard measured a yard and a half in length.

*Hippocrates* mentions the names of two bearded women, whose masculine appendage was no obstacle to matrimony, namely, *Phœtusa*, wife of *Pythias* of Abdera, and *Hanysia* the wife of *Gorgippus*, of Thases. *Schenkias* mentions several modern instances of the same kind.

*Bulwer*, in "Anthropometamorphis," affirms that there is a mountain in Ethiopia, near the Red Sea, where the women have prolix beards and whiskers.

The great Margaret, governess of the Netherlands, had a very long stiff beard.

Madame Fortunne, a native of Geneva, lately exhibited in London, had a beard of enormous length. She was married, aged twenty-five, and the mother of a young child. This case is mentioned in the *London Lancet*, of 1852. Numerous other instances of bearded females are on record.

The famous General Haynau, of Austria, whom the brewers of London, whilom mobbed, for his tyrannical propensities, and cruel treatment of Hungarian women especially, had a moustache half a yard long! Still greater was the beard of the carpenter depicted in the Prince's Court at Eidam, who, because it was *nine* feet long, was obliged, when at work, to sling it about him in a bag.

We have elsewhere alluded to women having the hair of the head so luxuriant as to envelop the whole body, when allowed to fall down. It has been frequently seen *twelve* feet in length among some of the women of the Pacific Islands.

Mr. *Walker* mentions in his work on Physiognomy, that he was informed by Mr. Chamberlain, clerk of the church at Hythe, that when examining the piles of Saxon bones in the crypt, he had found red hair still adhering to some of the skulls of those who had fallen in the contests on that coast with the early Britons.

## F. OTHER PECULIARITIES OF HAIR.

Hair is highly susceptible of electricity. Most persons have seen the sparkles and listened to and felt the tiny shocks elicited from the hair of a cat by friction, and many have doubtless while brushing their hair observed the peculiar manner in which, under certain states of the atmosphere, and especially in frosty weather, each individual hair will fly apart and avoid the contact of its neighbor. This will also occasionally occur in certain states of the body, and in persons of nervous and sensitive temperament. Another peculiarity of hair is its hygrometric demonstrations, the curious way in which it will uncurl and lengthen itself under the influence of damp or moisture, contracting again gradually as the atmosphere becomes dryer. This has been ascribed to the animal portions of it, which, having in their composition saline particles, attract the moisture in the atmosphere, and, by absorbing it, distend the body of the hair.

The hair of a man's head is finer, generally, than that on the head of a woman; but if left uncut, it will not grow to the same length. A woman's back hair is an appurtenance entirely and naturally feminine. The hair upon the scalp, so far as it concerns its mechanical use, is no doubt the most important of the hair-crops grown upon the body. It preserves the brain from all extremes of temperature, retains the warmth of the body, and transmits very slowly any impression from without. The character of the hair depends very much upon the degree of protection needed by its possessor. The same hair, whether of head or beard, that is in Europe straight, smooth and soft, becomes crisp and curly in hot climates, and will become smooth again after a return to cooler latitudes.

According to *Erasmus Wilson*, the hair of women is coarser than that of men. It is not established that hair cut short tends to render it coarser and stronger. He states the average thickness to be from $\frac{1}{250}$ to $\frac{1}{600}$th part of an inch, and its ordinary length twenty inches, or now and then from that to a yard. Flaxen and chestnut hair are the finest, and white and black hair the coarsest. *Withof* confirms these views. He adds that five hundred and ninety-eight black, six hundred and eighty-four chestnut, and seven hundred and twenty-eight flaxen hairs, are about the average number produced on a square inch of the skin of the head. In some people the hair has a natural "disposition" to curl. In some it is very crispy; in others, stiff, straight and spering, while in another cl: s the least moisture will cause it to hang in what children not inaptly call "rat tails."

The distribution, concentration and location of hair are deserving of some attention. While in most quadrupeds the whole of the body is covered with long hair, in the human race only a small portion has much that is visible to the naked eye. In main the hair on the limbs varies considerably in length; in some, being merely pubescent, while in others it is nearly an inch long, giving to the limbs a hairy aspect. It is always met with on the back of the hand and foot, but never on the sole or palm, a circumstance of great importance to the delicacy of the touch. No animal in creation experiences from his main such inconvenience as man would do from the hair of his head, if obliged to walk on all fours—an evident proof that he was intended by his Creator to maintain an erect position. The hair supplies a sort of pad to the head, by which it is protected from mechanical injury, and guarded from the inclemencies of the weather.

The growth of the hair is limited. It grows longest in the female, waving over the neck and shoulders, screening and protecting them from injuries which might be sustained by free exposure to air, light, etc. In the softer sex it usually reaches to the waist. Sometimes its length is very great. Sir *Charles Bell* mentions a woman who had hair six feet long. Tennyson thus speaks of the Lady Godiva:—

> "Anon she shook her head,
> And showered the ripple ringlets to her knee."

Sir Charles *Wilkins* saw at Benares a fakir, the hair of whose head reached twelve feet. The tails of hair of the Chinese frequently reach the ground. Their moustaches are sometimes seen eight or nine inches in length. Mr. *White* mentions an Italian lady whose hair reached to her feet when she stood up. The Greek women are celebrated for long hair. English ladies have it from five to six feet long. Sometimes a head of hair is met with of the length of four feet, with a strong and continuous curl throughout. Such hair is exceedingly valuable to the hair-dresser.

The strength of the hair lies in its fibrous portion. In *Robinson's* "Essays on Natural Economy," we read that a single hair from the head of a boy only eight years of age, supported the weight of seven thousand eight hundred and twelve grains, while one taken from the head of a young man aged twenty-two supported fourteen thousand two hundred and eighty-five grains. *Weber* attributes some portion of this extraordinary strength to the elastic nature of the hair. A hair ten inches long can be made to stretch to thirteen inches.

The imperishable nature of hair arises from the combination of salt and metals in its composition. In old tombs and on mummies it has been found in a perfect state, after a lapse of over two thousand years. There are many curious accounts proving the indestructibility of the human hair.* Mr. *John Pitt*, on visiting a vault of his ancestry in Farley Chapel, Somersetshire, England, saw the hair of a young Lady

* See Gentleman's Magazine for 1840, p. 140.

Chandos, which had in a most exuberant manner grown out of the coffin, and hung down from it. She had then been buried upward of one hundred years. The body of Lady Audrey Leigh, who died in 1640, was recently found in the ruins of an old chapel at Nuneham Regis, in Worcestershire, England, with the eye-lashes and eye-brows perfect. The hair of Lady Chichester, her mother, who died in 1652, was also found as fresh as if she lived; it was long, thick, and as soft and glossy as that of a child, and of a perfect auburn color. *Wulferus** tells of a woman buried at Nuremburg, whose coffin, forty-three years after death, was found plentifully sprouting with hair; on being opened, the whole corpse, in its perfect shape, was found covered over with a thick-set hair, long and curled, but when the head was handled, there was neither skull nor any other bone left, yet the hair was very solid and strong. Mr. *Gough* mentions the discovery in Woolbridge Church, in 1792, of a lock of hair, braided, two feet and a half long, in perfect preservation, though surrounded by nothing but the bones crumbled to powder. In the choir of Norwich Cathedral was found, in 1780, some hair, supposed of a bishop or person of eminence, without any place of coffin or bones.†

In man the hairs are tubular, the tubes being intersected by partitions, resembling in some degree the cellular tissue of plants. Their hollowness prevents incumbrance from weight, while their power of

* Chambers's Cyclopedia; Philosophical Transactions.

† Sepulchral Monuments, Vol. II., 103.

resistance is increased by having their transverse sections rounded in form.

According to *Youatt*, hair, although sometimes covered with scales or rugosities, has no serrations or tooth-like projections. The difference between wool and hair is that hair is imbricated or scaly, while wool is toothed or serrated. *Bichat* also asserts that hair is of an imbricated or bristled texture. The projections all point in one direction from the root to the tip, analogous to the feathered part of a quill.

The various uses and economical purposes of the hair are not clearly understood. There is little doubt, however, that, like the pubescence and leaves of plants, the hair performs some useful operations for the skin in absorption and ventilation. The leaves of plants and trees, we know, are mainly instrumental in absorbing the noxious carbonic acid gas of the atmosphere, and, after retaining the carbon, gives out the oxygen purified. Plants which are divested of their leaves are invariably weakened in their growth or destroyed. So, a deprivation of the human hair is usually found to weaken and enervate the frame. The history of Sampson proves that strength lies in the luxuriance, vigorous growth, and proper functions of the hair. Of special purposes fulfilled by hairs, we have instances in the eyebrows and eyelids, which are beautifully adapted for the defences of the organs of vision; in the small hairs which grow in the apertures of the nostrils, and serve as guardians to delicate membranes of the nose; and in similar hairs in the ear tubes which defend their cavities from the intrusion of insects. They perform, also, the office of an apparatus of touch. We feel distinctly the disturbance of the hairs of the head by the movements of a fly, although the little animal is at some distance from the skin.

When hair is boiled in water, a portion of it is dissolved, which on cooling, possesses the character of gelatine. The portion that is insoluble has the properties of coagulated albumen.

It is ascertained that a full head of hair, beard and whiskers, are a prevention against colds and consumptions. Occasionally, however, it is found necessary to remove the hair from the head, in cases of fever or disease, to stay the inflammatory symptoms, and to relieve the brain. The head should invariably be kept cool. Close night-caps are unhealthy, and smoking-caps and coverings for the head within doors are alike detrimental to the free growth of the hair, weakening it, and causing it to fall out.

### G. LONG HAIR PROPER IN WOMEN.

Long hair is considered a special adornment of woman. The beautiful features and personal attractions of the fair sex, are always enhanced by this ornament. Whether the auburn tresses fall in graceful fold, the rich and glossy curls are bound with roses, or

> "The long dark hair,
> Floats upon the forehead in loose waves unbraided,"

either style will equally serve to set off the *ensemble* of female loveliness.

The pillar of the Ionic order is constructed upon

the model of a beautiful woman, with soft, flowing hair—

> "Her ringlets unconfined,
> About her neck and breast luxuriant play."

The elegance and ingenuity displayed in this architectural pillar is in strong contrast with the Doric, which is formed after the model of a strong robust man.

The Goddess of Beauty, without this elegant ornament of hair, though she had the brightest eyes, the fairest complexion and the most fascinating charms, would appear hideous and deformed. *Homer* speaks of the fair one who set all Asia in arms, as the "beautiful-haired Helen." *Apuleius* maintains that no bald Venus could ever please even swarthy Vulcan. *Petronius* describes the tresses of *Circe*, the enchantress, as "falling negligently over her beautiful shoulders." *Apuleius,* also, praises her trailing locks, thick and long, insensibly curling, disposed over her divined neck, softly undulating with carelessness—

> "Whose golden hair
> Around her sunny face in clusters hung."

*Ovid* speaks of those beauties who plaited their braided hair like spiral shells. *Amasia* is described with long flowing hair, distilling the perfume of myrrh and roses, and that of *Venus* as diffusing around the divine odors of ambrosia. *Coleridge* speaks of

> "Mirth of the loosely flowing hair."

While the bards of Hellas boast of a *Hypsipyle*, that gorgeous beauty, whose hair fell flowingly to her feet.

These, and a thousand other examples, show that in all ages and among all people, flowing hair was considered an essential element of female beauty.

We repeat, to women, long hair is an ornament, and adorning. It is an instinctive prompting of Nature that women should allow her hair to grow long. It gives her a sort of natural covering, and indicates the propriety of her wearing a veil. It answered the purposes of a veil when it was suffered to grow long, and to spread over the shoulders and over parts of the face before the arts of dress were invented or needed. We have already intimated that the hair of woman actually grows longer than that of man, which fact proves that flowing tresses are intended for some *especial* purpose in the economy of Nature. The value which Eastern females put on their long hair may be learned from the fact, that when *Ptolemy Euergetes*, king of Egypt, was about to march against *Selencis Callinicus*, his queen *Berenice* vowed, as the most precious sacrifice which she could make, to cut off and consecrate her hair if he returned in safety.

*Milton*, in his "Paradise Lost," Book IV., gives a description of the hair of Mother Eve:—

> "*As a veil*, down to the slender waist,
> Her unadorned golden tresses fell
> Dishevell'd, but in wanton ringlets waved."

The poets and writers of ancient times, whatever their predilection in regard to the *color* of the hair, are unanimous in their admiration of luxuriant and flowing locks in woman.

## H. PREDILECTIONS FOR CERTAIN COLORS.

The predilection for certain colors of the hair differ in various countries. In the East black hair has ever been held in the highest estimation. The most polished ancient nations were passionately fond of red hair. The Turks are fond of women with red hair. The inhabitants of Tripoli give their hair a red tinge by the aid of vermlilion. The women of Scinde and the Deccan dye their hair yellow and red, as the Romans did, in imitation of German hair. In Spain red hair is admired almost to adoration. Lately an English naval commander, who luxuriated in fiery locks, while in that country, was greatly caressed in consequence by the Spanish women and looked upon as a perfect Adonis. In China a red-haired person is termed "*Hung Maow Kwie*," literally red-haired devil. Red is beautiful to the Chinese. They extol the peach flower because of its form and delicate red color; all the fronts of their houses are red; they use the vermillion pencil. The word *Kwei* is a general term for spirits, whether good or evil, and equivalent to our word spirits. Thus "red-haired devil," instead of having an offensive signification, becomes "beautiful spirit." The Brazillians regard light hair and a ruddy complexion as enviable marks of nobility.

The Germans were in the habit of using a kind of soap of goat's tallow and beechwood ashes, to stain their hair red or yellow. The Roman ladies used to disguise their hair by wearing wigs composed of the hair of Germans. The peruke-makers of Rome, according to *Ovid*, bought up all the spoils of German heads to gratify those of his countrymen, who were determined to conceal their fine black hair under a wig of light or flame color. Hair from Germany was sold at Rome for its weight in gold. Red hair has been almost universally given to warriors and golden tresses to ladies. In heathen mythology, the golden locks of Apollo, the red hair and beard of Mars, the yellow tresses of Venus, and the flaxen braids that were twisted under the helmet of Minerva, demonstrate how much this color was appreciated by the ancients.

Sir *Walter Scott*, in his description of King James in "Marmion," says:—

> "Auburn of the darkest dye,
> His short curled beard and hair."

It is a favorite subject of description with our amatory writers;—

> —— "Her soft, unbraided hair,
> Gleaming like sunlight upon snow, above her forehead fair."

Another invites us to contemplate a picture—

> ——— "Where
> Streamed its long tresses of golden hair,
> Like straggling sunbeams of softest glow,
> Tinging the splendor of stainless snow."

Modern poets seem to be very partial to golden hair. *Milton* speaks of it in a variety of places; "Usa, golden-haired," and "Hecærge, with the golden hair." In his drama of "Adam" he thus apostrophizes:—

From that soft mass of gold that curls around it
Locks like the solar rays!
Chains to my heart, and lightning to my eyes,
O let thy lovely tresses,
Now light and unconfined,
Sport in the air, and all thy face disclose."

In another place—

" Her breast
Met his, under the flowing gold
Of her loose tresses hid."

Petrarch again—

" Loose to the wind her golden tresses streamed."

The royal poet, James the First of Scotland, writes of his lady's "golden hair."

Sir Walter Scott thus describes Clara in Marmion:—

" Now her bright locks with sunny glow
Again adorned her brow of snow."

" And down her shoulders graceful rolled
Her locks profuse of paly gold."

In the Lay of the Last Minstrel:—

" All loose her golden hair."

And speaking of Margaret, he says:—

" Her blue eyes shaded by her locks of gold:
His skin was fair, his ringlets gold."

*Shakspeare* seems to have delighted in golden hair:

" Her sunny locks hung on her temples like the golden fleece."

Bassanio, in the "Merchant of Venice," beholding Portia's portrait, enraptured, exclaims:—

" Here in her hair
The painter plays the spider, and has woven
A golden mesh to entrap the hearts of men,
Faster then gnats in cobwebs."

In the "Two Gentlemen of Verona," Julia says of Sylvia and herself:—

"Her hair is auburn—mine is perfect yellow."

Other passages will suggest themselves to every reader. Shakspeare mentions black hair only twice throughout all his plays, showing that he considered light to be the peculiar attribute of soft and delicate women.

The old poets had a similar partiality for the color touched with the sun. Old *Homer* sings of this kind of hair.

An ancient song has it—

"Still for glyittering lookes and gaze
Thou wilt ever cite the sonne;
Here's a simple tress—I praye,
Hath he such a golden one?"

Numerous other extracts might be quoted showing partiality for this color, but we need cite only a few more.

"And parted hair, of a pale, pale gold,
That is priceless every curl."

"'Tis sweet to part the sunny hair,
And look upon the brow of those we love."

"The breath of heaven came from the summer bowers
And stirred upon her cheek the golden curl,
That floated there as if it loved to kiss
Its alabaster beauty."

The old painters had the same fondness for golden tresses. In the English "National Gallery," the highest ideal of female beauty, from *Corregio* down to

*Rubens*, are represented with golden or flaxen hair. There is not a single black-haired female head among them. It is to the fineness and multiplicity of hairs that blonde tresses owe the rich and silk-like character of their flow. In the days of the elder Palma and Giorgione yellow hair was the fashion, and the paler the tint the more admired. The women had a method of discharging the natural color by first washing their tresses with some chemical preparation, and then exposing them to the sun. In some districts of Africa, they prefer light hair. The Gauls, the ancestors of the modern French, had the same preference, though that color is now in disrepute with their descendants who like black hair.

Red hair is often considered a deformity, but why it is hard to say, since in all cases the hair and complexion suit each other admirably. The "golden locks" and "sunny tresses" of the poets, invariably accompanied the blonde, frank and manly faces inherited from Saxon ancestors. "Villainous red hair," "horrid red whiskers," are terms of contempt and ridicule; but hair is only "villainous" and "horrible" when dirty and improperly worn.

The prevailing sentiment in modern times seems, however, to be in favor of dark or black hair. In the East black hair is held in the highest distinction. The Persians especially cannot tolerate any other color. The Song of Solomon says: "His locks are bushy, or curled, and black as a raven." Black hair characterized the prophetic virgins of the Druids. The women of Caraccas, Venezuela, are seldom blondes; but with hair of the blackness of jet, they have the skin white as alabaster. Jet black eyes and raven tresses have their admirers in all countries. *Ainsworth*, in his "Thirty Requisites of Perfection," enumerates three black: "Dark eyes, darksome tresses and darkly-fringed lids. What can be more seducing than jet black hair, falling in undulating ringlets upon the bosom of a youthful beauty!"

Some people prefer brown:

> "She has ringlets richly brown,
> Lovelier than a jewel'd crown."

Some poets also have sung of black hair, and others of blue:

> "Jet locks upon the open brow,
> Madona-wise divided there;
> And graceful are, I know not how,
> Descending to the shoulders fair."

A Portuguese poetess sings thus:

> "Black hair and brown, you may every day see,
> But *blue*, like my lover's, the gods made for me."

The Zinder ladies of Central Africa color their hair with macerate indigo. They also color their flesh with this dye, the dark blue replacing the yellow ochre of the ladies of fashion in Aheer.

The eyebrows are usually of a darker shade than the hair, which serves to give a tone of character to the forehead.

> "Black brown, they say,
> Become some women best, so that there be not
> Too much hair there; but in a semicircle,
> Or half moon, made with a pen."—*Winter's Tale.*

The ancient Romans considered it indispensable for a beauty to have her eyebrows meet, and in Scotland, persons whose eyebrows are so formed are considered lucky. In the East, a powder composed of antimony and bismuth is used to darken the eyelashes. In Circassia, Georgia, Persia, and India, the growth of children's eyelashes is promoted by tipping and removing the fine gossamer-like points with a pair of scissors when they are asleep. By repeating this every month or six weeks, they become, in time, long, close, finely curved and of a silky gloss. The practice never fails to produce the desired effect, and it is particularly useful when, owing to inflammation of the eyes, the lashes have been thinned or stunted. *Byron* in his "Bride of Abydos," alludes to the beauty of long eye-lashes in the following exquisite lines:

"As a stream late concealed
By the fringe of its willows,
Now rushes revealed
In the light of its billows.

"As the bolt bursts on high
From the black cloud that bound it—
Flashed the soul of that eye,
From the long lashes round it."

Another poet says:—

"Half-drooping lids, deep-fringed, they shade
The large blue orbs that shine below:
Bright eyes! by their own lashes weighed,
Still, still they languish to and fro."

The Japanese have a tradition that tea sprang from

the eye-lashes of their pagan saints. This fable, like that of the alleged discovery of coffee by goats browsing on the leaves and becoming frisky, and monks thence testing their properties, took its rise, probably, from its effects in promoting wakefulness.

# CHAPTER IV.

## A. STYLES OF WEARING THE HAIR IN ALL AGES AND AMONG ALL NATIONS.

CERTAIN modes of wearing the hair have distinguished particular nations. The Armenians and other Asiatics twisted it in the form of a mitre. The Parthians and Persians kept it long, floating and curled. It was thick and bristly with the Scythians and Goths. The Arabians, Abantes, etc., had it cut upon the crown of the head, while the Athenian Bacchantes kept it floating only. Girls wore it fastened upon the top of the head, and matrons had it tied and fastened upon the nape of the neck. To "remain in the hair," signified unmarried girls, who wore their hair long and not twisted into knots like that of married women.

At a mediæval period the modes of arranging the hair were very varied. It was lost beneath the hat in the time of Henry VIII. It was a cloud upon the head in the reign of George III. During the same period in France, it was curled on the temples and collected behind in distinct tresses by means of clasps. Margaret of Navarre frizzed her hair on the temples, and turned it wholly back in front. Puffing the hair and using white and yellow powder extravagantly were adopted. The Têtes, or head-dresses, were built or plastered up once a month, and sometimes at longer intervals; so that, it is stated, on one occasion, a family of young mice was discovered on taking down the hair. Some flat bottles, containing water, were introduced into this pyramid to receive and give a freshness to the stems of the flowers with which it was adorned. The Spaniards parted their hair at the side, and so destroyed all balance of outline. Sometimes the coiffure resembled a mushroom. The Greeks wore their hair in a simple and elegant manner. It was divided on the crown of the head, turned at the temples, falling gracefully in loose ringlets on the neck and shoulders. If these were turned up, they were fastened with a single ornament, such as a golden stylus or pen.

The ancient Greeks, at various periods, wore quantities of false hair, plaited their tresses into elaborate braids, curled them in pyramid of curls, frizzled and pomatumed them; and it was only now and then that the classic head-dress we term Grecian predominated.

The ancient Roman ladies made hair-dressing an absolute science, taught their slaves how to rear the hair into marvelous edifices of curls or frize, with flowers, jewels and coronals; or to plait it in multitudinous plaits, which were enclosed in a silken caul, or a net woven of gold and silver thread and gems, or fastened with large pins, arrows, or even dagger-shaped jewels of gold, silver, or metal.

The Egyptians perfumed and pomaded their tresses, and suffered them to float in braids or plaits about their necks and down their backs, enwreathed with flowers, or gems, or bands, and confined by a fillet round the head. They, too, wore false hair, both with their own and in wigs.

There is in the British Museum a wig said to have been found among the ruins of the temple of Isis, at ancient Thebes; and although so many centuries have elapsed since it was fabricated, the hair retains its extraordinary hue, the curls their form, and the whole thing its *vraisemblance*, affording a proof that the *perruquiers* of those days possessed a secret ours have not,—that of preserving the curl of hair. If we may judge, however, from the few authentic descriptions and specimens of their art which have come down to us, we should say that they were by no means like ours, ambitious of emulating and imitating Nature, for they seem to have painted, frosted, gilded, silvered, and stiffened the hair until its actual identity was lost or destroyed.

In the early times in England, the style in which women wore their hair was very plain. It was dressed very simply, being parted in the middle, put back off the face, and then wound up under the hood, or coif, or cap, or suffered to float at length in curls down the back.

We find Berengaria, Eleanor of Provence, Isabella of Valois, and Philippa of Hainault, thus represented. Elizabeth, Queen of Henry VII., wore her hair thus on the day of her marriage, with a "calle of pipes over it." One portrait of Anne Boleyn represents her in a similar manner. Jane Gray is pictured with her hair parted in the middle and braided over the forehead, while the back hair is concealed beneath a veil or cap; indeed, it was not until the reign of Elizabeth that we begin to perceive those elaborate headgears which a century later became so ridiculous in size and height. We find this "goode Queen" delighting in marvelous structures of curls, frize, gems and gold; in some portraits her hair appears to be folded over a cushion—we say "her hair," but history strangely belies her if the false portion did not far exceed that supplied by nature; and indeed, if she had not several entire wigs. In *Ellis's* letters we find the following entry among the items composing her wardrobe:—

> "Item. One caule of haire, set with pearles in number xliij.
> " One ditto, set with pearles of sundry size and bigness.
> " One caule set with nine true loves of pearle and seven buttons, in each a rubie."

About 1630 the hair began to be worn in a sort of crop, curled in short fine curls over the forehead, and falling in ringlets on the neck—*à la* Henrietta Maria, Queen of Charles I. In the reign of Charles II. perukes were very much worn. It was then the fashion for ladies to match or contrast their com plexions and dresses with wigs of divers hues. Perukes came into fashion in England in the latter end of Queen Elizabeth's reign. The making of them furnished employment for decayed gentlewomen. So much was hair worn at that period, that false hair became high in price, while it was scarcely possible to to obtain the requisite quantity by any means. Poor women were bribed with large gifts to part with their natural tresses; children were enticed into lonely places and robbed of theirs, while even the dead in their graves were despoiled. The custom of dyeing the hair was also then very prevalent. *Stubbs* says: "If any have haire of her owne naturall growing, which is not fine ynough, then they will die it in divers colors." In short, it was about this time that Art began to assume the rule over Nature. France was the originator of the changes of the fashion in wearing hair, as she is the inventor of new styles at the present day. Perukes were an importation from that country. *Stowe* says that they were introduced into England about the time of the massacre of Paris.

*Randal Holmes*, speaking of costumes and coiffures in 1690, mentions this peculiarity: "The ladies wore false locks set on wires to make them stand out a distance from the head."

In the beginning of the next century, 1700, the hair was suffered to grow very long, and either curled or allowed to float over the neck in a multitude of wavy ringlets, interspersed with ribbons and jewelry, or built up into an edifice of curls and frize, and surmounted with feathers, or gauze and flowers, or ribbons.

Fifty years later, the absurd fashion of putting a cushion on the head, and combing the hair smoothly over it, prevailed. Some of these cushions were of a ridiculous height. Sometimes the extreme ugliness and stiffness of this coiffure were occasionally softened by a few thick curls being suffered to wander over the neck and shoulders.

Powder and pomatum were profusely used in the reign of George II., and ladies wore as much false hair as they conveniently could. Various stiff and unnatural-looking curls also came in vogue, such as the French or sausage-shaped curl, and the German or roll-shaped curl, which had to be well frizzled underneath to give it amplitude and roundness. These elaborate head-dresses took much time to adjust, and required the skill of a hair-dresser to rear them properly; hence it was impossible that they could be done up every day, or even every week, so ladies slept in them—how, they best know. About the same period, wigs closely resembling those of the opposite sex were worn by ladies, the only difference between the head of a man and that of a woman consisting in the former terminating behind in a *queue toupé*, and the latter in a club or fold of hair, termed a *chignon.*

From 1790 to 1800 the use of powder began to be discontinued. Wigs and false hair began also to decline, and women were proud of their own unsullied locks. The hair was curled in a profusion of thick ringlets, and these were allowed to fall like a veil over the forehead and face, as well as on the neck and shoulders, seldom confined save by a fillet or bandeau, which supported a flower, or knot of ribbons.

Crops, in which the hair was parted down the middle, and curled all around in rows of short curls reaching nearly to the crown of the head, or in which the parting was over the temple, and the curls were raised on one side, the head almost in a "*Brutus*," succeeded. Afterward the back-hair began to be worn long; tied nearly at the crown of the head and raised in curls, or rolls, or folds at the top of the head and these backed up by a high comb resembling that of a Spanish woman, while the front hair was disposed in French curls, like so many sausages. These in turn gave place to elaborate plaits looped down each side of the face, and surmounted by bows of plaited hair at the back. Then, in turn, gradually stole in the simple bands, the graceful curls, the classic braids of the last twelve or fifteen years, as seen in England and the United States especially, which combine elegance, neatness and artistic grace.

In the earlier periods, in France, the women hid away their hair beneath their head-dresses, as was the fashion with the earlier queens of England. Then came the more elaborate styles and perukes. One portrait of Marguerite of Navarre represents her with powdered hair, curled over the head, and sprinkled with diamonds. It was, however, not until the beginning of the eighteenth century that those turrets and mountains of hair were piled on the heads. Cushions, whalebone, and sundry other things were used to train the hair over and support it.

A head-dress in the reign of Louis XIV., was one of the most becoming of its kind. It consists of rows of full curls raised one above the other to the crown of the head. Between each row is a string of pearls, and in the centre of the head dress a *sevigné* is so placed that its pendants shall touch the top of the forehead. The long back-hair is curled and floats over the neck and shoulders, and often has gems or flowers carelessly entwined with it. In the reign of Louis XV. the hair was combed up from the forehead, and all around, and arranged in perpendicular rows of frizzled French curls; the whole surmounted by a species of ruff which passes under the chin and there fastens.

During all this period, however, there were many elegant women who dared to be "out of fashion," and had the good sense and taste to wear their hair naturally in curls, in bands, or plaited, or wound around the head. Occasionally a royal caprice sanctioned such innovations on the aristocratic discomfort of powder, promatum, and periwigs. Various modes of wearing the hair succeeded each other rapidly, during the period of the French Revolution. Powder and all those pet *penchants* of the disgraced *noblesse* were banished, although the wigs were generally retained. The beautiful Madame *Tallien*, toward the end of the Reign of Terror, and immediately after her rescue from prison, introduced the fashion of cutting the hair quite short all around, like that of a man, "*à la sacrifiée;*" and subsequently, (we imagine as her hair began to grow again) the clustering crop of short curls *à la Titus.*

Many grotesque and extraordinary styles of head-dresses were introduced at the beginning of the nineteenth century. There was the "*Giraffe,*" a pyramid of rolls or bows of hair supported by a tall comb, and heightened by flowers. Then there was the "Casque," wherein all the hair was combed together, and tied up at the very top of the head, like that of a Chinese woman, and there raised in bows or plaits over wire or whalebone foundations, into a kind of reversed pyramid.

The Spanish, the modern Greeks, and the Swiss modes of wearing the hair are familiar to all. The Portuguese and some of the Italians plait or braid their hair and then enclose it loosely in a silken net; or according to *Lady Morgan*, comb it back behind the ears, and dividing into tresses, confine each of these at intervals into beads or ribbons, and let them float over the neck and shoulders in a very graceful and picturesque fashion. Turkish women, too, divide their hair into innumerable tresses, or plait them or gem them with coins or jewels. The Americans have a similar fashion, but they add masses of false hair to their own, and when seated appear half buried in a heap of partially dishevelled locks.

A fashionable mode of wearing the hair in the eighteenth century is thus described: It was raised from the forehead to the temples and brought over a crape cushion, a small portion was confined and curled at the top of the head, whence a plume of ostrich feathers fell gracefully over the left side, while a single curl waved on the neck beneath. The remaining quantity was divided into ringlets, and brought back over the right shoulder. Another mode of wearing the hair prevalent for a long time in France, was having it slightly curled on the temples, and collected behind into distinct tresses by means of bands or clasps of various kinds.

The distinguishing fashion of the ninth and tenth

centuries was to twist and plait the lower half of the hair, so as to form two separate tresses which were turned up on each side of the cheek. In the next century, the hair on the forehead of women disappeared entirely under the bottom of a head-dress peculiar to the time. Subsequently, a tasteful mode of dressing the hair, with but few interruptions, seems to have prevailed till the close of the fourteenth century.

In the reign of Charles V., the luxurious Isabella of Bavaria introduced a remarkable style of head-dress, which was thrown aside about 1483 for more tastefully arranged head-dresses. These, however, were obscured by black veils a few years afterward.

As before intimated, early in the sixteenth century, the ladies began to turn up their hair. Queen Margaret of Navarre frizzed her hair at both temples and turned it back in front. Various fantastical and ridiculous modes of wearing the hair prevailed from time to time. At the commencement of the last century the ladies puffed out their hair, and used hair-powder to an excessive degree. The French women wore their hair short and curled round their faces; but so loaded with powder that it looked like white wool.

The accompanying figures give striking illustrations of the most peculiar and stylish modes of wearing the hair, prevalent at different periods, as handed down to us in veritable portraits.

## GROUP OF PORTRAITS, ILLUSTRATIVE OF THE STYLES OF WEARING THE HAIR IN DIFFERENT REIGNS.

Fig. 82. Fig. 83.

Fig. 82—Miss G——, a reigning belle in London, in 1776.
Fig. 83—Madam Elizabeth, sister of Louis XVI., A. D. 1790.

Fig. 84. Fig. 85.

Fig. 84—Mademoiselle de Pompadour, A. D. 1750.
Fig 85—The Right Hononorable Lady Charlotte Berthe, from a painting by W. Peters, A. D. 1777

FIG. 86. FIG. 87.

Fig. 86—Diana de Poitiers, A. D. 1550.
Fig. 87—Julia de Rubigne, from a painting of John Hoffner, A. D. 1786.

FIG. 88. FIG. 89.

Fig. 88—Marie Antionette, A. D. 1790.
Fig. 89—Mademoiselle Damoreau Cinti, of the Acadamie de Musique, A. D. 1832.

Fig. 90.

The Right Honorable Catharine Compton, Countess of Egmond.

In some satirical songs and poems on costume, written in 1755, we find the following description of the hair, as then worn:—

"Be her shining locks confined
In a three-fold braid behind;
Like an artificial flower,
Set the fissure off before;
Here and there weave ribbon in,
Ribbon of the finest satin."

The follies of the head-dresses then worn by the ladies, are thus indicated in the *London Magazine* for 1777:—

"Give Chloe a bushel of horse-hair and wool,
Of paste and pomatum a pound;
Ten yards of gay ribbon to deck her sweet skull,
And gauze to encompass it round."

Byron's description of Haidee may be appropriately cited here:—

"Her brow was overhung with coins of gold,
That sparkled o'er the auburn of her hair,
Her clustering hair, whose longer locks were rolled
In braids behind; and though her stature were
Even of the highest, for a female mould
They nearly reached her heel."

In Syria, the ladies decorate their heads with dollars and different kinds of money; sometimes the coins hang down to both ears and must be a great weight. This fashion is occasionally practiced in some parts of Greece.

Among the Jewish women a high forehead was considered an indispensable mark of beauty, and to prevent the hair from growing low, they were in the practice of wearing a bandage round the forehead of scarlet cloth. *Petronius,* to give an idea of a perfect beauty, says that her forehead was small, and showed the roots of her hair raised upwards. This fashion, adopted by the Chinese, was not long ago a modish coiffure in France.

*Sterling,* in his work on "Spanish Artists," says:—"Luxuriant tresses were twisted, plaited, and plastered in such a shape that the fair head that bore them resembled the top of a mushroom; or curled and bushed out into an amplitude of fizzle that rivalled the cauliflower wig of an Abbé. An ungainly mode also prevailed of parting the symmetry and balance of its outline; of which some wretched portraits in the Spanish gallery of the Louvre, impudently ascribed to Velasquez, might be cited as examples sufficiently offensive and deterring."

The custom of having children's locks braided in

long plats, and tied up with bows, which was prevalent a few years ago, was not a new fashion, for there is a portrait extant of the son of Villiers, first duke of Buckingham (1637,) with his hair thus ornamented. The fashion for young people to cover the hair with a silken net, which was lately prevalent both in England and America, as well as in France, was in vogue several centuries ago. Some of the nets were very elegant in form.

The tribes and people of all nations have some peculiarity in the mode of dressing the hair. Whether Ethiopian, Creole, or Indian, women have always given much attention to dressing the hair. In many instances extreme good taste is displayed, but in the majority the styles of wearing hair has not been much admired by the ladies of enlightened and civilized nations. In other instances, the head-dresses are uniquely fantastical and picturesque; but we will not now attempt a description of them.

## B. MODERN METHOD OF DRESSING THE HAIR.

### THE LAWS OF ART AND TASTE.

For a period much longer than is usual in such matters, the hair has been, until of late, worn Madona-like, drawn plain over each cheek, after the fashion adopted by Queen Victoria of England. It has, however, been reserved for the regal beauty of an allied nation to modify this fashion. The Empress Eugenia has introduced a style that is equally in good taste with that of the British Queen. It accordingly may perhaps be said that with these illustrious ladies for a guide, we can hardly deviate from the sounder canons of taste. This idea, nevertheless, involves a plausible fallacy. Whatever the prevailing fashion, it must necessarily be modified to suit the immense diversity of contour in the facial line. The fashion of hair-dressing four or five years ago was almost identical with the styles of the reign of Louis XIV.

We have already referred to the odious fashions which prevailed in the olden time, and we may here remark that the present tasteful and truly picturesque modes of wearing the hair induces us to lay down some certain rules for the guidance of all ladies who would wish to arrange their hair in an elegant and becoming manner.

To speak broadly and generally, we cannot be too attentive to lines. By forcing the hair upon the cheeks, and squaring it over the forehead, we give to the face a sort of pinched hatchet-shape, any thing but attractive. In truth, the *oval* should be sedulously preserved by any and by all means of art. When the line of beauty does not exist, the hair should be so humored that the deficiency may not be remarked. Nothing is more common than to see a face, which is somewhat too large below, made to look grossly large and coarse by contracting the hair on the forehead and cheeks, and then bringing it to an abrupt check; let the hair fall partially over, so as to shade and soften off the lower exuberance.

To a lady who would preserve her high privilege —the supremacy of beauty, the annexed collection of examples of mistakes, defects, etc., will prove of extreme value. Confining ourselves still to general observations, we may state that some ladies press the hair down close to the face, which is to lose the very characteristic of the hair—ease and freedom. "Let the locks," says *Anacreon*, "lie as they like;" for, poetically at least, the Greeks give them life and a will. There are some of the beautiful sex, who wear the hair like blinkers, which is apt to suggest that they may "shy" on near approach. Let a lady's head-dress, whether for a likeness or for daily adornment, be arranged as in the portraits of Rembrandt or Titian. Let it subside imperceptibly into shadow so as not to exhibit too hard an outline. It should not, in fact, be at any time isolated, and by such means out of sympathy with all surrounding media. They should at least have the merit of floating into the back ground, and, in their fall, softening the sharpness of the contours of dress about them. We may further remark, before giving some examples of mistakes and defects, etc., that as the human hair forms so striking an addition to personal beauty, it will naturally be supposed that the utmost ingenuity has been put in practice to increase it in glossy thickness and delicate pliancy, to perfect its color, and above all, to *arrange* it in the most tasteful manner; and yet, by some strange perversion, the most fearful *mistakes* have arisen in adapting the hair to the peculiar physiognomical characteristics.

In the following examples will be perceived how much there is to correct with a view to the development of what Hogarth has so convincingly established as the line of beauty.

## DESCRIPTIVE REFERENCE TO ENGRAVINGS.

Fig. 91.

A large forehead and masculine features, worthy of a Roman Empress, are here exaggerated by the exceedingly inappropriate school-boy style of brushing back the hair from the forehead and sides of the face

Fig. 92.

Corrected by a classical mode of treatment

Fig. 93.

A narrow brow and a broad base to the visage, are rendered more obstinately prominent by shaving the hair close to the head and turned back.

Fig. 94.

Corrected.

Fig. 95.

Here both the thinness and length are increased by the hard mechanical lines.

Fig. 96

To obviate this we must avoid formality, and give variety and flowing character to the hair.

Fig. 97.

The large curvilinear lines of the hair tend to carry out the natural sweep of the full face; in fact, they repeat the original defective form.

Fig. 98.

Play of line, it will be perceived, is a great improvement and the small curves break up and distract from the larger ones.

Fig. 99.

This mode is exceedingly unbecoming to a stout person. It shortens and "dowdifies" both face and neck.

Fig. 100.

An obviously better result is here produced by narrowing and giving apparent length to the facial lines.

FIG. 101

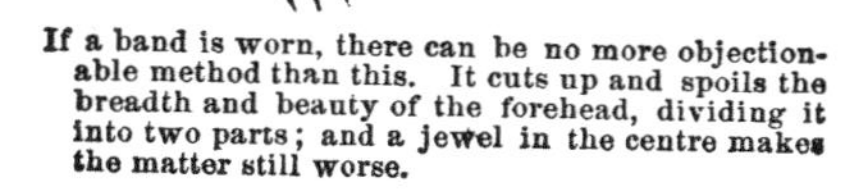

If a band is worn, there can be no more objectionable method than this. It cuts up and spoils the breadth and beauty of the forehead, dividing it into two parts; and a jewel in the centre makes the matter still worse.

FIG. 102.

The band, by a different arrangement, is rendered very much less objectionable.

## MONSTROCITIES.

BLINKERS.—We have alluded to the danger and inconvenience of hair dressed in this style in another part of this chapter

FIG. 104.

Blinker Styles.

FIG 103.

Fig. 105.

Fig. 106.

The Full Moon and Cloudy Style.

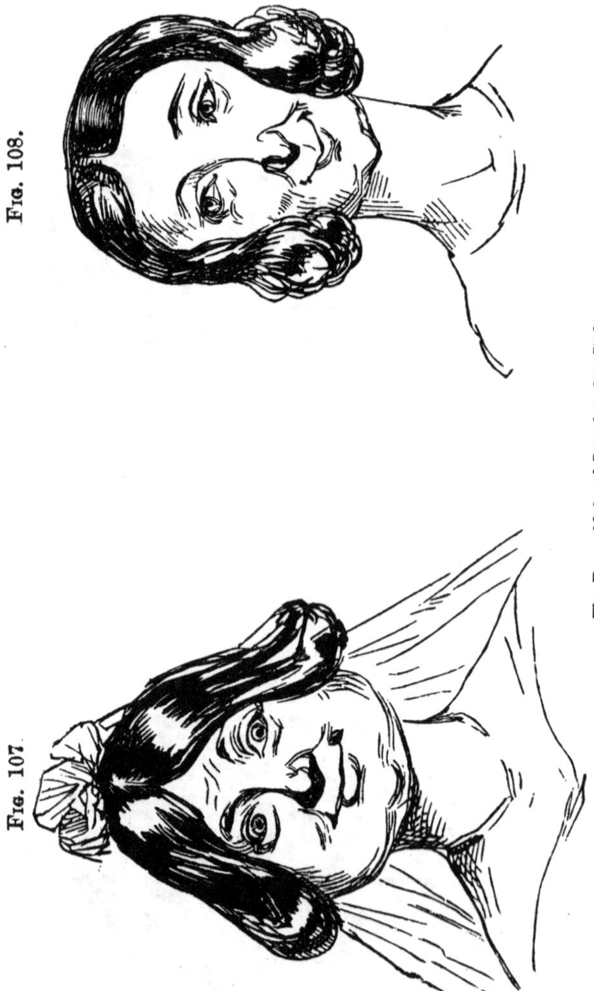

Fig. 107. Fig. 108.

The Pyramidal and Door-knocker Styles.

FIG. 109.

FIG. 110.

The Square-root and Architectural Styles.

### SENTIMENT.

As the modes wherein the hair may be arranged are very numerous, notwithstanding a certain adhesion to the prevailing fashion, it may be interesting to remark the way in which an especial sentiment may be preserved and rendered still more engaging by a due management of the *chevelure.*

Fig. 111. Fig. 112. Fig. 113.

Fig. 114. Fig. 115.

Fig. 116.

Melancholy result of permitting the curls to be too high-minded.

Fig. 117.

The Remedy.

Fig. 118.

Beauty Adorned.

Fig. 119.

Unadorned.

FIG. 120.

Successful manifestation of uncertain age.

FIG. 121.

And vice versa.

FIG. 122.

The Innocent and Debonair.

HOW TO DRESS THE HAIR.—Light hair is generally most becoming when curled. For an oval face, long and thick ringlets are suitable; but if the face is thin and sharp, the ringlets should be light, and not too long. Open braids are very beautiful when made of dark hair. A simple and graceful mode of arranging the hair, is to fold the front locks behind the ears, permitting the ends to fall in a couple of ringlets on either side behind. Great care should be taken to part the hair directly in the centre of the forehead. Persons with very long narrow heads may wear the hair knotted very low at the back of the neck. If the head is long, but not very narrow, the back hair may be drawn to one side, braided in a thick braid, and wound around the head. When the head is round, the hair should be formed in a braid in the middle of the back of the head. If the braid is made to resemble a basket, and a few curls permitted to fall from within it, the shape of the head is much improved.

FONTAGNES.—By this title is designated a ribbon, which forms an important ornament in certain styles of coiffures. The following is its origin: Mademoiselle de Fontagne, maid of honor to the Princess Palatin, by the favor of Louis XIV., the great duchess, who spent from fifty to a hundred thousand crowns a month, was the embodiment of the graces, and the leader of the ton. While at a hunting party, the wind having disarranged her head-dress, she fastened it with a ribbon, the bows of which fell over the forehead. This fashion was immediately adopted by all the ladies of the Court, and it passed with the name of Fontagne throughout France.

## C. SUGGESTIONS FOR GRACE AND BEAUTY.

We have already given the modes of arranging and dressing the hair in all ages of the world. We may here present some of the peculiar means by which the grace and beauty of females are heightened among many modern nations, whether enlightened or uncultivated.

In Asia the hair has always received elaborate attention both by male and female. The hair, eyebrows, and eyelids are kept stained with Kohl, a black dye.

The Persians use the henna to dye their beards. The women braid their hair, and dye their eyebrows and eyelids with plumbago.

The Bedouin Arabs wear their hair curling in ringlets over their shoulders.

The toilet of the Arab ladies in Egypt is the only thing they study, and usually with great success. Their dress is rich, graceful and picturesque. Long curls and plaits of their beautiful black hair, with ornaments of gold suspended to them, hang over their neck and shoulders. They dye the eyelids with a black powder, called Kohl, and the inside of their hands and nails with a red stuff called Henna (the leaves of the Egyptian privet).

**"Who has not heard of the Vale of Cashmere?"**

A Mussulman gentleman, attached to the Court of Jehangur, writing to a friend at Delhi, of the lovely damsels of this beautiful valley, after exhausting the powers of language in his description of their various attractions, among other details says: "The musky and wavey ringlets of those heart-ravishing plunderers, turn into a thousand wily snares like the links of a chain. When they let loose their flowing tresses from their soul-enchanting heads, the point of each hair can captivate a thousand hearts. They can draw a thousand Josephs from the well where his brethren have immersed him." The Moslem writer seems to have paraphrased Pope's lines:

> " Fair tresses, man's imperial race ensnare,
> And beauty draws us with a single hair."

The Sindhian Beluchi allow the hair to fall in wild luxuriance over their shoulders. The hair is dyed black when it becomes gray. The holy characters use the henna plant to impart a red tinge to the beard and hair.

Among the qualifications of a Singalese belle are that "her hair should be voluminous, like the tail of a peacock; long, reaching to the knees, and terminating in graceful curls, and her eye-brows should resemble the rainbow."

The ebon hair of the Kandian women is twisted into a knot at the back of the head, where it is confined by gold, silver, or tortoiseshell-pins, which are usually most exquisitely chased. This style of arranging the hair is adopted in Ceylon, by every native woman, and the coiffure of the hair, at the back of the head, is classically elegant. The four hair ornaments of a principal chief's wife, when studded with ambers and other gems, have often been valued at $250.

In Burmah the hair of both sexes is worn long, and tied on the top of the head in a knot.

The Chinese females wear their head uncovered and decorated with beautiful artificial flowers.

The Japanese women decorate their hair with flowers and ribbons, and use gold and silver bodkins to confine the hair. They anoint it with cocoa-nut oil, and plait it Chinese-fashion.

The desert-tribes of Africa dress their hair with ghee or butter, which in that climate is entirely fluid. I give a representation of a Bisharee woman, in which the style of wearing the hair is pleasing and tasteful.

Some Negresses use false tails as well as false locks, as our belles do, the long flowing curls being preferred by the sooty Nigertian beauties, in spite of such an ornament being unnatural to them.

The aboriginal ladies of Australia are conspicuous for their head-gear. Glowing in grease and red ochre, the ringlets of these "dark angels" are decorated with opossum tails, the extremities of other animals, and the incisor teeth of the Kangaroo.

In New Zealand, married women permit their tresses to flow loosely over their shoulders. Oil is employed in beautifying the hair. They use two kinds; shark's oil and that obtained from the seeds of a tree called *titoki*, the odor of both of which oils is very offensive. Young girls let their hair fall over the forehead, cutting it a little above the eye-brows. Bunches of the white feathers of the albatross or of the gannet, and of the beautiful tail feathers of the *luria*, which are black tipped with white, are worn in the head of both sexes, and form a strong contrast to the raven blackness of the hair.

The people of the Australian and Pacific Islands have similar peculiarities in dressing the hair.

The Oceanic Islanders pay great attention to the adornment of their persons. The hair of the females is arranged in short, loose curls, while the eye-brows are reduced. The head is ornamented with elegant native flowers, sometimes in great profusion, at other times only a few Jessamine blossoms, or a small wreath, being woven in their black, shining ringlets. They display great taste in the use of flowers in adorning their hair. They may be frequently seen with garlands of yellow flowers around their brows, and branches of the brilliant scarlet *Hibiscus rosæ Chinensis* fastened in their hair. They dress the hair with a gummy substance obtained from the trunk of the cocoa-nut tree, called *pia*, or in the viscid gum of the bread-fruit tree, which gives it a shining appearance, and fixes it as straight as if it had been stiffened with rosin.

The hair of the South Sea Islanders is worn in various fashions, according to the taste of the wearer. The natural color of the hair of the females can scarcely be ascertained, as they use lime and pigments, which make it red, brown, white, or black, according to the taste of the individual. They wear a *sala*, or *kerchief*, of very thin gauze-like paper-cloth, thrown loosely over the hair, and tied around the head in the form of a turban. The color of the hair is usually red or yellow, by the universal method of powdering it with burnt shells and coral, of which powder they usually carry a small gourd or box filled with it about them.

The Fejees smear their hair with red ochre and grease. The married women wear their hair short, the girls rather long.

The natives of the Wallis Islands and the Navigator's Group, wear their hair long and matted, which serves as a protection against the hot sun and heavy rains.

The natives of the Britannia Islands take great pains in dressing their hair. So with those of the Loyalty Islands and the Isle of Bornobi, where they use a variety of perfumes mixed with cocoa-nut oil. Both sexes wear round their heads at feasts and other occasions wreaths of beautiful, sweet-scented white and yellow flowers. The female has often a few pale blossoms wreathed round her hair, richly contrasting its jetty curls.

Among the natives of South America, the hair is worn in endless variety—in some places with singular taste, and in others in a very slovenly manner.

The Indian women of Peru allow their hair to flow loosely and copiously over their shoulders.

The Auracanians have long hair plaited into two tails, ornamented with strings of brass or gold bells, which make a tinkling noise at every movement of the head.

Some of the Patagonian women twist their black hair with ribbons of divers colors. Others let it hang carelessly down their backs.

The fashion, aboriginal with the Oregon females, of wearing the hair in two lateral braids, is also widely diffused in Spanish America, and as far as Chili.

The native females of Vancouver's Island have long hair, dressed in different styles, and ornamented with the white down of birds.

The hair of the Indians of Behring's Strait, is done up in large plaits on each side of the head. The edges of the eyelids are blackened with plumbago rubbed up with a little saliva upon a piece of slate. This is a very ancient practice, and is often alluded to in the sacred writings, and the custom now prevails extensively among Eastern ladies. (See 2 King, ix. 30; Jer. iv. 30; Ezek. xxiii. 40. Also *Eadie's* Dictionary of the Bible.)

According to *Eadie*, the Eastern ladies tinge their hair and the edges of their eye-lids with a fine black powder moistened with oil or vinegar. The manner of doing it in the East is thus described: A smooth cylindrical piece of ivory or silver, shaped like a quill and about two inches long, is dipped into the composition and placed within the eye-lashes which are closed over it. This "eye-salve" is made with lead ore and other ingredients.

The Esquimaux women consider it disgraceful to cut off their hair. It is only done in deep mourning, or on a resolution never to marry. The act of cutting off the hair is of greater importance to an Esquimaux woman than that of assuming the veil to an European woman, as she is then doomed to perpetual celibacy. Usually, they weave their locks into a double ringlet on the crown of the head, and ornament it with ribbons and beads.

The North American Indians in every part, usually have long hair, arranged in various ways; sometimes flowing loosely, other times in braids, and generally ornamented with feathers, ribbons, etc.

Frequent allusions are made in Scripture to the fashion of wearing the hair. A bald head was considered a great curse among the Jews. It was the custom for the men to wear it cut short, but the women were required to wear it long.

In the time of David however, the hair was considered a great ornament, and the longer it was the more it was esteemed. They were in the habit of powdering it with dust of gold.

The Emperor Commodus is said to have powdered his head with gold. It is singular how old fashions are revived. Not long since, some fashionable ladies in Paris reintroduced the practice of wearing powder in the hair. Some carried the matter to the extreme of using gold and silver powder; gold for brunettes, and silver for blondes. There were five or six *merveilles* in gold and silver powder. They might have been called the *Danae* powdered by Jupiter. The most remarkable of the brunettes in gold powder, was Madlle. Fould, a lady of the high financial circle. The silver powder was most adorably wedded to the locks of that Spanish blonde, Madlle. *Montigo*, since become Empress of the French.

*Lady Mary Wortley Montague* thus describes the modern mode of wearing the hair by the ladies in the East:—"Their hair hangs at full length behind, divided into tresses, braided with pearls and ribbons, which is always in great quantity. I never saw in my life, so many fine heads of hair. In one lady's, I have counted one hundred and ten of these tresses, all natural."

The dancing-girls of India pay great attention to dressing their hair. Mr. *Roberts*, when speaking of the Hindoos, says, "When a dancing-girl is in full dress, half her long hair is folded in a knot on the top of her head, and the other half hangs down her back in thick braids."

Miss *Pardoe*, in the "City of the Sultan," tells us,

that, "after taking a bath, the slave who attended her spent an hour and a half in dressing her hair."

## D. DISEASES OF THE HAIR AND DIRECTIONS FOR ITS MANAGEMENT.

There are numerous disorders of the hair, predisposing to baldness, ringworm, premature gray hair, etc. Bodily infirmity, disease and mental irritation, sudden change of climate, have an injurious effect upon the hair. Many of the morbid states and conditions of the hair, owe their virulence and connection with diseases of the skin.

The hair of the head may become weak and slender, and split at the extremities, from a deficient action of the bulb, in consequence of debility or impaired vital power, frequently connected with disorders of the assimilating organs.

To preserve the hair and keep it healthy, all ex cesses or extraordinary excitement should be avoided. Mental and bodily over-stimulation are injurious. An equable temperament of mind and body are essential to the health and beauty of the hair.

Curling the hair in strong or stiff paper has a very injurious effect. The more loosely it can be folded or twisted, the better for its free and luxurious growth. Soft paper or silk, should be used for *papillottes* when curling the hair. Those who wear the hair in bands and braids, ought to twist or fold it up very loosely at night, when retiring to rest. It should always be liberated from forced constraints and plaits. It must be well combed and thoroughly brushed every morning. After oil has been applied, the hair should be nicely smoothed with the palm of the hand. To prevent the hair from splitting, and to increase the length and strength, the ends should be tipped once a month.

Many mothers cut the hair of their daughters when young, in the idea that it will prevent baldness, and cause it to grow longer, thicker and more abundant. This is a mistaken notion. Cutting has a tendency to injure its beauty and retard its maximum growth. It is quite sufficient to tip or clip the ends once a month.

Hair has turned gray in a single night, from the effects of mental emotions and violent passions. Disappointment, bereavement, deep grief, intense care, produce devastating effects on the hair. Dr. *Wardrop* in his work on "Diseases of the Heart," states that the changes which are induced by arterial disturbance upon the cutaneous capillaries, are illustrated in a remarkable manner in persons where the hair of the head has suddenly become white, from increased action of the heart caused by violent mental excitement. He knew a lady who was so deeply grieved on receiving the intelligence of a great change in her worldy condition, that she had her dark hair changed into a silver white in a single night.

Sir *Walter Scott*, in "Marmion," says of Mary Queen of Scots,

> "For deadly fear can time outgo,
> And blanch at once the hair."

M. *Bichot* tells of a man whose hair turned white in a

few hours after receiving some dreadful news. *Sir Thomas More* became gray during the night preceding his execution. *Lord Byron* alludes to this generally received opinion in "The Prisoner of Chillon":—

"My hair is gray, though not with years,
Nor grew it white
In a single night,
As men's have grown from sudden fear."

Falstaff, in *Shakspeare's* King Henry IV., says: "Thy father's beard is turned white with the news." Madame *Campon* states that Marie Antoinette's hair turned white during her transit from Varennes to Paris.

When the Duchess of Luxembourg was caught making her escape during the terrors of the French Revolution, and put into prison, it was found the next morning afterward that her hair had become perfectly white.

A Spanish officer distinguished for his bravery, was in the Duke of Alva's camp, and an experiment was made by one of the authorities to test his courage. At midnight the provost-marshal, accompanied by his guard and a confessor, awoke him from his sleep, and informed him that by order of the viceroy he was to be executed, and had only half an hour to make his peace with Heaven. After he had confessed, he said that he was prepared for death, but declared his innocence. The provost-marshal at this moment burst into a fit of laughter, and told him that they only wanted to try his courage. Placing his hand upon his heart, with a ghastly paleness of face, he ordered the provost out of his tent, observing that he had done him an evil service. The next morning, to the wonder of the whole army, the hair of his head from having been of a deep black color, had become perfectly white.

There are many other similar cases on record. *Vanquelin* is of opinion that this phenomenon is to be attributed to the sudden extrication of some acid, as the oxy-muriatic acid is found to whiten black hairs. *Parr* thinks that this accident is owing to the absorption of the oil of the hair, by its sulphur, as in the operation of whitening woolen cloths.

Most persons on sudden exposure to cold, and experiencing any emotion of fear or horror, feel a creeping sensation pass over the head. This sensation is accompanied by a certain degree of erection of the hair, but not to such an extent as to cause it to "stand on end."

Macbeth says:—

> "What horrid image doth unfix my hair."

And again—

> "The time has been—
> * * * and my fell of hair
> Would at a dismal treatise move and stir,
> As life were in it."

Sir Walter Scott alludes to this:—

> "Back from her shoulders streamed her hair,
> The locks, that wont her brow to shade,
> Stared up erectly on her head."

In the Book of Job, at the appearance of a super natural presence, Eliphaz states that the hair of his "head stood up."

A description is given of the result of terror by Shakspeare in the Ghost's speech to Hamlet:—

> "I could a tale unfold, whose lightest word
> Would make * * *
> The knotted and combined locks to part,
> And each particular hair to stand on end,
> Like quills upon the fretful porcupine."

There is no doubt of the *fact* that alarm or fright may cause the hair to turn grey, or make it assume a certain degree of erection. Dr. *Hassall* says that the sensation or emotion which causes the erection of the hair, is the result of the distribution of fibres of elastic and contractile tissue, throughout the substance of the corium, and their interlacement among the hair follicles. The *cause* may be, that sudden fear drives the blood to the heart; and the extremities being left cold; the skin thus contracts, and the effect is to raise the hair.

The decay or fall of the hair usually commences at the crown or on the forehead and temples. It often takes place from disorder of the digestive organs, or of the constitution, or of a local affection of the scalp extending to the hair follicles. It indicates premature exhaustion of the nervous energy. Premature loss of hair may extend to all parts of the body.

According to Dr. *Copeland,* the remote causes of baldness are any thing that debilitates or exhausts the system, such as dangerous hemorrhages, low fevers, care and disappointments, the depressing passions, anxiety of mind, excessive study, the contact of rancid, septic, or putrid animal matters with the scalp, and the frequent and prolonged use of mercury.

Paleness may also be caused by exposure to the sun's rays, by the fumes of quicksilver, by the friction of a military cap or helmet, by chronic eruptions of the scalp, and by the use of tobacco. The salts of sea water, left in the hair, will cause it indirectly; hence, in sea-bathing, ladies, especially, should wear an oil silk cap, else it will be found difficult to dry the hair thoroughly. Baldness is endemic in some places. *Les Africanus* says that it is common in Barbary. *Tournefort* found it universal in Mycone, of the Cyclades, while *Sir R. Sibbard* says it is frequent in Shetland, owing to the fish diet of the inhabitants.

Baldness may arise from contraction or relaxation of the skin of the head. Strong local irritation, which produces a tendency of blood to the part, is frequently efficacious in restoring the hair in bald places on the head. Blistering, the application of caustic potash, and an ointment of lard and cantharides, have been used with more or less advantage. They are however dangerous applications, and cannot be generally recommended. If the bald part becomes red after friction with the hand, there is every chance that the skin may become soft and permeable for a renewal of the hair.

It requires unremitting attention to restore hair. The action of the blood through the deadened tissue of the skin must be promoted; the tubes relieved of obstruction, and a free secretion of the fluid by which the hair is nourished, excited. Where the constitutional powers remain unimpaired by age or disease, there is always sufficient vitality in the part to ensure activity and renewal of the hair.

According to *Dzoude, Dieffenbach, Wiesemann*, and *Hassall*, hair may be transplanted and grow after such transplantation, in consequence of the adhesions and organic connection established between them and the adjacent tissue.

Baldness was considered a curse among the Jews. Among all nations a premature loss of hair has been considered humiliating and degrading. The loosening of the hair, if neglected, will terminate in baldness. Blanching of the hair is mostly common in persons of swarthy complexion and black hair.

Baldness is quite common among men, but seldom seen among women. Literary ladies however are subject to this defect. Farmers, and those who exercise, or pursue manual labor out of doors, usually retain their hair; while the man of science and literature, the merchant, the shop-keeper and the factory operative often become bald. In short, all who over-exert the intellectual powers, and neglect or are ignorant of the precautions necessary to preserve the hair, are subject to the affliction, for such it really is, of baldness or general loss of hair.

White and grey hairs are natural to old age, owing to the decay of system and the exhaustion of the coloring matter of the hair. There is a general dislike to the approach of grey hairs. The prejudice is equally shared by male and female. Philosophers consider grey hairs honorable; they are certainly venerable in appearance, but there are few persons who would not prefer youth and beauty to age, baldness, or grey hairs, however honorable and venerable they may appear. Baldness and grey hairs, however, are not unseemly in the aged, although a great blemish in the young.

Grey hairs are not the natural indication of old age. Grey hairs have been known in children of six years, while it is common to see persons of both sexes, from twenty to twenty-five, looking as though seventy winters had passed over them. On the other hand, there have been frequent instances of persons over seventy years of age who had not a grey hair in their heads.

It is stated in "Chambers's Encyclopedia" that the people of ancient Troy were so disgusted with gray hairs, that they would hold their heads for hours over the steam of boiling herbs, in vain attempts to change the color of the hair.

A lady once said to Douglas Jerrold, "I cannot imagine what makes my hair turn gray, unless it is the 'essence of rosemary' which my maid is in the habit of dressing it with." "I should rather be afraid," replied the wit and satirist, "that it is the 'essence of *Time!*' "

Men usually begin to get gray about forty, many between thirty and forty, and others not till a more advanced age. *Meckel* considers that the hair begins to turn gray at thirty, but *Elbe* gives forty as the period of life at which this change first makes its appearance; much, however, depends on the habits and constitutions of individuals.

Fineness and silkiness of the hair are esteemed as beautiful, but fineness must not be confounded with neatness. The hair, however, of a *healthy* person is as strong as if it were coarse; but the *thinness* of the substance from ill health of body or over-growth, shows a want of strength and a tendency to break—the one cannot be mistaken for the other. Shaving the head is injurious to the hair, and should never be resorted to unless absolutely necessary, as in cases of sickness. Shaving the head increases the irritation, on which the loss of hair depends. It may cause the hair to grow *thicker*, but it will induce it to fall earlier and more easily.

There are several varieties of a disease affecting the hair known as *Porrigo.* That known as *Porrigo furfurans* is common with adult females. It is usually confined to the scalp, but sometimes extends much further. *Porrigo lupinosa* may be hereditary, and is not exclusively confined to the scalp. *Porriyo decalvans* is a bald or *ringworm-scald.* It may be cured by shaving the hair away from the spot, and steadily applying some stimulating liniment. It is common with both children and adults. There is another form of the eruption called *Porrigo favosa*, frequent with children under four years of age. All crude vegetables and fruits, saccharine preparations, and stimulating substances are to be avoided in this form of disease. *Porrigo scutulata* is a troublesome ringworm, and appears spontaneously in children of feeble habit, who are ill fed, and not sufficiently exercised. It originates in a great measure from uncleanliness. A medical man should always be consulted in this disease. The disease is as virulent as it is contagious. It may be contracted from the thoughtless interchange of hats, bonnets, caps, etc., and the use of combs and hair-brushes promiscuously. When the scalp is inflamed and tender, the blotches should be sponged twice a day with warm water, and covered by a light clean linen cap. Irritating applications must be avoided. A blister applied to the scalp may sometimes remove the complaint, but cannot be relied upon. The hair ought to be kept cut close, and the head perfectly clean. This with suitable food and open exercise will generally cure the disorder in a few weeks.

The removal of the hair was enjoined by the Levitical law in leprous indications. The long hair of persons who neglect it frequently becomes matted or inextricably interlaced. This false *Plica* is favored by a morbid secretion from the scalp, from *Porrigo favosa*, and other chronic affections of the part. In *Plica polonica* the hair is agglutined by a morbid secretion from their bulbs and from the scalp, and has an offensive smell. This disease, however, is rare, except among persons who are proverbially negligent of their persons.

M. *Cazenave*, physician to the hospital of St. Cours, Paris, in his treatise, as translated by Dr. *Burgess*, gives the following general directions for the management of the hair:—

"Pass a fine-tooth comb, at regular intervals every twenty-four hours, through the hair, in order to keep it from matting or entangling; separate the hairs carefully and repeatedly, so as to allow the air to pass through them for several minutes; use a brush that will serve the double purpose of cleansing the scalp and gently stimulating the hair bulbs. Before going to bed it will be desirable to part the hair evenly, so as to avoid false folds, or what is commonly called turning against the grain, which might even cause the hair to break. Such are the usual and ordinary requirements as to the management of the hair. There is, on the other hand, a class of persons who carry to excess the dressing and adornment of the hair, especially those who are gifted with hair of the finest quality. Thus, females are in the habit of dragging and twisting the hair, so as to draw the skin with it; the effect is to break the hairs and fatigue the scalp, and finally to alter the bulb itself. The fine-tooth comb is also too freely used, especially when the hair is divided—a part that the most particular attention seems to be bestowed upon. These separations, and the back of the neck whence the hair is drawn, in females, toward the crown of the head, are parts which first show signs of decay, or falling off of the hair."

Little more need be added to the views of M. *Cazenave*. In a hygienic point of consideration, as intimated elsewhere, the dress of the hair best adapted for females, especially for young girls, is that which keeps the hair slightly raised, drawn as little as possible, carefully smoothed, and arranged in large bands so as to admit the air to permeate; to unfold it morning and evening, and brush it lightly, but carefully; in a word, to dress it in such a manner as will not require dragging or twisting, but leave it free. If fashion requires it to be tied and drawn, and the individual yields to the mode, it should be unfolded morning and evening, and allowed to hang loose for several minutes.

Long, luxuriant and glossy tresses are the admiration of every person of taste and sense. A fine head of hair is the pride and joy of every woman's heart. The more *naturally* it can be worn, the better, not only for its preservation but its elegance and richness.

## E. TREATMENT OF THE HAIR.

In the language of Miss *M. A. Youat*, in an article on Hair, which appeared in the *Ladies Companion* for July, 1851, we may well exclaim: "How ignorant, how indifferent are we often to the nature, the properties, and history of the most common things which surround us. The beautiful gift of bountiful Nature, the human hair, we see and admire, and we weave it into all the fantastical forms dictated by the capricious goddess Fashion; but we seldom pause to reflect upon it, to marvel at its growth and beauty, to mark how it obeys the laws of vegetation, how it flourishes for a time, reaches to a certain length, falls and is replaced by a succession of new shoots, and eventually decays from age."

"Truly," continues the same writer, "the hair is one of the crowning beauties bestowed by Nature on human beings. What poet has neglected to sing its praise? All hues have been celebrated from the

'Lassie wi' the sunny locks,'

of *Allan Cunningham*, to the aged man whom *Crabbe* describes with

'Those white locks thinly spread
Round the bald polish of that honored head.'

"To woman particularly is hair an adornment. Take that from her, and she loses one of her greatest ornaments. Surely Venus herself would cease to be Queen of Beauty if she had her head shaved. And how busy Fashion has been, throughout all ages of which we have any record, with female tresses; how she has twisted and tortured, disfigured and confined them; dyed, variegated and blanched them; greased, stiffened and frizzled them! In short, how she has done her best in some portion of every age to nullify their graceful effects, and convert that which should have been a beauty into a deformity.

"Much has been said relative to treatment of the hair; and oils, balms, pomatums, creams and greases have been recommended without number for its nourishment and preservation. Cleanliness, however, and friction are its best stimulants and improvers. We do not advocate the use of sharp-pointed scratching combs, neither do we approve of those very hard brushes with which some persons delight to torture themselves; but a moderately stiff brush, with bristles from about three quarters of an inch in length will cleanse the hair well and also produce a warm glow on the skin, and this should be well used morning and evening every day, and then the hair polished with a softer brush. Cold water is the best wash for the hair. Soaps, generally, contain too much alkali and pungent matter to act beneficially on the skin of the head; but boiling water poured on bran, left to stand until cool, and then well-strained off, washes long hair very nicely. If the hair has a tendency to fall off, the skin of the head may be brushed with a small, hardish brush dipped in honey-water, or rosemary-water, or distilled vinegar, morning and night for a few days, and then brushed with the hair-brush until it glows."

To the foregoing judicious remarks of Miss *Youat*, little more need be added. The hair should be kept scrupulously clean by brushing, etc.; but never be roughly handled. By improper treatment the hair may be irretrievably injured. Brushes applied to the skin of the head should be soft and pliable than otherwise, but stronger ones may be employed for the long hair. From the respectable perfumers excellent lotions may be obtained which are effectual in removing scurf and cleaning hair, while well-prepared vegetable oils may be advantageously employed in promoting growth and gloss.

Every people, however savage, have had their own peculiar greases or oily preparations for the hair. The vegetable oils are always to be preferred. Animal fat, with some few exceptions, is exceedingly injurious to the hair, being often the cause of scrofulous disease of the scalp. Fluid vegetable oils should be selected as the best means for obviating a deficiency of oleaginous products in the cells of the hair-tubes.

Ladies often wonder why it is that their hair loses its curl and becomes straight and flaccid. The secret of this is, it readily imbibes moisture from both the skin and the atmosphere, when the natural secretion of the lubricating fluid in the tubes of the hair is impeded; and by degrees the latter becomes coarse, harsh and scurfy. Obviously, therefore, the hair must be supplied naturally or artificially with its necessary nourishment, and pure fluid vegetable oil is the only desirable application for this purpose. It should be well initiated into the roots of the hair as well as throughout the general texture, but it should not be lavishly employed, as in that case it would become a cloy.

As before remarked, every people employ some kind of oil for the hair. The Esquimaux and Greenlanders patronize train and seal oil. The South American fair ones of the Amazon and Orinoco, use the more delicate turtle oil. Others use the fat obtained from the alligator. The Zealanders adopt shark's oil. In the South of Europe, and throughout the Mediterranean, olive oil is in constant request. Cocoa-nut oil is much used in the West Indies. In the Pacific Islands, cocoa-nut oil and castor oil are used. The oils of the palm, butter tree, and earth-nut, are in vogue among the African people. Cleopatra was the first to lead the fashion in bear's grease. The fat of ducks, moles and vipers have not survived the age of William and Mary, while beef's marrow and hog's lard play a distinguished part in the hair dresser's laboratory, and greatly economize the destruction of Bruin. We are told by *Melville*, that the Typee girls devote much of their time in arranging their fair and redundant tresses. They bathe several times a day, and anoint their hair with cocoa-nut oil, after each ablution. Melville observes that this oil is fit for the toilet of a queen. Mrs. Osgood, an American poetess, thus sings in praise of this sunny clime:—

"The glowing sky of the Indian isles
Lovingly over the cocoa-nut smiles,

And the Indian maiden lies below
Where its leaves their graceful shadows throw;
She weaves a wreath of the rosy shells
That gems the beach where the cocoa dwells;
She binds them into her long black hair,
And they blush in the braids like rosebuds there.
Her soft brown arm and her graceful neck,
With those ocean blooms she joys to deck.
O, wherever you see
The cocoa-nut tree
There will a picture of beauty be!"

No doubt enough of the cocoa-nut oil would answer a valuable purpose in beautifying the hair, but the oils which hold a pre-eminence are a combination of the choicest vegetable products scientifically prepared, so as to conduce to the preservation and improvement of the hair.

## F. HAIR DYES AND OTHER MEANS FOR ITS BEAUTY AND RESERVATION.

It should be borne in mind that no artificial means will preserve the richness and strength of the human hair, or prevent its premature decay or falling out without good health, regular habits, frequent ablutions of the body in water, early rising for walking and riding. Though the *natural* hair is always to be preferred, yet every lady may be freely pardoned for using such innocent appliances of art and science as may tend to heighten the native graces and loveliness of her person, and remedy any abnormal or constitutional defect of whatever kind, particularly such as may affect or have a bearing upon the hair. Hair dyes, pomades, oils, etc., and even *false* hair, braids, curls, etc., are all perfectly justifiable, under a suitable discrimination concomitant of propriety, good sense, taste, and refinement.

"If a woman have long hair, it is a glory to her," says the Apostle. Especially in young females, it should be allowed to fall in graceful ringlets, "unconfined and free," over the snowy shoulders and swan-like necks of our American fair—alike models of grace and loveliness.

That this ornament may be rendered as tasteful as it is capable of being made, it should be kept free from scurf and other impurities.

It is advisable for those ladies who engage in domestic offices to wear a light bonnet or cap, to preserve the hair from dust and keep it glossy and clean.

The following receipts are in common use—some of which are considered harmless, and may therefore be used with propriety.

1. To Promote the Growth of the Hair.—The following receipt is a favorite one among ladies of the higher circles. It has all the elements of excellence in its composition.

℞ Bay rum,........................4 ounces.
Tinct. cantharides,..............1 "
Hartshorn,......................1 "
Olive oil, pure,................. 2 "

Shake before using. This should be applied to the head once a day, and the hair thoroughly saturated with it.

2. General Twiggs' Receipt for Hair.—The following is General Twiggs' celebrated Hair Restorer. It is also good for itching of the scalp.

℞ Sulphur, ........................1 drachm.
Sugar of lead, ..................½ "
Rose-water,......................4 ounces.

Mix them well. Shake the vial on using it. Saturate the head thoroughly with it at bed-time, and bandage the hair to prevent soiling the pillow. In the morning wash with soap and water. It does not dye the hair, but seems to restore the original color.

3. A Capital Pomade.—Dissolve thoroughly over a slow fire two ounces of white wax and half an ounce of palm oil, with a flask of the best olive oil. Stir it till nearly cold; then add one ounce of castor oil and about threepenny worth of bergamot or any other perfume you please.

4. To Promote the Growth of Hair.—The following is a good oil to promote the growth of the hair:—

℞ Palma-christi oil, ...............3 ounces.
Oil of lavender,..................1 drachm.

Apply morning and evening to those parts where the hair is weak and deficient, in consequence of a deficiency of moisture.

5. Baron Dupuytren's Pomade.—The famous pomade of the celebrated Parisian physician is made as follows:—

℞ Boxwood shavings,..............6 ounces.
Proof spirit,...................12 "
Spirits of rosemary,.............2 "
Spirits of nutmeg, ..............½ ounce.

The box-wood shavings should be left to steep in

the spirits, at a temperature of sixty degrees, for fourteen days, and then the liquid should be strained off and the other ingredients mixed. The scalp to be thoroughly washed with this night and morning.

6. AN EXCELLENT HAIR CLEANSER.—The celebrated Lola Montez, the Countess of Landsfeldt, gives the following hair-cleanser, as used by a great beauty of Munich, who had the handsomest hair of any lady in the Bavarian capital.

Beat up the white of four eggs into a froth, and rub that thoroughly into the roots of the hair. Leave it to dry on. Then wash the head and hair clean with a mixture of equal parts of rum and rose-water. This is said to be one of the best cleansers and brighteners of the hair ever used.

7. HONEY-WATER.—This celebrated wash, known to fashionable ladies all over the world, is made as follows:—

| | | |
|---|---|---|
| ℞ Essence of ambergris, | 1 | drachm. |
| " musk, | 1 | " |
| " bergamot, | 2 | " |
| Oil of cloves, | 15 | drops. |
| Orange-flower water, | 4 | ounces. |
| Spirits of wine, | 5 | " |
| Distilled water, | 4 | " |

All these ingredients should be mixed together, and left about fourteen days, and then the whole to be filtered through porous paper and bottled for use. This is a good hair-wash and an excellent perfume.

8. TO PREVENT HAIR FROM TURNING GRAY.—A retired Spanish actress warded off the approach of

grey hairs by using the following preparation whenever she dressed her head:—

> ℞ Oxide of bismuth,...............4 drachms.
> Spermaceti,.....................4 "
> Pure hog's lard,.................4 ounces.

The lard and spermaceti should be melted together, and when they begin to cool stir in the bismuth. It may be perfumed to your liking.

9. How to Color Grey Hair.—The following recipe was given by an old physician and chemist, at Lisbon, to a fashionable Parisian lady.

> ℞ Gallic acid,....................10 grs.
> Acetic acid, .................... 1 ounce.
> Tinct. of sesqui-chloride of iron,.. 1 "

Dissolve the gallic acid in the tincture of sesquichloride of iron, and then add the acetic acid. Before using this preparation, the hair should be thoroughly washed with soap and water. A great and desirable peculiarity of this dye is, that it can be so applied as to color the hair either black or the brighter shade of brown. If black is the color desired, the preparation should be applied while the hair is moist, and for brown it should not be used till the hair is perfectly dry. The way to apply the compound is to dip the points of a fine comb into it until the interstices are filled with the fluid, then gently draw the comb through the hair, commencing at the roots, till the dye has perceptibly taken effect. When the hair is entirely dry, oil and brush it as usual.

10. Pomade against Baldness.—The following is

considered a most valuable preparation:—Take of extract of yellow Peruvian bark, fifteen grains; extract of rhatany root, eight grains; extract of burdoch root and oil of nutmegs (fixed), of each two drachms; camphor (dissolved with spirits of wine), fifteen grains; beef-marrow, two ounces; best olive oil, one ounce; citron juice, half a drachm; aromatic essential oil, as much as sufficient to render it fragrant; mix and make into an ointment. Two drachms of bergamot, and a few drops of otto of roses would suffice.

11. PALMA CHRISTI OIL.—Take an ounce of Palma christi oil; add oil of Bergamot, or lavender to scent it. Let it be wéll brushed into the hair twice a day for two or three months—particularly applying it to those parts where it may be most desirable to render the hair most luxuriant. This is a simple and valuable oil, and not in the hands of any monopolist.

12. HOW TO DARKEN THE HAIR.—Wash the head with spring water, and comb the hair in the sun, having dipped the comb in oil of tar. Do this about three times a day, and in less than a fortnight the hair often becomes quite black.

13. A QUICK HAIR DYE.—Hair may be dyed black in a few seconds by moistening it first with a solution of nitric of silver in water (one to seven or eight), and then with a weak solution of hydro-sulphurate of ammonia. Constantly using a leaden comb darkens the color of the hair.

14. HAIR-WASH.—A good hair-wash is soap and water, and the oftener it is applied the freer the surface of the head will be from scurf. The hair-brush should also be kept in requisition morning and evening.

15. To Remove Superfluous Hair.—With those who dislike the use of arsenic, the following is used for removing superfluous hair from the skin:—Lime, one ounce; carbonate of potash, two ounces; charcoal powder, one drachm. For use, make it into a paste with a little warm water, and apply it to the part, previously shaved close. As soon as it has become thoroughly dry, it may be washed off with a little warm water.

16. Hair Depilatory.—It is proper to remark that all depilatories either act mechanically or chemically. To the first belong adhesive plasters, which on their removal from the skin bring away the hair with them; equal parts of pitch and resin spread on leather, has been used for this purpose. To the second class belong those substances which act upon the bulbous roots of the hair, and destroy their vitality. The former method is more painful, but less dangerous than the latter one. The following is a depilatory at present very much employed in the fashionable world:—Quicklime, two ounces; orpiment (or arsenic), half an ounce; strong alkalin lye, one pound; boil together, until a feather dipped into it loses its flue. It is applied to the skin, previously soaked in warm water, by gentle friction, for a very short time, followed by washing wlth warm water. This is one of the most certain and powerful depilatories made, but rapidly loses its strength unless kept in a well-stoppered glass bottle.

17. Hair Unguent.—The following is an admirable preparation for the hair:—Into a perfectly clean and well-tinned stew-pan put one pint of very fresh oil of

sweet almonds; set it over a slow fire, and gradually melt in it one ounce and a half of spermaceti, and two ounces of very fresh hog's lard. The heat must be barely sufficient to melt these substances, for a high temperature would make the oil rancid in a few days. The whole being melted, pour it into a china or earthenware basin; and when almost cold, stir into it whatever essential oils will communicate the perfume you prefer. Then put it into pomatum pots, and as soon as it is quite cold tie paper over the pots. This unguent would be still better if oil of ben were substituted for oil of sweet almonds, and purified beef-marrow for hog's lard. Beef-marrow may be purified by gently boiling a quantity of it in water, until the fatty part floats upon the liquid; it must then be allowed to cool, and the purified marrow removed.

18. Coloring for Eyelashes and Eyebrows. —In eyelashes, the chief element of beauty consists in their being long and glossy; the eyebrows should be finely arched and clearly divided from each other. The most innocent darkener of the brow is the expressed juice of the elder-berry, or a burnt clove. The following innoxious compound, however, will have a more permanent effect:—Dissolve in one ounce of distilled water, one drachm of sulphate of iron, and one ounce of gum-water, and a teaspoonful of *Eau de Cologne;* mix, and having wetted the eyebrows with the tincture of galls, apply the wash with a camel-hair pencil. The deepening the color of the brow is a most venial artifice, for light eyebrows always impart a very vacant and simple expression to the countenance and invariably counteract the effect of the

most brilliant eyes or the finest features. The flashing fullness of the eye depends, of course, chiefly on its form and color; but the eyelashes assist the effect considerably; and as it is only over these we possess any power, it may be considered a secret worth knowing, to learn the system adopted for their improvement by the Circassians. Observing that hair left to itself seldom grows long, but either splits at the top into two or more forks, or becomes smaller, with a fine gossamer point which never increases its growth, they remove with a pair of scissors the forked and gossamer-like points of the lashes, and, their growth being renewed, they become long, finely curved, and of an enviable silken gloss. The clipping may be repeated every six weeks, but no more should be removed than these points.

### HAIR SPECIFICS, DYES—GENERAL REMARKS.

Hair can be dyed any color by the same processes and chemicals as those used in coloring wool; but these are not applicable to hair on the living animal, as in almost every case, wool requires to be boiled in hot liquors. It has been found that the salts of some metals are adapted to the coloring of hair in a cold state; and these have been, and are, applied to change grey and red hair into brown and black. As grey hair imparts the appearance of advanced age to persons who may have become prematurely so by sickness, or other causes, it is quite natural that such should have a pardonable desire to make the color of their hair correspond with their years. In oriental countries the practice of coloring the beard has existed from time immemorial; and some of the inhabitants of Persia exercise a queer fancy in the choice of color. All dyes only color to the root of the hair; they must, therefore, be applied as often as the natural hair grows out and shows itself. The cheapest hair dyes are powders principally composed of lime and an oxyd of lead.

The following is one of these:—

HAIR DYE, No. A.—Take two ounces of powdered litharge, half an ounce of calcined magnesia, and half an ounce of powdered slacked lime. They are mixed intimately together, and are ready to be applied by reducing them to a cream-like consistency with soft water. When thus made into a paste, it is laid on the hair in a good coating, and then covered up with a silk handkerchief. The best time to apply it is before going to bed. In the morning it has to be rubbed off with a hard brush, for it sticks like mortar, and is a disagreeable, although an effectual dye. The hair is rendered harsh by it, and has to be softened with grease or oil. It is too troublesome for coloring the hair on the head, but may answer for dyeing the whiskers. This is the white powder sold for dyeing hair.

HAIR DYE, No. B.—Another receipt of the same kind is as follows:—Take one ounce of litharge, two ounces of carbonate or white lead, and three ounces of powdered quicklime. It is applied in the same manner as the former. Litharge and lime alone will also color the hair.

HAIR DYE, No. C.—The hair dyes principally composed of nitrate of silver are the most convenient and best. This salt of silver, when applied in solution to hair, and exposed to light, converts it either into a dark brown or black, according to the strength of the solution; but it possesses the defect of staining the skin while it colors the hair. This result, however, can be avoided if moderate care be exercised, as herewith described:

*a.* Take twenty grains of gallic acid, and dissolve them in an ounce of water in an ounce vial; then take twenty grains of nitrate of silver, and dissolve them in half an ounce of soft water, to which should be added a weak solution of gum Arabic or starch, and forty drops of ammonia, so as to fill an ounce vial. The gallic acid is now applied to the hair with a sponge, and allowed to dry; the nitrate of silver solution is then applied in the same manner, and allowed to dry under exposure to bright light. In about ten minutes let the hair be washed, and it is found to be colored from grey to a dark brown.

*b.* The above is a good hair dye, and although it colors the finger-nails and the hair, it scarcely stains the skin—the gum Arabic and gallic acid preventing it from doing this. Considerable of the coloring matter is washed off loosely, but enough is taken up by the capillary tubes to dye the hair. The ammonia may be omitted, and a weak solution of the hydro-sulphuret of ammonia used as a wash upon the top of the silver, after the latter has been on about five minutes. This is called the "Magic Hair Dye," because it is so rapid in its action.

*c.* Either ammonia or hydro-sulph ıret of ammonia is necessary to color grey hair black; a strong solu tion of galls or sumac may be substituted for the gallic acid. The sulphuret of potassium (in solution) may be substituted for the gallic acid, the ammonia and sulphuret of ammonia, by applying it to the hair first, and then allowing it to dry before the silver solution is put on. It has a disagreeable odor, however; but this may be counteracted by a perfume, such as oil of bergamot, lavender, or rose-water. In applying any nitrate of silver solution to the hair, some care should be exercised to prevent it touching the skin.

*d.* Another hair colorer is as follows:—An ounce of sugar of lead, dissolved and mixed with six ounces of the sulphuret of alcohol, (alcohol in which flour of sulphur has been steeped,) darkens the color of the hair and restores it, in a measure, if grey, to its natural color. Some perfume must be added to this mixture—rose-water is commonly used. This lotion is called "Hair Color Restorer." It is miserable stuff, and ought never to be used.

Remarks.—These hair dye specifics may be greatly increased in number without any increase in useful knowledge. We have given the best that are used, so far as we know.

The nitrate of silver costs one dollar per ounce; the other ingredients are cheap. For a few cents a person may color his red or grey beard by the above methods a splendid black, rivalling that of the darkest crow.

## CHAPTER V.

### A. STRUCTURE OF THE TEETH.

EVERY tooth is divided into three parts The *Body*, or portion projecting from the gum and covered with the enamel; the *Root* or fang, which is received into the socket; and the *Neck*, which connects the body and fang together. The body of the tooth contains a central cavity, that extends into the fang or root, which is the seat of sensation and nutriment.

The *first* teeth are called *deciduous* or milk teeth, and are twenty in number, ten upon each jaw.

The *second* teeth are called *permanent* teeth, and consist of thirty-two, or sixteen upon each jaw.

The structure of the deciduous and permanent teeth are the same, and composed of three distinct parts, viz., *Dental*, *Enamel*, and *Cement*.

1. DENTAL.—This substance is called the ivory of the tooth and enters into the formation of the greater part of the body and fangs. It is of a yellowish color and of fibrous structure, which fibres are tubular. These fibres are too small to contain blood-vessels, but are filled with a fluid, having the appearance of blood serum, which is the nourishing principle of the tooth.

2. ENAMEL.—This covers the grinding surface and the body of the tooth. It gradually tapers to an edge

near the gum—is white, brittle, and extremely hard, consisting of solid fibres of an hexagonal form.

3. CEMENT.—This covers the surface of the teeth not invested by the enamel. It has the character of true bone and contains the same chemical constituents.

Each tooth fits into a bony socket so firmly as not to admit of motion in the healthy condition, and surrounded by a delicate and vascular membrane called the periosteum. The teeth of the upper and lower jaws are supplied by their respective arteries and nerves, which pass into the cavity of the tooth at the lower part of the root.

## B. DEVELOPMENT OF THE TEETH.

The process of development commences at a very early period of fœtal life—about the seventh or eighth week. At this period the jaw becomes grooved, and is divided by septa into *alveolar cells*, or follicles, corresponding in number with the deciduous or first teeth. The follicles contain at first a yellowish-white fluid, which, after a time, takes on a granular form. This granular pulp, about the fourth month becomes enclosed in a distinct dental sac that subsequently becomes the periosteum of the tooth. Attached to the top of the sac is the dental cartilage. This is pierced by the tooth in dentition and produces in some children very alarming symptoms. Within this sac and from its contents is deposited the enamel and cement of which mention has already been made. This deposit generally commences about the middle of pregnancy and is perfected a short time before the tooth protrudes through the gum. The protrusion takes place, as a general rule, or rather commences, at six months, and terminates or is completed at two and a half years.

The *second* dentition, or the appearance of the permanent teeth, usually commences about the sixth or seventh years, in the following order:—

The first *molars* between the sixth and seventh years of age. The *incisors* between the seventh and eighth. The *bicuspids* between the ninth and tenth. The *cuspid* or canine at twelve. The *second molars* from twelve to fifteen. The *third molars* or wisdom teeth, from eighteen to twenty-five.

The germs of the permanent teeth may be traced in the jaw at birth, on the inner side of the deciduous teeth. These sacs are nourished by the same vessels as the milk teeth. A curious connection exists between the two sets of teeth. A cord passes from the sac of the permanent to that of the deciduous tooth. This was formerly supposed to give direction to the tooth. According to Dr. *Thomas Bell*, the sac of the deciduous tooth gives off a bud or shoot which subsequently becomes the permanent tooth. The cord-like appendage, therefore, is merely the connection existing between the offshoot and parent tooth. It becomes gradually atrophied as the permanent tooth develops, and finally appears as a mere thread.

The development of the permanent teeth causes the absorption of the deciduous teeth, so that the fangs entirely disappear, or are only retained within the socket of the jaw by a small portion of the gum that surrounds the body of the tooth.

## C. MODE OF PRESERVING CHILDREN'S TEETH.

When a tooth commences to decay, it is upon the external surface, gradually extending toward the internal parts of the tooth. If no effort is made to arrest the decay, the destruction of the tooth proceeds rapidly on toward the internal cavity, while the exposure of ths pulp or nerve causes the toothache. When a tooth commences to decay, it should be examined by a dentist, and the decayed part removed and the cavity filled with gold.

The decay of teeth is often hereditary. This might be avoided, in many instances, by proper attention to them in childhood. After the first teeth make their appearance, care should be taken to keep them in a cleanly condition. The mouth of the child should be washed once or twice a day with a linen rag saturated with cold water, while the first appearance of decay should be attended to at once by a dentist.

Some mothers are exceedingly anxious for their children to present an attractive appearance, and will spend several hours a day in dressing and curling their hair, while they appear totally indifferent about the teeth. What is more offensive than decayed or blackened teeth, in a child or female? It presents a more unseemly appearance than uncombed hair or tattered garments. When a child becomes old enough it should be taught to use, and made to employ a tooth-brush night and morning, while a piece of floss silk should also be passed between the teeth after every cleansing. This will prevent the tartar from forming on the teeth.

Children's teeth when they are undergoing decay, sometimes cause intense pain to the individual. When such is the case, dissolve four parts of mastic in one part of ether, in a well-stopped bottle. With this solution, which is of an oily consistency, saturate a piece of cotton wool and press it into the cavity of the tooth. The ether soon evaporates and the mastic forms a coating to the diseased surface and protects it from the air and food.

Children's teeth should not be removed even if they are decayed, unless they are loose and creating mischief, because of the existing connection between them and the permanent teeth, inducing them to assume an irregular position.

At from five to seven years of age, it will be observed that the arch of the jaw elongates posteriorly, and that an entirely new double tooth has taken up a position behind the last double one of the first set. This occurs on the upper and lower jaw, and upon both sides, and is indicative of the commencement of the second set. Spaces may also be noticed between all the teeth, showing that the arch of the jaw is expanding for the reception of the second supply of teeth, which teeth are much larger than those of the first set.

When the double teeth make their appearance, the front ones of the first set become loose, and should be at once removed, in order to prevent the second set from being crooked or having a wrong direction. This changing of teeth continues until about the twelfth year, when all the teeth of the first set will be superseded by new ones. At from twelve to fourteen years, another double tooth will appear in the rear of the arch on both sides, upper and lower, when there is seemingly a pause or suspension of their growth until the sixteenth year. From that time until the twenty-fourth year, and sometimes later, the wisdom teeth make their appearance. Thus we find that there are three important facts to be borne in mind in regard to children's teeth, viz.:—

1. The first teeth should not be removed too soon.
2. They should be removed when the others have appeared, and are interfering with them.
3. Whenever a new tooth has not sufficient space to assume a regular position, a dentist should be consulted.

The children's teeth should be examined every sixth month during the shedding of old and the development of new ones, in order to keep the latter regular, clean, and sound. The advice already given, if attended to, will not only preserve the first teeth, but assist materially the beauty of the permanent ones.

## D. THE ART OF PRESERVING PERMANENT TEETH.

Every individual can do much toward the preservation of the teeth. The principal means to this end is to keep them clean. To do this properly, they should be well brushed inside and out and on the surface, night and morning, while the interstices between them should be manipulated by using a linen or silk thread, so as to prevent particles of food from accumulating about them, thus inducing their decay and a fetid breath. The tooth-brush should be rather hard but not too wide, while the bristles should be reasonably loose, pliable and elastic. Should the brush be even hard enough to produce slight bleeding of the gums, it will not prove prejudicial.

Tooth powder should be used once a day; in the morning in preference to the evening, inasmuch as the teeth during the night are more liable to become coated with impurities. The utmost care must be observed in selecting a proper tooth-powder. Some of those that are highly recommended contain certain acids, which will injure the teeth if not utterly destroy them. The tooth-powder should be composed only of such ingredients that will exert a cleansing effect and preserve the healthiness of the gums.

When the tooth-brush is properly used twice a day with cold water, it will generally be sufficient to cleanse the teeth and prevent the tartar from forming. Castile soap is easily procured, and will prove an excellent means to neutralize any acid secretion, remove tartar, clean the teeth, and purify the breath.

The following dentifrice is much recommended by dentists, viz.:—

Prepared chalk, two parts.
Pulverized orris root, two parts.
Pulverized pumice-stone, one part.
Any of the essential oils, a few drops.

This may be used twice a week, in the morning particularly, should there be any accumulation of tartar. The Castile soap and cold water should not be omitted even for a single day. Rinse the mouth with cold water after using the foregoing dentifrice.

A few drops of Eau-de-Colonge, Pellitory of Spain, or other tincture, may be used as a fragrant and salutary addition.

Rinse the mouth with cold water after every meal. The tooth-pick should not be of metal, but made of a piece of wood or a quill, not omitting to pass a silk or linen thread between each tooth, as before directed, daily.

During an attack of fever the teeth are very liable to decay. They should therefore be the more frequently cleansed every day, using the dentifrice likewise the oftener than in ordinary cases. Always rinse the mouth after taking medicine to prevent its injurious action upon the teeth. Sometimes mercury is given to produce salivation; the teeth become tender to the touch, the gums inflamed, and the breath offensive. It also makes the teeth more liable to decay.

In case the patient should become salivated, the mouth ought then to be rinsed frequently with tincture of myrrh and chloride of potash. One or two grains of the chlorate of potash may be taken internally three or four times a day. This is said to be a *specific* for salivation. Sulphur is also a preventive of salivation. It may be given in small doses, if the other should not answer the purpose.

As before remarked, frequent examinations by a dentist, and the utmost care to keep the teeth clean, can alone prevent their decay, and avoid much pain and anxiety concomitant of defects and impurities.

## E. DISEASES OF GUMS.

The gums are liable to disease, and produce by consequence much suffering and trouble. They first become inflamed, swollen and congested with blood. Sometimes the edges become thickened and upon pressure discharge matter. They are also sensitive and bleed freely. If this condition be not arrested, the disease will extend to the sockets and affect the teeth, causing suppuration, so that they become loose and drop out. This affection of the gums is generally called scurvy, and is principally occasioned by the accumulation of tartar upon the teeth. The same condition may result from disease, or decay of the roots of the teeth, or from the improper use of mercury.

*Treatment.*—First remove the cause of irritation. Should it be tartar, have it removed. If a decayed tooth, have it extracted. If it be mercury, abandon its use, and resort to the remedies already mentioned.

When the cause is removed and the gums continue much inflamed, leeches should be applied; or the gums may be scarified and warm water held in the mouth to induce or promote bleeding. After this, use some astringent wash. A very good one is as follows:—Take a pound of the inner bark of white oak, add three quarts of boiling water, and boil it down to a quart; strain and wash the gums several times a day with the preparation.

Or the following may be substituted:—

℞ Tanic acid, .................... ½ ounce.
Pulverized alum,................ ½ "
Spring water,................... 1 pint.

Where the gums are much swollen and painful, a strong tea, made of poppy heads and chamomile flowers, equal parts, kept hot, with two pieces of flan nel alternately dipped therein and applied to the swollen part of the face, as hot as possible, bandaging the jaws before going to bed. The following may also be taken internally:—

℞ Tincture aconite, *fol*................f ʒjss.
Tincture belladonna,...............f ʒj.
Morphia, ...........................grs. ij.
Water, ............................℥iv.

Mix—Dose, one teaspoonful every one or two hours until pain subsides.

Should there be much swelling and accumulation of pus, the gums ought to be lanced and the impure matter be pressed out in a gentle manner.

# CHAPTER VI.

## CAUSE AND TREATMENT OF FOUL BREATH.

FOUL breath is occasioned by a variety of causes. Some of the most common are: Decayed teeth, perverted secretion of the salivary and mucous glands of the mouth, uncleanliness of the teeth, etc. The more obstinate cases result from an imperfect assimilation, or vitalization of the food, dependent upon a derangement of the liver or mesenteric glands; or it may be occasioned by a foul stomach.

A frequent cause of foul breath is a torpidity of some one of the excretory organs, such as the skin, kidneys, or bowels. I have known the most offensive breath arise from obstinate constipation of the bowels, the lungs eliminating a portion of what should be thrown off from them.

Should any one of the excretory organs, as the skin, kidneys, bowels, liver or lungs, cease performing their functions, one of the others will be called upon to perform an extra office. In this way, when the bowels or skin become affected, the lungs, being an excretory organ, will be called upon to throw off an additional waste from the system. If so, the breath becomes tainted.

Again, if the food is improperly assimilated by the liver or mesenteric glands, it cannot serve the purposes of nutrition. It is broken up or disintegrated by coming in contact with the oxygen of the blood, and eliminated by one of the excretory organs. If by the lungs, the breath becomes tainted. The excretory organs are all to be regarded as outlets of the system, for the purpose of eliminating decayed and waste material.

*Treatment.*—We must find out the cause that produces the foul breath. If the teeth be decayed, they are to be removed; those not too far gone should be plugged. The teeth are to be frequently cleansed with Castile soap and water. If the secretions of the mouth are in fault, the teeth and mouth may be washed two or three times a day with eight to ten drops of the chloride of soda in a tumbler of water. Where the bowels are inactive, or where there is deficient assimilation, one of the most effective remedies is the tincture of Nux Vomica, three times a day. It may be prepared as follows:

℞ Tincture nux vomica,..............f ʒj.
Camphor water,...................f ℥iij.
Syrup of orange peel,..............f ℥j.

Mix.
Dose.—One teaspoonful three times a day in water.

Should the foul breath be depending upon the stomach it must be corrected by proper diet, and judicious treatment, recommended by some skillful physician. If the skin be dry and flaky, it should be well-sponged once or twice a day with salt and water, or with soap and water. A small quantity of common whiskey may be added, and the skin, after the sponging, be well rubbed with a coarse crash towel. It is of the utmost importance to keep the skin in a clean and pliable condition, in order to maintain good health. This can only be done by the free use of water. Bathing should be resorted to once a day during the summer season or warm weather, and two or three times a week during the winter season. The chill may or may not be taken off the water during the cold weather, at the option of the patient.

The following may be used when the secretions of the mouth and teeth are in fault:—

TO SECURE A FRAGRANT BREATH.—Take two ounces of powder of myrrh; eight ounces of Peruvian bark; thirty-two drops of oil of cinnamon; thirty-two drops of oil of cloves; twenty-four ounces of prepared chalk; eight ounces of orris powder; three ounces of rose pink. Mix well together and use the brush.

A BAD BREATH.—Gum catechu, two ounces; white sugar, four ounces; orris powder, one ounce. Make them into a paste with mucilage, and add two drops of veroli.

**THE END.**

# INDEX

OF THE

## SUBJECT MATTERS IN THIS VOLUME.

# GLOSSARY

OF THE

## MEDICAL, SCIENTIFIC AND OTHER TERMS EMPLOYED IN THIS WORK.

*Abdomen.* The cavity situated between the lower part of the thorax and the region of the pelvis, containing the intestines, etc.

*Abnormal.* Unhealthy, unnatural.

*Abortion.* Miscarriage.

*Abrasion.* Excoriation.

*Abscess.* Cavity containing pus.

*Absorbents.* The lacteals and lymphatic vessels.

*Absorption.* The act of taking or sucking up.

*Acacia.* Gum Arabic.

*Acetate.* A salt containing acetic acid, united to a base.

*Acetic Acid.* Vinegar.

*Acetic Tincture.* A tincture made with vinegar.

*Aconite.* Monkshood. A native of Europe. This plant is cultivated in gardens as an ornament. It is extensively used as a febrifuge.

*Acme.* Height of disease.

*Adipose.* Fatty.

*Afferent.* Name of lymphatics conveying lymph to the glands; also, nerves which convey impressions to the brain and spinal cord.

*Afflux.* The act of flowing to.

*Ague-chill.* The cold stage of an intermittent.

*Albumen.* A substance found in animals and vegetables, and which constitutes the chief part of the white of eggs.

*Alcohol.* Rectified spirits of wine.

*Aliment.* Any kind of food.

*Alimentary Canal.* The entire passage through which the food passes from the mouth to the anus.

*Alkali.* A substance having a metallic base, which neutralizes acids, as potash, soda, ammonia, etc.

*Aloes.* The inspissated juice of the Aloe spicata.

*Alteratives.* Medicines intended to change the morbid action by restoring the healthy functions of the secretions, etc., by a gradual process.

*Alum.* Super-sulphate of alumina and potash.

*Alvine.* Relating to the intestines.

*Ammonia.* Volatile alkali.

*Amenorrhœa.* Absence of the menses.

*Anæmia.* An impoverished state of the blood.

*Analysis.* Resolution of a compound body into its elements.

*Anatomy.* Dissection. Knowledge of the parts of the body.

*Androgyni.* (*Plural.*) A term applied to Hermaphrodites in whom the male characteristics predominate.

*Androgynæ.* (*Plural.*) Those Hermaphrodites in whom the female peculiarities are most apparent.

*Androgynus.* A Female Hermaphrodite.

*Androgyna.* A Male Hermaphrodite.

*Aneurism.* Morbid enlargement of a vessel or vessels.

*Anima Mundi.* Soul of the Universe.

*Antidote.* A medicine given to destroy or counteract a poison.

*Antimony.* A metal used in medicine.

*Anus.* The inferior opening of the rectum.

*Aorta.* The large artery passing from the heart.

*Aphides.* Plant lice.

*Aphis.* A plant louse.

*Areolæ.* The interstices between fibres composing organs.

*Artery.* The name of a blood-vessel which conveys blood from the heart.

*Astringents.* Medicines used to contract the animal fibre.

*Athletæ.* Men trained to feats of strength, endurance, etc., among the ancient Greeks.

*Axilla.* The arm-pit.

*Balsam Copaiva.* Liquid resin used for inflammation of mucous membrane.

*Battery,* Galvanic. A connected series of copper and zinc plates, alternately arranged, with acid and water.

*Belladonna.* Deadly Night-shade.

*Bicuspides.* The first grinding teeth, molars.

*Bifurcate.* To divide into two branches.

*Bile.* A yellowish fluid secreted by the liver.

*Camphor.* A valuable antispasmodic and nervine.

*Canula.* A hollow tube.

*Cantharides.* Spanish flies, for blistering.

*Capillaries.* Hair-like vessels for conveying the blood from the arteries to the veins.

*Capsicum.* Red pepper, or Cayenne.

*Cartilage.* Grizzle.

*Catamenia.* The menstrual flux.

*Catheter.* A hollow silver tube used for evacuating the bladder.

*Caustic.* A substance which destroys parts by combining chemically, or disorganizing them.

*Celibacy.* The unmarried state.

*Cervex Uteri.* Neck of the womb.

*Chalazæ.* The dense internal albumen of the egg, in the form of spirally-twisted bands, produced by the revolving motion of the egg in its descent through the ovaduct.

*Chlorine.* An elementary gas.

*Chlorosis.* Green sickness.

*Cholera Infantum.* Summer complaint of children.

*Cicatrix.* A scar.

*Cicatrization.* Process of healing.

*Citric Acid.* Acid of lemons.

*Ciliary.* Resembling small hairs, attached to cells of the mucous membrane.

*Clitoris.* A body resembling a male penis, situated below the mons veneris, above entrance to vagina, within the labials.

*Colostrum.* An unhealthy condition of milk, or of the lacteal secretions.

*Coma.* Insensibility.

*Conception.* The impregnation of the ovum by the positive contact of the male sperm, whence results a new being.

*Congestion.* Overfullness of the blood-vessels.

*Congenital.* Being present at birth.

*Constipation.* Costiveness.

*Consumption.* Wasting away.

*Contagion.* Propagation of disease.

*Continent.* Virtuous. Abstinence from venereal or sexual indulgences.

*Corpus Luteum.* A cicatrix or scar. A small yellowish body, perceived in the ovarium, and left after the rupture of one of the ova vesicles.

*Corrugated.* Wrinkled.

*Croup.* Inflammation of the trachea.

*Cyst.* Sac, bag, or pouch.

*Decoction.* Preparation made by steeping.

*Dental.* Appertaining to the teeth.

*Dentition.* Process of cutting the teeth.

*Depletion.* Diminishing the fullness of a part by evacuating remedies.

*Derangement.* Applied to functional disturbance of the organs.

*Dermoid.* Resembling the skin.

*Desideratum.* Something needed.

*Desquamation.* Scaling off.

*Determination.* Unnatural flow of blood to the part.

*Diagnosis.* Distinction of maladies.

*Diagnostic.* Characteristic of disease.

*Diathesis.* Constitutional tendency.

*Digestion.* Conversion of food into a liquid substance called chyme.

*Disorganization.* Destruction of an organ or tissue by disease, etc.

*Dissection.* The anatomical examination of the parts of the body.

*Drachm,* or *dram* (ʒ). Sixty grains by weight, and an ordinary teaspoonful by measure.

*Drastic.* Powerful purge.

*Dysmenorrhœa.* Painful menstruation.

*Element.* A simple constituent or principle of the body, or any other substance.

*Emaciation.* Wasting away.

*Emesis.* Vomiting.

*Emetics.* Medicines provoking vomiting.

*Emmenagogues.* Medicines believed to have the power of acting on the uterus or womb and exciting the menses.

*Ecrasseur.* A surgical instrument.

*Erotic.* Excessive venery.

*Enamel.* Outer surface of the teeth.

*Embryo.* The young being in the womb.

*Encysted.* Covered with a sac.

*Enema.* Injection into the rectum.

*Epithelium.* The thin layer of cells which covers the nipples, lips, mucous membranes, etc.

*Epigenemal.* Relating to generation.

*Epigenesis.* Generation. A theory of conception, according to which the new being is created entirely anew, and receives at once from each parent all that is necessary for its formation.

*Evolution.* Development of germs.

*Exacerbation.* Aggravation of fever or other disease.

*Excretion.* Substances secreted and thrown off from the body, as urine, perspiration, etc.

*Exhalants.* Vessels which throw out.

*Fallopian Tubes.* The ducts which convey the ova from the ovaries to the womb, and the semen toward the ovaries.

*Febrifuge.* Medicine to subdue fever.

*Febrile.* Belonging to fever.

*Fecundation.* Impregnation. The power to produce young.

*Fistula.* Deep-seated ulcer, with a tube or canal opening externally.

*Flaccid.* Soft, pliable, relaxed.

*Fœtus.* The young being in the womb passed from the embryo stage, four months after conception.

*Follicle.* A little bag or depression in the mucous membrane lined with secreting cells.

*Formula.* Prescription for preparing medicine.

*Function.* The action by which vital phenomena are produced in the living body.

*Generation.* Producing kind, procreation, formation, etc.

*Genus Homo.* The human race.

*Gland.* Applied to those organs which separate from the blood any fluid whatever.

*Globule.* A small globe. The blood is composed of globules, the red and white.

*Gonorrhœa.* Flux or discharge from inflammation of urethra.

*Hermaphrodism.* A blending of the male and female sex in one person.

*Hermaphrodite.* Partaking of the character of male and female in one person.

*Heteradelphia.* A monstrosity, or double animal, or having duplicate organs.

*Homunculi.* Miniature representations of men, which the ancients imagined to exist in the semen. Animalculæ of the male sperm.

*Hybrid.* An unnatural mixture of distinct animals, as the male ass with the female horse. A mule.

*Hydatids.* A species of encysted entozoa.

*Hygiene.* The art of preserving health.

*Hymen.* Vaginal valve. A thin membrane stretched across the orifice of the vagina, in virgins.

*Hypothesis.* A theory, supposition, law, or doctrine.

*Imperforate.* The congenital closure of any foramen or opening.

*Imperforate Hymen.* Unbroken curtain at the entrance of the vagina of virgins.

*Incision.* A clean cut by a sharp instrument.

*Incisors.* The front teeth.

*Induration.* Hardness of a tissue.

*Inflammation.* A state in which the capillaries of the affected parts are intercepted in their proper functions, and morbidly relaxed and over-distended, causing increased redness, pain and increase of temperature.

*Infusion.* Watery decoction.

*Iufusoria.* Minute animalculæ diffused through the atmosphere or water. The lowest microscopic types of life or existence.

*Injection.* Clysters. Fluids forced into the urethra, vagina, uterus, rectum, etc.

*Integument.* That which covers any thing; as the skin, etc.

*Iodine.* Elementary body obtained from sea-weed.

*Irritability.* Susceptibility of excitement from any exciting cause.

*Irritation.* The effect of stimulants.

*Kalogynomial.* Compounded from three Greek words, beautiful, woman, law; meaning, the law of female beauty.

*Labia.* Lip.

——— Majora. Large, or external lips of the vulva.

——— Minora. Small, or internal lips of the vulva.

*Lactation.* Yielding milk. Giving suck to the young.

*Laxative.* A mild purgative.

*Leech.* An aquatic worm.

*Leucorrhœa.* Whites, a sexual weakness or discharge from vagina, peculiar to females.

*Lymph.* A thin, transparent fluid, which circulates in the lymphatics.

*Lymphatics.* Glands or vessels carrying lymph.

*Maceration.* Softening in water.

*Magnesia.* One of the earths having a metallic basis.

*Malaria.* A noxious gas arising from decomposition of vegetable matter.

*Malformation.* Deformed, defective, irregular, unnatural, ill-formed.

*Mammæ.* The breasts or the bosom of a female.

*Measles.* An eruptive fever.

*Meatus.* A passage.

——— Urinarius. Channel or outlet for the urine.

*Mens Divina.* The Divine Mind.

*Menses.* } The catamenial or monthly discharge from the
*Menstruation.* } womb and Fallopian tubes.

*Modus operandum.* Mode of operation.

*Mons Veneris.* Prominence above the external opening in the vagina, covered with hair at puberty.

*Mucus.* Secretion taking place in all mucous membranes.

*Nausea.* Sickness of stomach.

*Nervine.* Medicine allaying nervous excitement.

*Natura naturans.* Nature of Nature herself.

*Opium.* The concrete juice of the poppy.

*Organs.* Parts performing a definite function.

*Os.* A bone.

*Ova.* Eggs.

*Ovaducts.* Fallopian tubes.

*Ovaries.* Two small oval bodies attached to the uterus, one on each side.

*Ovasacs.* Sacs or bags containing ova

*Oviparous.* Producing young from eggs, by hatching, after the eggs have passed from the body, as with fowls and birds.

*Ovum.* An egg.

*Oxygen.* One of the most extensively diffused elements in Nature. A constituent of atmospheric air.

*Pancreas.* The gland situated behind the stomach.

*Pancreatic Juice.* The secretion of the pancreas.

*Parenchyma.* The texture of glandular organs, as the liver, etc.

*Parturition.* The act of bringing forth young.

*Pathological.* Morbid changes.

*Pathology.* Doctrine of disease

*Pelvis.* A basin. The bony cavity which contains part of the intestines, and the urinary and genital organs.

*Peritoneum.* Serous membrane lining the abdominal cavity.

*Phthisis.* Consumption.

*Physiology.* Science of life.

*Placenta.* A soft spongy body adhering to the uterus, and connected with the fœtus by the umbilical cord.

*Polypus.* A tumor growing in the cavities of the body.
*Pregnant.* With child.
*Procreation.* Fecundation. Generation.
*Prolapsus.* Falling of the womb.
*Purulent.* Resembling pus.
*Pus.* Matter produced by suppuration.

*Rash.* Patches of redness on the skin.
*Regimen.* Regulation of diet so as to promote health.
*Roseola.* Rose rash.
*Rubeola.* Measles.

*Scarlatina.* Eruptive fever.
*Schirrous.* Hard.
*Sebaceous Glands.* Glands that secrete the oily matter that lubricates the skin.
*Sedative.* A remedy that lessens arterial and nervous excitement.
*Semen.* The fluid substance ejaculated by the male in the act of copulation.
*Serous.* Watery.
*Sexual Congress.* Coition.
*Spermatic Fluid.* Semen.
*Spermatozoa.* Animalculæ contained in the male semen, which impregnate the ova.
*Spermatozoon.* Singular of spermatozoa.
*Stamina.* Substance, strength.
*Sudorific.* Producing perspiration.
*Sudorific Glands.* Sweat Glands.
*Superfœtation.* Impregnation of a woman already pregnant.

*Tannic Acid.* Astringent property of oak-bark.
*Tartar Emetic.* Tartarized antimony.
*Testes.* Testicles. Organs in the male which correspond with the ovaries in the female. Generative organs.
*Tribades.* Women having abnormal clitorides, or who act toward women as if they were males. A society of women among the ancient Greeks, who indulged in the vice of "Lesbian Love," or unnatural connection with their own sex.

*Ulcer.* A morbid solution of the continuity of the part.
*Umbilical.* Naval.
*Urethra.* Canal or passage to the bladder, through which the urine is evacuated.
*Uterus.* The womb.

*Vagina.* The canal leading to the womb, penetrated by the male organ in the act of copulation or coitus.
*Vascular.* Belonging to vessels.
*Vesicle.* Bladder of water. A sac.
*Viscera.* Entrails.
*Vis Medicatrix.* Vital power of the living body, possessing the power of resisting disease. It also possesses the power of developing organic matter into organized forms.
*Vis Vitæ.* Life. Living spirit.
*Vital.* Connected with life.
*Viviparous.* Animals which bring forth their young alive and perfect, as a female her child.
*Vulva.* The whole of the external genital organs of the female, entrance to vagina, etc.

*Womb.* Uterus, the pear-shaped pouch or organ in which embryotic or fœtal life is nourished into a full development of a child or other animal being, situated within the pelvis, etc.

*Yelk* or *Yolk.* The yellow ball or inner body of an egg.

---

## EXPLANATIONS OF THE ABBREVIATIONS OCCURRING IN THE FORMULÆ OF THIS WORK.

℞. Recipe.
*M.* Misce. Mix.
*gr.* Granum. A grain.
*O.* Octavius. A pint.
*ss.* Semi. Half.
*aa.* Of each ingredient equal parts.
℔. Libra. Pound.
℥. Uncia. An ounce.
ʒ. Drachma. A drachm, or dram.
*Gtt.* Gutta. Drop.
*Tinct.* Tinctura. Tincture.
*Ext.* Extractum. An extract.

www.ingramcontent.com/pod-product-compliance
Lightning Source LLC
LaVergne TN
LVHW021225110826
845150LV00002B/252

* 9 7 8 1 4 2 5 5 6 3 9 5 0 *